PUBLICATIONS

OF THE

NAVY RECORDS SOCIETY

VOL. CI

A MEMOIR OF JAMES TREVENEN

THE NAVY RECORDS SOCIETY was established in 1893 for the purpose of printing rare or unpublished works of naval interest.

Any person wishing to become a Member of the Society is requested to apply to the Hon. Secretary, Royal Naval College, Greenwich, S.E. 10, who will submit his name to the Council. The Annual Subscription is Two Guineas, the payment of which entitles the Member to receive one copy of each work issued by the Society for that year, and to purchase back volumes at reduced prices. The subscription for those under the age of 30 is One Guinea.

MEMBERS requiring copies of any volume should apply to the Hon. Secretary.

Subscriptions should be sent to The Hon. Secretary (Admin.), Crown House, Aldwych, W.C. 2.

CAPTAIN JAMES TREVENEN

IN THE UNIFORM OF THE IMPERIAL RUSSIAN NAVY

A MEMOIR OF JAMES TREVENEN

Edited by

CHRISTOPHER LLOYD

F.R.Hist.S.

Assistant Professor, Royal Naval College, Greenwich

and

R. C. ANDERSON

LITT.D., F.S.A.

PRINTED FOR THE NAVY RECORDS SOCIETY

MCMLIX

PRINTED IN GREAT BRITAIN BY
SPOTTISWOODE, BALLANTYNE AND CO. LTD
LONDON AND COLCHESTER

THE COUNCIL

OF THE

NAVY RECORDS SOCIETY

1958–59

CONTENTS

GENERAL INTRODUCTION

The manuscript from which this volume is printed is entitled *Memoirs of James Trevenen, by C. V. Penrose*. The preface is dated 1805, but it is evident that additions were made after that date. One copy of the MS. was purchased in 1954 by the National Maritime Museum, Greenwich, and there is another copy in the Alexander Turnbull Library at Wellington, N.Z. Both copies have about the same number of pages, viz. 835 closely written folios which have, however, a variety of pagination on account of the number of appendices included.

The author of the MS. was Admiral Sir Charles Vinicombe Penrose (1759–1830), who married Trevenen's sister Elizabeth in 1787. He entered the Royal Academy, Portsmouth, shortly before Trevenen went there, and passed for lieutenant in 1779. He became a captain in 1794, but his service at sea was interrupted by spells on shore on account of fever contracted on the West Indies station. Hence between 1803 and 1810, when the memoir was written, he was captain of the Padstow Sea Fencibles. In 1813 he was advanced to flag rank in order to command a squadron under Lord Keith which co-operated with Wellington's advance on Bordeaux. After the war he was commander-in-chief in the Mediterranean, but saw no further service after 1821. He was a devout Evangelical and the composer of a number of religious tracts; on service matters he contributed to the *Naval Chronicle* and wrote a pamphlet on corporal punishment in the Navy which was printed in 1824. In 1850 his nephew, John Penrose, published *The Lives of Sir C. V. Penrose and Captain James Trevenen* in which some selections from the present MS. are printed, and to which is prefixed the portrait by Allingham which forms our frontispiece.

The genealogical ramifications of the Penrose-Trevenen connection are described in *The Penroses of Fledborough Parsonage* privately printed by the Rev. A. B. Baldwin in 1934. The facts, as far as they affect the subject of the present volume, are that John Penrose the first, 1713–76, vicar of St. Gluvias near Penryn in Cornwall, married Elizabeth Vinicombe, by whom he had seven children, of whom the youngest was the author of the memoir of Trevenen, whose sister he married. His elder brother, John Penrose the second, married another sister and became vicar of Camborne on the death of his father-in-law. It was his son, John Penrose the third, who published the *Lives* referred to above, and who married Eliza Cartwright, the daughter of the inventor of the power loom and the authoress of *Mrs. Markham's History of England.*

James Trevenen's father was the Rev. John Trevenen of Rosewarne and vicar of Camborne in Cornwall until his death in 1775. He left six children to be brought up by his widow: Elizabeth (the 'Bess' of the following letters, who married C. V. Penrose); Jane, who married John Penrose; John, who died in 1825; Matthew, who died in 1785; Thomas, who died in 1816; and James, the subject of this memoir. In February 1789, shortly before his death, James married at Kronstadt Elizabeth Farquharson, by whom he had one daughter who died unmarried in 1823. Mrs. Trevenen made a second marriage, to Thomas Bowdler (1754–1825), the editor of the *Family Shakespeare*, whose name has become immortalized in the word 'bowdlerize'. She died at Bath in 1845.

The method upon which Penrose composed this memoir of his brother-in-law was to write a narrative which either paraphrased or connected the letters and journals preserved in the family. His religious beliefs result in an unfortunately priggish style which contrasts strongly with the more natural flavour of Trevenen's letters to his family and friends, such as Captain Riou, and the lengthy journals of his tours in Britain and on the Continent, where he was an indefatigable tourist noting down everything which he saw.

The editors of the present volume have included everything of naval interest which Trevenen himself wrote, but they have omitted a good deal of Penrose's editorial matter. To obtain a chronological sequence, many of Trevenen's letters, which Penrose relegated to appendices, have been transferred to the body of the narrative. The whole of Trevenen's evidence with regard to Cook's last voyage and to his service with the Russian navy has been included, but from the three hundred pages describing his tours only those passages have been transcribed which are of naval or general interest. Such are his descriptions of the Carron foundry at Falkirk, or life in Venice as seen by an intelligent young officer on half-pay. The fact that Dr. Johnson once drank thirty-two cups of tea at a sitting seems worth recording, but not how much it cost to get from Nice to Marseilles.

The story of Trevenen's career provides much of naval interest. His letters from the Royal Academy, Portsmouth, are the only ones which appear to have survived. His service as a midshipman on Cook's last voyage provides a new angle from which to judge the latter's character, though it is to be regretted that Trevenen's account is only in the form of notes to the printed version. His subsequent career shows how the circumnavigators continued as a band of friends and throws new light on some of Cook's shipmates, particularly his First Lieutenant who completed the published narrative—Captain King. Trevenen's is also one of the only two narratives we have of a British officer in the navy of Catherine the Great, the other being an account of the operations in the Mediterranean in 1770. His prophetic plans for the development of the Russian Pacific seaboard, his description of Russian naval life and the war with Sweden in which he lost his life, his criticism of Paul Jones and his eulogy of Greig provide much that is new and valuable.

EDITORIAL NOTE. Editorial summaries of the original MS. are either in italics or enclosed in square brackets. Copies of original letters or documents are shown by single quotation marks. The remainder of the text is Penrose's biography.

OBITUARY BY DAVID SAMWELL

in *The Gentleman's Magazine*, August 1790

July 9. Died in Russia, aged 31, James Trevenen Esq., a Lieutenant in the British Navy and a post-captain in the Russian service. In the action with the Swedish fleet off Viborg on the 4th. he carried a broad pendant and after having gallantly distinguished himself, was mortally wounded by the last shot fired by the enemy. He was a native of Cornwall, and of a very respectable family in that county. He received his education at the Royal Academy, Portsmouth, and in the year 1776 embarked as a midshipman with Captain Cook on his last voyage to the South Seas. In taking astronomical observations and surveying the various coasts, he proved an able assistant to the great navigator, who justly considered him as a young gentleman of ample promise to do honour to the service and to his country. On his return from that expedition in 1780 he was promoted by the Earl of Sandwich to the rank of lieutenant, in which capacity he sailed till the conclusion of the war with his friend Captain King, who had the highest esteem and friendship for him.

He accompanied that worthy man to Italy on his illness, and was with him when he died. He afterwards visited Rome and travelled over the greater part of Italy and France. Returning to his own country and being impatient of an inactive life, he solicited employment of Lord Howe, then at the head of the Admiralty. But unfortunately for the naval service of this country, his application proved ineffectual. This refusal, added to a hint he received from a brother officer who knew his great talents and ardent spirit of enterprise, induced him to draw up a plan of discovery and a proposal of opening an intercourse by sea between Kamchatka and Japan and the southern parts of China, which was laid before the Empress of Russia, and so well approved by her that she immediately sent an officer express to invite him over to carry it into execution. He arrived at Petersburg the latter end of 1787, but the war with the Turks breaking out, put a stop to the intended expedition, and he was prevailed upon to accept the command of a ship of the line.

In the various engagements which have taken place in the Baltic since the commencement of hostilities between Russia and Sweden he has borne a very active part and has been honoured with repeated marks of the

Empress' favour; and doubtless had he lived would soon have arrived at the first rank in her service. He was a man of strong natural abilities, greatly improved by cultivation, and possessed a high sense of honour and a liberal enlightened mind. To the manly courage and open generosity of a British sailor, he united in an eminent degree the education and the manners of a gentleman. To those who had the pleasure of knowing him, his death is deeply distressing, and to his country the loss of so accomplished an officer will not easily be repaired.

PART I

SERVICE IN THE BRITISH NAVY

Chapter 1

THE NAVAL ACADEMY

Introduction

The Naval Academy, Portsmouth, later known as the Royal Academy, of which Trevenen became a scholar in 1772, was founded in 1729, though the buildings were not completed, nor the staff appointed until 1733. The next year the brig *Success* was rigged in the harbour for instructional purposes. This academy in the dockyard (the buildings of which are now the R.N. Staff Officers' Mess) was designed to accommodate forty young gentlemen, but as the years went by the number diminished until new regulations were required in 1773. From its inception, the Naval Academy had a poor reputation. The scanty records which have survived in the shape of letters to the Secretary of the Admiralty or to the Navy Board suggest a low rate of efficiency and a high rate of drunkenness and expulsion. Matters reached a climax when, in 1766, the Port Admiral was directed to enquire into 'a dispute which has arisen between the masters, and between the masters and the scholars', the consequence of which was the dismissal of the head-master, the mathematical usher and a number of scholars.

According to Penrose's testimony in the following pages, matters did not improve greatly under the new headmaster, Witchell. Because of the low rate of entry—most boys going to sea direct as captain's servants—a new type of 'Volontier-per-Order' (as he was called) was instituted, consisting of fifteen sons of officers to be educated at the public expense. It is not clear how Trevenen gained entry to the Academy, but his letters (childish as they may be) are the only scholar's letters which have survived.

Some idea of the conduct of the Academy when he was there may be gained from the following extracts from the rules—

> 'None shall be admitted into the Academy but the sons of noblemen or gentlemen, who shall not be under 12 years of age, nor above 15 at the time of their admission, except fifteen young gentlemen, the sons of commissioned officers of H.M. fleet, who are to be educated at the public expense and may be admitted at the age of 11 years.
>
> 'The Commissioner of H.M. Dockyard shall be the Governor, and the Masters, Ushers and Scholars shall be obedient to and observe his directions.

'The scholars are to lodge in separate chambers and all to board with the Master, at £25 a year, in consideration of which he is to keep them a decent and proper table and to find them in washing, fire, candles, towels, table and bed linen and the messing utensils of the house.

'A yearly suit of blue cloth, conformable to a pattern suit lodged with the Master, to be donned on H.M. birthday at the price of £5.'

The subjects of study to be covered in the 'plan of learning', many beautiful copies of which have survived, include writing, arithmetic, drawing, navigation, gunnery, fortifications, dancing, fencing, 'the useful parts of Mathematicks and the use of the Firelock'. (A report of 1774 complains that scholars are 'too talkative when under arms'.) No boy was permitted to leave the dockyard without permission, nor could he remain more than five years to complete his plan of learning. Three weeks' leave was granted at Christmas. A discharge certificate (of which an example is printed on p. 4) was given to each boy when he joined a ship.

The 1773 reforms do not seem to have attracted many new candidates, a failure which is perhaps explained by a report of July 1774: 'Kitchen utensils are amazingly dirty. The scholars heads abound in vermin. Scholars to have three clean shirts, etc., a week and clean sheets once a month. Not to throw stones over the wall, or go to a billiard table'. Similarly, in December 1776, three scholars were expelled and eight 'confined for insolent and riotous behaviour when the Head Master was gently correcting Charles Hurt for ill behaviour'. In 1793, when Jane Austen's brother was a scholar, only twenty-eight names are recorded. Occasionally a boy who had already gone to sea as a captain's servant stayed at the Academy for a short time, especially if his ship was in port. Such a one was James Anthony Gardner, who was there in 1780 when the Master's name was Orchard—'a very good man he was; but who the devil taught him navigation is more than I can say. He was a great disciplinarian and used to flourish with direful sway an infernal horsewhip that I have reason to remember'. The few pages of his recollections devoted to the subject do not suggest that discipline was in any way improved thereby. It is not surprising that in 1801 St. Vincent wrote, 'The Royal Academy at Portsmouth, which is a sink of vice and abomination, should be abolished.'[1]

In 1806 the buildings were enlarged to accommodate seventy scholars and the constitution of what henceforth became the Royal Naval College was altered. Under the Rev. James Inman, of *Tables* fame, a much higher standard was aimed at, and the vanguard of the modern Royal Corps of

[1] Gardner's *Recollections*, p. 16. St. Vincent in *Naval Miscellany*, Vol. IV, p. 472.

Naval Constructors was admitted in 1809 under the guise of 'a superior class of shipwright apprentices'. In 1837 the Academy came to an unlamented end.

Among the scanty records, we are fortunate in possessing a 'list of young gentlemen in the Royal Academy', dated January 1773:

Date of Admission	*Name*	*Date of Passing Out*[1]
1770 March 21	Charles Burt	1773 Sept. 6
1770 May 17	John Sutton	—
1771 Feb. 9	Francis Phipps	1774 Feb. 12
1771 March 7	Peter Dupuy Abbott	1773 Nov. 10
1771 April 6	Chas. Alex. Macrae	1773 Oct. 11
1771 May 23	Richard Gomm	1773 Oct. 30
1771 Sept. 30	Thomas Sotheby	1774 Feb. 12
1772 Feb. 7	Chas. Vinicombe Penrose	1775 May 2
1772 April 18	William Carthew	1774 Feb. 5
1772 July 11	John Gwatkin	1774 Oct. 10
1772 July 24	John Incledon Webber	—
1772 Sept. 19	Conway Spencer	—
1772 Sept. 19	William Delater (expelled July 1774 'for eloping and for decoying Henry Wray and for having a bad character')	
1772 Dec. 18	James Trevenen	1775 Dec. 23
1772 Dec. 18	James Ward (discharged at request of his father, Dec. 23, 1775)	
—	William Charlton	1775 Nov. 8

Most of these boys became Trevenen's shipmates in later years and at least two sailed with him in the *Resolution*.

The following are specimens of documents issued by the Admiralty to a scholar:

A. *Passing Out Order*

'Whereas we have appointed Mr. —— to go to sea in H.M. —— the —— you are hereby required and directed to cause him to be discharged from the Academy and to direct the Head Master to give him a Certificate of the time he has spent in the said Academy from the day of his appearance to the day of his discharge; taking care to deduct

[1] P.R.O. Adm. 1/3504. I am indebted to Cdr. May for the passing-out dates drawn from a document in the National Maritime Museum, POR/D 19.

the time he has been absent, excepting three weeks at Christmas allowed yearly at Christmas.

'To the Commissioner of H.M. Navy and Governor of the Royal Academy Portsmouth.'

B. *Certificate*

'Whereas Mr. —— has been educated at the Royal Academy at Portsmouth and is well qualified to serve His Majesty at sea, you are hereby required and directed to receive him on board H.M. —— under your command and enter his name as one of her complement.

'You are to take care that he applies himself to the duty of a seaman; and he is to have the privelege of walking the quarter-deck. You are to allot him a proper place to lie in, without setting up any cabin; and you are to rate him Volontier-per-Order, which will entitle him to Able Seaman's pay.

'You are to oblige him to keep a journal and to draw the appearance of headlands, coasts, bays, sands, rocks and such like; and you are to take care that the Master, Boatswain and Schoolmaster do instruct him in all parts of learning that may qualify him to do the duty of Able Seaman and Midshipman.

'After two years at sea you are to rate him Midshipman Ordinary, or Midshipman if he be qualified for it.

'When your ship shall be at Spithead or in Portsmouth harbour, you are to direct him to attend the mathematical master in order to his examining his journals and representing to us how he has improved himself. And at the end of the service in the ship under your command you are to give him such a certificate of his sobriety diligence and skill as he shall deserve; as also of the length of time he has served with you, either as a Volontier-by-Order, or as a Midshipman.'

C. *Entry Warrant to the Academy*

'You are hereby required and directed to cause the bearer, Mr. ——, to be entered and received as a scholar in H.M. Royal Academy in Portsmouth Yard for educating young gentlemen for sea service, and to be instructed and provided for there according to the Rules and Constitutions thereof. For which this shall be your warrant.

'To the Commissioner of H.M. Navy and Governor of the Royal Academy.'

I SHALL NOT DETAIN my readers with long particulars respecting the family of the subject of the memoirs I am about to write. To strangers such narration would be uninteresting, and the inhabitants of the part of England it is situated in are already well acquainted with its respectability and its worth.

James Trevenen was born on New Year's Day, 1760. His father was for many years the officiating clergyman of the large and populous parish of Camborne in the county of Cornwall, where he was much and deservedly beloved by those under his charge for the upright and regular discharge of his duty as a minister; and respected by all ranks for his estimable character as a gentleman, and enlightened knowledge of political and mercantile interests of the county. This gentleman died suddenly on December 4, 1775, leaving the minds of all who knew him deeply impressed with sorrow at the loss which society had sustained of a useful and irreproachable member.

His mother is still living: a memorable instance of that fortitude derived from the strength of genuine Christianity which has enabled her with cheerful resignation to submit to some heavy dispensations at the hand of Providence by giving her such command of reason in the hour of grief as to seek for comfort where she was sure to find it, and also to impart it both by precept and by example to her children and friends. There are also surviving two brothers and two sisters, of whom from my new and intimate connection with them it would not become me to speak as they deserve.

James Trevenen received his first rudiments of a classical education under his father, but was placed at an early age at the grammar school at Helstone, of which Rev. Marshall was the master. Here he remained until, on account of an early propensity discovered towards sea life, he was entered at the Royal Academy, Portsmouth, in the year 1773.

At this place it was that I had the happiness of forming and cementing with him that friendship which afforded me many years much solid advantage and genuine pleasure which made me always highly interested in his concerns, earnestly to lament this loss; and confers on me the power and right of endeavouring to do justice and honour to his memory, by delineating a character which all who knew admired and describing the scenes of a life which, by its early termination only, was prevented from being conspicuous to and admired by the world at large. The boyish part of his life is not to be long dwelt upon in such a work as this. Such part only is necessary which tends to develop the general character of the subject of it in a clear light, and to trace the expanding powers of the mind as experience and reflection invigorate and improve it.

From my personal knowledge I am enabled to describe the conduct of my friend during his stay at the Academy. This was so different from that of his contemporaries at that place, or of the persons of his age in general, that even then it raised the expectations of something marked and superior in a more advanced age.

Indefatigable in the pursuit of learning, he kept steadily at his books, without those interruptions of fatigue and idleness so common with boys in general, and even with those whose capacities are above the common run; and seemed always impressed with the idea of what vast consequence his then acquired knowledge would be to him in his progress through life, when more action would deprive him of the leisure requisite for making improvements in science. In this particular he stands wholly unrivalled as far as my observation and experience extend. His diligence was rewarded by the honour of finishing at the Academy several months before the allotted period; and the late Mr. Witchell, who was the first master, has often declared that he never knew any person leave that seminary so much benefitted by his stay there as James Trevenen. The merit of this improvement, I am competent to declare, is principally due to the learner. For although, at this period, the masters were gentlemen of extensive knowledge in the several branches they superintended, and of great respectability in all parts of their character, yet the unfortunate declension of discipline had rendered it too much the pupil's option whether he would or would not pay attention to his studies. Consequently this noble institution had lost great part of its intended value. For from its excellent regulations and fortunate situation it certainly is, in preference, to any other place, calculated to form officers for the British Navy. But from want of attention to restrain habits of idleness, which most boys will fall into unrestrained, it has frequently happened that the time has been thoughtlessly wasted till the remaining part of that allotted for the finishing of the whole plan has been too short to complete it properly; and those who have been backward suffered to bring it to an apparent conclusion by cursorily looking into some parts and copying the rest. I am sensible of my digression, yet the general mode of proceeding at the Academy throws by its contrast a bright light on that of James Trevenen; and I may plead an excuse also that the vast importance of a nursery of British naval officers cannot be too often recalled to the minds of British readers.

But to return to my subject. It is remarkable that during the two years and a half he passed at the Academy he never received or merited any sort of punishment from his masters, or was involved in any quarrel with his schoolfellows; which is all the more striking as from a quickness and great strength of spirit, he could ill brook submission, and of a great activity of mind and body he was eager at, and concerned in, all the plays and exercises of his companions, and excelled in most of them; but a certain early habit of propriety occasioned his weighing all the consequences and acting from conclusions of judgment instead of the impulse of passion. . . .

After a lengthy description of how his friend saved his life in a swimming accident, Penrose prints the earliest surviving letter by Trevenen.

No. 1

Portsmouth,
December 23, 1772

DEAR FATHER,—I received your letter dated the 10th with great pleasure and am now about to answer it. A few days after I arrived here there came another from London, so I have got a junior already. His [Ward's] warrant and mine came down together, but as I had been here the longest I am the senior. He is a good natured young gentleman and always keeps his word, but swears greatly. Not quite so tall as I am, nor so big. Some of the young gentlemen have very uncommon names, viz. Peter Dupree Abbot, Charles Pam Burt, John Newton Ingleton Webber, etc. I will give you the characters of the young gentlemen as I think. Sutton is a most amiable young gentleman, rather taller and bigger than myself; not so amiable in his mind, for he swears greatly and brags of his singing. But his virtues are not quite overcovered by his vices. The next is a second Humphreys. Mackie the Scotchman is a most good natured, obliging, virtuous young gentleman; I will give you a description of him another time. Next comes Burt, very slight and thin, taller than me but not so big; swears, good natured enough and almost blind. Next a *macaroni*, viz. Abbot, is taller than Mackie, a great swearer and a great drunkard—what a waster! Stays out whole nights drinking at bawdy houses, together with Phipps, who is just the same character. They conceal it from Mr. Witchell I can't tell how. I beg you would not speak about it. Next comes Gum [or Gomm] a Russian who is very kind to every one, and does not swear in the least. Sotheby is ill natured, but does not swear. Carthew is a merry fellow, tall and slight, does not swear. Pringle is very good natured, spends all the money he gets as soon as he has it, does not swear, is idle and throws away his time. Gwatkin is coming on fast in wickedness, very fast. Webber is very bad, and follows the steps of Abbot and Phipps, who hate Mackie. Spencer and Delater come next, are two ill natured fellows and are at Coventry, *id est*, none of the young gentlemen speak with them. I am next and then Ward.

I must now beg leave to subscribe myself your dutiful son, JAMES TREVENEN.

Duty to Mama. My love to sisters, and little dear brother, and tell him I will write to him soon. I have written to my brothers and Mr. Bennablack and have received their answers.

No. 2

Royal Academy,
March 10, 1773

HONOURED FATHER,—Pardon my neglect this once and I promise never to be so again, if possible, but it was not willingly done, for I write so many letters to one or another that I do not know to whom I write. I have had a letter from my brother Jack lately in which he gave me an account of St. John St. Aubyn, and described him as a most sensible and good natured young gentleman, and did not leave out his itinerary with my brother Thomas. I give you and Mama my most grateful thanks for the token of your affection which you were so kind as to send me, and will for the future endeavour to deserve it. I am very sorry to hear of my sisters' illness and hope they will soon recover, which I shall be very glad to hear as soon as possible.

Master Penrose gave me an account of the proceedings of the tinners in Cornwall and of the mischief they have done at Penryn, which is not very inconsiderable from a letter which he received from his father. The other day when I told him of Mrs. Commins' death he appeared most concerned for her and asked me a great many questions about it, with such apparent concern that I greatly pitied him. He and I are very intimate together and are very seldon separate from each other if we can help it. He is one of the most good humoured gentlemen I ever saw. But Gwatkin is quite the contrary, for he is the most ill-natured fellow I ever saw. Carthew is another excellent character and so is Gomm. Though I do not like to praise myself I may safely say I have won the affections of my masters, particularly of Mr. Jeffrey's, the drawing and arithmetic master in whose hands I now am. Spencer the Irishman, when I first began my plan was above fifty before me and now is is not upwards of thirty seven. I hope this pleases you, from yr. ever dutiful son, JAMES TREVENEN.

No. 3

Portsmouth,
November 15, 1774

HONOURED MOTHER,—I received my father's letter of the 29th of last month in due time, but could not answer it till now, my time being almost wholly taken up by one thing or another. However I hope for the future to have more, for I have worked so hard of late that Penrose says he thinks I may finish easily by next Whitsuntide, when I expect to leave the Academy nem. con. If I had not promised to exert myself to the utmost in order to finish in that time I should nevertheless have numbers of incitements to do it and what Papa mentions would not be a slight one, viz. that soon there will be no Cornishmen left. Indeed I do not much care for Gwatkin, for I never liked him, but the Academy would have no charms which could make me desire to stay here when Penrose is gone; he is the life of it, and without him to would be very insipid. Among other incitements and a principal one is that my brother Jack will leave Westminster at that time; but enough of this, I shall now treat of something else. I believe I told you that Delater ran away from hence and was afterwards expelled, but I will now tell you of something worse. He lately wrote a letter to Charlton (who favoured me with a sight of it) and told him all his story. He says that when he arrived at London he was almost dead, for having disobliged all his friends (who now refused to have anything to say to him) and that later having spent the little money he had, in gambling and brothels, he pined away for about a month with hardly anything to support him, lying all night in the streets, but could not get a wink of sleep; but that one day walking in the Strand after having eaten nothing for two days and nights he met an acquaintance who gave him two or three shillings, treated him to a dinner and hired a lodging for him. He does not mention him any more, but says that his landlord soon began to dun him for money and threaten him; that one day walking out he happened to see a bill for enlisting soldiers and that he went and listed himself as a common soldier in the 70th Regiment of foot. There ends his account and I hope you will excuse my subscribing myself your dutiful son, JAMES TREVENEN.

No. 4

Portsmouth,
September 5, 1775

DEAR BROTHER TOM,—Once more before you leave Cornwall I write you that your last (letter I cannot call it, not even ticket, but rather a scrap of paper) did not deserve an answer. However, relying on your promise of writing to me soon, I've begun this. There are two ships now here fitting out to go round the world and to carry Omiah the Tahitean back to his native country. Now if Mama and Papa please I should like to go out in one of them. I believe they will sail in or about November. In their last voyage they lost but four men. It will be a most excellent breaking in for

me. I shall experience all climates, hot and cold to an extremity, and consequently shall always be prepared for any other station whatever. Charlton, another Academite, intends to go. Besides there are no ships fitting out for the Mediterranean, nor will there be I believe for this long time. I doubt not but that you and brother Jack came off with honour in your part of the play. I think you must be very happy all of you together, indeed I know you are. I had a letter lately from Mr. Wood, together with the shirt and two handkerchiefs which Mama sent me. Here I have been an hour racking my brains for something to say and what have I produced? Very little; however, that little must serve and I leave nothing more to do than to subscribe myself your loving brother, JAMES TREVENEN.
Pray write soon for I have been much disappointed since Christmas at not receiving a letter every fortnight. . . .

No. 5

Royal Academy,
January 16, 1776

DEAR BROTHER,—With a heavy heart I take up my pen to write a few lines on a subject altogether new to me, and which I wish had remained so much longer. What a loss we have sustained, and so unexpectedly![1] It is almost too much to bear. The post before I received the melancholy news I learned all was well. Grieved as I am, I do not feel so much for myself as for my mother and sisters at home; but let us not grieve too much, for that is in my opinion accusing the allwise dispensation of Providence. We must all die sooner or later and I heartily wish that I had passed the dangerous and unsteady paths of youth in the same manner our late honoured parent has done before me. I should then wait for death without any repining and with tranquillity. . . .

I hope soon to see you in London, but am not quite certain. The *Resolution* is in commission, so I shall soon get my discharge and then I shall wait upon the Captain (I suppose) at Deptford to get leave to go into Cornwall, and I dare say I shall obtain it. I imagine that Mr. Edwards will be our guardian. Brother Jack will soon be on his own. Before I return from my voyage our late father will almost be forgotten, but that will recall the memory of him, as I shall go out about the time he died. I hope there will be some alterations in our family by that time. The greatest pleasure I could now possibly receive would be to see my two sisters properly and happily disposed of. Dear girls, how I love them! We boys are of no consequence. Mr. Edwards first wrote to Mr. Witchell of my father's death and one morning coming into school he called me to him and asked me how old

[1] James' father died on December 4, 1775.

my father was. I said I believed not far from seventy. 'Have you heard of his being ill?' I then began to suspect and, says he, 'He is dead'. I could scarce believe it, but he gave me the letter. Then said he, 'Go into my parlour and read it'. I went up to my own room and cried a long time before I could prevail on myself to look into it. I was very much afflicted, so there I stayed till Mr. Witchell came to me. He then took me with him to his apartment and gave me two or three glasses of wine. He has behaved extremely well to me ever since. I drink tea and sup with him, as I dare say he imagines the noisy company of scholars does not well agree with my present melancholy condition, and indeed it is very true. Adieu, your afflicted brother, JAMES TREVENEN.

No. 6

Royal Academy,
February 19, 1774

DEAR SIR,—Master Trevenen having informed me that you desired to have his bills for the last six months, I have taken the opportunity of enclosing them in his frank. The young gentleman is extremely well in health and I have the satisfaction to add that he still maintained his former good character and what is indeed singular I do not remember that a single complaint has ever been made against him by any of the Masters since he has been at the Academy. This is truly a striking circumstance to be met with in a youth of his age.

I am, Rev. Sir, your most obedient humble servant, G. WITCHELL.

The following paragraph of a letter written in 1775 is inserted in the biography: 'I have spoken to Mr. Witchell about my going in the *Resolution*. He said he had no objections in the least but that it was a very hard voyage. That I knew before. Mar[?] came home lately from the West Indies and he told he that there was no life in the world so unhappy as that of a midshipman on account of the numberless hardships he must undergo. But I told him I was prepared for them all. I myself can see no pleasure in knocking it about at sea and eating nothing but salt beef; but then even that gives the greater relish to your enjoyment when you come ashore. What joy! after having been out three years to come home to your friends and what pleasure is seeing foreign countries and exploring new worlds! I should fill my sea chest with curiosities of all sorts. I think at least I could make myself comfortable at sea.'

Early in 1776 having gone through his studies in a manner highly honourable to his head, and pursued a line of conduct redounding as much to the credit of his heart, he was discharged from the Academy and gratified in his wish of being appointed to the *Resolution* under the command of the immortal Cook. The capacity in which youths are first entered on board ships of war after leaving the Academy is styled Volunteer by Admiralty Order. They are entitled only to Able Seamen's pay but wear the uniform and do the duty of Midshipmen and are looked upon as the first to receive the rating of Midshipmen as vacancies occur.

Having visited and taken leave of his friends in the west, he paid his first visit to London, where his time was busily employed preparing for his voyage. A letter to his brother at Cambridge dated April 22, 1776, amuses me as a good specimen of his impetuosity—

'The chest I had ordered to be carried on board the *Resolution* does not answer well. So I trudged to Captain Cook to take his directions concerning it. He was very dark and inconsistent. So I went from him rather dissatisfied and was in great doubt whether to take it or not, as I was afraid to disoblige him. While I was in this most miserable of all situations—suspense—in came Captain Mowat and his advice determined me to take two small chests instead of one large one. Then there were a thousand little things which I had not thought of. Upon this Wood and Nichols began with their comments, telling me what I should have done, etc., etc., and a parcel of stuff and nonsense which they knew no more about than your Cambridge hack. In short they teased me so much that I had a great mind to call them a couple of ignorant fellows. However, I governed myself for some time till they became so provoking that I started up and kicking the chairs about in a frenzy exclaimed with violence: "What do you keep preaching me about what should have been? I know that as well as you or anybody else. Tell me what I shall do now and I shall be obliged to you, or else hold your tongues!" '

A letter to his sister dated June 1776 gives an impression of London: 'I think the first thing that struck me was a post, which I ran against as I was gazing about, but I suppose you will say I struck the post and not the post me. Hah, Hah, Hah! But speaking seriously, of all places and things in London I am partial to St. Paul's because it is of service to me, for whenever I am out of my way I steer for it and am then in my right latitude. Mr. Knight is intimately acquainted with Captain Cook and will speak to him in my favour: "better and better", quoth I.'

Chapter 2

THE *RESOLUTION* AND *DISCOVERY*

Introduction

The *Resolution* sloop of 462 tons, which Cook had commanded on his second voyage round the world, was commissioned for his third voyage on February 9, 1776. Another Whitby-built ship, the *Discovery* (originally the *Diligence*) of 295 tons, was purchased to accompany her in place of the *Adventure*, Cook's other ship on his second voyage, because the latter was on service elsewhere. She was commanded by Captain Clerke, who died during the voyage, after which Lieutenant King transferred into her, together with Trevenen and other junior officers.

James King, who became Trevenen's particular friend although he was ten years older, had an unusual career as a naval officer. Like Trevenen, he was a parson's son, but he had entered the navy at the age of twelve as a captain's servant. He served during the Seven Years War, but during the time of Cook's two previous voyages he was studying scientific subjects at Paris and Oxford. Shortly before the third voyage he was recommended to the Admiralty by the Professor of Astronomy at Oxford as a naval officer with an interest in astronomy, and it was his astronomical observations which later procured him a fellowship of the Royal Society From this we can understand why he was chosen to write the continuation of the narrative of the Third Voyage after Cook's death, the three volume account being published in 1784.

The complement of the *Resolution* was 112 men, together with 20 marines under the command of Captain Molesworth Phillips. Her senior officers included John Gore, First Lieutenant, James King, Second, and John Williamson, Third, who was in charge of the boats at the time of Cook's death and of whose character Trevenen gives a very unpleasant account. William Bligh of *Bounty* fame was her Master. On board the *Discovery* was Lieutenant James Burney, brother of Fanny Burney and later the historian of the Pacific, and two midshipmen who were to win fame—George Vancouver and Edward Riou.

Trevenen's name does not appear on the Muster Book of the *Resolution* until May, when it is spelled 'Trevanion' and he is rated midshipman.[1]

[1] P.R.O. Adm. 36/8048.

It is impossible to give the exact number of 'young gentlemen' who sailed with him, because some are rated midshipmen, some master's mates, some able seamen. One of the youngsters was David Samwell, surgeon's mate, who became a close friend of Trevenen and wrote the most reliable account of Cook's death. The surgeon himself was William Anderson, whose notes on natural history were incorporated in the account of the voyage after his death during its course. Two at least of the young gentlemen were fellow Academites—Ward and Charlton (or Charleton). Others whose names appear in the following pages are William Lanyon, master's mate until he was made Lieutenant on August 23, 1779, and Taylor, rated as able seaman (as was Ward). The name of midshipman Nugent mentioned by Trevenen does not appear on the books of the ships. Cook refers to them collectively as 'several young men amongst my sea officers who, under my direction, could be usefully employed in constructing charts, in taking views of the coasts and headlands near which we should pass, and in drawing plans of the bays and harbours in which we should anchor.' Trevenen supplies some interesting evidence on how these duties were carried out.

The official objects of the voyage were twofold—to carry Omai back to his native Tahiti, and to discover the western exit of the North West Passage. As Trevenen's notes are very disconnected, a short account of the course of the voyage may be included here. Trevenen joined the ship a few days after she was hauled out of dock at Deptford on March 9, 1776. She did not sail down the river until May 29, nor did Cook assume command until she was at Sheerness on June 24. As will be seen, the Cape of Good Hope was the last place from which letters could be sent home. After visiting New Zealand and Tahiti, Cook continued northward to discover Christmas Island and then the Hawaian group, which he named the Sandwich Islands after the First Lord. He then turned east towards the coast of America, failed to notice the narrow entrance of the strait of Juan de Fuca owing to thick weather, and anchored at Nootka Sound on Vancouver Island on March 30, 1778. The ships then followed the coast northward to Alaska and through the Behring Straits as far as latitude 70° 44′, when further progress was checked by ice. On his return to Hawai'i Cook was killed at Kealakekua Bay on February 14, 1779. Captain Clerke assumed command, but as he was a sick man Lieutenants Gore and King became the real commanders. After another attempt to penetrate the Behring Straits had failed, the ships returned to Kamchatka where, off the harbour of St. Peter and St. Paul (the modern Petropavlovsk), Clerke died on August 22. King with Trevenen and others transferred into the *Discovery*, leaving Gore in command of the *Resolution*.

A visit to Canton enabled many of the crew to sell the skins they had collected in America. When they returned to the Cape of Good Hope they hoped to be home in a fortnight, unless involved in operations connected with the American War which had broken out since they left home. However, contrary winds detained them and ultimately compelled them to spend many weary weeks at Stromness in the Orkneys before they anchored in the Thames on October 4, 1780.

On October 3 both Gore and King were promoted Post-Captain, the former being appointed to a captaincy at Greenwich Hospital left vacant by Cook's death, the latter to the command of the *Crocodile* frigate in the Channel. Most of the midshipmen were commissioned lieutenant, Trevenen's commission being dated October 28, 1780.

Some difficulty has been experienced in arranging the following section because the few pages of Penrose's biography are of small importance compared with the notes written by Trevenen in the margin of his copy of Cook's narrative (which copy has not been traced). These notes were transcribed by Penrose as an appendix together with the letters, and a few of them were printed by John Penrose in 1850. I have rearranged the material as far as possible in chronological order, giving in italics the reference and context of Cook's narrative which Trevenen is annotating. In spite of their sporadic nature, these notes give valuable details about the circumstances of Cook's death and they extend our view of his modest and reticent character. He is seen from the midshipman's point of view—at one time a god to be idolised, at another a passionate and irritable despot who seems to have treated the 'young gentlemen' with undue severity. Hitherto the rougher side of his character has been chiefly illuminated by the remarks of Zimmerman, a Swiss seaman who was rated coxswain on the last voyage. According to the latter, Cook's 'expression was somewhat stern and so hasty tempered that the least contradiction on the part of an officer or sailor made him very angry. He was inexorable regarding the ship's regulations and the punishments connected with them', though on occasion he could be 'exceedingly affable to the crew'. Trevenen's notes, scanty as they are, give vivid examples of both sides of his character.

The Resolution sailed from Plymouth on July 12, 1776. The first opportunity Trevenen had of writing home was from Teneriffe on August 1.

'HONOURED MOTHER,—I have only time to tell you that I am well and happy. I don't believe I have another moment to express what I would to you, my dear Mother, only I knew you would be happy to hear from me. I am going on shore. We sail this afternoon. This goes by an English brig, going to Senegal and after to England. Remember, I am happy. Love to everybody. I am, and ever shall be, your dutiful son, JAMES TREVENEN.'

Table Bay,
October 23, 1776

'MY DEAR MOTHER,—A letter from James! Oh! my dear creatures, how eager I see you break open the seal of this. Be happy then! for I know it will make you so to hear that I am well and like the sea as well as ever. What a great pleasure it would be to me to hear from you whom I so tenderly love! But I must content myself with my old way at the Academy, viz. thinking of the pleasures of meeting, and I have now more occasion than ever. There, I heard from you every fortnight; now I am quite in the dark with regard to your health and everything concerning you, but I will always hope the best. While at sea I often used to hold conversation with you and in the dead of night, during my watch upon deck, while others used to be variously engaged and trying different ways to amuse themselves, I used to seek some quiet corner where I was least likely to be disturbed and retiring within myself was soon at Rosewarne. Often when thinking upon you the pearly drop would steal silently down my cheek, and at last I would melt into tears, but they were not tears of sorrow. They were tears of gratitude for your tenderness and love for me; and I was quite happy at the time when, had you seen me, you would have taken me for the most miserable person in the world. In general I have the greatest spirits, and am remarked for it; but so great is the contrarity that I am most happy when I appear least so. Indeed, I am never otherwise than happy, but there are a thousand pleasures I perceive when I am thinking of you, which otherwise I am a stranger to. How heartily do I pity those rough sailors (of whom we have many on board) who have no idea or notion of sensibility, and who laugh at those persons who show any tenderness for their relations, or who cannot drink as much grog as themselves. They are strangers to those feelings which constitute my *summum bonum.*'

The appendix of Penrose's life of Trevenen contains the only record left by him of the voyage of the Resolution. *This record is in the form of 'notes inserted by Trevenen in the margin of his brother's set of Cook's last voyage'. About half these notes were printed by John Penrose in his book on Penrose and Trevenen.*

Vol. II, p. 182. (Christmas Island, December 26, 1777. Cook writes: 'I ordered Captain Clerke to send a boat with an officer to the south east part of the island to look for turtle; Mr. King and I went each in a boat to the north east part'. Christmas Island, lat. 1° 58′ N., long, 157° 32′ W., had been discovered the previous day.)

After mentioning that he (Trevenen) had the command of the small cutter during their stay at Christmas Island, he gives the following account of the service he was on, and of the humours of the seamen:

'The service was rather a perilous one, as we had to pull into the lagoon over a very high sea (which, however, never broke) through a narrow passage with which we were little acquainted, and where we could see the bottom the whole way; had any sunken rocks projected higher than the rest, we had been destroyed, but luckily we never encountered any. On every side of us swam sharks innumerable, and so voracious that they bit our oars and rudder, and I actually stuck my hanger into the back of one while he had the rudder in his teeth.

'The boats fished for cavallos etc. in shallow water and carried long pikes to keep the sharks from the bait on board the ships. The sailors caught hundreds of them, and as these two species are always at war with each other, contrived abundance of ways to torment them. Sometimes they were tied together by their tails and turned adrift; others had large pieces of board tied under their heads; this is called *spritsail yarding* them and prevents them sinking, so that we saw them floating and vainly attempting to dive as far as the eye could reach.

'Besides turning the turtle when asleep, the common mode of catching them, we took another way, which afforded great sport. On the tide subsiding there remained about a foot of water (more or less) on the reef, which extended half a mile from the shore, where it is bounded by another ridge. But there were many deep holes where the turtles used to remain until the rising of the water again. The water was so clear that we could see them in these holes, and as all our people could swim to perfection, they could dive down and catch them by the fins, or pull them out; and then the chase and sport began, we, as well as the turtles, dashing through thick and thin and very ludicrous scenes occurred. In deep water they had the advantage; but when it was not deeper than six inches we could come up with them and catch them by the fins; but as one had often not strength enough to hold them, he would be dragged sometimes up, sometimes down, till others came to his assistance. On meeting with a large pool, into which the sailor would be dragged head foremost, perhaps the turtle would escape; and I have seen some larger than common thus taken three times and at last escape through a passage in the reef to the open sea. This chase was chequered with all the vicissitudes of hope and fear that can enliven any other, and was surely equally interesting—the more so, perhaps, as our dinner depended on the success of it. We once caught forty-two in half an hour.'

Not long after leaving Christmas Island the discovery of the ever memorable Sandwich Islands took place. I understand that they were first seen by Trevenen's friend Ward. It has generally been the practice to mention the names of those who have first been the discoverer of places far less important than this, and as there is a species of honour attached to it, I mention it here.[1]

Every anecdote relative to those islands must be interesting. I shall therefore omit no note that relates to them.

> *Vol. II, p. 251.* (Cook, describing the early history of the Pacific, points out how useful these islands would have been to the Spaniards for their Manila galleon, and also to the English buccaneers 'who sometimes used to pass from the coast of America to the Ladrones with a stock of food and water scarcely sufficient to preserve life. Here they might always have found plenty'.)

'Clipperton,[2] who commanded two privateers from England, after parting with his consort Shelvocke and lost his own ship, crossed the Pacific ocean in a small vessel of about 20 tons in the latitude of 18° north. The south part of Owhyhee discovered on our return to these islands lies in 18° 15′ N., so that he could not have been twenty leagues from them.'

> *Vol. II, p. 273.* (April 1, 1778. Cook describes the 'great concourse of Indians visiting the ships as they anchored in Nootka Sound.')

'An anecdote I shall relate may not be amiss here and will serve to illustrate what is afterwards said of the hasty, violent disposition of these people and their fearless independent spirit, which apprehended no danger from any other than the person with whom they had particularly quarrelled as well as manifesting that phlegm which enters strongly into their tempers. An old North Briton of a most irascible spirit had been fixed upon as boatkeeper, the station to which he was best fitted by his infirmities, and that might render him useful from his known care and vigilance. In despite

[1] This was Atooi, sighted on January 18, 1778 (mentioned below), but Cook does not say by whom. Owhyhee is the modern Hawaii.

[2] Clipperton's ship *Success* (260 tons) parted from Shelvocke's *Speedwell* in 1720 to intercept the Manila galleon. According to the account in Harris' collection of voyages (1705, Vol. I, p. 184) Clipperton crossed from Mexico to Guam in fifty-three days in latitude 13°: 'In this passage they lost six of their people, and the rest were so weak and low that nothing could be a more joyful sight to them than this island.'

of this, however, he had been so often outwitted and of course reprehended for neglect of duty, that he was become as savage as the most savage tribe around him, with whom he had perpetual quarrels; and at last in an attempted theft, resolving to take full vengeance on the offender, he made a blow at him with the boat's stretcher, a thick, heavy piece of wood which would effectually have done his business had it taken place, but missing him it fell with such force on the side of the canoe as to break it down to the water's edge. His antagonist, withdrawing the canoe out of his reach, was preparing to return the compliment by transfixing him with an arrow that he had most deliberately drawn to the head for that purpose, when Mr. Phillips,[1] who had that instant made purchase of a bow and arrow from another Indian, let fly at the savage with such good aim that the arrow passed close to his ear and called off his attention from the old man in the boat; when, seeing the number of his adversaries increasing, and that the affair was likely to come to no good, he quietly laid down his arms and paddled off in peace.'

No anecdote relative to Captain Cook can be uninteresting to a Briton, although it might not perhaps be right to expose the rougher part of his character, if the world was not already aware that this great man was of a hasty and somewhat tyrannic disposition to his inferior officers and crew, and that mankind know themselves so well as not to expect perfection in a fellow mortal. Captain Cook's character might perhaps be best given in a few words—'He was the best and most successful navigator that ever lived.'

Vol. II, p. 279. (April 20, 1778. Cook writes: 'I set out to take a view of the Sound' i.e. Nootka Sound on Vancouver Island.)

'I with several other of our midshipmen attended Captain Cook on this expedition, in which we rowed him not less than thirty miles during the day. We were fond of such excursions, although the labour of them was very great; as not only was this kind of duty more agreeable than the humdrum routine on board the ships, but as it gave us an opportunity of seeing different peoples and countries; and also another very principal consideration we were sure of having plenty to eat and drink, which was not always the case on board on our usual allowance. Captain Cook also on these occasions would sometimes relax from his almost constant severity of disposition and condescended now and then to converse familiarly with us. But it was only for a time; as soon as on board the ship he became again the despot.'

[1] Molesworth Phillips, Captain of Marines, who married Susan, sister of James and Fanny Burney, in 1782.

Vol. II, p. 283. (April 22, 1778. Cook describes a second visit to the village at the west point of Nootka Sound.)

'There was another reason for our revisiting this town. In making a sketch of the Sound I had been employed in taking the necessary bearings the last time we were here, and on our return nothing could be made of them. Of course I had a *Heiva* of the old boy (MS. NOTE—*Heiva*: The name of a dance of the southern islanders which bore so great a resemblance to the violent motions and stampings upon deck of Captain Cook in the paroxysms of passion into which he frequently threw himself on the slightest occasions that they were universally known by the same name, and it was a common saying, both among officers and men, 'the old boy has been tipping a heiva to such and such a one'.) But in this second visit, going to the same place, and placing the compass in the old station, it was found that there was some magnetic quality in the rocks which threw it quite out of its proper direction. On examination all the rocks were found covered with a sort of iron sand.'

Vol. II, p. 306. (April, 1778. Cook is describing the appearance of the Nootka Indians and the way their faces were 'smeared with tallow mixed with paint'.)

'This is an operation of much importance, on which they bestow much time and pains. They are assisted in it by a piece of polished slate, which, when dipped in water, is a tolerable substitute for a looking-glass, and serves them in its stead. I have seen them discontented with the first and sometimes second attempt, and after rubbing all off their faces begin again. A ground of grease and red ochre is first laid on, then the iron sand or glimmer, and the rest of the operation performed by the finger before the slate.'

The indefatigable ingenuity of a Nootka Sound thief can hardly be better illustrated than by the following anecdote. 'One of them had nearly got off with a double cross cut saw, used by the carpenters ashore, which he had contrived to twist round his body, and hide under his clothes so ingeniously as almost to avoid suspicion.'

When in King William's Sound (Alaska) he gives a remarkable instance of the vast profits of the earliest fur traders to North America. 'To give some idea of the vast profit to be expected here in a trade for skins, I may mention the following circumstance. Mr. Bligh, the Master, while at Otaheite (Tahiti) had given a shilling hatchet for thirty large green Spanish beads on which the natives there set little value, but which he thought might be useful on the course of the voyage; accordingly in this country he purchased six sea otter skins with twelve of the beads. These skins might have sold in China at a low average of £15 each. Here we find a quick return of £90 for one shilling!'

A little adventure which befell Trevenen at Owhyhee during the first stop of the ship at that island strongly evinces the friendly footing our countrymen were then in with the inhabitants. 'A constant exchange of good offices and little acts of friendship obtained among us. I once had occasion to experience the good effects of it, where the assistance received seemed to flow entirely from a desire to be of service to those who wanted it without any view to interest. Having occasion with two other midshipmen to go off to the ships at night through a considerable surf, the canoe we had engaged filled and sank at about twenty yards from the shore, to which we had to swim and land on a rocky beach difficult of access. Some little children playing near the spot had observed us, and whilst one or two ran to the houses near by for better assistance, the rest came down to us crying and, leaning over the rock, reached out their little hands to endeavour to help us up it. They afterwards conducted us to a village, running by our side, and uttering the most endearing expressions of pity and concern. We were equally well received at the village: another large canoe was immediately launched and we were conveyed to the ship in safety without any demand whatever for pay or reward.'

The Death of Captain Cook. The notes are in their nature so unconnected that without material and borrowed aid I cannot form them into a narrative, but as the account of the voyage is very generally spread through this kingdom, the possessors may be pleased to add to it such additional information as I can give them.

Vol. III, p. 46. (*Conclusion of King's account of Cook's death.*)

'The man who stabbed Captain Cook was, according to the best accounts of such a sudden and confused transaction, an old thief, whom Captain Cook himself had kicked out of the ship the day before with many expressions of anger for having committed a theft. He was immediately shot dead by John Perkins, a marine from the boats.

'From this circumstance it appears probable that though the rage of the islanders had risen to such a pitch before the fatal blow was given, that still their respect for Captain Cook's person was such that it required the strong stimulative of a personal resentment to raise a hand to such a bold action. The mortality of this idolized man being now made apparent, the savage thirst for blood prompted their hitherto checked hands to satiate their brutal fury by mangling the body with wounds. May we not hope, however, that these reiterated wounds soon placed the gallant man beyond reach of pain and anxiety, and thus mercy may have been the fruit of their brutality?'

Vol. III, p. 54. (King describes the efforts to cover the retreat from the shore after Cook's death. The *Resolution* put out 'a small boat, manned by five of our young midshipmen (which) pulled towards the shore'.)

'The five gentlemen who were in this boat were Messrs. Lanyon, Ward, Taylor, Charlton, Trevenen. Although we had not seen Captain Cook in the other boats when they pulled off to the ships, and now saw the dead bodies lying on the beach, we did not think of Captain Cook being killed, therefore we also pulled off. The fact is that I, as well as the others, had been so used to look up to him as our good genius, our safe conductor and as a kind of superior being, that I could not suffer myself—I could not dare to think—he would fall by the hands of the Indians, over whose minds and bodies he had been used to rule with absolute sway.'

Vol. III, p. 62. (King describes how, after Cook's death, the chief Koah swam 'off towards the boat with a white flag in his hands' and an invitation to come on shore. King put off in a boat, sending Midshipman Vancouver to ask the opinion of Captain Clerke, who was sick, whether he should land. The latter ordered him to return to the ship.)

'It has been seen that Koah put himself in our power by swimming off to our boat, and it may be a query whether we might have trusted equally to them. If it be true that suspicion always haunts the guilty mind, we may conclude the reverse of the position to be true also, and that confidence and openness belong unfailingly and almost exclusively to the generous and undesigning; yet our respective conduct here was contrary both to the one and to the other. We had certainly no treacherous designs against the natives, yet were afraid to trust ourselves among them. Koah's behaviour was open and unsuspicious, yet we thought we had reason to suspect his designs, and therefore did not return his confidence, even though he put himself wholly in our power. The case, however, was somewhat unequal. He was a chief, but not a supreme one. They thought that Captain King was now become our principal commander, therefore to get him in their power might be worth hazarding something for, as leading to consequences which might be ultimately fatal to both ships. The object for which we were to trust him with them was not equally important, therefore we thought our mutual confidence unwarrantable and were unanimously of opinion that he should not go on shore.'

Vol. III, p. 65. (Those on board the ships could see the natives on the beach using 'the most insulting and contemptuous gestures . . . among them a chief was handling Captain Cook's hanger and a woman was holding the scabbard.')

'I saw this from one of the boats which was scarce more than ten yards from the man. The hanger was bloody; he washed it in the sea, told us he had been cutting up the body of our chief, and that if we came ashore he would serve us in the same manner.

'Notwithstanding our state of hostility, the women swam off to the ship every night. Having the guard about midnight, and observing an Indian jump on board, I presented my musket and should certainly have fired had not I luckily been prevented in time by being told it was a woman.

'By the light of the fires we could plainly see the Indians in motion about them, and this sight, joined to the stillness of the night, produced the most awful solemnity, now and then interrupted by their hideous cries and yellings, and was finely calculated to make impression on our already agitated feelings.'

Vol. III, p. 75. (A few days later a landing party made reprisal by burning a hut. Unfortunately the fire spread to the village and 'several natives were shot in making their escape from the flames, and our people cut off the heads of two of them and brought them on board'.)

'The heads had been, before they were carried on board, stuck on poles and waved to the crowds of Indians assembled on the hills about half a mile off. A cry of horror and an involuntary motion of starting back was instantly observed among them; and with the instance of exposing themselves to carry off the dead bodies of their friends, served to convince us that they have some superstitious notions with regard to their treatment after death, depending on their interment with proper ceremonies.'

Vol. III, p. 76. (After the fire the members of a deputation, led by a friendly Indian called Kaireekeea, were seized and brought on board.)

'When brought on board he had the paleness of death on his countenance, and appeared utterly insensible and stupid. It will be allowed he had reason for his apprehensions. He had seen several of his countrymen killed, and the heads of two of them were in the boat. A sailor presenting one of them to him, face to face, told him in a little while he would be like it. When first unbound and set at liberty, he put no trust in it, but sat silent and totally disregarded every thing and every person, till at last, being assured of his safety, he began to raise his head and look round him, but the mingled emotions of hope and fear were strongly depicted on his countenance.

By degrees he crept towards the gangway and at last seeing to a certainty that nobody stopped him, he returned quick as lightning and threw himself with rapture at the feet of the officer upon deck, embracing his knees with the most lively demonstrations of joy and gratitude. Then, flying away again, he went ashore, and in a little time returned with a canoe full of provisions, and was very useful afterwards. The two heads were thrown overboard in his sight, lest he should suppose us cannibals.'

Vol. III, p. 77. (April 18, 1779. Koah appearing alongside in a canoe, King 'ordered him to keep off. He went immediately on shore and joined a party of his countrymen who were pelting the waterers with stones. The body of the young man who had been killed the day before was found this morning and some of our people went and threw a mat on it.')

'The hatred of the ship's crew against this man (Koah) for his double-dealing and treachery was very great. After many escapes he had nearly fallen a sacrifice to it here, for Mr. Nugent, midshipman, pursued him up close to the body of his countrymen, where, being very near, he snapped his pistol, which unluckily misfired.'

Vol. III, p. 82. (February 22, 1779. Departure from Hawai'i.)

'An universal gloom and strong sentiments of grief and melancholy were very observable throughout all ranks on board the ship on our quitting this bay without our great and revered commander.'

Vol. III, p. 92. (March 1, 1779. The ship next anchored off Atooi, where a watering party under Captain King ran into trouble with the natives, 'who became every moment more daring and insolent. On this occasion I was indebted to the sergeant of marines for suggesting to me the advantage that would arise from sending off his party first in the boats.')

'Never did any people run greater risks than Captain King and his party did here, and nothing but the most consummate prudence and knowledge of the Indians saved them from a repetition of the Karakakoa scenes. I am confident it must have happened had not that late instance repressed the impetuosity and confident superiority of our people, and their fear kept them in good order. Indeed, I have been told by every one of the party that they never expected to have got off to the ship again, and were of the opinion that everything ought to be abandoned, and their attempts for that day confined to saving themselves; but Captain King resolved to perform the duty he was sent on, which he did with the most perfect judgement.

'The sergeant of marines was the same Samuel Gibson mentioned[1] in Captain Cook's first voyage as having endeavoured to escape from the ship at Otaheite (Tahiti). This was his third voyage with Captain Cook, with whom he was a great favourite, having saved his life once in one of the skirmishes with the Indians at New Zealand. He spoke the language better than anyone except Mr. Anderson,[2] and was always a very great favourite with the Indians. He was taken ill afterwards in the Straits of Sunda, but was recovering when we arrived at Stromness in the Orkneys, where he married, and died on our passage to the River (Thames). I should have said before that he was wounded at the same time and in the same manner as Captain Cook and Mr. Phillips, and like the latter escaped only by killing his adversary. He had fallen overboard, intoxicated, in the night a little before our arrival in Karakakooa bay, and was with difficulty saved from drowning by a machine called a *life buoy*, cut away as soon as he fell off the deck, and after remaining an hour in the sea, which here abounded with sharks, he was picked up by a boat directed to him by the ringing of a bell on top of the machine.'[3]

In a paper loose in the last volume of the voyage I find the following memorandum which appears to have been a sketch of the character of Captain Cook, and from the manner of its construction was clearly meant to have been extended. It will draw the minds of the readers to do justice to the memory of Cook and may close this series of notes, which however trifling some may appear, I dare say the possessors of the voyage, at least the generality of them, will be glad to enrich the margins with most, if not all.

'The coolness and conciseness with which Captain Cook passes over the relation of dangers, the bare recollection of which makes every one else shudder with horror, is very remarkable. These imminent dangers and hairbreadth escapes in other hands would have afforded subjects for many laboured and dreadful descriptions, and would even have justified them. The want of such may make him lose the credit of having avoided or surmounted them by his skill and prudence with readers who reflect not on causes and effects, or on natural and unavoidable consequences; but he who once revolves in his mind the immense extent of the coast that Captain

[1] On July, 9, 1769, Cook describes how two marines, Webb and Gibson, deserted and how he used a chief held as a hostage to ensure their return three days later, when they explained that an acquaintance contracted with two girls induced them to desert before the ship sailed. They were punished with two dozen lashes each. Molyneux's journal describes Gibson as 'a wild young man'. (Hakluyt Society's edition of the Voyage of the *Endeavour*, ed. J. C. Beaglehole, 114, 562.)

[2] William Anderson, the surgeon, whose notes on natural history were incorporated in the narrative of the voyage. He died of consumption when the ships were off Alaska.

[3] This appears to be the first recorded use of the words 'life buoy'. The bay where Cook was killed is now named 'Kealakekva'.

Cook has in this voyage surveyed, the earliness of the season when he began it, and the advanced state of it when he left off, the badness of the provisions which had already been three years from England, the intricacies of the coast, the inlets, rocks, and shoals that would make, when well known, the boldest pilot tremble to venture on it, the length of time which his crew remained in and bore with the consequent fatigue of such uncommon and accumulated circumstances of distress, passed among rocks and fields of ice in thick fogs, with the entire privation of fresh meat and such necessary comforts as alone can render men capable of undergoing extreme hardships; with the allowed hazard of navigating among ice; must wonder at and admire the boldness of daring and skill in executing projects big with every danger; but as his mind was more impressed with the thought of duty, and the general consequences of his undertaking, no danger or difficulty had the power of turning away his thoughts from this object. Nor is the good fortune of the discovery of the Sandwich Islands to be omitted, which saved us from wintering at Kamchatka, where a want of fresh provisions and a more [less?] genial climate would probably have proved fatal to many lives.'

In John Penrose's biography of Trevenen some verses in Cook's memory are printed which do not appear in the MS., but a in scrap book dated 1787.

O genius superior, in forming whom, nature
Had an eye to the moulding a great navigator,
And toward thy mids thou wert nor very nice,
Declaring thou 'dst have 'no more cats than catch mice,
'Not here do you come to see fashions, or folly, but
'To hold on the nippers, and row in the jolly-boat';
And though still wouldst thou send me, when by the wind steering,
To haul out the weather mizen topsail reef earing,
Yet now I'll remember thy wholesome severity,
Or remember 'twas meant but to give me dexterity.
No! rather I'll think on that happiest season,
When turned into thy boat's crew without rhyme or reason,
But proud of that office, we went a marooning,
And pulling 'gainst tide, or before the wind spooning,
Sometimes we were shooting and sometimes surveying,
With pleasure still watching, with pleasure obeying,
Till pleased with our efforts, thy features relax,
And thou giv'st us thy game to take home on our backs.
O day of hard labour, O day of good living,
When TOOTE[1] was seized with the humour of giving—

[1] The Polynesian pronunciation of 'Cook'

When he clothed in good nature his looks of authority,
And shook from his eyebrows their stern superiority.

During the long remainder of the voyage until the return to the Cape in 1780, when opportunities for writing letters occurred again, we must be content with fancying our friend an active sharer in the occurrences related by Captains Cook and King.

I recollect, however, one anecdote strongly marking the amazing profit which the earliest fur traders to the North-West coast of America must have made. When the ships were in Nootka Sound, Trevenen accidentally holding the rim of a broken buckle in his hand, observed a native with looks of admiring envy gazing on the lovely trinket. It was immediately accommodated as a bracelet to his arm and an offer made to treat for it. The Indian thought he had made a very advantageous bargain when a very fine sea otter's skin was accepted as an equivalent. This skin, on the return of the ships to China, sold, if I am not mistaken, for three hundred dollars. At any rate its value was such as to enable Trevenen to purchase not only what he wanted to supply his own necessities, but silk gowns, fans, teas and other articles, which he brought home as presents to his sisters and friends.

When the fatal dispute with the natives of Owhyhee on February 14, 1779, which deprived the world of its greatest navigator, took place, he was employed in one of the boats; and I well remember always expressed much dissatisfaction that greater exertions were not made to recover the body of their adored commander, which he thought might easily have been done. He was highly pleased with the general spirit with which his friend Samwell's account of that transaction was written; yet he expressed himself not so thoroughly satisfied as he expected to have been from the very high opinion he entertained of the gentleman's abilities. But although he says in a letter to a friend: 'It is not what I expected from him. Some things are represented different from my conception, and in situations which should seem to render minute detail impossible,' I perfectly recollect his earnest recommendation of the work to his friends, suggesting it to be bound up with Captain King's continuation of the voyage as highly useful in giving a clear insight into the business of that eventful period, and in some measure accounting to the public why some serious notice was not taken of the supposed defaulter.[1]

Trevenen was on this occasion in the small cutter, which boat was manned by the midshipmen only, who, however they benefitted by the great example

[1] An MS. note to this passage runs 'Perhaps better omitted'. The defaulter was Lieut. Williamson, in command of the boats. He was challenged to a duel on the voyage home by Phillips and was later cashiered for cowardice after the battle of Copenhagen. Samwell supports Trevenen's opinion that more could have been done to rescue Cook's body. His narrative was printed in 1786.

of Captain Cook, and on the whole may have profited by his rigid manners towards them, yet, during the time when they were under his command, perhaps underwent more hardships than any other description of men engaged in the undertaking. For besides their constant watching and unwearied attention to looking out for land, rocks, etc. for which they receive in a handsome way the merited acknowledgement at the end of Captain King's continuation of Cook's voyage, they were frequently sent on the severest boat-service, acting at once as officers and common seamen. This mode of treatment, carried to an extreme, is prejudicial to the service, by placing those who are so often to command on a footing with those who are to be commanded by them. And although it may not perhaps be so hurtful as the now too prevalent system of entire relaxation, yet it is a great injustice to men of education and science, whose minds and bodies are formed by habit for far different employments.

On the death of Captain Clerke,[1] Trevenen removed with Captain King into the *Discovery*, as this gentleman had always shown a very friendly attention to him, and found him of great service in the astronomical observations and calculations during the voyage. Honourable mention is made of his ability and attention in this part of the labours of the voyage in several places of Captain King's continuation.[2]

From November 1776 to May 1780 he had no opportunity of writing to his friends. Having given his letter of October 23, 1776, describing his feelings at the beginning of the voyage, I now extract some parts of that of May 1780 on their return to the Cape of Good Hope after a tedious absence from all communication with his country or connections—

'My Most revered Mother,—An address to a mother after so long an absence, and entire ignorance of what may have befallen at home, is a circumstance altogether so new to me that I find myself at a loss how to behave. The darkness and uncertainty with regard to events the most interesting cannot fail to give a serious turn to my thoughts, and I tremble with apprehension. On the other hand, when I recollect that I have once more a dawn of happiness breaking upon me—that I am once more in a fair way to see and converse with all I hold dear—the tide of joy is so tumultous as to render me equally unfit to express my sentiments. But I feel myself already excused by you for not being more full when I tell you that at least in a fortnight after your receipt of this I hope to be in your

[1] On August 22, 1779, off Petropavlovsk on the coast of Kamchatka.

[2] After stating that only on two occasions during the whole voyage did the ships lose sight of each other, King concludes—'A stronger proof cannot be given of the skill and vigilance of our subaltern officers, to whom this share of merit almost entirely belongs.' When he transferred to the *Discovery*, King says he took with him 'four midshipmen who had made themselves useful to me in astronomical calculations'.

embraces. Good God! the thought is too much. Far, far away, my eyes and steps have been directed from you, but my thoughts never. You still constitute my chief happiness amidst all the bustle and variety of sea life. I have written many a long letter to you, though I knew it could never be delivered; but it relieved my mind after the variety of business I had been engaged in—was indeed my most pleasing occupation; gave me a gleam of joy that helped to dissipate the gloom around me, and whenever I was melancholy proved a never-failing consolation.'

The remainder of this letter is mainly to acknowledge his obligations to Captain King, and to take care that those of a pecuniary nature should be discharged to his friends in case of any accident happening to the ship. After regretting the uncertainty of seeing his friends, at least for any long period, on account of the war, and feeling a little low on that reflection, he ends his letter by resolving. 'However, let us make the best on't. Nothing can hinder me from enjoying the pleasures of anticipation.'

On August 22, 1780, the ships anchored safely in the harbour of Stromness in the Orkneys, where they were cruelly detained by foul winds. And it was October 4 before they arrived at the Nore, after an absence of four years, two months and twenty-two days.

I

Stromness,
August 23, 1780

'I fancy by this time you have received my letter from the Cape of Good Hope. Long ere this I hoped to be happy in your company, but by a set of untoward accidents, vexatious disappointments and other unaccountable causes we have been so delayed in our passage from the Cape that I fear my confident assertion of being with you within a fortnight of the receipt of it is already rendered vain; though with regard to the delays of wind and weather, the *Sybille* frigate, in which I sent it, must have experienced the same as ourselves. We sailed five days after her and at the first outset were unfortunate, having a gale of wind off the Cape that not only hindered us from advancing on our way, but drove us considerably out of it. After this, constant calms were extremely mortifying to a set of people who, having been above four years absent from their native country, were eagerly impatient to revisit it, and could ill brook delays at such a critical juncture. You will guess by your feelings that I was not the least desirous, but my dear mother often used to tell me that I might go to sea to learn patience, and in truth our voyage has afforded some capital lessons; but they were all insufficient to make me even tolerably easy.

When expecting to go into Falmouth a most ill-natured wind drove us to this last corner of the world (the Orkneys, north of Scotland). I was happy as a prince, hugging myself in the thoughts of how happy and surprised you would all be on hearing I was so near you, and that perhaps while reading my letter I should come with a thousand fine things, amongst which I did not forget that Fanny Goodridge and her sweet sisters lived at Flushing [near Falmouth]. Under their hospitable roof I expected to learn the first account of your welfare, for otherwise I did not dare to think.

But all my castles are demolished, and at present we are safe lodged at Stromness, where I think myself as much out of the world as when freezing under the North Pole. In my letter from the Cape I wished we might have a safe passage through the French Spaniards and Americans. It was then very doubtful, for though our ships are of good size (at least one), our force was small and most privateers would have been an over-match for us, not being at all fitted for war. However, it was the appearance of our ships that preserved us, for we met with many who came to reconnoitre us, when by putting a good countenance on the matter we fairly bullied them and they sheered off.[1]

We have been on the whole about four weeks in our passage, perhaps one of the longest ever known, it being commonly done in ten or eleven [days]. But to have done with it, and think how long it may be before we leave this place for sweet England. An express is gone off for London, and as we are to wait here some time it cannot be less than three weeks before we arrive in the Thames, a dire space to be idle in whilst others are so heavily employed and every hour teems with great events. After that time we are uncertain how we shall be disposed. If so, I cannot say how soon I may yet see you. If we are ordered home the shortest way, unless ill luck continues, less than a fortnight will carry us to the Thames. I shall take care to inform you as I learn them which way our motions trend. Meantime, as calms and foul winds may detain us, a letter from you will stand a pretty good chance of reaching me; what a desirable thing it will be in my present uncertainty of how matters stand, you will easily judge.

If the war lasts I may yet hope for a lieutenancy, but if a peace is soon concluded, after that for many years there will be little chance of it, and although I am as much enamoured of a sea life as ever, it is not in the

[1] Trevenen need not have worried about enemy interference. Soon after Cook sailed, the French Minister of Marine issued instructions that 'as such discoveries are of general utility to all nations, it is the King's pleasure that Captain Cook shall be treated as the commander of a neutral and allied power, and that all captains of armed vessels who may meet with that famous navigator shall make him acquainted with the King's order on this behalf, but at the same time let him know that on his part he must refrain from all hostilities'. Similar instructions were issued in Spain, and by Franklin in France on behalf of the American government, but his order was revoked by Congress. See p. 33.

station of a midshipman that I shall approve it, or will you, for that length of time.

I am almost afraid some mischief has befallen my old friend Penrose, as his name is not down in the lists of lieutenants for the year 1779.[1] It is almost the only one except mine and one or two more in the ship of all the Academites who were above me, and a great many below me. I do not envy others, but I may think myself unlucky. However, I am resolved not to be unhappy on that account as yet. My captain's warm interest towards promotion I am sure of. I told you before that on the death of Captain Clerke I left the *Resolution* and went into the *Discovery* with one of our lieutentants, Mr. King. With him I may say I have lived ever since more as a friend (he is hardly old enough for me to say son) than as a midshipman. As I came in here almost naked, it will require some money to fit me out again. This I shall get of him.

This letter was written off Ireland. By foul winds were were disappointed of getting into Galloway [Galway] bay, and forced us here, where I find the post just ready to set off and absolutely have no time to write another letter calculated to my present situation.

Your dutiful son, JAMES TREVENEN.

II

Stromness, Orkneys,
August 31, 1780

MY MOST BELOVED AND HONOURED MOTHER,—[After three pages admitting that he has 'no material business' to tell his mother, Trevenen continues] Our Commander is certainly the only person in the fleet that does not eagerly will to get home, but his being not so is sufficient to keep us perhaps another month longer from the Thames mouth, and indeed there is a report of us going into Leith, a town not far from Edinburgh. What reason can be given for it, no one knows but himself, nor perhaps himself neither. I may speak too freely of my commander, but his conduct justifies it. At common times we were always glad to visit as many places as possible for reasons obvious, being travellers, and Edinburgh is a place to gratify curiosity in a high degree. But now everything gives way to the more natural and stronger emotions of filial and fraternal love. The Commander (I speak of Mr. Gore of the *Resolution*) is a good man, but he certainly keeps us out without any occasion. However, it is possible (but

[1] Penrose was commissioned Lieutenant on August 17, 1779; Trevenen on October 28, 1780. When the latter's ship was at Stromness the former, in the *Cleopatra*, was cruising north of Scotland and in a fog actually boarded a vessel which an hour previously had been hailed by the *Discovery*.

only possible) that there might be a hidden cause; any opinion may be too rash, therefore must not be seen by any outside the family, as walls have ears; it might do me harm. At any rate I only speak the general view.

The news we hear of the honours paid to Captain Cook's memory, and the reported intentions of the Admiralty towards his followers, flatter us with hopes of promotion, which however we are afraid to indulge too far for fear of disappointment at last. It is perhaps not very Christianlike to wish a continuance of the war, but we shall all be very sorry for it to be over without our having a share in it. We wish to contribute to its glory as Warriors as well as Discoverers; the dangers we have gone through have been chiefly of another kind. Besides this, the sight of a large American privateer just brought in here by two of our frigates excites our avarice and prize money tinkles in our ears. We ourselves are, it seems, franked by the French and Spaniards in consequence of the publicity of our expedition, but this recollection only renders us uneasy that we did not take advantage of the circumstances to come up the English Channel, by which means we could have saved a month in the time of our arrival in the Thames. However, 'tis best to be content. We are used to vexations and armed against them by habit. For my part I am as happy as the above circumstances will admit. Shall I finish with 'dutiful son'? 'Tis too lame an expression of my feelings. I am your ever dear loving and (I know) beloved son, JAMES TREVENEN.

III

Stromness,
September 7, 1780

MY DEAR MOTHER,—Again to my sorrow I am obliged to prefix Stromness to my letter. A constant foul wind again detained us another week, and still blows with as little likelihood of change as ever. From this circumstance you will perhaps find a spirit of discontent throughout my paper, and I must acknowledge that I can hardly help indulging it, or thinking that it so much longer delays my commission as lieutenant, which at least I hope for. It is indeed delay alone that will be the most likely thing to keep me from it. What a deal we have to hope for from a fair wind, and how much to fear from the continuance of a foul one. By the former I may gain the wished lieutenancy, and what I still more impatiently expect, the sight of all that's dear. By the latter the first is risked and the last cruelly put off.

We have now been three weeks idle in this place, whereas if that time had been properly managed I might ere this have been blessed in your company, and again at sea, joining with others in the glorious task of defending my country. Constantly hearing of engagements, victories and defeats, it is with the greatest indignation I look upon our now useless idle ships, hitherto so active and vigorous in their motions. I mean when when actuated by the sublime and soaring genius of a Cook. . . .

That the wind may soon alter and waft me to happiness in your company is the ardent wish of your impatient son, JAMES TREVENEN.

IV

Stromness,
September 9, 1780

MY DEAREST MOTHER,—Since my last letter a new and unexpected manoeuvre has taken place, which gives me another opportunity of writing, and perhaps to more purpose than my former letter. Captain Gore of the *Resolution* (our commander-in-chief) has taken it into his head, on account of the continued easterly winds, which afford no prospect of us getting away from this place, to send Captain King of the *Discovery* (which ship you already know I am in) to London with all the papers, etc., relating to the voyage. He goes in a Customs House cutter that sails remarkably well, and makes good her way against any foul wind, as far as Leith; the rest of the way by land. It is probable that he will get to London long before our ships, and in that case he has promised to me his interest as far as it will go, for the advantage of all his shipmates. I have reason to think, nay, I am sure, that I shall be at least one of the first he will consider, as he wishes to have me (and I, wishing the same, have promised to go with him) in his next ship as a lieutenant, if a commission can be obtained. If it were not my sincere desire, gratitude for his unnumbered favours would engage me to sail with him. He is a nephew of Sir Fletcher Norton, Speaker of the House of Commons.[1] Had Sir Fletcher still been in the Ministry, Captain King would have been sure of getting everything he asked, and readily granted, but as the Speaker has lately gone over to the minority this will be more doubtful. It will therefore be necessary if my brother can make any interest by speaking to Mr. Buller,[2] or elsewhere, that it should be applied so as to co-operate with my Captain. He has most obligingly, the better to effect this purpose, agreed to take my letter with him and in London to hold correspondence by letters or personal, if waited on (as it is impossible for him to find people out whom he knows not, and to whom I cannot direct him) with anyone who will

[1] Sir Fletcher Norton, 1716–89, a distinguished lawyer chosen as Speaker in 1770, but quarrelled with the Court in 1777 and later attacked Lord North.

[2] Perhaps Sir Francis Buller, 1746–1800, a Cornishman who, at the age of thirty-two, became the youngest man ever to be created an English judge.

take so much trouble for me. I shall therefore subjoin his direction. It is a little melancholy that I know no person in London. Was I sure of Mr. Woods being still there, I should in that instance apply to him. Indeed, I shall now at a venture write to him, and as perhaps any of my brothers may be in London to them through his channel. Of their readiness to exert themselves on my behalf I am quite certain. My good Tom has already done it quite sufficiently—I mean in the trouble he took with Mr. Buller on my coming out in the *Resolution.*

I have already mentioned the hopes we have from the reported intentions of the Admiralty which we hear, from the merits of the voyage alone, to prefer all such as shall be found capable. In this case all other interest will be needless and may serve for another opportunity. At any rate I cannot trust to a better agent than Captain King. None that wait upon him need fear the haughtiness of power, or insolence of office too often the accompaniments of favours to be granted. In short, as one of the best, he is also one of the politest, genteelest and best bred men in the world.

I have still something to say of him, which is that he has at different times in my want most good naturedly supplied me with money to the amount of over £40 (I don't exactly know, but I believe he has notes of it all). I could wish it paid to him as expeditiously as possible. I fear that I have committed a great fault in not before desiring my most sincere and hearty thanks to be returned to Captain Wallis for his kind recommendation to Captain Cook on my coming out.[1] If not in my words, I have had him in my thoughts and when we expected to have gone into Falmouth meant to have waited on him immediately and thanked him in person.

I have just learned another instance of Captain King's good will towards me. He wished me to go to London with him and mentioned it to the commander-in-chief, but that old conceited American who never conformed to any scheme of which he was not the proposer, who never took advice in his life, and consequently never took a right step in his life, refused—for what reason I am sure he knows not.[2] Could I have gone, the time would not have been long ere I should have been blessed in your company at Rosewarne. At present there is a foul wind, but foul or fair while under the command of an indolent old man, it is impossible to say when we shall sail home, or when come in the Thames. Thank God the lieutenant (a Mr. Burney) appointed to act as captain in the absence of our own is not only a good man, but a good seaman, a good officer, and much of a gentleman. With him I flatter myself to be in favour. Our first

[1] Samuel Wallis, 1728–95, the discoverer of Tahiti on the circumnavigation preceding that of the *Endeavour*. His connection with Trevenen is probably due to the fact that he was also a Cornishman.

[2] Gore?

lieutenant (Williamson) is a wretch, feared and hated by his inferiors, detested by his equals, and despised by his superiors; a very devil to whom none of our midshipmen spoke for above a year, with whom I would not wish to be in favour, nor would receive an obligation from, was he Lord High Admiral of Great Britain. Our second lieutenant is Mr. Lanyon, our countryman; he desires to be remembered to all hands. And now having, I believe, finished all my budget of news I subscribe myself your dutiful son

JAMES TREVENEN.

V

London
October 30, 1780

To the Junta. Sing tarantarrara, drunk all! drunk all! Sing tarantarrara, drunk all! I am now in a very good humour to sing, laugh, and dance, as well as yourselves, and having a commission in my pocket might easily be prevailed upon to get tipsy too! You will have learned before this by the droll circumstance of Captain King's letter (which was wrote in the supposition that I had set out for Cornwall) that my brother Jack's, or Matt's or Betsy's or Mama's or Lydia's or John's letter was not wrongly directed to *Lieutenant Trevenen*, for I am now in fact 4th Lieutenant of H.M.S. *Conquestador*. 'Tis true I have not yet taken up my commission, or sworn allegiance, but I have seen it made out and my name affixed to it in black and white, never to be recalled. The white lapels are putting upon the old midshipman's coat[1] and tomorrow I go through the necessary ceremonies. I cannot tell you when I shall get leave of absence. My scheme of going to Cornwall to you is all knocked on the head; and all the noble foundations I had laid for growling at clerks, Lords of the Admiralty etc. is now entirely removed; but I bear this frustration with becoming fortitude. . . .

Tomorrow I set out for my ship and to endeavour to get leave of absence, and if I am successful shall have nothing to detain me from the long-wished presence of my dear mother. On every score but this my heart is quite at ease. All doubt and uneasiness about a commission is removed, and I feel quite comfortable in the change from midshipman to lieutenant, that is from the lowest state of wretchedness to at least a decent station in life. . . .

JAMES TREVENEN.

Among the most important consequences of this voyage was the friendships he formed and cemented during its progress. Among these we

[1] I.e., are being put on. A midshipman's coat was buttoned across the front, whereas that of a lieutenant was open, with white lapels and cuffs.

must highly mark that with Lieutenant, afterwards Captain King, which was manly and sincere on both sides, and on the part of Trevenen mingled with a lively gratitude for friendly attentions, instructions and assistance afforded when of infinite value. We shall see in its proper place that this friendship was retained and practically evinced until death severed the friends.

Among those who, like himself, served in the humble capacity of midshipman he gained and returned the warm friendship of Riou,[1] whose steady perseverance in the midst of danger and active gallantry of service have since been so well known.

With his old schoolfellow Ward[2] he bound close those ties by which their younger hearts had been united. He formed a strict intimacy with Hergest,[3] whose turn of mind towards discovery was somewhat similar to his own, though his views soared not so high, and who was to have accompanied him in his intended expedition to the North West of America, of which I have to speak hereafter.

Samwell, first surgeon's mate and afterwards surgeon, always possessed a warm share of his regards, as did this gentleman always remain a warm admirer of Trevenen. He performed a last act of friendship by recording his friend's life and actions in the obituary of the *Gentleman's Magazine*.

[1] Riou, Edward, 1758–1801, described by Brenton as 'a perfect officer'. For his command of the *Guardian* when she was wrecked in 1790 see *Naval Miscellany*, Vol. IV, ed. L. Kennedy. He was killed when in command of the frigates at Copenhagen in 1801.

[2] Ward, James, Lieut. August 1782. A portrait of him as a midshipman hangs in the National Maritime Museum.

[3] Hergest, Richard. Lieut. December 22, 1780. Commanded the supply ship *Daedalus* on Vancouver's voyage, in the course of which he was murdered at Oahu in 1793 in circumstances which recall the death of Cook.

Chapter 3

H.M.S. *CONQUESTADOR*

For an active young man to be appointed to a ship lying guard ship at the Nore in war time was a mortifying circumstance, but it was intended as the best way of ensuring his being in the way to join his friend Captain King whenever he took command of another ship. Another consolation offered itself to his mind, which was the greater possibility of getting leave of absence from the *Conquestador* than from any other ship in more active employ. But on joining her he found to his great mortification that her situation with respect to officers was such that he could not be spared. He had, however, the polite and friendly attention of Admiral Roddam[1] to make his disappointment lighter than it might have been by a more abrupt refusal from an officer of less consideration.

Conquestador
November 10,1780

'MY BELOVED MOTHER,—Half pleased and half angry, I am sat down to write away the fervour occasioned by my disappointment in not being able to see you, which was what I more anxiously wished for than a commission. . . . I was appointed to be lieutenant of the *Conquestador*. When I joined her at the Nore Admiral Roddam, who commanded there, received me very politely and on my telling him the circumstances of my case said that I certainly deserved and might have leave, but that it was impossible at that time as there was no Third Lieutenant appointed to his ship, and more than one ought not to be absent at a time. A young man was acting in my place before and he could not act as Third Lieutenant above me, mine being a real commission and his only an acting one. Nor, on the other hand, could I take the place of the Third Lieutenant, so that I made no increase in the number of officers in the ship. There was a great deal of truth in all this, but it was not very striking to me at first, as I was exceedingly unwilling to find it out. The public service has nothing to do with the feelings of an individual. So here I must remain till the Third Lieutenant is appointed—hard fate—cruel stars. . . . [Further expressions of devotion

[1] Robert Roddam, 1719–1808; served under Anson and Hawke, and from 1778 was commander-in-chief at the Nore.

follow at length. He was, however, able to meet his brothers Tom and Matthew on board.] JAMES TREVENEN.'

It was not, however, long before the arrival of another lieutenant enabled Admiral Roddam to gratify his wishes by leave of absence to visit Cornwall. My readers are by this time sufficiently acquainted with the affectionate warmth of his disposition to fancy with what exultation the power of gratifying his ardent longing to see his long absent friends was realised. With them he remained until January 1781, when he returned to the *Conquestador* and by so doing felt as strong a contrast to his domestic situation as could well be experienced. Having no other sphere to exert his abilities in than the *Conquestador* but that most painful of all duties—pressing seamen from homeward-bound ships—I am not surprised to find that on all accounts he was very uneasy, and now more so, about the inglorious state he was cooped up in, as far as reaping laurels by the defeat of our numerous enemies was concerned.

In a letter to his mother of January 25, 1781, he thus complains of his situation: 'Captain King is not yet returned from Ireland. So I intend to finish the charts on board the *Conquestador* and shall afterwards endeavour with all my might to get quit of her. My present wish, if Captain King does not soon get a ship, is to go out Volunteer on the home station, where I may be seeing service and not lose my time in this old hulk doing nothing. I am terribly afraid the war may be over before I can come to action, which will be mortifying indeed. For then in peace I shall be insulted by every pitiful fellow with accounts of engagements in which they did wonders, whilst I must hold my peace and say nothing; though certainly our late voyage will always be a standby on which to pride myself. I shall by and by explain with Cloton in Lear that every Jack fool can have a bellyful of fighting whilst I must look on.'

At this period it was my good fortune to pass and enjoy many happy days in the society of this dear friend of whom I am writing. The rich topic of our mutual friends occupied our chief conversation. . . . The *Cleopatra* frigate, to which I belonged, was refitting at Sheerness. Shall I be excused in inserting Trevenen's just and pleasing character of my long tried and valued friend Admiral Murray, then my captain?[1] 'I never knew a more agreeable man than Captain Murray. More solicitous to create in his officers a love of his person than an awe of his office, he threw aside that affected state and reserve by which most naval captains think they

[1] Hon. George Murray, Lieut. 1762, Captain 1768, Rear Admiral 1794. Died 1797. He became captain of the *Cleopatra* in 1790. He is to be distinguished from Captain George Murray, who became Lord Elibank in 1781, and Admiral Sir George Murray, who died in 1819.

preserve their authority; and though not hail-fellow-well-met with everyone he meets, his behaviour is such a well-tempered mixture of easy affability, cheerfulness and becoming dignity as cannot fail of prejudicing those who know him in his favour.'

The service of an officer on board a ship in the situation of the *Conquestador*, which at this time was the receptacle of all the pressed men and volunteers of the navy at the Nore, is certainly highly irksome from the nature of the duty itself, as well as the mortification of being deprived of the means of increasing either fame or fortune. But a moralist would find more subjects of reflection in the strange vicissitudes of life than in any other scene he could be placed in. Here he would frequently witness the most distressing situations, by seeing men after many years absence and on the point of being united with their wives and friends, snatched at once from all their hopes, and doomed to severe trials and greater dangers than ever in the course of many more long years of absence. Here he would see almost daily arrived vessels from all parts of Great Britain and Ireland with hundreds of men on board. Those whose fortunes have been broken by calamity, ruined by extravagance, and dissipated in gaming, all promiscuously huddled together with the drainings of the jails and the outcasts of society from town and village. The variety of characters to be examined, and the extreme contrareity of circumstances which have brought these groups together, are often too strange for the powers of fiction to equal, and baffle the strength of the imagination. The real seamen, who are sometimes mingled in the collections, soon find themselves a comfortable situation on board from the respect their brother tars show them and from experience. But the poor unfortunate man who has, perhaps, been burnt out of a comfortable dwelling and deprived by the flames of family and prospects; and the miserable wretch who compounds to risk his life in war to save his person from transportation are alike subject to every species of distress, as they labour under that greatest misfortune in this place, being lubbers and landmen.

I shall insert an anecdote which I find in a letter to his sister: 'I hope I shall always be able to muster a laugh at the world and sometimes a tear. This thought brings to mind a circumstance that caused tears to flow by the emotions raised in harder hearts than mine. On board the *Conquestador* with me were two old soldiers who had served together all the late war in Germany, and were bound by the most indissoluble ties of friendship. One was married and had two children; the other single. The husband died, to the great grief of the friend's wife and children. But this lasted not long, for the surviving soldier gave the most convincing proof of the heroism of his friendship by marrying the wife and adopting the children as his own. . . . Sometime after this the marine officer, in order to lighten the old man's burden, took care of one of the boys, made a drummer of him and sent him on board a ship going abroad. Most evidently did this foster-father's love of the helpless lamb left under his care appear when the silver-headed veteran, after much good advice to the youth to behave himself bravely in the service of his king and country, turned blubbering to the other infant. 'Ah, Poor Tom!' says he, 'I have now only thee to take care of, and it shall go hard with me if I can't get thee a livelihood and make thee as good a soldier as thy father'. And then, unable to say more, he wiped his sleeve across his eyes and retired.'

Chapter 4

H.M.S. *CROCODILE*

Introduction

Some additional glimpses of life on board Trevenen's next ship, the *Crocodile*, one of the smallest class of frigates, are afforded in the correspondence of his friend David Samwell, surgeon of the *Resolution*. Writing from Portsmouth on June 5, 1781, he tells a friend that she is 'a beautiful little frigate, but I should like her better if her force, which is not despicable, was a little greater. . . . There are so many of us circumnavigators on board that it is current over Portsmouth that we are going on discoveries and it is difficult to persuade intelligent people of the contrary.'[1]

It was a tribute to King's personality that so many of Trevenen's companions joined his new ship. 'I am very agreeably situated in the *Crocodile* with Captain King and the rest of my old shipmates,' continues Samwell on November 21. 'We are all hearty and in good spirits, and as none of us made our fortune at Otaheite we are all keen hunters after prizes. . . . No less than seventeen lieutenants have been made out of our two ships. We are perhaps somewhat partial to one another, for it is an article of faith with us that such a collection of fine lads, take us for all in all, never got together as there was in the *Resolution* and *Discovery*. 'Much to his regret, Samwell could not accompany King to his next ship: 'I never in my life knew a warmer friend or a worthier man than he is.' Nor could he continue his close friendship with Trevenen; but when he heard of the latter's death in 1788 he described him as 'as fine a young fellow as ever I knew, and a real loss to the naval service of this country'.

The truth of that remark is obvious from the way King advanced the fortunes of his young friend by making him his First Lieutenant. As such it was Trevenen's duty to keep the ship's log, which is now preserved at the National Maritime Museum. The following details are abstracted from it—

April 25. When the ship was launched at Portsmouth 'there were present many spectators and a band of musick'. While she was being coppered, thirty-six tons of iron pigs and twenty tons of shingle ballast were taken in.

July 6. When cruising in the Channel a fleet of merchantmen was sighted.

[1] Liverpool Record Office, Gregson Correspondence, Vol. XVII.

'Hoisted out the pinnaces and cutter. Sent them a-pressing. At 10.0 our cutter returned with 3 men; at 12.0 the pinnace returned with 13 men.'

July 18. 'In the evening the people refusing to work, and behaving in a disobedient and mutinous manner, were obliged to draw the marines up on the quarter deck with their arms to quiet the disturbance. Punished six men with a dozen each for mutinous behaviour and disobedience of orders.'

April 25, 1782. The account of the chase of the French privateer *Prince de Robecq* (described in a letter given below) appears in the log as follows— 'Gave chase. Gave him a broadside and kept up a constant fire. Some cartridge between decks took fire, which disabled 8 men and put our people into a little confusion, which was soon over. Sheered off a little, but in 10 minutes came alongside again. Kept up a constant and heavy fire. For the two last broadsides she could not answer a gun. At 9.0 our pilot would not keep chase of the ship and refused to proceed any further on account of the shoals off Gravelines. . . . We supposed the enemy to be the *Prince de Rebecq*, mounting 6–9 lbs and 4–18 lbs.—carried 300 men, just left Dunkirk, commanded by M. Vanstabel.' This was Jean Vanstabel, a merchant skipper who joined the French navy in 1778. He was promoted lieutenant in 1788, captain in 1792 (when he commanded the convoy from America at the battle of the Glorious First of June) and died an admiral in 1797.

In April 1781 Trevenen had the pleasure of getting freed from the guardship and of being appointed lieutenant of the *Crocodile* under the command of his friend Captain King. The *Crocodile* mounted twenty-four guns and was still on the stocks at Portsmouth when this appointment took place. In her were also collected together several of the gentlemen circumnavigators, whose attachment to the virtues of Captain King made them eager to serve again under him.

When ready for sea, a period which was hastened very much by the active exertions of Trevenen, his captain being most of the time in London preparing the account of the late voyage round the world, the *Crocodile* was ordered to the Downs, on which station she remained till sent to join the squadron under Lord Mulgrave,[1] the object of which was supposed to be the reduction of the port of Flushing in Zeeland. But whatever was intended, the squadron attempted nothing, but peacefully came out and as peacefully returned to port again, perhaps no one more mortified than the Noble Lord who commanded it. Report at the time gave out that this

[1] C. J. Phipps, Lord Mulgrave, 1744–92. When in command of the *Courageux*, captured the *Minerva* and *Monsieur* frigates in January, 1781 off Flushing.

expedition was set on foot from the representation of someone who pretended a thorough local knowledge of the port of Flushing, and asserted that many pilots could be found who would take the large ship into harbour even by night, and therefore they need not be collected or consulted till on board ship, for fear of leading to a discovery of the destination of the squadron. Unfortunately on examination it was found that not one pilot would venture to take ships of the line into Flushing without every advantage of daylight and tide.

The next service the *Crocodile* engaged on was cruising with the grand fleet the remainder of the summer of 1781 till she received orders to proceed to Ireland, and in pursuance of them arrived at Cork on October 25, having met with little success.

To Rev. T. Trevenen

H.M.S. *Crocodile*,
Cape Finisterre,
August 17, 1781

'DEAR THOMAS . . . .—'Tis at the dead and dreary hour of night when ghosts do walk etc.; in other words, 'tis now twelve o'clock and I am just come off deck from a four hour watch, cold and stiff and a little wet to be sure, but not hungry, not quite famished and starved as in the days of yore; besides I am a lieutenant and have a cabin of my own, quite comfortable, quite a paradise to those days of yore. Matt will tell you what sort of a paradise it is, but I have made great alterations since, and he is prejudiced against being on board ship.

My habitation, then, is six feet square, which six feet is now completely filled up as an egg. My cot in which I sleep is two feet broad and five and a half long, allowing half a foot on each side for swinging (and this is too little when it blows hard). I wish I had not mentioned the cot, for it blows hard now, and brings to memory that I shall have a bad night's sleep. Allowing half a foot then for swinging, my cot will take up just half my cabin, and there will be left six feet by three feet. A very small bureau will take up three feet square, and my chair and myself will pretty well complete the rest of the space. Right against me stands Captain Cook like the knight of the woeful countenance and pointing to a map of the South Sea.[1] Ay, ay, old boy, I remember all very well, especially the many hungry guts I have experienced whilst you lived in clover—but it is a horrid life altogether. If there is any neatness in my cabin I give all credit to William, who has the

[1] Probably an engraving of the portrait by Nathaniel Dance.

sole management of everything save my papers. These are sacred, all piled up in regular confusion, such as nobody but myself could extricate them from—signals, sketches, orders, letters, etc. Tom boy, good night. I am sleepy and shall turn in.

Torbay, August 26. The former part of this letter was written off Cape Finisterre, where we cruised in high spirits till a Portuguese brig gave us information of a French fleet of 90 sail (56 of the line) being in sight. This has brought us with all speed to Torbay, keeping close all the while to the French coast. Tomorrow we are going to moor our whole fleet in a double half moon, ready for the reception of the monsieurs, come when they will.[1]

Since the *Crocodile* joined the grand fleet we have taken but two prizes and those of little value, therefore can have little to say about our operations except that they are infinitely more troublesome than if by ourselves. What with signals, chasing, manoeuvring, etc. we have not a moment's time on our hands. The news we hear is by no means favourable to old England. Tobago and west Florida taken beget melancholy reflections upon what shall fall next. The engagement in the North Seas is honourable to both sides, but we have too many enemies to deal with.[2] If we had no employment for our line-of-battle ships there, they might join and help us to thrash the combined fleets supposed to be off the Lizard and known to be fifty-six, while we have only twenty-one. I am sorry the *Cleopatra* was not engaged, as Penrose might have won honour and a captaincy. I am myself much mortified at having been so long in commission without seeing anything of the kind. God knows, a sea life is extremely dull without it. We are so long dilly-dallying, doing nothing but following old Darby (I might say Joan) that our enthusiasm for the honour of old England has quite time enough to evaporate. 'Till we met the Portuguese who gave us the intelligence of the combined fleets, we jogged about without the least thought of fighting or doing any service. We have not regarded ourselves as meant for it. I begin to be disgusted with a sea life, and if I do not get made commander before the war ends—adieu—but I grow ill humoured and will write no more.

August 27. Being despatched yesterday to look for the French, which we saw nothing of, hindered me from putting an end to this letter, and on retrospection I find it so full of folly that I am in doubt whether to send it, but I can securely trust in the generosity of my dear Tom that he will not indulge the least ill-natured smile at the nakedness of a brother's heart. . . .'

[1] Admiral George Darby succeeded Geary in command of the Channel fleet in 1780. In August 1781 the combined fleets were reported off Scilly, but 'after a useless parade for a few days' they returned to port. (Charnock, *Biog. Nav.*, Vol. VI, p. 41).

[2] Hyde Parker's action with the Dutch off the Dogger Bank on August 5, 1781.

To John Trevenen

Crocodile,
At Sea,
October 16, 1781

'MY DEAR JACK,—[After lengthy congratulations on his brother's marriage, he is interrupted by being called on deck]. Why, man, I am ten guineas richer than when I left off writing. I told you we would take a Scotch prize,[1] but I never told you where we are. You know we sailed with the fleet from Torbay. After cruising for some time to the west of Scilly for the West India fleet, hearing they were safe at home, we bent our course the same way. We saw no enemy except once when the *Crocodile*, being the nearest ship, chased and on getting near found her to be either a line-of-battle ship or a very large frigate. We were coming up with her very fast, but about four in the afternoon it fell calm and we could not proceed till about twenty boats came from the fleet, and taking us in tow we again began to gain on her fast and should certainly have got into a noble scrap but that about eight at night from a perfect calm it came on to blow a very hard gale of wind, with rain and fog, so that we entirely lost sight of her. But this was of little consequence as the men in the boats were in danger of being lost. In this case we were obliged to bear away for the fleet, the boats following as well as they could, for it was in vain for them to come alongside, too high a sea was running.

It was the most disagreeable situation I ever was in in my life. Every now and then we could hear them hailing us to stop or they should sink. Some boats began to fill with water, and we were obliged to take the men out of them and let them sink. Thus we continued all night and in the morning found ourselves among the fleet, which was very much scattered. The weather moderated a little, and the boats got on board their own ships. On enquiry afterwards we found to our great joy that not one life had been lost. Three of them were alongside of us and it was with infinite difficulty we saved the people. Captain King got great praise for his care of them from the Admiral and the Captains, except one or two who did not agree with the Roman notion that it is more worthy to preserve the life of one fellow subject than destroy two enemy. However it would have been impossible for us to have kept sight of him [i.e. the enemy].

When we came into the Channel the Admiral despatched us to cruise off Cape Clear with the *Flora*, Captain Peere Williams, who formerly took the *Nymphe* and a Dutch frigate. The *Minerva*, Captain Pakenham, who behaved so well in the same action in the *Crescent*, and the *Monsieur*, Captain Phipps (two frigates of great force) were ordered to cruise thirty

[1] I.e., a mistake, or worse than no prize.

leagues to the west of us.[1] We had hardly arrived on our station, the two frigates not out of sight, when, as I was writing to you the first part of this letter, we perceived ourselves chased by a ship a little to windward of us and astern. While he came up we were in a line with him at twelve o'clock. He perceived our force, put about, and we after him. Having by this manoeuvre gained the wind of him, he put before it and by six o'clock we had run him into the mouth of the two other frigates, and all four being then near, he struck in Yankee colours and we find her to be the *Hercules*, privateer of 20 guns and 116 men, from Boston two months and had taken nothing. The captain had been taken four times during the war. He had the most exact information concerning all our outward and homeward bound fleets, with the ships appointed for their convoy, and even in what longitude and latitude they were to part company.

We have some information from him, but what I do not know. The *Hercules* having nothing but her guns on board, I instantly upon hazard sold my prize money for ten guineas, and as we expect to go into Kinsale immediately, a gale of wind only hindering us, I inclined to make good the proverb 'lightly come, lightly go' after a day or two at home. I dare say you have heard a good deal of Captain Peere Williams, but he is a blunt-willed hero, not much liked by the captains in general on account of his pride and stateliness. There is as much sound sense in the little finger of my captain as in his whole carcase. He will never set the Thames on fire, but the man will fight. Love to Lydia and the younker.

October 23, *Cork*. We have come here instead of Kinsale, not having met with any more success. Yours, JAMES TREVENEN.'

From a letter to his sister Betsy, November 21, 1781. '. . . As for Lord Chesterfield's letters, I have read very little of them. From what I have read I think them very improper to be put into the hands of any but such as have arrived at sufficient maturity of judgement to distinguish which is the most amiable character—the honest upon heart, or that too great keenness and circumspection which lead to suspect even the good deeds of others to proceed from selfishness. . . .

I don't like to be laughed at, but fear you must laugh at me in some scenes I shall describe, if pity does not take the place of mirth. I told my mother that I went to dine with Lord Inchiquin, being introduced to his lordship by Captain King. His seat was about two miles from the ship (at Cork), and one day Captain King, who constantly lived with him, sent me

[1] Williams (who later changed his name to W. P. W. Freeman) was a captain in 1771, admiral 1794, died 1832 at the age of 90. Hon. Sir Thomas Pakenham, a captain in 1780, captured *La Nymphe* off Ushant on August 10, 1781, the first action in which a carronade was used, according to Marshall, *Naval Biog.*, Vol. I, p. 33.

his invitation to dinner. I wished it much, but am such a careless fellow that I had not a single article of dress decent enough to appear in. I had let my hat and coat grow old in the service. My buckles were broke, and I could not borrow or steal any other. I regretted it much, but there being no help I acquainted Captain King with my distress and begged him to make some excuse for me to Lord Inchiquin. Instead of this he showed him my letter, and laid open the nakedness of my wardrobe, to their no small diversion and my no small embarrassment when next day another message came to the same purpose, adding that I must make no excuse. I began scrubbing and cleaning in the greatest hurry and Stephen Tippit happening to be on board to see me at the time with a fine pair of buckles in his shoes, I immediately seized on them as lawful plunder, and soon strutted a complete magpie in borrowed plumes.

Being thus equipped, I proceeded on my journey, but not without feeling a little awkwardness at going in the company of lords and ladies, to which I was never used. This palpitation, however, was dissipated on my arrival by his lordship taking me by the hand with all the frankness and cordiality of an old acquaintance. To be sure I was a little taken aback when he stepped back and, surveying me from head to foot, cried out: "Why, Mr. Trevenen, this does not agree at all with what Captain King has been telling me. Upon my word, you are quite smartly dressed, much better than he himself." This was true enough and I should have come off with flying colours had not Captain King maliciously intervened by saying: "But, my lord, you labour under a mistake. He has borrowed his coat; the buckles are none of his; and the hat belongs to the surgeon. In short, his whole dress is a collection from others, just made up for the occasion." And he continued taking me to pieces with great success until I luckily happened to recollect myself and laid claim to my own sword which at the very time he had by his side. This turned the laugh against him. . . .'

All the winter of 1781 and the beginning of 1782 the *Crocodile* was employed in very severe service in the Channel, and in the month of November was for twenty-four hours maintaining a hard struggle with a violent gale. Providentially the result was escape from shipwreck, which for sometime had seem inevitable.

Captain King during this winter's cruise evinced not a little of Captain Cook's perseverance in beating to the westward against long and repeated gales, being anxious to be as far advanced as possible to protect the valuable trade in the Channel. To reward his assiduity he had the great satisfaction to preserve several very valuable Jamaican ships, which had been separated from their convoy from being taken; and recaptured several from the *Robecq* privateer, Captain Vanstabel, who was at that time the most daring and successful of the enemy's cruisers. This man was too well acquainted with the superior management of a British ship of war to risk an action, although his force was not on the whole unequal to that of the *Crocodile*. But he had two or three narrow escapes effected only by the cunning use of light airs, when his ship had the superiority in sailing.

One of the ships retaken was the *Active*, Jamaica-man, whose crew, put on board by the *Robecq*, had been so captivated by the rum in her that the prize-master took her down to the *Crocodile*, although his own ship was in sight to windward, and in jovial humour hailed to enquire how Captain Vanstabel was. One of the captured crew, perceiving the Frenchman's mistake, joyfully proclaimed who they were, and the *Active* was accordingly secured.

Early in 1782 their station was changed for the Irish, whence several voyages back to England with convoys, or unsuccessful cruises took place in miserable weather, attended with no notable occurrences. In a passage to Ireland they saved several vessels by protecting them from privateers which, however, they could not overtake. In one of these vessels—the *Edward*—was the person and family of that infamous deserter, General Arnold, whose life was saved by their timely intervention.[1]

In a letter of this period is a well-penned account of the uproar and confusion sometimes attending sudden danger: 'I really thought we were all gone one night, for we saw a light close to leeward which everyone thought was the Gaskets (off S.W. Ireland). Our only way to clear it was to veer round in an instant. This is done by putting the ship before the wind, instead of bringing her head up against it, as used in fine weather. So all hands were turned up, naked, in the rain and snow, and away we went amidst uproar, confusion, noise, horror, distraction and every passion that could present itself to the minds of so many different persons who thought themselves on the brink of destruction. But that I had my hands full of work, I should certainly have very energetically repeated a prayer of Ajax, which struck athwart my mind:

> Great Lord of earth and air!
> Oh king, oh father, hear thy suppliant's prayer.
> Dispel this gloom; the light of Heaven restore;
> Give but to see, and Ajax asks no more.
> If Greece must perish, we thy will obey,
> But let us perish in the light of day.

We soon got clear of the dreaded danger, and were congratulating each other on our narrow escape, when daylight convinced us of the vanity

[1] Benedict Arnold, 1741–1801, the American general who, after a successful campaign against the British, deserted in 1780 and sailed for England in 1781.

both of our fear and our rejoicing, by presenting us with the view of a ship not far off which had carried the light and thrown us into so dismal a stownd.[1] But a sea life is a continuation of hopes and fear, dangers and escapes, so sudden, so miraculous and so unavoidable that custom itself can hardly reconcile it to a thinking mind, or to any but such as nature may have formed in a particular manner and adapted to the occasion.'

Another anecdote is as follows: 'In one of these violent gales we met with the melancholy accident of losing a man overboard from the main topsail yard, while furling the sail. Two, indeed, fell headlong from the yard, but one had the miraculous good fortune to catch hold of a loose rope, which lowered him safely down upon deck, whilst he observed with the most perfect indifference that he was "learning to fly".'

On the *Crocodile*'s arrival at Portsmouth with a convoy in March she was ordered once more on the Downs station, where Captain King left her, being appointed to the *Resistance* of 44 guns, then on the stocks at Deptford. It had previously been determined that Captain King should use his utmost endeavours to get Trevenen appointed his first lieutenant in the *Resistance* as soon as possible, and then, if the service permitted it, give him leave of absence to visit his friends in Cornwall. His impatience for these two events is strongly expressed in his letter to his mother of April 14, the ship being ordered to sea in a hurry. He says: 'I was indeed sorry to have it put out of my power to visit you, but there is a tide in the affairs of men, etc. I comforted myself by reflecting that I should run no risk of losing my tide, or having to blame myself afterwards for preferring a month's ease to the chance there might be of something falling out during that month which might turn to advantage. This opinion operated so strongly that I resolved not to quit the *Crocodile* at present.'

Captain King was succeeded by Captain Albermarle Bertie,[2] under whose command they had the pleasure of seeing once more their old acquaintance the privateer which had taken the Jamaica ships. She now, as before, used all possible efforts to escape. But as daylight and the breeze favoured the pursuer, she was brought to action. Captain Bertie bore the fire of the Frenchman for some time, reserving his own till the *Crocodile* was placed within half musket-shot of the enemy. Her guns were then so well served that in about an hour the fire of her opponent was nearly silenced. At this time an unfortunate accident, caused by the dastardly fears of an individual, snatched the near-approaching reward of

[1] Usually spelled 'stound', a state of stupefaction.
[2] Sir Albemarle Bertie, 1755–1824. Captain, March 1782. He later fought at the First of June and was promoted Rear Admiral in 1804, Admiral in 1814.

valour from his braver shipmates. A marine, seized with fear which robbed him of his senses and prevented him from standing upright, crawling like a wretch upon the deck with a cartridge of powder in his hand, laid it down upon a lighted match, which instantly exploded on the quarter deck, under which the accident happened. Every person was thrown off their legs by the deck rising near a foot from the violence of the blast. The flames coming up the hatchway, the darkness from the smoke and the confusion necessarily attending such a scene obliged Captain Bertie to back his sails, naturally concluding that the ship was thoroughly on fire. Ten men, among whom was Trevenen's servant, were miserably burned by the explosion, but all recovered. Some, after having been dressed by the surgeon, returned to their quarters, although the next day they were quite blind. The smoke being dissipated, the action was renewed on the part of the *Crocodile*, but the Frenchman could scarcely return a shot, trusting wholly to the shoals off Dunkirk, which soon afforded him shelter and boats came out and towed him in. Captain Bertie persisted in his pursuit till the pilot refused to take any longer charge of the ship and till the enemy was nearly in port. The *Crocodile* mounted 24 guns, 9 lb.; her crew was 160 men. The *Prince de Robecq* mounted 28 guns, 9 and 12 lb.; her crew was 220 men. She was afterwards taken by Captain, now Sir Edward, Pellew in the *Artois* [July 1, 1782].

The French pursued what is generally styled their 'policy' in this action, firing at the rigging only, by which means the *Crocodile* had not a man killed or wounded on board by their shot; whereas there were fifty wounded landed from the *Robecq* at Dunkirk, and we may indeed conclude her killed to be in the usual proportion. There certainly happen situations in which it may be right to aim principally at the masts and rigging of your enemy, but the old British mode of proceeding has succeeded admirably (as the French, Spanish and Dutch can witness). For my own part, I do not give our enemies credit of intentionally firing at the masts and rigging, as I have seen many of their general, as well as their particular, orders directing the contrary. I attribute their firing high principally to that want of presence of mind which so eminently attends British seamen in action; owing to which deficiency they point without precision after the first broadside, and the beds and quoins once thrown out of the guns by the recoil are seldom replaced.[1] But whether in the present instance the *Robecq* would have been disabled had she lost ten ropes more, or ten less we are not now to dispute. It is certain, however, from his confession that Vanstabel was about to strike his colours when the dastardly conduct of the marine blew up the

[1] I.e., guns thrown out of their beds and the quoins, or wedges on top of the beds, were not replaced.

hopes of the English and gave him time to escape among the shoals of his own coast.

I should finish my account of the action by extracting from a letter to his mother his own description of his feelings when entering into the first battle he ever witnessed—'My private feelings could not be known. To say that I had not any fear about me would be false. But I may truly say that those fears were on account of my reputation, not my life. My fears then were lest human nature might fail, and in a frail moment I might lose the mastery of my passions and do something unworthy of myself. I trust I also found support in that sense of religion which the precepts of my parents had always inculcated. For I prayed to Heaven with a good conscience, and as we approached the scene of action found myself inspired with a cheerful confidence and serenity of mind.'

Chapter 5

H.M.S. *RESISTANCE*

Soon after this engagement Trevenen was appointed first lieutenant of the *Resistance* and that ship being still on the stocks he had another opportunity of paying a visit to his friends in Cornwall, and it was July [1782] before he was again able to exert himself as an officer. His destination was for some time uncertain, and in the midst of this suspense I find the following reflections in a letter of October 16 from Portsmouth, to which place they had sailed in a great hurry in consequence of orders to join a squadron appointed to guard Guernsey and Jersey against an expected invasion—'But now, whether we shall be sent against the Dutch, or whether we shall again fit for foreign service, is uncertain. For my part I care very little, though the sooner we come to action the better. If we go on a foreign station, I care not the least where it is. All places are equal; and if we observe its care, the same divine Providence overlooks us in prosperity and adversity, in heat or cold, under the torrid or frigid zone.'

The alarm about our little islands having subsided, the *Resistance* was ordered to the West Indies with the charge of a very valuable convoy. Having been accompanied the first part of the voyage by a squadron of line of battle ships, they proceeded on their way to Barbados, meeting with nothing memorable on the passage. To those, however, who can judge of the real worth of an officer's conduct, Captain King and his assistants in this voyage will gain more credit than would have redounded to them had they, by the exertions of force, beat a very superior enemy. The usual route to the West Indies is to run at first directly to the southwards, passing in general not at any great distance from the island of Madeira, and thence as direct as possible into the Trade Winds, which blow constantly from the east; and when arrived within their influence, steer to the westward for Barbados. By this means, being always enabled to be nearly correct in latitude, the errors in longitude become of no consequence, provided a good look-out is kept in time. But Captain King, whose scientific knowledge was too complete to allow him to hesitate about trusting firmly to it, and relying also on the long approved skill of Trevenen, depended on the accuracy of the lunar observations for determining the longitude, and instead of the circuitous route above mentioned, steered from the first a direct course for his intended port. Nothing could exceed the surprise and terror of the masters of the merchant ships who, used only to the old jogtrot of their ancestors, were soon bewildered and lost all kind of tolerable accuracy in their reckoning. But when they found that the skill of the circumnavigators had brought them exactly to the desired point, nothing could exceed their admiration and astonishment. There still unfortunately exist in our naval service many officers, even of high rank, who profess an utter dislike to all calculations and cannot bear to see others soaring so high above the centre of ignorance they are placed in. This run to Barbados should be drawn out upon a chart and served up to them every morning with their breakfasts. Beside the example set to others, this new course saved a valuable convoy from the enemy. For the French, as usual, had obtained accurate accounts of the sailing of the convoy, and had despatched three sail of the line and two frigates to the usual track, where they could not fail to have encountered them, but for the superior skill of the circumnavigators.

Having thus safely disposed of the convoy at Barbados, the *Resistance* proceeded to Jamaica, on which station she proved a valuable cruiser, as her good sailing admirably seconded the activity and perseverance of her commander. But the peace which soon followed on their arrival on this station put an end to their hopes of benefiting by these advantages; not, however, till they had captured several prizes and been once in keen expectation of rendering service to their country which would have been brilliant to themselves.

In their route to Cap François, off which they were bound on a cruise, accompanied by the *Du Guay Trouin* sloop of war (which was soon left astern because she sailed so badly), having to pass through the Turk's Island passage, they were agreeably surprised at the sight of an unexpected opportunity to exert themselves. The Turk's Islands had been settled by us, having then a governor and about a hundred fishermen whose employment was to gather salt, which they sold indiscriminately to all nations. So little was their consequence that, far from being fortified, they had scarcely a musket in the place and were of course unprepared for resistance.

However an officer had found means to persuade the French governor at Cap François that these miserable islands, which did not afford water for their inhabitants, were of great consequence and had a force allowed him to take them, and a pension was to be his reward. Possession of course was taken, and the French had been masters of the islands about a fortnight when the *Resistance* was passing them. Captain King and his officer were much surprised to find here two French frigates, which immediately cut their cables and stood from the *Resistance* with all expedition. Her fast sailing, however, now brought her near them, when the foretopmast of the smaller went by the board and she hauled away among the shoals in order to draw the attention of the *Resistance* to the larger. Even the carrying away of the mast was found afterwards to have been a manoeuvre, the more effectually to persuade the *Resistance* to pursue her. But the approach of night had ruined all hopes of capturing both, and the larger ship was the proper object.

After passing within random shot of the smaller and giving her a broadside *en passant*, they soon got within reach of the shot of the larger, whose stern-chase guns were plied for some time without effect, till the *Resistance*'s guns beginning to bear from her broadside, the French ship, after the common vapour of firing her guns that a ship belonging to the Grand Monarque should not be taken with them loaded, struck her colours, when Trevenen boarded and took possession of her. She proved to be the *Coquette* of 28 guns and 200 men, commanded by the Marquis de Grasse, nephew to the Count of that name, and of an older branch of the family.

Two days after this capture they fell in with Captain Nelson in the *Albemarle*, with a small squadron under his command, who, after hearing Captain King's account of the French being in possession of Turk's Island, determined to make an attempt to dislodge them. Taking the *Resistance* and her prize, which remained under the command of Trevenen, with him, some inefficient attempts were made, both by landing and attacking the batteries. But the French had made better use of their time, and had a larger number of men than was expected, and the undertaking failed of success. The *Resistance* and the *Coquette* returned to Jamaica.[1]

After this no naval event of moment occurred, but while waiting orders for their further proceedings, Trevenen was seized with a violent fever from having made too free with his constitution by overheating himself with exercise on shore. Soon after his recovery, the peace having put an end to all further expectation of fame and fortune, and the bad health of his excellent friend Captain King having made it necessary for him to come home, which he was about to do in the *Diamond* frigate, Captain Bartholomew Rowley (son to the admiral of that name), Trevenen, whose fever had perhaps abated his zeal for a journey through America, which he had planned, got an exchange into the same ship and in her arrived safe at Portsmouth in July 1783. In the beginning of August the *Diamond* was ordered round to Plymouth and paid off. The party at Rosewarne were soon made happy in the society of their dear wanderer, and he had to try an entirely new scene of life in the tranquility of retirement and the converse of his friends.

[1] For Trevenen's comment on this expedition, see p. 56. Nelson's despatch is printed in Nicolas, Vol. I, p. 73. According to the Bridport MSS. in the British Museum, for 'this surprise action Nelson was severely lectured by Lord Hood'.

I

To his mother

Resistance,
Port Royal,
April 5, 1783

'MY DEAR MOTHER,—As I have already finished a letter to my brother with an account of our proceedings since the date of my last, a recapitulation of the same to you would be needless. You will there see that, considering the time of our stay in this country, we have been lucky in taking a French frigate and three other prizes. We were soon afterwards unlucky in losing one of them, and with the peace coming so soon, the *Coquette* was to have been brought into service in three days' time, and the price to be given was about £8,000. The news of the peace arriving in the interval, the Admiral could not buy her, so we were obliged to sell her to the merchants at the reduced price of £3,500. The two other prizes were also lessened in their value and my prize money reduced from the expectation of £500 to a reality of £100. Had we sent down our prizes when we first took them, I should have had nearly the first of these sums. But the ridiculous expedition against Turk's Island, undertaken by a young man merely from the hope of seeing his name in the papers, ill depicted at first, carried on without a plan afterwards, attempted to be carried into execution rashly, because without intelligence, and hastily abandoned at last for the same reason that it ought not to have been undertaken at all, spoilt all. It was necessary to have all the force we could, therefore our two prizes were carried with us and delayed a long time. This has spoilt the sale of the *Coquette* and occasioned the loss of the other vessel which was worth above £3,000.

'My mother will suppose that the exultation I felt in the hopes of being made a captain when we first fell in with the *Coquette* and her consort, which we took to be two French frigates. I probably said that I should have now no one but myself to thank for my promotion. But I since find that the smallness of their force has spared me the mortification of proving by experience [the vanity of?] whatever good fortune the chance of war may throw in our way. The Admirals here at Jamaica do not think themselves placed on this station to reward success, or to make captains of the officers who may merit it from their services, but of their own sons, nephews and creatures who have not perhaps been three years in the service. This is openly acknowledged, that the Admirals leave it to their superiors at home to judge of the merits of an officer from any engagement. They cannot take upon themselves this privilege, but they take the privilege of buying into the service vessels not at all fit for it, merely to make boys of fifteen and sixteen captains.[1] This custom has been so much abused that the Admiralty at last sent orders to buy nothing into the service without their orders, and this for some time delayed the Admiral's resolution about the *Coquette*, that at last he said he would buy her upon the presumption that the Lords would have no objection, as she was a French *king's ship*. Accordingly, his nephew was named for the command, when the peace obliged him to alter his intentions and they are now selling all the small things to the merchants again.

'This peace is a sad blow to us who were in a fair way of making our fortunes. Captain King is esteemed a keen cruiser and we should have had good stations. But when we come to talk of the merits of peace and war and their effects upon the happiness of mankind, such trivial considerations must drop and we console ourselves that it is a blessing to the world.'

[After a lengthy discussion of his plans for the future, he continues] 'Why then, I'll exercise my curiosity in a view of America. A new people rising into an independent and new nation, modelling their form of government, making their laws and regulations, and emerging by degrees into greatness, will furnish ample room for remarks. . . . It is not impossible but an opportunity might offer for me to go into their naval service and with honour, and my gratitude to my native home for what I have gained in her service is not of magnitude sufficient to influence me further. . . . Therefore I intend, if the ship is ordered home, to quit and take a passage to America. If she stays here, to amuse myself first with a view of these islands, and afterwards set out for the continent. Captain King intends to go home as soon as possible, that he may live in the country and endeavour to recruit his constitution impaired with fatigue and long service. He thinks I am right in my American scheme, all but the going into their service, against which he gives reasons of prudence and weight, tending to knock down all ambitious hopes. But of this I shall better judge by and by. . . .

'The news from England mentions a war between the Turks and the Russians. Here will be another drain for all the idle humours discharged on the close of our war. I should not dislike going into the Russian service, if I could get a command. At the same time I bear such a grudge against those false friends of Britain that, were they not such an impracticable set of wretches to act with, I should prefer the Turks.'

Sunday, April 6. 'I am just made happy in a letter of Betsy's sent me from the *Ulysses*. Captain Spry has quitted that ship at least for a cruise.

[1] The admirals on the station were Samuel Hood and Hugh Pigot. Rodney's son, John, became a captain at fifteen in 1780. Hood's nephew, Alexander, was appointed to the *Amiable* prize instead of the *Coquette*.

I have not seen George Davey.[1] I shall enquire about him. His brother in the last cruise he was in off the Havana had the good fortune to take five Spanish ships of great value. I have never yet seen him. I never received either letters or potatoes by the *Mercury*, nor indeed have I heard of the arrival of such a vessel. The *Thynne* packet sails tomorrow, so I make haste to finish. The *Monarch* 74 is expected to sail soon, when I will write again. My dear mother etc.' JAMES TREVENEN.

II

To His Brother Tom

Resistance,
Port Royal,
May 17, 1783

'DEAR TOM . . . Captain King's health is so bad lately that I much fear he is in a consumption, in which case he will also quit, should his ship be ordered to remain here. We are in eager expectation of Admiral Pigot, who comes down in the *Formidable* to arrange all naval matters before he goes home. Our fate depends on him. Captain King is a favourite with him, but does not like old Rowley, who is a perfect brute.[2] We wish as much for a packet, not having had one from England these two months. . . .

'The peace was liked by few or none here. Tobago is a most improving island, and St. Lucia, from its situation near Martinique the rendezvous of the French force in time of war, of the greatest consequence.[3] Had we not had possession of St. Lucia, 'tis not only possible but highly probable the event of April 12 could not have happened. St. Lucia commands a view of Port Royal in Martinique, consequently Sir George Rodney had immediate intelligence of the sailing of M. de Grasse and therefore pursued him with success. Had he been at Barbados or any other of our islands, De Grasse would have got so far the start of him that he would not have overtaken him before he reached Cape François, where he would have been joined by the Spaniards and his force become too superior to Sir George's for him to have engaged in battle.

May 30. 'How vain is the wisdom of man! How fragile his schemes! I have had a horrible fever which has brought me so low I could scarce

[1] Spry, as Thomas Davey, was in command of the *Ulysses* 44 in 1780, when she was dismasted by a hurricane. He became admiral in 1805, when he changed his name to Spry to inherit the Cornish estates of Admiral Sir Richard Spry. His brother, George Davey, was a lieutenant in 1780; in 1783 commanded the *Prothée*, 64; he died in Cornwall in 1829.

[2] Admiral Sir Joshua Rowley, 1747–90. On Pigot's return home, he assumed command of the station. King returned in the *Diamond* commanded by his son; Trevenen procured an exchange into this ship, which was paid off at Plymouth in August 1783.

[3] Both these islands were restored to France at the Peace of Versailles.

move without help. Judge how uncomfortable it must be for me to lie in bed four days who never was twenty-four hours sick before. I caught it by overheating myself ashore in too great confidence of my constitution. In three days it has reduced me to a skeleton, but by that time I had conquered its violence. The bark [i.e. quinine] has restored me to some degree of strength, but this is not a country to recover in, therefore I give up my American schemes and shall pay you a visit as soon as possible—perhaps as soon as this letter. I shall soon go to Mr. Burke's in the country: he is a friend of Captain King and a distant relation of Edmund Burke. There I shall have more convenience than on board and besides have the care of the ship off my mind. Captain King had not paid us a visit for six weeks before, but as soon as he heard of my illness he came down immediately and brought with him an old practitioner in these fevers. However our own doctor had followed the best methods and by incessantly purging and vomiting expelled the fever and made a clear stage for the operation of the bark, which I then took in large quantities. 'Tis the constant way here in intermittent fevers—everything depends on taking it in time, purge and vomit away as fast as possible, till they get an intermission for the bark which is the universal nostrum.

'I am ashamed of myself for not having mentioned Humphrey Cole who is here as a lieutenant of the 79th Regiment. He has behaved in the kindest manner. I have been at the camp and he has often visited me on board. He has now pressed me to take up my lodging at the camp for the recovery of my health. It lies in a fine air and he has a kittereen [chaise] which he has offered me to ride out in the mornings and evenings. Besides this I am tempted to suck in the nourishing milk of a fine goat he has. He bears the universal love and esteem of his regiment from the colonel to the private, as not only appears to me, but as I am informed by one of the officers.

'Admiral Pigot has been down here but brought with him no arrangements for the ships on this station. He went away a few days ago. I meant to have sent this by him, but was so ill at the time I could not.

'We have had no packet, but the merchant ships have brought letters and newspapers. I am glad to see the Rockinghamites are the leading party, as economy is their principle and what we are much in want of at present. When Admiral Pigot came in, I looked out with a glass for Carthew Reynolds[1] and was sorry when I thought I discovered him, but on going on board I was glad to find myself mistaken and that he was Master-Commander of the *Dauphine* storeship. The sloop which in my former letter I mentioned we had taken was run away with by the people

[1] Robert Carthew Reynolds. Lieutenant 1777, Captain 1790, Admiral 1810.

but taken and carried into New York, where they are now. Remember me to all hands. I hope to see you soon.' JAMES TREVENEN.

The peace of 1783, which came upon military people by surprise, made instantly a grand revolution in all their plans and hopes of life. Instead of looking forward to the chance of war for riches, honour and promotion, a new scene unexpectedly opened to them. . . . Such were the changes in the prospects of the man I am writing of. But not long could a tranquil life please him, even in imagination. He could not bear the idea of ceasing to struggle for knowledge and superiority. And although the peace did not shine upon a man of more affectionate heart, yet what he esteemed the great duties of a young man made him forego all hopes of long enjoyment in the delights of home.

The pursuing the steps which he had before trod with the immortal Cook was the favourite undertaking, but an individual had no means of pressing forward such a scheme. The war between the Russians and the Turks, which then seemed approaching, afforded a field of action. But to join the standard of such an impracticable set, as he calls the Turks, was out of the question, and no naval man of spirit could as yet forgive the Armed Neutrality so much as to fight under the banner which flew in it.[1] The tour of Europe was pitched upon by him as the essay during the peace, and afterwards America, just rising from subject colonies to an immense independent nation, formed the ground on which he built the expectation of much rational instruction.

Men and manners, when first forming in a new society, are much more interesting to a keen observer than a view of nations already receiving their highest polish and refined into artificial conduct on all occasions. The sight and acquaintance of so many brave men, nurtured into warriors and states men by the love of freedom, and changed from simple planters and peaceful cultivators into daring soldiers by the mere ardour of liberty, was a treat expected with the greatest delight, and formed the basis of his intended peaceful occupation. . . .

(*MS. Note.* Such were the speculations formed by people in general, both then and now, respecting America. But experience has proved the fallacy of them. America, with all its vast extent of country, variety of soil and climate, navigable rivers and excellent harbours, is never likely to be a great nation. In its exertions to rise to wealth and power it had to struggle against an insurmountable obstacle, being laden in its infancy with all the weight of vice which Europe can scarcely sustain in its prime,

[1] The alliance formed in 1780 by Holland, Russia and other northern powers in protest against Britain's exercise of the Right of Search.

and under which we have indeed seen one part of it overwhelmed. The vices of America are indeed different to those of Europe, in that they are gross, naked, unvarnished and destitute of that polish which sometimes hides their deformity and even gives them a semblance of virtue. The policy of an American statesman is like the chicanery of a pettifogging lawyer. What is meant to answer the purpose of a jovial meeting is a drunken debauch. Games of billiards or cards are detestable gambling matches. Freedom of speech in the men is the most foul-mouthed language, and in the women only one stage above obscenity. The valour of an American is savage, his cowardice the extreme of pusillanimity. General Washington was the soul of the American army, which was a body infinitely too gross to exert its faculties with full effect, and I cannot for a moment think the Americans gained freedom, as they call it, by their own merits but by—to say what would be foreign to my subject. But no Briton who knows the comparative worth of the two countries can refrain his surprise and indignation at the frequent attempts made to depreciate the mother country by a false statement of her lately revolted colonies. The Americans think themselves a mighty nation, and particularly a maritime one. But they have not one grain of true patriotism, not enough to submit to taxes to equip six frigates for the whole of their immense continent. A Virginian, who will squander his whole year's produce of tobacco in one night at cards, would vilify the government which should demand a dollar of him as his proportion of a sum which would save his country from slavery. The Bostonians, perhaps, have not less religion for not being such rigid puritans as heretofore, and the commerce of New York has been of a nature to render that port distinguished for liberality. Above all, Connecticut has uncouth union. And why? It has preserved inviolate the manners of those ancestors which they only maintain honourable memory of. On the whole, the mob of America being an abominable tyrant, he who seeks shelter there will find himself a slave to the most savage commonalty on earth, except their ground pattern—the dregs of Paris and Nantes. He will find that religion is hardly remembered in most parts of it, and that decency, economy, and morality is less practised there than in any other part of the globe.

A pencil note adds: The above was written in 1805. Great moral and religious improvements have since taken place. 1823.)

Having conducted my reader to the first period of my friend's life, when a prospect of a little tranquility was allowed him, I quit my pen in order to prepare for the second intended portion of these memoirs.

Chapter 6

A TOUR OR ENGLAND AND SCOTLAND

From the general peace in 1783 to September 1784, including Trevenen's journal of a tour through part of Great Britain.

The general peace which reigned during the winter of 1783 giving Trevenen no employment in the line of his profession, he planned, in concert with his brother Matthew, a journey through England and Scotland. A state of inaction was neither agreeable to his disposition, nor reconcilable to his conscience, as he esteemed it a fixed point of duty to be always aiming at improvement and be in a state of progression in knowledge. Indeed, during his stay in the country he was indefatigable at perfecting himself in the French language and practising his drawing and mathematics. But a continuance of all these pursuits he thought practicable when travelling from place to place as when fixed at home, with the greater advantage that the former enabled him to reduce his theory to practice, and render his accomplishments useful.

Quotations from his letters and journal follow—

1783. November 6. In the way from Exeter to Bristol we took in a female passenger of about 300 lbs. weight. Just entering Bristol the coachman, being drunk, ran foul of a stone and upset us all in the mud. I never felt a more pleasing sensation than when we were going over, and should have laughed outright had I not been alarmed for what might have become of my brother Tom under the pressure of so enormous a weight as the above-mentioned female, who sat at the same side and fell on top of him. As soon as we were over and quiet I hailed him to know if all was well, and was happy to hear he was not quite suffocated. As soon as we were assured that no one was hurt, we indulged ourselves in hearty horse laughs, which I verily believe operated better than all the salts in the world on the fat lady. From Bristol we went to Bath, and into the Rooms, drank the stinking water, etc. and Saturday morning set out for London. Last night we saw Henderson in *Richard III.* Sometimes I thought him delightful, but in general a ranting, roaring buffoon.[1]

[1] John Henderson, 1747–85, known as 'the Bath Roscius', a friend of Gainsborough and Garrick, though the latter was jealous of his popularity.

December 16. Captain King has been in town, but is again departed [to Woodstock] having engaged me to assist him in some works relative to correcting the charts, etc. in order that he may be able to bring out the voyage in January next, for which his honour is engaged. One of our shipmates employed in a principal part has failed in his performance and therefore without some help he is fearful he shall not be able to fulfil his engagements, which are to no less a person than the King himself. In the meantime Sir —— —— [Joseph Banks?], that sulky, envious cur, is the enemy of the voyage and ready to do it all the ill offices in his power, because he could not be permitted to have the entire direction of the publication. There have been many consultations with Lord Sandwich and other great men about the price of the book, his Lordship wanting to make it a guinea and a half a volume. Others are afraid lest the public should be disgusted and not purchase.

(*MS. Note:* That publication did, however, come out in so handsome and liberal a manner and afforded such general satisfaction that the price was never complained of. The contrast between the quality, as well as the quantity of that and Sir G. Staunton's late account of a voyage—for I believe we have more of the voyage than of the embassy to China—is very striking).[1]

Having purchased a gig and a horse, the two brothers set out on May 5, 1784.

1784. May 5. At St. Albans we visited the ancient church and surveyed the remains of the good Duke Humphrey through a hole made in the lid of his coffin.[2]

May 8. Among the things at Derby worthy of attention we did not omit seeing and of course admiring Mr. Wright's paintings. Their excellence is now well known and allowed.[3]

May 9. Arriving at Dovedale and having procured a little girl as a guide, we proceeded to examine the romantic scene. We followed in general the course of the river Dove, but were sometimes from the nature of the road obliged to quit it and mount the hills, always sure to have some new and picturesque views opening us at every change of situation. . . . A finer school for the landscape painter cannot well be imagined than this dale.

[1] In 1792 Sir George Leonard Staunton accompanied Lord Macartney on the first embassy to China and in 1797 published *An Authentic Account of an Embassy to the Emperor of China.* His son, George Thomas, went with him as page and interpreter, though only eleven years old, and accompanied Amherst on the embassy of 1817.

[2] Humphrey, Duke of Glocuester, was buried at St. Albans in 1447. In 1703 the tomb was opened and the body found 'lying in pickle in a leaden coffin' (Gough's *Sepulchral Monuments*, Vol. III, page 142.)

[3] Joseph Wright, 1734–97, called Wright of Derby to distinguish him from Richard Wright the marine painter. In 1784 he was elected to the Royal Academy.

May 10. Matlock is fullest at the time of the Nottingham races, when it is resorted to as a public place for amusement and dissipation. But it never fails to be visited during the whole summer by those who expect to benefit from its waters, attracted by the fame of its excellent society and agreeable and familiar intercourse. . . . The company on our arrival was small but choice, each person presenting to an observer some amusing particular. A Welch parson was quite an original character and preferred his joke (not always the most decent) and good ale to everything else in the world. Two agreeable young ladies from Mansfield were a most important part of the company, not only on account of their good qualities, but because their sex imposed a necessity of the observance of decorum, and prevented the licentiousness of conversation too often introduced in companies of men only. Though some of our fine gentlemen would have pronounced these sisters hoydenish and wanting in polish, and complained of their country dialect, yet those who value things at their intrinsic worth would think their open ingenuousness of manners and evident sincerity and goodness of heart (those truly brilliant female ornaments) illy exchanged for that polish which engenders sulkiness and suspicion, reserve in public and satire in private. With us in Cornwall the dialect or brogue is confined nearly to the lower ranks, but here the better sort are by no means free from a strong provincial manner of speaking.

May 13. Chatsworth. In the town is a good inn, kept, I suppose, merely for the accommodation of those who come to see the ducal house and grounds, as there is no thoroughfare. The Chapel painted by Verrio, and some carvings in wood by Gibbons, were the most remarkable objects, and amongst a great number of bad paintings we were struck only with two, which were of the Holy Family. None of the rooms were large, and the furniture, though elegant, not remarkably so.

May 14. Buxton. The season beginning here before Matlock, the place was already pretty well attended; consequently everyone busy, and we had to wait some little time before ourselves and baggage could be accommodated. Our equipage was not sufficiently grand or noisy to impress the waiters with an idea of consequence and we found ourselves rather neglected at first. But this was the only place where we had experienced a coolness of reception.

May 15. From Castleton we went to survey the underground wonders and pass into the bowels of the earth, our hostess having given us a paper containing some account of the different parts and the common price paid to the guides at each, but in general we found it of no use to us.

May 16. The rapid increase of its [Sheffield's] size, the appearance of riches and the busy employment of its inhabitants, afford a striking idea of the advantage of commerce and the utility of industry. Having examined some of the neat manufactories, we made our next day's journey to Leeds.

May 17. In York was the dwelling of a Mr. Beckwith, who had been our Lieutenant of Marines in the *Resistance.* A note from me brought him to us, and I had the great pleasure of shaking my old shipmate by the hand, experiencing, according to Dr. Johnson, one of the most pleasing emotions which life affords in a place where a meeting could never have been expected. With my friend we went to the play and were liberally entertained in a handsome theatre. It being the last night of the season, the house was much crowded and all the beauty of York seemed assembled. Indeed, it was an observation we made now that as we advanced northwards, the human form divine, especially in the female sex, increased in stature and elegance of figure. . . . The Assembly Room, which was designed by the Earl of Burlington, and is called the Egyptian Hall, is vastly elegant and is esteemed the best room in the kingdom (being 122 feet long), except the Banquetting Room at Whitehall. . . . In every part of York you find stones of excellent worksmanship in sculpture applied to purposes of utility and convenience in the streets, and many of the watering places for horses are supplied with Roman coffin stones. In a cliff near the Ouse we saw the ends of three of these coffins appearing about four feet below the surface. The third was discovered while we were there and some gentlemen talked of digging them out.

May 24. The town of Shields was almost obscured in the clouds of smoke and dust issuing from the salt pans, collieries, etc. The entrance of Newcastle bore in every respect strong marks of opulence and populousness, but having crossed the bridge we entered the narrowest street and the dirtiest town I ever saw.

May 25. Alnwick. After breakfast we followed the porter to the ancient seat of the Percies of Northumberland. The effect of the first approach is fine, but as Mr. Pennant observes, somewhat hurt by a number of figures representing warriors, with their different arms. (*MS. note:* As I have a thorough reliance on the taste and veracity of my friend, I cannot but surmise that Mr. Pennant must have been terribly out of humour while here, as he cannot find one pleasing trait in all the characters at Alnwick.)[1]

May 29. Edinburgh. We stopped at the Prince's Street Coffee House where we were accommodated with two bedrooms and a dining room for £1 16*s.* 0*d.* a week. Finding this somewhat like a settled situation, we fancied ourselves very comfortable and congratulated each other on having performed so great a part of our journey without let or accident.

[1] Thomas Pennant, whose *Tour of Scotland* appeared in 1771. The Trevenens largely followed his route.

June 7. We now intended to depart, but seeing the door of the theatre now so much crowded as usual, we resolved to attempt getting in to see Mrs. Siddons in *Lady Randolph.* After a severe squeeze we were lucky enough to get good seats and did not repent letting slip another day.

June 8. At last we arrived at Falkirk. On enquiring for an inn, we were directed to the best in the place, but the outside was enough to sicken us by the dirty appearance of everything, and the inside did not bely the expectations we had formed from the out. An *olio* of stinks assaulted our noses. . . . We were surprised to find that our host was an Englishman, for I could not have thought one of our countrymen would have lived in such an Augean hole, but concluded that either he had been long in Scotland and was used to it, or that he was prevented from attempting a reform for fear of the cabal it would have raised against him. . . . The town of Falkirk is the nastiest, worst built, blackest and most stinking place I ever saw. Falkirk is, however, growing rich from the neighbourhood of the Carron works and wharf. At the latter great quantities of goods are landed for Glasgow and carried by a canal which unites the German ocean and the Irish Channel. In the morning we went to the foundry at Carron. From this foundry our enemies, particularly the Spaniards, have been supplied with abundance of these cannon with which they have fought against us. Is not this something like Liberty forging chains for herself? Mr. Gascoyne, who was for many years the manager of the works here, and was, I believe, the inventor of the gun called carronade from the place of its first formation, has now for a considerable time been at the head of an immense foundry in Russia, established by the late Empress.[1] The foundry, about two and a half miles from Falkirk, is the largest in Great Britain, probably in Europe, and is well worth seeing. On applying to the porter, he took down our names and we were admitted by a ticket he procured for us. The number of furnaces melting iron ore I don't know, but I think there are five of the large blast furnaces. The noise of these blasters is terrible when close to them, as may easily be perceived from the immense quantity of air forced through a single muzzle. These blasters are immense bellows, worked by large water wheels and a strong power of water. The furnaces are 27′ deep and in all of them they use coke, a kind of charcoal made from coal which yields infinitely more heat and less smoke. The consumption of this article must be immense, but the collieries of Burrowstoneness are not far off. I took the proportions as put into the furnaces. Four baskets of coke, seven of iron ore and stone and two of chalk or limestone to run it. We saw

[1] Catharine II. Charles Gascoigne established a foundry at Olonetz near Lake Ladoga with the connivance of the British government, but against the will of his associates in the Carron Company. The carronade was introduced into the British Navy in 1779 and into the French Navy in 1785.

them make several casts for pots, shot, chimney pieces, etc. The patterns for them are first worked in iron, which is laid on a fine black sand properly tempered with water to prevent it flying. Having made the impression, it is removed and a frame is laid over to determine the thickness and prevent anything falling in. The metal is then poured in through a small aperture. The battering hammers surprised and pleased us. They are 600 cwt. each, worked by water and used with as much ease and quickness as a common hammer. All their hammers, bellows, etc. being worked by water, two large reservoirs are kept up; and in case of failure a steam engine, which when at work costs £24 an hour, draws water from the river Carron. Casting of cannon is performed with as much ease as things of less magnitude; but the boring being kept a secret, we could only learn that the cannon turn round and the instrument stands still.

Having examined this immense magazine of iron wares, we returned much gratified to Falkirk; but I must mention that twenty years ago, when these stupendous works were begun, the country round was a desert, but now is all enclosed, well cultivated and tolerably wooded. The town built for the workmen is quite regular and the houses neat. Since the first going to work there has been a vestal fire kept up at the foundry, never having been extinguished.

June 9. Stirling. At dinner our talk was enlivened by the conversation of the waiter, one of the invalids at the Castle, who had been long in the army and had served in America under Generals Wolfe and Amherst. The former, he said, was the idol, the latter the abhorrence of the soldiers. He had been wounded at Quebec and gave us an account of the battle.

June 19. Aberdeen. In the ancient chapel is now the library and a school, concerning the connection between which and the college we could get no regular account, for here, as well as in many other places in Scotland, it was our misfortune to have a cicerone whom we could not understand. All the students we saw were very young, quite boys. . . . The library had many curiosities as John Trevisa's translation of Higden's *Polychronicon* of 1383 in manuscript. In the hall some good paintings by Jameson.

June 25. Inverness (from a letter to his mother). We are just arrived here in the most dismal weather and seated snug by a good fireside and have been thinking that it will afford my mother some pleasure to know that we have turned our backs on the bleak north and are more than twenty miles on our way home. Cromarty was the *ultima thule* of our journey. We rest here a day or two and then proceed on our journey through the Highlands to Glasgow.

We have been in Scotland more than a month and I don't think there has been a single day without rain, and such cold weather that we never put off our greatcoats even in the middle of the day. The people themselves say it is extraordinary but that it is good for the land and they have a fine prospect of corn for the season to come. The two last were such as brought the greatest distress and poverty into the country. The gentry do not reside, and the poor emigrate to America because they starve at home. . . . Of Scottish hospitality I can only say that I have heard much of it. In what it consisted I had no opportunity of experiencing. Dr. Johnson speaks highly of his treatment in Scotland, but the hospitality which extends only to the rich and great I think not much praise is to be given. . . . The only civil person we met with was the son of a clergyman and schoolmaster at a small town in Ross-shire, who did us the honour to come and sup with us. The conversation was entertaining and full of information. From him we learnt the opinions of Scotsmen with regard to Johnson's and Pennant's tours. The former is execrated, the latter pretty well liked. The reason is obvious. Dr. Johnson though he praises when he can, tells too many truths. Pennant very liberally bedaubs them with praise and gratifies their vanity by odious comparisons with their southern neighbours. Dr. Johnson's personal behaviour also makes against him. One clergyman tells a story of him when in Scotland which he had from Mrs. Macleod, the Lady of Ramsay, his relation. The doctor spent some time there, as he mentions in his tour, and she declared that she made for him, without once rising from the table, thirty-two cups of tea; and that during the whole time he never spoke a word.

July 10. Glasgow. . . . which take it for all in all is the best built and cleanest city I ever saw. This appearance strikes a stranger the more forcibly as commercial towns are in general remarkable for dirt and irregularity of buildings; but at Glasgow there is not much of the dirty part of commerce carried on, as the shipping are unladen and laden at Greenock and Port Glasgow, where the cargoes are deposited in warehouses.

July 19. Borrowdale. To give a summary character of this lake, I shall say that it is a collection of Scotch beauties in miniature; a beautiful and happy mixture of the horrible, the gloomy, the picturesque and the pleasing.

I have no account of the subsequent journey to London, at which place our travellers arrived safely in the middle of August. James Trevenen had been apprised while on his route that his friend Captain King was in such a state of health as to render it necessary for him to gain a milder climate before the approach of winter, and on his arrival in London found him preparing for his journey.

To his Mother.

London,
August 24, 1784.

'I have delayed writing so long in order that I might speak with more certainty with regard to Captain King and myself. Wednesday last I went down to Mr. Burke's at Beaconsfield to learn his intentions from his own mouth and found they were to set out for France as early as possible in September. I was sorry to observe that from appearances it is highly necessary for him to make haste. He is much emaciated, coughs and spits much, has short breath and every symptom of a consumption; but is in good spirits and talks very cavalierly of his situation, allowing that he has no chance for his life but in going abroad. A Captain Young of the Navy also goes with us.[1] I never saw him before, but his reputation is great in the service and Captain King says he is a most agreeable man. They were midshipmen together. Captain Young has already travelled over every part of France, speaks the language perfectly well and will be of good service in preventing frauds and the impositions always practised against English travellers with more money than wit. The French carriages being very miserable things, Captain King purchases a chaise to take all the way and I am commissioned to look out for one. . . .

'With the prospects of such advantages before me, I trust that my mother will have no objections to my leaving England. The times called for our departure is so short that it would be very inconvenient to visit Cornwall before we go.'

[1] Sir William Young, 1751–1821, captain in 1778, rear admiral in 1795. Trevenen revised his opinion of Young as the tour proceeded; for a hostile picture of him as a port admiral, see Dundonald's *Autobiography of a Seaman*, Vol. I, p. 171.

Chapter 7

A TOUR OF THE CONTINENT

From his embarking for France in September 1784 to his return from the continent in June 1787.

The two brothers with whom we made the tour of the north of England and Scotland now separated. Matthew pursued his solitary journey to Cornwall, with the horse and gig which had so long befriended him; and his brother set out on Sunday, September 12 with his friend Captain King, their fellow traveller Captain Young, a French servant of the latter gentleman's and William Bennets from Dover, on their way to France.

I

To his Mother

Calais,
September 16, 1784

'MY DEAR MOTHER. I write in a hurry and while at breakfast. The matter uppermost in my mind is the misapprehension you lie under with regard to the sense of my last letter to my brother John. I never meant that I would ramble I know not where, but that if I had a command of money travelling would be the chief business of my life for some years. At present I have nothing in view except attending on Captain King, and when that attendance is dispensed with I hope to visit you. . . . We have had hitherto a very pleasant journey and Captain King bears it pretty well. Our passage yesterday from Dover to this place was only three hours and a half. Captain Young is a most worthy man and grows every day more agreeable. Of my other dear little captain I have little hopes. He is so far gone that I think it would be miraculous to recover him. But whilst there is life there is hope. . . .

II

To his Mother

Paris,
September 22

'MY DEAR MOTHER. We arrived at this place on Monday last and intend leaving it tomorrow. You will therefore easily conceive that our hurry is not small and that our time is sufficiently taken up with viewing the sights of Paris. . . . Our passage (from Dover) cost us a guinea a piece, and fees etc. much more. The duty at Calais for our chaise and a saddle amounted to 38 livres (tenpences). Our baggage underwent a narrow inspection and after tumbling our things about they seized on Captain King's bark and sago as contraband. It cost us 12/– to recover them out of their hands again. I thought we should never have done with fees, yet we were certain of paying no more than was necessary from Captain Young having been in the same circumstances before, and from his consummate prudence. He is the best cashier I ever knew. He gives to everyone the least possible and has a fine captain-like way of stopping their clamours.

'At Calais we were at M. Desseins', of famous memory. His Hotel d'Angleterre is, I suppose, the finest in the world. It is built round a spacious garden of about fifty yards square. Two sides are allotted to apartments: one is a theatre, and the other is occupied by the *remise*, at the door of which Sterne had his tête-à-tête with Madame L——. I went to the spot to pay my respects. In the *remise* are contained about 130 carriages of different sorts for sale or hire. Dessein keeps seven or eight cooks and is supposed to dine fifty families daily. He was himself a cook in the same house thirty-six years ago.

'Travelling in France is conducted in a different manner from what it is in England. The government has the profits arising from the horses. If you have not a chaise of your own, you hire one at Calais to take you all your journey. The road is divided into posts of about five English miles each, and you are charged at these posts instead of by miles. A stage in general takes in only one post, at the end of which you find, if not a town, a single house or stable belonging to the government where the horses are kept. In the towns the posts are often inns or hotels, but not always, and if you do not drive to the posts you are obliged to send to them for the horses you want. You sometimes travel five or six posts without meeting with an inn. They do not consult the traveller on the number of horses wanted, but determine it by fixed rules, the number of persons, quantity of baggage. Thus a four-wheeled carriage must have three horses, and if three persons are in it, four; and you pay for one more than you have, which is a tax. Of course from Calais we had four horses and paid for five; but on the road we made interest and took but three, paying for four. Such horses! Such harness! The traces are pieces of old rope. It is, however, much cheaper travelling than in England. You pay 25 sols (12d.) per post for each horse. Living on the road is nearly as dear. We order a dinner at two livres a head and one bottle of Burgundy of the second quality, which costs three livres. Altogether it is about a third cheaper travelling than at home.

'The roads are excellent and within about forty miles of Paris it is a continued pavement as good as that of Portland Place or any other of the best streets in London. Paris, although it has the advantage of being built of stone, must not compare with London. The streets are narrow and without foot pavements, so that it requires care and caution to avoid being run over. There are more public buildings, and their royal palaces are much superior, but I have seen nothing to equal Greenwich Hospital. The Seine and its bridges are diminutive, not to be compared with the Tay at Perth or the Clyde at Glasgow.

'We went to the Duke of Dorset's to procure passports, but his Grace and his secretary had gone to play cricket. . . .

III

From a Letter to his Mother

Lyons,
October 6

'After leaving Paris we got in three days to Auxerre in Burgundy and rested five days at a Mr. Parisot's, a friend of Captain King's. It was exactly the time of gathering the grapes. The time when is not at the will of the proprietors, but is appointed by proper officers of the government. The country people then go about in gangs and make their bargains. If you do not choose to begin, you must wait perhaps till everybody is served. Their wages are five sols a day (2½*d.*) and victuals. At dinner time and after supper they all get together to dance, but not with that life and spirit which I expected; altogether as heavy as Englishmen could be.

'The white grapes were first trod in a large tub by naked feet and then pressed, stones and all, by a machine on purpose; the juice put into casks and left to ferment. This is done as soon as they come in from the vineyard. The red grapes are separated from their stems by rubbing them with a kind of rake without teeth over a large stiff net through which they drip into the tub below and are left to ferment, skins and all. The fermentation only lasts for a few days. The red grape makes the best Burgundy, and the juice of the white is made red by a mixture of a little of the other. A son of the house, from acquaintance with the Burkes, purposes carrying to England 30 casks yearly, which he is to sell at 6/6 a bottle. . . .

IV

To his Brother

Nice,
October 22

'MY DEAR JOHN. We arrived here on the 16th, five weeks from London. It cost me six louis (according to our exchange, 20/6) to hire a boat down the Rhone from Lyons to Avignon, 150 miles, to carry chaise, baggage and all. The trip would have been delightful had not the weather been so cold as to oblige us to take shelter in the chaise.

'Avignon is a very handsome town, regularly built of freestone, but its beauty is entirely hid by the narrowness of the streets. Many English families live there on a small fortune quite in style, provisions being very reasonable. This city, though in France, belongs to the Pope and is governed by a vice-regent from Rome. . . .

'From Aix we came in three days to Fréjus. The first sight of that sea, the scene of so many a great event, was a circumstance attended by some pleasurable sensations. (*MS. Note*: Knowing Trevenen's enthusiastic admiration of Dr. Johnson, I cannot avoid recollecting his remark on the subject of the Mediterranean—"the grand object of travelling is to see the shores of the Mediterranean"). Nice is but a small place, the resort of many English on account of its fine air, and, as is always the case wherever they come, provisions and everything become very dear. Captain King bore his journey very well, but I believe it was the hurry and agitation of it that contributed to keep up his spirits, for since we have been here he has sunk into a very loose state. He begins to be a little better, but is so much reduced in flesh that I much fear he can never recover. . . .[1]

V

To his Sister

Nice,
November 20

'Blessings on thee, Bess, for thy letter. It came exactly on the time I wanted to have it recalled how many dear friends I still have in the world and threw a gleam of light across the gloom occasioned by the loss of my dearly loved Captain King. He died the day before I received it, worn to a shadow by his disorder, yet exhibiting a noble picture of the independence of the soul upon the body—every mental faculty bright and unclouded to the last moment. He might have said with Addison, "See how a Christian can die". I have no doubt that the journey hastened his end. Easy as we made it, the fatigue was too great for his weak state and his decline advanced rapidly from the time of our coming to Nice. He had all along been sensible of his true situation, and never flattered himself

[1] A letter to Lieut. Riou, dated October 26, adds 'I delivered your letter to Law, who is by no means well. We see him often'. Thomas Law, surgeon on board the *Discovery*, was now surgeon in the *Trusty* stationed at Civita Vecchia. He attended King in his last illness.

with false hopes; yet his cheerfulness scarce ever left him, and if anything could alleviate the melancholy of our situation, it was his example. . . .

Captain Young has shown a degree of sensibility on this occasion which I did not think belonged to his character, and which has raised him much in my esteem. I am sure, however, that he will soon resume the hauteur of his character, but he is so very respectable that I can often allow it to him without disliking him.

How I shall dispose of myself now, I am not in the least determined. My first emotion on receiving your letter prompted me to return immediately. But on reflection I find that it would be losing a great end in travelling, and that it will be best, now I am here, to do away as much as possible the occasion of visiting these parts again. . . . The number of rich and foolish English, constantly resorting here at this season, renders everything intolerably dear. But the climate and the situation of Nice are indeed charming and the society often very agreeable. There are no other amusements here but a decent opera and *conversaziones*, alias routs, open every night at the houses of the *noblesse*, where you go to play cards and chat. These are the only places where you can see anything of the people of the town, for the nobility are too poor to think of giving entertainments, and the *bourgeosie* cannot aspire to that honour.

VI

To Captain Riou

Nice,
December, 1784

'I should have answered your letter but for the unhappy event of Captain King's death. It is painful to go over the subject again, therefore I shall only inform you that his consumption advanced very rapidly and reduced him so low that we expected his bones to come through his skin; that he was perfectly sensible of his approaching dissolution, yet kept up his cheerfulness and sweetness of disposition to his last moment, and that he expired at least almost without a struggle, or without pain, except about an hour before his end, when he complained of feeling a great deal. He retained his senses to the last, and spoke till a few moments before his last breath. Death, even when easy like this, is a very shocking thing and surely nothing but a conscience so perfectly free from guilt as his, can abate its horror.

Having paid my last duties to so dear and excellent a friend, and shed a tear over his grave, I am now at liberty to pursue my own inclinations and ramble wherever interest or fancy may lead me. . . . Tomorrow I set out for

Marseilles, where I intend to spend the greater part of the winter. I had intended to go by sea in a *tartane*, a nasty little vessel, but there have been many Algerines cruising lately and as the King of Sardinia is at war with these gentry I have embraced the opportunity of going by land in a returned coach. . . . Our friend Law attended Captain King with great affection and friendship. He is much better than when we came here. Being in want of a servant, he has taken mine. Captain Young stays here the season. I hardly know what to make of him yet. I have infinite regard and esteem for him, but I fear very little love. His principles of honour are strict and rigid, punctiliously so. I am sure he has an excellent heart, but his manners are so austere, his opinions on mere trifles so severe, his behaviour so constrained, and his whole character so made up of prudence and reason that he is by no means a pleasing companion. . . .

VII

From a letter to his mother

Marseilles,
December 17

'I assure you I have met with no small civility merely from having been with Captain Cook, whose name has much greater *éclat* here than in England. It has served both as an introduction and to prevent me from being silent in company. A copper medal from those of gold struck by the Royal Society in Captain Cook's honour and given me by Captain King just before he died, as a memento, has also stood me in great stead and given great satisfaction to the curious.[1] On mentioning Captain King's name I reproach myself from having so much seemed to forget him throughout this letter. Dear little fellow! I shall never see him more! He who has been so much to me so long a time.

VIII

From a letter to Captain Riou

Marseilles,
January 26, 1785

'We now only wait a fair wind to carry us to Naples. My companions are a Mr. Ellison, a man of fortune from Yorkshire, and two Irish officers from Gibraltar, Captains Vesey and Macartney, both excellent young men. I

[1] The Cook memorial medal, showing him in a tie wig; inscribed IAC, COOK OCEANI INVESTIGATOR ACERRIMUS. REG. SOC. LOND. SOCIO SUO.

am afraid Mr. Ellison may lead us into expense, but he has promised to conform to our economical plan of living and seeing everything on the least possible. From Naples we travel by land to Rome, Florence, Venice and Turin and then part, they to return home, and I mean to cross the Alps to Switzerland. Meet me there, Riou. It is an excellent place to learn French, and we will walk all over that country with a mule to carry our portmanteaux.

IX

From a letter to his sister

Naples,
March 11, 1758

'It is so long since I wrote to any of you that I am almost grown out of the fashion. Immediately after writing to my brother [from Rome] my fever, which I mentioned as being very slight, returned with great violence and confined me to my bed for a week. . . . We have driven about to Pompei, Herculaneum, Baiae, etc. The former is exceedingly curious: a Roman town buried for 1700 years and now exposed to light again: a very small part of it indeed, but sufficient to show the size of their apartments, streets, etc., with all the utensils for their houses, for agriculture, gardening and most other things.[1] Two days ago we made an attempt at Vesuvius, which is now making an eruption of stones and lava every day. My companions mounted with difficulty to the top, but I found myself unequal to it, and after ascending to the burning river of lava I descended again.

X

From a letter to his mother

Leghorn,
April 23, 1785

'You will not be surprised to see that I again date from this place after having said in my last that I was about to set out for Florence. The first reason for my staying was my finding a young English doctor, under whose hands I placed myself in order to get rid of the fever which I told you had again attacked me. . . . My doctor now advises me to go to Venice, as he says the motion of the carriage in travelling will rather be of service than otherwise.

[1] Systematic excavations began in 1763. By this date Ellison, the 'nabob', had left the party.

XI

From a letter to his brother

Venice,
May 6, 1785

'We hired a gondola rowed by two men for 5/6 a day. Imagine a hearse put into the middle of a London wherry of twice the common length and you have a perfect idea of a gondola, except that it is a little raised at each end. The hearse is provided with commodious seats for two persons, and incommodious for two more, and with blinds and windows. In general the boatmen go through the water about as fast as a pair of sculls on the Thames, but I think a pair of oars would have hard work to beat them when they exert themselves, which they do at what they call their promenades on the great canals, where on a particular day the nobility go in their gondolas and the gondoliers gaily dressed vie with each other who shall go the fastest. . . .

'Tis time I should come to the great day, May 5, and the so-much talked of marriage of the Doge to the sea, which in my opinion is tantamount to My Lord Mayor's Day. I must acknowledge myself egregiously disappointed. We arrived in our gondola among the crowd just as the Doge entered the *Bucentaure*, which is a large galley so built upon as to have a deck above the rowers, covered over, where the Doge and Council of Ten remain in the after part, and the rest is crowded with noble Venetians of all sorts and sizes. The vessel is covered all over with red velvet, adorned with carvings very richly, and gilt from the water's edge to the top. It must be confessed she makes a very magnificent appearance, and then I have said all there is to be said about the grandeur of the ceremony, except that about half a dozen ambassadors had their boats very beautifully and gaily adorned to attend him; whereas I had expected that all the gondolas should be so. On the contrary, they were all in their usual melancholy black.

The time of his departure was announced by two or three small guns from a galley, and an irregular fire immediately commenced from the galleys and merchant vessels lying in the canal, each ship firing as he passed. The *Bucentaure*, besides using her 42 oars, was towed by several boats and advanced at a tolerable rate. She went about three miles in all in the canal when, being within sight of the open sea, she was turned about and the Doge advancing to the stern, threw the ring into the sea through a kind of window let down for the purpose. In doing this he was hardly visible to any but those immediately astern, and I thought looked ashamed at the frivolousness of the business, as he turned his back immediately and the window was closed. . . .

The Arsenal. On presenting our order and giving our names, a man was sent to be our conductor. This arsenal is far more complete than our dockyards in that it has within itself everything relative to war either by sea or land, as gunfoundries, armouries etc. which ours' want. But I am not certain there is any advantage in this, and I should rather think that our plan of separating the dockyards from them is a better one, as the business of ship-building and gun-casting and cleaning arms are very different. I may add that perhaps it is better to keep such fires as are necessary for gun-founding as far distant from our dockyards as possible. Their plan of having all their slips for building ships enclosed and covered over is, I think, a good one. Indeed, it seems to be an acknowledgement of it when in our dockyards we cover with caps of wood all the timbers of a ship that is meant to remain any length of time on the stocks, to season before she is finished. Of these covered slips I counted eleven with ships in an advanced state, except one destined to carry 84 guns. One ship of the same rate was in the basin ready to carry the ambassador to Constantinople. The *Bucentaure* lay in a covered dock. On board her we were entertained with excellent oysters which they take in plenty in the canals. They talk much of the great extent of their arsenal and perhaps we may not have seen all of it, for being under the care of our conductor we were not at liberty to go where we pleased. It did not seem to me that in the whole we walked above two miles in it, and if we saw all of it it will be by no means equal in size to the dockyards at Portsmouth and Plymouth. Either our view was a very imperfect one, or there is a great deficiency in naval stores for, except in the rope walk, we saw no kind of ship necessaries except a quantity of anchors. It is true that the Venetian marine is by no means equal to what it was. . . .

XII

From a letter to his sister

Venice,
June 5, 1785

'Besides the pleasure of the place, the society easy of access to a stranger, and its good air, my vanity has furnished another motive to prolong my stay. A lady will easily conceive the pleasure one finds in being stared at, in hearing the whisper "He made the tour of the world", "He was with the famous Captain Cook when he was killed. 'Tis a pity he should be ill, etc.," of which I assure you I have had plenty launched at me in Venice. And the good folk not content with that, have paid me the highest compliments to my face. 'How happy they were to be acquainted with so extraordinary a personage!' I was often obliged to bite my tongue that I might not laugh in their faces, at my being of consequence to the world in general and the strange questions sometimes put to me which arise from the extravagant ideas they have of Cook's voyage. Some have got it into their heads that all the officers were destroyed except myself. Others that officers, crew and all were killed and I only escaped to tell the news, with a thousand others as curious fancies, from which arise many curious questions. One lady that thought like Lord Anson's midshipman who swore that there was no Red Sea for that he had been all round the world and had never seen it, asked me what time our voyage took place, for though older than me she did not remember our coming to Italy. Another with much sprightliness, on observing me as she thought very serious, asks me 'Whether like Alexander I was sad because there were no more worlds to discover?' However, notwithstanding the general ignorance with regard to such matters, there are many sensible people in Venice who have read Cook's voyages with attention and as philosophers, for they are eagerly read and sought after in Italy; and to such I had real pleasure in explaining the plates, etc. Amongst others I had the pleasure of doing so to the niece of the Doge, a most sensible and accomplished woman. . . .

The manners and dress of this city are as singular as its inhabitants. The nobles turn night into day; the citizens keep the same hours as the rest of the world; and from hence it arises that the same concourse of people is to be found in the streets at all hours, one class going to bed whilst the other is getting up. The opera in its season begins at ten o'clock at night and ends at two in the morning. From hence they resort to each other's *casinos*, that is, houses which the richer nobility keep to receive company in, distinct from their palaces; a strange custom which arises from the great desire they all have to avoid ceremony, yet to enjoy society. In their *casinos* they are in *dishabille*. I mean to say that no pomp of dress is necessary. You may go there in frock, when you please, make your bow to the master or mistress, mix in chat with whosoever you find, and walk off when you like without troubling anybody. Thus you make the tour of as many as you like at the season when there is no opera. It is almost the only way of employing their time. They generally retire to rest at three or four in the morning, and you may well suppose that they are no more visible till past noon, when you are then again walking on the place of St. Mark. . . .

In most of the houses I was in, the lady seemed to be the master. Indeed, the husband was seldom or never seen, but she is always attended by her *cicesbeo* or *cavaliere servante*, as they are now called. This seems to be rather a despicable office. They are entirely servants at the ladies' beck, and hover about her person to prevent her wants like so many guardian angels. The *cicesbeo* and his sovereign mistress are never seen asunder. He squires her to all public places and must never quit her. It is the most abject, though perhaps the most gentle slavery, I have ever heard of.

The Venetian nobles are very proud of the antiquity of their families and it is true that they can boast of a more ancient pedigree than the nobles of most countries. They rank themselves with princes, and are so far right that their sovereign authority rests entirely in their body, but there are above a thousand of them. Their pride, however, seldom incommodes anyone. They keep it to themselves and mix in the coffee houses with strangers, and even with some of the citizens with a degree of familiarity almost unknown elsewhere out of England; and the *haute noblesse* of England have certainly much more *hauteur* than that of Venice. The inhabitants of Venice, however, are not perfectly free in their conversation, for they are not allowed to talk on their government and a stranger that should give himself any liberties on that subject would speedily be sent out of their dominions or worse. They are famous for political abilities and extremely jealous on that subject. They have served the Freemasons a sad trick lately. Their papers and furniture was seized and burnt in a public place, and two or three banished from Venetian dominions. There had been a fire lately in the Arsenal and the government seemed to throw the odium of it on the Freemasons, but their papers were found perfectly innocent: nothing but N., S., E. and West and such other cabalistical terms. . . .

I was the other night at a most magnificent fishing match given by a noble Venetian to a lady he was in love with. We were forty persons in all, but only five ladies. About ten at night we embarked in three large rowing boats and rowed out into the lagoon with music, and proceeded to the spot where a number of boats were ready to haul in their nets, which they did like our pilchard fishers, and caught a number of fish. About midnight we rowed back to an elegant *casino* and were served with a most splendid supper of three courses. Oh, how they did eat! Such sauces and strong things, with all sorts of rich wines! The Venetians are remarked for having more of the French ease and gaiety than other Italians and I must join my suffrage that they are witty, sprightly and shine in conversation. But I must say at the same time that the ladies here excel those of England in this point in their having a most unbounded licence in their discourse, and less of real modesty and virtue. I was shocked at some of the jokes passed about as good things. Love is a very different matter here and in England. With us it is a passion looking forward to a connexion for life. Here there are none but temporary amours. Conjugal fidelity is hardly looked upon as a virtue. The husbands are no longer jealous. They attach themselves as *cavalieri servanti* to other ladies and leave their wives at liberty. Sentiment and sensibility are entirely unknown here. They have been laughed out of countenance with us, and those who possess them keep them to themselves. Here they have not an idea of them.

June 1785. Padua. At the church of the Arena the walls are painted by Giotto, one of the first revivers of painting in Italy. Accordingly they have little merit as paintings, but deserve notice as the first buds of that art, then breaking through the dark ages, and since arrived at such perfection.

July 1785. Milan. Saw the churches. In the refectory of S. Maria della Grazie is the famous picture by Leonardo Vinci of the supper in Gallilee painted in fresco on the wall at one end. It is admirable for the expression and disposition, and also for the architectural perspective part; and it is much to be lamented that the damps have begun to injure it essentially. It was once so far effaced that it became necessary to employ an artist to restore it, which he has done in a very masterly manner.

XIII

From a letter to his mother

Turin,
July 18, 1785

'I was to have set off this minute on a six days' journey across the Alps to Geneva. My *voiturier* is come to beg me to delay till tomorrow morning. I still live *solus* and therefore I have taken a place in a carriage bound to Geneva in which goes another person I know not: I suppose a watchmaker, as they are all watchmakers at Geneva. At Milan I was always a *milord anglais*, as are all the English who keep good company. When I lived in this way I was taken for a French vendor of wares and am hail-fellow-well-met with every bagus[1] that occurs. At Milan I stayed seventeen days because I had all I could wish, was introduced to the Archduke of Milan, the Emperor's brother, and knew everybody. The presence of the King of Naples made everything gay. . . . I still am free from fever, but as my tongue continues somewhat foul I consulted a physician, who told me I should take some mineral waters. Therefore at Lausanne I mean to consult the famous Tissot.[2]

In crossing the Alps I quit Italy, where I have been more than five months, and though I have been so unfortunate as to be deprived of my health the whole time, yet I quit it with some regret. In the people in general there is very little real virtue or worth, but some of all sorts are to be found, and they are remarkably civil to strangers, particularly to the English, who still preserve their consequence on the Continent in private opinions, whatever they may have lost in cabinets or public councils. The manner in

[1] I.e., commercial traveller.
[2] S. A. Tissot, 1728–97, famous for his treatment of smallpox, and the author of a popular book on medicine.

which we supported the last war against so many powers is regarded as a prodigy in the annals of the world, and more than one Italian has assured me that his countrymen during the whole time were so many English patriots. . . . I have also been singularly fortunate in procuring such letters as were necessary to introduce me into the societies I wished, and in enjoying them without being obliged to cut such a dash and to run into such expense as my richer countrymen. The title of *voyageur autour le monde* has been a capital travelling one, and has stood me instead of liveries or equipages. I have experienced so many pleasures that I cannot regret the expense, which has certainly been above my ability. Yet even that, I have reason to believe, has been much less than any Englishman since the day of Goldsmith has travelled through Italy for; and I fancy he only saw the things and very little of persons or society.

XIV

From a letter to James Ward

Turin,
July 18, 1785

'MY DEAR FRIEND,—Let me grasp thee by the hand and offer thee my sincere congratulations on thy return from India.[1] What an immense space of time has elapsed since I have seen you! . . . I know you will regret him [King] as I do, and that it is not to you it is necessary to make his elegy. . . . Devil take me, but I am sometimes tempted never to go to sea again, but to love at home at ease on little or rove at large where fancy directs. Do me justice. Such thoughts have been but momentary, and my reason tells me that man was not born for himself alone. . . .

Not long before his [Captain Clerke's] death he told Captain King that he had not one good action to boast of throughout his life, except that of always having served his country with zeal and fidelity, and in some reason having fallen a sacrifice in its service. He comforted himself much with this idea. (*MS. note*. I understand him to have been one of those who are said to be no man's enemy but his own, and that a warm and benevolent heart may have often led him to injure himself by folly and intemperance. I am told that one of the last actions of his life was destroying the papers which were drawn up to criminate Lieut. Williamson for his conduct at the time of Captain Cook's death. For an account of Captain Clerke's death I refer my reader to page 280 of King's continuation of Cook's voyage.) . . .

Mont Cenis is a bugbear to frighten children withal. I was much disappointed with it, though I can hardly say disagreeably so, for so much fatigue

[1] Trevenen's shipmate, who had just returned from the East Indies, where he had been with another shipmate, Captain James Burney.

saved is an object to such a poor wretch as I am at present. After rising by degrees from the fertile plains of Lombardy, we came to the foot of it, where we quitted our carriages and mounted mules. When a traveller has his carriage with him they take it to pieces with great dexterity and mount it upon their mules. But I do not travel in such style. Therefore I left my hack on the other side and got another on this. The road is everywhere wide enough for two mules abreast and at this season free from danger. In the winter, when the snow is on the ground, it is by no means so, as it is stony and steep. In an hour's time we came into the region of pines and, about five in the morning, of cold. I buttoned my great coat. In another hour we had the clouds about us, and in two hours and a quarter reached the top—i.e., the top of the valley between two mountains, where the snow lay pretty thick. Here is the lake Cenis where you get excellent trout and bread and butter. The keenness of the weather gave us appetites and we devoured enormously. After a mile of plain we began to descend in the same kind of road, and in two and a half hours were at the bottom of Mont Cenis. Here you again find a carriage road.

August 1785. Lucerne. Having met with a young man at Geneva about to make the tour of Switzerland I seized the opportunity of going with him, for a Swiss tour *solus* would be a great bore. My companion is a very accomplished and a very agreeable personage, but has not the least *gout* for lakes and mountains and therefore is for hurrying through them as fast as possible for the say-so (*sic*) of saying, I have seen it. I on the contrary am in no hurry and would rather sit down for a week or two when I am at an agreeable place and amuse myself with drawing. You will easily conceive that we differ sometimes and I have been tempted to quit; but as the youth is really very amiable, and as the expense is considerably lessened, I resolve to finish the tour with him. . . .

My present companion whose name is Summer is not altogether so much to my taste, leaning very much to the fine gentleman, with a dash of affectation. However, he has many good points about him. Through him I have got acquainted with Mr. Wilberforce, the friend of Pitt, and we have spent the last two or three days in company together on the lake.[1] He travels for his health, accompanied by a sick family of ladies. He seems a most excellent little man, and I was much struck by the resemblance between him and Captain King—the same quickness in his manner, the same ease in his behaviour, the same mildness, gentleness and persuasion: I am sorry to say also the same apparent state of health; and was I obliged to prophecy of him I would say he would not see another year pass over his head. May

[1] William Wilberforce, then aged 36, lived to be 74. He was returning to England with his mother and sister on the tour which converted him to a stricter religious life.

Heaven avert the omen! for he appears to me one of those men in whose breast private interest could not be preferred to public good.

Mont Blanc. We mounted the Mont Alvers [Montavers], a stiff tug up the hill for two hours ten minutes. From the top you look down on what is called the Sea of Ice, the same glacier extending horizontally for nine miles. It is certainly a curious and fine sight. Several of the party, while I sketched, descended on the other side of the hill to walk on it. They said it appeared of much greater dimensions in that situation, and they found rents or chasms in the ice to which they could see no bottom, and a stone thrown down sounded a long time. Without care it is dangerous walking here, and sometime past one of the guides slipping, hung suspended over one of these chasms by his pole, which reached the opposite side; his companion relieved him. . . .

XV

From a letter to his brother

Lausanne,
September 2, 1785

'This town, or rather its environs, contains a colony of English, and it is said that there have been at one time eighty families established near it, and indeed as much English as German may be heard in the streets. How much did I regret that I did not understand German, for it is the universal language of the Swiss. French extends no further than here and the Pays de Vaud. The boasted simplicity of manners that reigned formerly among the Swiss, and so delightfully portrayed by Rousseau, is quite swept away by the inundation of the English and other travellers that visit them, or at least is only to be found in some obscure valleys where they have not yet found their way. They have learnt the value and use of money, and the desire of acquiring it. For this purpose they do not scruple at the most glaring impositions and in a manner more disagreeable than in Italy. There they cheat you behind your back, cringe, fawn and treat you very civilly with *my lord anglais*. In Swiss (*sic*) the innkeepers charge you three times the value of what you have need of, and will tell you they do it because they choose it, that they have no need of you, and do not want your company; you may stay at home and save your money if you please. No redress can be had, as perhaps the innkeeper is the principal magistrate of the place and thinks himself very superior to you and any stranger that visits him. They know their rights and privileges, care for nobody, and despise all foreigners, whom they consider in a state of slavery. This is a picture of Swiss given by many travellers whom I have met violently enraged against them. . . . However, in going through the country I have found those people who had no interests to manage with you very civil and serviceable in directing you the way. It is true that at the same time you may perceive in them an opinion of their own consequence when placed in comparison with you; and in passing through the villages, when the country people chance to be assembled, you may distinguish in them, while regarding you, the smile of superiority and the negligence of independence. Englishmen must not quarrel with them for this: they find the same in their own country. . . .

As to the better sort of people whom you find in the cities, opinions are as various in reporting them. From what I have myself seen, I am a strong advocate for them, and it appears to me that every Englishman coming from France or Italy must be strongly struck with the difference of the society of this country and with the great resemblance to that of his own. They have not all the unmeaning civility and apparent warmth of friendship that is found in France and in Italy, which imitates it. Therefore many may find them cold and uninteresting. But they are affectionate, sincere and open, capable of real friendship and even ready to do kind offices. There is one striking feature in their societies resembling the English, which is the clubs and parties consisting of men only, unknown in France or Italy, where the women are the soul of everything. The ladies will therefore find the latter much more amiable. But look on the morals of both sides and perhaps it will be found that the universal conjugal infidelity prevailing on one side, and the universal respect in which the married state is held on the other, proceeds from this sole cause.

XVI

From a letter to his Mother

Geneva,
November 9, 1785

'My Beloved Mother,—It is impossible that I should at present say another word[1] than that I am following this as fast as possible, and I shall not be long behind it. I dare not flatter myself that our meeting will not be without some faint melancholy sentiment of pleasure, and that you will take me to your breast and cherish me. Nothing happens to us without the express direction of the Almighty, and his goodness, more extended than our foresight, orders everything for the best, though the stroke sometimes falls too heavily for human affections to bear. Adieu, my adored mother, until I clasp you in my arms.

[1] About the news of the death of his brother Matthew, with whom he toured England, on October 27.

From a letter to Penrose from M. Pictet

The following extract of a letter from M. Pictet to myself written some years after is in answer to my enquiries relative to the time spent at Geneva: 'At twelve years distance there can be few circumstances which can be safely traced back. I can only say that he (Trevenen) frequented the best company here and was courted by it. The sweetness of his temper, and the politeness of his manners, rendered him extremely welcome everywhere, independently of the powers he had of gratifying curiosity with an inexhaustible complaisance. I remember having seen him take off his coat two or three times in an evening at the Duke of Gloucester's (then residing here) to exhibit to some curious ladies his tattoed arms. I was ill with an ague when he was here. He was then so kind as to come every day to a country seat of my sister's two miles from the town. He took them a friendly dinner and read with me the whole afternoon Cook's last voyage, delightfully intermixing his own sensible comments with the author's narrative. He wrote some of them on a few sheets, which I have unluckily mislaid.'

Chapter 8

RUSSIAN PLANS

Introduction

Trevenen spent the winter of 1785–6 in Cornwall, where James Ward, his shipmate on the voyage round the world, paid him a long visit. Tiring of an inactive life, he applied to the Admiralty for employment and narrowly missed two interesting appointments—that of the first ship to Australia, and that of the *Bounty*.

The idea of a colony in New South Wales was first proposed by Sir James Banks and James Matra. The latter, who accompanied Cook in the *Endeavour* as an Able Seaman, proposed in 1783 to colonize Australia with American loyalists. The plan was revived by Admiral Sir George Young in 1785, but was transformed into a scheme for a penal settlement by Lord Sydney, Secretary for the Home Department, who persuaded the Admiralty to provide the frigate *Sirius*, to which after some discussion Captain Arthur Phillip was appointed in September 1786, instead of Trevenen. By a similar mischance he was not appointed to the command of the *Bounty*, though recommended by Alexander Dalrymple (Cook's rival), Bligh being appointed in December, 1787.

His own scheme, when he failed to find employment in the British service, was to memorialize the Empress Catharine with a project for discovery and fur trading in the North Pacific. This scheme, strangely prophetic of modern times, fell through because of the outbreak of the second Russo-Turkish war after Trevenen had reached St. Petersburg.

He was by no means the only person interested in such a project. After Behring's ship had brought back to Kamchatka the first cargo of sea otter furs from North America in 1742, Russian traders had virtually occupied parts of Alaska and the Aleutians. A map of the area presented to Catharine by Vassili Shilov in 1764 aroused her interest and a scientific expedition was despatched under Captain Kremitsyn in 1766–70. Then Cook appeared on the scene, the news of his death being sent overland by Clerke from the harbour of Petropavlovsk (St. Peter and St. Paul), where he himself was buried shortly after. The high prices paid for their sea otter skins at Canton inspired Trevenen and others to develop this trade with North America.

John Ledyard, an American who served under Cook as a marine and had published an account of the voyage in the United States, was aiming at the same thing at the same time as Trevenen. Having failed to secure a backing in America or in London, he reached St. Petersburg in 1787 and even penetrated to Siberia before he was arrested and deported to Poland.

Meanwhile, in 1784 the Russians Shelykov and Golykov had fitted out three ships to sail for Alaska. After claiming all territory north of California for Russia, they formed the Russian-American Fur Company, for which Alexander Baranov, the first colonial governor, built the first Russian ship in the Pacific. The next year Spanish traders appeared (not for the first time) at Nootka Sound on Vancouver Island. Similarly English traders, licensed by the East India Company, such as James Hanna, Nathaniel Portlock and James Meares, sailed across the Pacific from China. In 1786 the French explorer La Pérouse visited the area before his mysterious death in the Pacific. And in 1789 the American Captain Gray reached Nootka to find Meares and the Spaniards at loggerheads. His vessel, the *Columbia*, continued her voyage to China, where she sold her cargo and then returned home, the first American vessel to go round the world. Meanwhile the English and the Spanish appealed to their governments to support their claims, the resulting embroglio being known as the Nootka Sound Crisis or the Spanish Armament of 1790. Vancouver, the only one of Cook's men to appear a second time in these seas, reached the island which bears his name in 1793 to settle the matter.

As for Trevenen's scheme for opening a trade with Japan, nothing came of it until the visit of Commodore Perry in 1853. The Russian ambassador carried to that country by Krusenstern in 1805 was rebuffed even more preremptorily than the Macartney embassy of 1787 had been by the Chinese. Only the single Dutch ship continued to be permitted her annual visit.

The subject I am about to enter upon of my friend's last departure from England and its consequences are so very interesting that I would gladly trace the causes which led to it, but I am afraid that all my diligence will still leave me deficient in many essential points.

He applied to me to engage with him in a voyage to Nootka Sound and Cook's River to carry on the fur trade. He had been previously applied to by Mr. Danbruz of Falmouth on behalf of a company of merchants for information respecting the proper means of entering upon the trade above mentioned, and a request that he would command the expedition to be carried out in two ships. I apprehend that the sum appointed for their equipment was sufficiently liberal, and all his terms complied with and in consequence of this negotiation he set out for London in November (1786) in order to arrange the matter with the government. A petition was accordingly prepared and by him presented to Mr. Rose of the Treasury. On the back is written 'Promised to be complied with'. I never knew exactly why it was not, but I understand this expedition was checked in its early career in consequence of some ships being detained upon the plea of the South Sea Company that their rights were invaded.

From a letter to M. Pictet

London,
November 16, 1786

'I am now in London, for what purpose I can hardly tell you. You may perhaps have heard of our projected settlement at Botany Bay in New Holland. That was one reason for my coming to this place. Uncomfortable as must necessarily be the prospect of such a scheme, with such colonists as whores and rogues, the desire of doing something in the world rather than pass away my time in inglorious obscurity made me offer my services, but I was too late.

Commercial schemes are carrying on here with great spirit, and among others the fine furs we discovered on the coast of America are carried thence to China and exchanged with great profit. If I do not get employed under government, I shall most likely engage in that trade. Indeed, I am in some measure already, but some difficulties are to be got over which concern charters and monopolies.'

From a letter to his sister

London,
December 4, 1786

'I have seen *Cleone*, a tragedy, in which Mrs. Siddons exerted herself with wonderful effect. She is in a lone wood with her child, and an assassin sent for the purpose appears. She snatches up the infant, and running off crying in all the agony of fear "Murder, Murder" she sounded in it such a note of unison to the feelings of the house that in an instant everyone cried "Murder" too, and ladies screaming and fainting were carried out by dozens.'

During his stay in London, James contracted a violent antipathy towards the gentlemen at the head of affairs, and was not very moderate in his anger at their not employing him in the way he wished. In fact, however, the Lords of the Admiralty, Lord Howe being then at the head of that department, did not know the mind of the applicant and therefore no blame is imputable to them, although I deem it a very great national loss that they were ignorant of it.

Mr. John King, brother of his old and tried friend, had been secretary to the late Marquis of Rockingham during his short administration, and at this time was violent against all the measures of Mr. Pitt. James also at this time spent some days at Beaconsfield with Mr. Burke, and was highly captivated by his brilliant conversation and engaging manners. He also passed several days with his old acquaintance Lord Inchequin at Cliveden. At neither of these places were to be found men or sentiments likely to assist my friend in pushing his fortunes under the auspices of his own government, but on the contrary, gave him a high disgust both to the men and to their counsels.

It was then that his ardent mind embraced the world as his country, and he formed the plan which I shall present to my readers. Both that and the letter which precedes it are in French, which I shall translate with all the justness in my power. It was offered to the Russian Ambassador in London, who instantly saw its merits and transmitted it to his mistress, then on her journey to Chersonese. Her journey was checked in its progress by the unexpected war made against the Great Autocratrix by the Turks, unless indeed her army of attendants might justly be called the opening of the campaign.

February 1787

'Sir,—It is for a considerable time past that the plan which I have the honour of presenting to your Excellency's consideration has made a strong impression on my mind. I had conceived hopes that the parts which relate to the proposed discoveries on the coasts of China and Japan would have been adopted in England, and that I should have command of the ships destined for their service; and in truth Captain Cook, before his death, had intended employing the ships under him for this purpose.

To all appearance this project is no longer thought of here, and therefore I have taken the resolution of offering my services to the Empress of Russia, whose dominions are better situated than those of any other European power to draw from it all the advantages of which it is capable, and whose character for penetration and magnificence appears to me calculated to conceive at the possible consequences and to put it into execution in the manner which alone success may be hoped from.

I have detailed my opinion at great length, but that does not prevent the plan from receiving all the modifications which the wisdom of the Court of Petersburg may judge proper, and I shall think myself too happy to bear a part in the discoveries from which I foresee glorious consequences. I have, etc., J. T.

Enclosure. The plan has for its immediate objects—

1. The augmenting the consequence of Kamchatka and its value to Russia by increasing its commerce to America for furs.

2. A consequence of the first—the increase of trade with China. The accomplishment of these will open the prospect of others, secondary indeed, but no less important and by no means chimerical.

1. The opening a trade with Japan, which may offer a large and more advantageous vent for the said furs, as well as for the iron and other products of the eastern part of the Russian empire.

2. The creating an excellent nursery for the Russian seamen by means of a navigation which will make them acquainted with the varieties of climate and manoeuvre.

3. The augmenting the Imperial revenue, a necessary consequence of the expansion of commerce.

We will begin with the first article. In order to carry this prospect into execution with effect, it will be necessary to equip three stout vessels in Europe and sending them round Cape Horn to Kamchatka. These vessels must be loaded with those articles which are best adapted to commerce with the inhabitants of America and which are not to be procured in Kamchatka. The assortment of the cargo will consist principally of coarse clothes, blankets, looking glasses, glass beads and all the different sorts of toys which are liked by savages and which are not manufactured in the eastern part of the Empire. Besides these, provisions, naval stores and whatever most needed in Kamchatka. It will be proper to embark on the ships a more than ordinary proportion of armourers, smiths and ship-wrights. These artisans will establish themselves at Kamchatka, at which place there were none when we were there with Captain Cook. The smiths will employ themselves in fabricating the iron which may be sent them from Siberia, according to the various tastes of the savages; and the shipwrights will be necessary as well for the unavoidable repairs of the vessels which we propose to send as to improve the construction of those that may hereafter be built in the country.

The ships which ought to sail from Europe in the month of September, will touch at some Spanish or Portuguese part of South America, and after having doubled Cape Horn, will proceed to some of the islands in the South Sea for the same purpose. From thence they will steer for that part of the coast of America which is situated to the north of California and employ the summer in collecting furs the whole length of the coast, as well as to the southward and eastward of Cook's River, or among the Russian settlements already established on the island of Oonalaska.[1] The vessels employed at present in this traffic from the bay of Awatchka are neither of a size nor a construction fit for the navigation, and therefore do not venture on those parts of the coast where the furs most abound. The ships which I propose to conduct from Europe to Cape Horn will examine the whole extent of the coast from the lowest latitude in which the precious furs of the sea otter are to be found; and collecting a great quantity of furs infinitely superior to what is at present produced, will accomplish the first proposed object of augmenting the commerce from Kamchatka to America.

The second object, viz. the augmenting of trade from Kamchatka to China, naturally follows the first; for it appears to us beyond a doubt that the consumption of China will be equal to any quantity of furs that America can supply. Judging both by the distance, and by the experience I have had of it, it appears that the passage from Kamchatka to Canton will not in general prove longer than six weeks. We have reason to believe that it will be very possible to open communications with ports nearer to Pekin. To effect this, we propose that two out of the three ships shall quit the coast of America early enough to be able to arrive at Kamchatka, disembark the artisans and all the provisions for that colony, and to be ready to depart by the beginning of the month of September, leaving the third ship on the coast of America employed in collecting furs as before pointed out. [The two ships to explore the coast on their way to Canton, and one of them to return to Russia to report.]

I apprehend that to keep this commerce in train no more will be wanting than to send annually a ship or ships to Kamchatka via Cape Horn in order to carry by the quickest possible means whatever it may be necessary to draw from Europe. These ships will return by China and the Cape of Good Hope, and will bring home to Russia the productions of the East.

If it is found that anything is wanting to complete the settlement of this plan, I shall be ready to contribute everything in my power towards it.

We have left these two ships in those seas. One will be kept in prosecuting an annual commerce between Kamchatka and America, and the other between Kamchatka and China. We imagine that we have sufficiently demonstrated the advantage of this plan, and the great profits that may be hoped by those who may be concerned in the fitting out of the ships. We

[1] Cook's River is actually an inlet lying west of Prince William's Sound in Alaska. It was discovered on June 1, 1778, and was so named by Sandwich on the return of Cook's ships. Awatchka is now the harbour of Petropavlovsk on the cost of Kamchatka.

come now to those objects which are more remote in point of time, but which perhaps are at no great distance.

First, the opening of trade to Japan. The probability of such an event taking place is not unknown in Russia, where they have been pointed out by Mr. Muller in his account of the voyages of Captain Spankov and Lt. Walton to that country.[1] And besides these reasons it cannot be imagined that when the communication between Kamchatka and China shall be established, when the Kurile islands belonging to Russia shall have made themselves known to those of Japan in this neighbourhood, when perhaps the commerce for furs shall be carried on direct from America to China, and the ships so employed passing near to Japan; when, in short, the world around them, now torpid, shall be animated and set in motion by commerce, it will not be possible that they shall any longer maintain their separation from the nations, or lock up their treasures in the bosom of their country.

And here there is reason to entertain the most flattering hopes, as well respecting the commercial interests of Russia by the trade which may be opened between Kamchatka and this new rich country, as at the prospect of fame and glory which must redound to the Empress in being the first to give her empire this communication and to open this traffic: a traffic the probable importance of which defies speculation to penetrate, which may give a new era to the history of commerce, which may change the useless and uninhabited wastes of the bay of Awatchka into the flourishing neighbourhood of a commercial city which may extend its influence over the whole country of Kamchatka and produce a revolution throughout the affairs of the eastern world.

We now come to the second object, viz. the establishing a nursery of Russian seamen, in which subject little remains to be said. We have already remarked the advantage which must result to the seamen in regard to practical manoeuvre, to which we must add that the success of the voyages will principally depend upon the health of the crew. In order to ensure this advantage, it will be absolutely necessary to form the seamen and inferior officers to the scrupulous observance of the numerous regulations which the experience of navigators has proved to be requisite; and I hope it will not be thought too presuming of me when I say that, having made my first essay under Captain Cook, and having been First Lieutenant with Captain King, I look upon myself as able to ensure to my ships' companies all the health that the attentions of officers can procure them. . . .

[1] S. Muller, *Voyages from Asia to America for completing the discoveries of the N.W. Coast of America*, London 1761, translated from the Russian. Cook was familiar with this book. G. F. Muller produced a map of this area in 1754.

Our plan is finished, but it may not be improper to remark here that when it shall be carried into effect in its full extent, Russia will be supplied with all the produce of the East Indies in her own ships, it will afford a considerable exportation of her own manufactures, and create an equally considerable nursery of seamen. All other means apart, it is perhaps yet worthy of remark that when the English and other nations, who have already sent vessels to carry on the commerce in furs between America, Japan and China, and are preparing others, shall prosecute a considerable trade in those seas, it will become as necessary as advantageous to Russia to keep always a respectable force at Kamchatka.

If it is thought proper to establish other colonies in America, or to reinforce those which are already established at Unalaska, the respectable appearance and superior force of the ships which we propose to send from Europe will give a much greater facility to the measure than has been hitherto found. . . . Some little islands of little consequence may remain undiscovered within the immense extent of the South Seas, but after this there will exist no considerable portion of land unknown, and the Empress of Russia will have the glory of putting the finishing stroke to the so much celebrated discoveries of the maritime nations, and of rendering the geography of the globe perfect.

I have not been willing to obscure the more prominent parts of this plan by entering too much into inferior details. I have therefore reserved for this place to mention some circumstances which have regard to the consequences which may be drawn from it hereafter. That there is an immense extent of country which possess resources of furs equally inexhaustible as the trade which the Hudson's Bay Company carry on from England. That it is a country very rich in metals, the inhabitants all being provided with knives and other pieces of native copper. For all these reasons we imagine that an inferior sort of nagivation in small vessels, which will go from port to port, may be established independent of the large ships. But the means to have them? Captain Cook's ships came provided with such, built in England, taken to pieces again and arranged within the ships, all ready to be reconstructed in case of need. Our large ships may be equally provided with such. There remain, however, yet many resources. They may be bought cheap in China, or they may be built at Kamchatka, or we might take them from Europe in company with the large ships, for there is no danger in passing Cape Horn in vessels of a hundred tons. I would willingly do it myself in the proper season.

Of the three ships that go out from Europe, one ought to be of 500 tons, the others of 300 tons each. These vessels going from Kamchatka to America may bring back wood proper for building vessels, or at least to make masts and yards. For making this voyage it will be necessary to be provided with a good timekeeper, sextants, and all the instruments necessary for making astronomical observations, as well as for making charts and plans of the coast to be examined and of the ports and harbours which may be entered.

MS. Note. Two ships are at present on a voyage from Russia presenting nearly this plan, one of them having on board an ambassador extraordinary to Japan, with magnificent presents. The commander of the expedition, Krusenstern, and the captain of the second ship, Lisyanskii, I am intimately acquainted with and have long known of the determination of the former to embark in this expedition if he could. No men can be better fitted for such a task.'[1]

Having presented this plan to the Russian ambassador, James did not long remain in London, but in the month of February returned to Cornwall to await the answer of the Empress. . . .

(*Penrose having in the interval married Trevenen's sister Bess and having opposed the Russian plan*) all my persuasion was in vain. His mind had long been occupied with a magnificent object; his ardour and his merits led him into hopes that his name would descend to posterity on a footing with the immortal Cook. As soon as I saw that such was the situation of the ardent feelings of my friend's mind, I only urged further the question of the propriety of showing a plan of this important nature to the British government before embarking on it, and to make this the ground of asking leave of absence when it might be wanted. James was satisfied with offering his services a short time before. . . .

The Admiralty in reply granted leave of absence for one year and he prepared to set out for London. In a letter to his friend Riou of March 5 he details to him many parts of his plan, and mentions Hergest and Samwell, two of his old circumnavigation associates, being to embark with him in his voyage of discovery, if it be brought about. . . . On arriving in London, after some consultations with Count Vorontsov, James determined not to leave London till the Empress' answer arrived, which not being expected till May he immediately commenced such studies as tended to assist him in the projected enterprise. During his absence Count Vorontsov had found means of enquiring into his character, and had become very anxious that his mistress should possess the services of such a man as he found the proposer of the plan to be and paid him every polite and kind attention.

[1] This expedition, with M. de Resanov on board as ambassador, sailed from Kronstadt in 1803. They were refused entry at Nagasaki, continued to Petropavlovsk and returned in 1806, having taken on board at Macao a cargo of furs brought from America in another Russian vessel. Captains Krusenstern and Lisyanskii in the *Nadezhda* and *Neva* were the first Russian circumnavigators in 1803–5. See M. Mitchell, *Maritime History of Russia*, p. 226.

The month of April seems to have passed without any particular occurrence, unless it appears that some negotiations took place respecting the command of the *Bounty*, then about to be fitted out for the voyage since made so memorable by the uncommon infamy of her crew and the dreadful hardships sustained by her gallant commander. This offer was made to him by Mr. Dalrymple, who has rendered himself conspicuous from his eminent knowledge of the geography of the globe and his admirable collection of voyages. But the plan having been previously presented to the Russian ambassador, and that nobleman having assured James that there were no doubts of the Empress entering fully into it, the scheme of the *Bounty* was instantly declined.

About the month of May the answer of the Empress arrived and stamped the fate of the expecting hero. I here subjoin a translation of the letter of the Great Autocratrix on this occasion—

'To Lt. General Count Vorontsov.
Sir,—You will acquaint Lt. Trevenen, whose plan you have sent with your letter to Count Bezborodko, that I read it with satisfaction and find him an able man in his art, and well acquainted with such matters. Being very willing to employ this officer in my service, I leave you to forward this affair; and as there is nothing to intercept such an expedition as he proposes to make further discoveries for the benefit of commerce, he may rest assured that by quitting the English service he not only shall lose nothing, but shall find it much to his advantage, as you well know yourself how distinguished and rewarded were those who have been employed on such expeditions. What money he shall want for his journey you will supply him with it, and draw for the same on the Cabinet.'

Catharine

Kiev. April 2, 1787.

The acceptance of his services by the Empress forms a proper finish to the third part of my labours, which I shall therefore draw to a conclusion after inserting an extract from the last letter written by my friend in England.

To his Mother

May 28, 1787

'You will not, I fancy, do me the injustice to suppose that I leave England with a tranquil heart, or that I do not feel the sacrifice I am making of country and friends. Nevertheless as far as reason, hopes, or conscience are concerned, I find myself quite acquitted and encouraged. . . . My brother and Ward promise to go with me to Harwich to see me take my leave of England.

Your dutiful son, James Trevenen.'

PART II

SERVICE IN THE RUSSIAN NAVY

INTRODUCTION

It seems strange that Trevenen's elaborate Plan for the Pacific should have been received with such apparent enthusiasm in Russia and such inducements should have been offered him to put it into effect, since we know that a few weeks before its presentation to the Russian Ambassador in London an expedition on very similar lines had been planned in Russia and an officer selected to command it. The Russian project was, indeed, concerned chiefly with exploration, but there would have been little difficulty in enlarging its scope to include trade in accordance with Trevenen's suggestions. Possibly, if he had not been delayed by his accident, the scheme of the expedition might have been changed and he might have replaced the commander already chosen, but even then the Plan would have had to be abandoned, because the outbreak of war with Turkey made it necessary to retain the experienced seamen who would have been needed for such a voyage.

This war had been made almost inevitable by the Russian annexation of the Crimea and the obvious intention of the Empress Catharine and the Emperor Joseph to enlarge their dominions at the expense of Turkey. It began, as Turkish wars usually did begin, with the imprisonment of the Russian Ambassador to Constantinople on August 5,[1] though the Russian declaration of war was not actually issued until September 9.

At the outbreak of the previous war in 1769 Russia had had no fleet in the Black Sea and no base from which a fleet could have operated. Now the base was available at Sevastopol and there was at least a small fleet, but it was very doubtful whether it could stand up to the full strength of the Turkish fleet and the natural course was to repeat the successful strategy of 1769 and send another fleet from the Baltic to make a large-scale diversion in the Grecian Archipelago.

Very few ships had been in commission in 1787 and it was too late to put this plan into execution before the winter, but for the next year it was arranged to send out a Mediterranean fleet of 15 battleships under the command of Admiral Samuel Greig, who had been Orlov's flag captain in the previous campaign in those waters. Trevenen's ship, the *Rodislav* 66, was to be included in this fleet and he fully expected a leisurely voyage to

[1] All dates are in Old Style, to correspond with those in Trevenen's papers.

the Levant with plenty of time for training crews before meeting an enemy of no great reputation at sea. What actually happened was very different; instead of fighting the Turks after some months in which to 'shake down', the Russians found themselves face to face with the Swedes within a fortnight of their first sailing from Kronstadt.

War between Russia and Turkey had seemed to Gustaf III of Sweden to give him an opportunity of recovering the Finnish territory ceded to Russia in 1721 and 1743. This he hoped to achieve, not by an advance over the Finnish frontier, but by a sudden direct attack on Petersburg itself, the fleet having first cleared the way for a landing close to the Russian capital. The scheme may have had its merits, but its execution was faulty enough to make its failure almost inevitable. Not only was the attack made too soon, while the bulk of the Russian ships destined for the Mediterranean were still in home waters; it was also made with too small a force, less than three quarters of the available strength of the Swedish navy. As a result, when the two fleets met, it was on equal terms and a drawn battle followed. The Swedes fell back on Sveaborg and all ideas of a short decisive campaign had to be abandoned.

On their side the Russians seem to have gone out of their way to make their enemy's task easier. News of the Swedish mobilization had reached them at the end of April, but it was not for another month that Greig was told to send scouts to investigate off Karlskrona and Sveaborg, and even later, on June 5, when the Swedes were well on their way northward, the three 100-gun ships belonging to the Mediterranean fleet were allowed to leave Kronstadt for Copenhagen, so that they might have time to lighten ship for the passage of the Sound before the arrival of the rest of Greig's force.

These three ships, with a frigate and three store-ships, under the command of Vice Admiral V. Fondezin[1] met the Swedish fleet off Dagerort[2] on June 11. War had not yet been declared, but the Swedish Grand Admiral, Prince Carl, Duke of Södermanland, the King's brother, did his best to find an excuse for fighting by demanding a salute. Fondezin insisted that in complying he was paying tribute to the Prince's personal rank and not to the Swedish flag, but fired the necessary guns and had to be allowed to go on his way.

A week later 'incidents' on the frontier led to a Swedish advance against Nyslott and war began without a declaration by either side. On June 24 the Swedish fleet left Hangö, where it had been since the 17th, and on the 27th

[1] There were several officers of this name in the Russian service from 1745 onwards. It was probably originally Von Dessen.

[2] The westernmost point of Dagö (now called Khiuma) marking the entrance to the Gulf of Finland on the south side.

it met and captured two Russian frigates not far from Revel; but then, instead of going on towards Petersburg, Prince Carl returned to Sveaborg, to await reinforcements, and remained there until July 3, when he at length put to sea to meet the Russians. The King with the galley fleet and the bulk of the army had reached Helsingfors ten days before this.

The Russian fleet under Greig had left Kronstadt on June 23, but had then waited to be joined by the ships originally allotted to the Baltic squadron and did not begin to work westward until the 28th. The two fleets met to the west of Hogland on July 6.

The Swedish line consisted of fifteen 2-deckers and five heavy frigates, the Russian of one 100-gun ship and sixteen 2-deckers; in the matter of guns they were almost exactly equal. The Russians came down before a light breeze at E.S.E. and the action began about 4.30 p.m. with both fleets on the port tack. With the fleet in reversed order, as it then was, the *Rodislav* was the leading ship of the Centre squadron and should have been No. 6 in the line, but a misunderstanding of signals had caused three of the five ships of the leading squadron (nominally the Rear) to steer for the other end of the Swedish line and left Rear Admiral Kozlyaninov to lead the line with only one ship between him and Trevenen.

Greig's flagship, which should have been No. 10 in the line, was now No. 7, but he still looked on the Swedish flagship as his proper opponent and this brought seven Russian ships against eleven Swedes. The ten Russians astern of him had nine Swedes opposed to them, two of them frigates, but their third squadron (nominally the Van) under Rear Admiral M. Fondezin, tended to hold aloof and most of the fighting in this part of the line was done by the sternmost ship of Greig's squadron, the *Vladislav*, and the three strays from Kozlyaninov's.

After some three hours the Swedes wore to the starboard tack and the Russians soon followed suit. Greig had previously passed the two ships ahead of him and now engaged the commander of the former Swedish Van, Count Klas Wachtmeister in the *Prins Gustaf*. This ship had already suffered severely and was in no condition to meet so powerful an opponent, but fought on unsupported for an hour or more against several Russian ships before surrendering. At about the same time the *Vladislav*, which had drifted into the Swedish fleet and could get no help from her own side, also surrendered. Soon after this firing ceased. The Swedes steered for Sveaborg, while the Russians, after two days more or less on the field of battle, withdrew to Seskär, some 40 miles west of Kronstadt, and there anchored.

They had suffered more damage than the Swedes and had lost more men, but they had done more than enough to upset the whole of the enemy's plan of campaign, in which a decisive victory at sea was essential. Besides this they were in the better position as regards repairs and reinforcements, since the Swedes were far from home and the resources of Sveaborg were very limited.

This advantage was driven home by Greig's appearance off Sveaborg on July 26 with a force of sixteen battleships and the capture and destruction of one of four Swedish ships found at anchor off that port. From then on there was no attempt on the part of the Swedes to make any use of their sailing fleet; it was not until the middle of November, when the Russians had returned to harbour for the winter, that Prince Carl even ventured to sail for Karlskrona.

Trevenen was one of four captains of private ships who received honours for their part in the battle of Hogland, but only after a somewhat undignified protest at having been overlooked. It will be seen that much the same thing happened two years later. Greig and Kozlyaninov with their captains were also rewarded, but Fondezin was relegated to a shore appointment and three captains, already deprived of their commands by Greig, received severe sentences from a court martial for failing in their duty.

An attack on Petersburg from the sea was now out of the question, but there remained the possibility of an advance along the Finnish coast, though here it would be necessary to reduce two Russian fortresses on the way, Fredrikshamn and Viborg. The Swedish flotilla was overwhelmingly superior to the Russian and a combined operation against Fredrikshamn should have been easy, but the troops landed near the place on July 23 were re-embarked almost at once and the whole project abandoned.

This had to be done on account of a mutiny among the officers of the Finnish army on the grounds that the war had been begun without the approval of their national assembly. Many Swedish officers were openly sympathetic and matters went as far as an approach to the enemy for an armistice; nothing came of this, but operations on land came to an almost complete stop. Denmark, too, chose this moment to declare war on Sweden and Gustaf III found himself engaged in a war on two fronts with a large proportion of his own subjects hostile as well.

Russian control of the Gulf of Finland threatened the Swedish forces in the eastern half of the country with a shortage of supplies, but the nature of the coastline helped to avert this danger, since small craft could use inshore channels where deep-water sailing ships could not penetrate. Only at two places was coastwise traffic compelled to appear in the open and it was an obvious move on the part of the Russians to occupy one or other of them. The choice fell on the westernmost, Hangö-udd, about 65 miles from Helsingfors, and Trevenen, though only a very junior Captain, was given command of the detachment told off for this important post.

His separate command lasted from August 14 to October 17. In spite of many difficulties with his subordinates, all set out at considerable length in the Memoir, he had succeeded in preventing the enemy from making use of the coastwise route as long as he remained on his station. It might have been expected that with their great superiority in rowing vessels the Swedes would have made a serious effort to drive him off, but they never assembled a large enough force for this and the only fighting that took place, early in October, was quite inconclusive.

On his return to Revel Trevenen learnt that Greig had just died. For the moment Kozlyaninov was in command, but early in 1789 he was sent to Copenhagen to replace V. Fondezin, who even after being joined by three battleships from the Baltic and four from Archangel had deliberately failed to intercept the Swedes on their return to Karlskrona. The chief Russian command then passed to Admiral Tchitchagov, a man of very little experience of fighting and one whose dislike of foreigners 'amounted to antipathy'.

Trevenen had come to look on Greig as his patron and feared that the change would be harmful to his prospects, but at first there was no sign of this. Not only was he promoted to First Captain almost directly after his return, he was even summoned to Petersburg, though his ship was laid up at Revel, and asked to submit a general plan of campaign for the following year. This plan is summarized in the Memoir. It might well have shortened the war and ended it more favourably for Russia than was actually the case, but Tchitchagov was not the man to put it into effect and the operations of 1789 left things very much as they were.

Before the opening of that year's campaign, Denmark had withdrawn from the war and Gustaf III had engineered a counter-revolution which assured him of the support of his own people. It was true that the Russian navy was potentially much stronger than the Swedish, but it had wintered in three divisions, at Kronstadt, Revel and Copenhagen, and climatic conditions ought to have enabled the Swedes to deal with these separately.

Unfortunately sickness, which had begun in the previous autumn, increased to such an extent during the winter and early spring as to paralyse both fleet and dockyard almost completely, and though the ice at Karlskrona broke up in the middle of April, it was not until the end of June that the Swedish fleet could put to sea. By that time the Russian ships in home waters had been concentrated at Revel for a month and might easily have joined or been joined by those at Copenhagen. Only extreme lethargy on the Russian side prevented this.

As it was, Kozylaninov's squadron did not move from Copenhagen till the middle of June and then remained at anchor in Kjöge Bay for another month, while Tchitchagov lay idle at Revel. His only activity was the sending out of a small detachment to repeat the work done in 1788 of preventing Swedish small craft from reaching Helsingfors from the west. Trevenen sailed for Hangö-udd early in May accompanied by a frigate and two cutters, but only to find that new Swedish fortifications made it impossible for ships to get in close enough to control the passage. He claimed to have suggested Porkala, twenty miles from Helsingfors, as an equally good place for the purpose and hoped to be sent there himself, but the task of occupying this new position was given to a Russian captain and Trevenen's hopes of a second independent command came to nothing, at least for the moment.

Tchitchagov's fleet consisted of three 100-ton ships and seventeen 2-deckers, while Prince Carl had twenty-one 2-deckers and nine heavy frigates, one of which was absent when their meeting took place. Kozlyaninov had three 100-gun ships, eight 2-deckers and one heavy frigate, the *Venus*, recently taken from the Swedes in the Kattegat, and could rely on help from a considerable Danish fleet as long as he stayed where he was. Of these three fleets the Swedish was the first to move, leaving Karlskrona on June 25. Tchitchagov sailed from Revel a week later, but Kozylaninov remained at anchor in Danish waters, and though Prince Carl came within sight, he soon moved eastward again. On July 14 he and Tchitchagov sighted one another and next day the battle of Öland, such as it was, took place.

The wind was north-westerly and the Swedes to windward with both fleets on the port tack in reversed order. Trevenen's station was then next but one astern of Tchitchagov's flagship. With a superiority in numbers, if not in strength, Prince Carl, or rather his Chief-of-Staff, Nordenskjöld, had planned to concentrate on the second half of the Russian line and even to double on its sternmost ships, while his leading squadron prevented the Russian van from coming to its help. To some extent these tactics suggest those of Trafalgar and it will be seen that on a later occasion Nordenskjöld again proposed a method of attack similar to that which Nelson afterwards adopted at the Nile.

The plan might be good, but it broke down at once, because the Swedish rear squadron took practically no part in the action. There was a good deal of long-range firing in the van and centre, but even there the attack was never pressed home and the two fleets parted after about six hours with very little harm done on either side. Ten of the Russian ships, Trevenen's among them, had no casualties and half the total loss of 210 in the remainder was caused by the bursting of guns in one ship; while the Swedes only acknowledged twenty-four killed and wounded all told, eighteen in their leading ship (from a burst gun) and six in the fleet flagship.

For the next few days the fleets remained for the most part in contact with the Swedes trying somewhat halfheartedly to force an action and the Russians avoiding it. At length on July 20 Prince Carl returned to Karlskrona and two days later Tchitchagov, now joined by Kozlyaninov, followed him. His orders had been to blockade the Swedes there, but this he failed to do. Driven off by heavy weather on the 26th he used the pretext of shortage of water to return home and anchored in Revel Bay on August 9 after ten days' aimless cruising at the mouth of the Gulf of Finland. A week later he took his whole fleet into Revel.

Neither side could well be satisfied with the result of this short campaign, but on the whole the Russians had done better than the Swedes. Tchitchagov had at least managed to join Kozlyaninov and to bring the combined fleet home without loss, whereas Prince Carl had achieved nothing whatever. Very naturally he blamed the commander of his rear squadron, Rear Admiral Lilliehorn, whom he had superseded immediately after the battle and now brought before a court martial. Lilliehorn was at first sentenced to death, but this was commuted to banishment from the kingdom and even this modified punishment was eventually relaxed. In Russia no honours were awarded and Tchitchagov was severely criticized for having failed to make use of his overwhelming superiority after the junction with Kozlyaninov, but was retained in his command.

As far as the main sailing fleets were concerned the year's fighting was over, for though Tchitchagov was at sea from August 27 to October 11 and Prince Carl from October 3 to 10, the one remained at the mouth of the Gulf of Finland and the other in the southern Baltic. On the other hand, there was much activity on the Finnish coast and in this Trevenen had a considerable share.

His doings are described very fully in the Memoir, but a still more important action, in which Trevenen was not concerned, is not even mentioned. This was the first battle of Svensksund, near Kotka, fought on August 13 between the whole available strength of the Swedish rowing fleet and a combination of two Russian squadrons, galleys and gunboats from the north and a miscellaneous assortment of larger rowing vessels and small sailing craft from the south. The first was under the direct command of Nassau Siegen, whom Trevenen had described with some justification as 'a sort of madman', and the second should have been commanded by Vice Admiral Kruze of the 'Reserve squadron', but that officer had disagreed with Nassau Siegen as to the method of attack and had been replaced at the last moment by Balle from the rowing fleet. Thanks to Nassau

Siegen's tardiness the southern attack was repulsed with heavy loss and the Swedes, though losing several vessels, were able to withdraw to the westward with the bulk of their force intact.

Trevenen's chief duty, first off Porkala and afterwards in Barö-sund, between there and Hangö, was to prevent the Swedish flotilla from being joined by reinforcements from Stockholm and this he did until forced to withdraw on account of the lateness of the season. Swedish accounts suggest that his departure was hastened by the arrival of a number of their gunboats on October 12, but there is no mention of this on the Russian side and the Memoir shows that a council of war had already decided on withdrawal as soon as the weather was favourable.

So far Trevenen had reason to be satisfied with his share in the operations of the year 1789, but now came a severe set-back, the loss of his ship on the way into Revel. This was due to the combined ignorance and obstinacy of his pilots and one of his Russian Lieutenants, but their counter-charges caused the ensuing court martial to be a long and anxious business, though it ended satisfactorily enough with their punishment and the complete exoneration of Trevenen and his second-in-command, the English Captain-Lieutenant James Aiken.

Although the sentence of the Court Martial was not pronounced until April, six months after the loss of his ship, Trevenen must have known that it would be favourable at least a month earlier, since he had by then been appointed to another ship, the *Netron menya.* This was one of those which had wintered at Petersburg and was to be included in the fleet under the command of Vice Admiral Kruze, for whom Trevenen had far more respect than he had for his former leader, Tchitchagov. Still, with the result of the Court Martial not yet declared, he felt justified in declining to take up this appointment, and when he might have done so, he was ill enough for his doctor to forbid it. The ship had to sail from Kronstadt without him and must have been in action only a few days after he joined her.

This year the Swedes made good use of their geographical advantage and were at sea some three weeks before either of the Russian fleets was ready to move. The idea of a direct attack on Petersburg had been revived and the general plan was, first to deal with the Russians at Revel, and then to meet and defeat those from Kronstadt, after which the sailing ships would be able to support the flotilla in an advance towards the mouth of the Neva.

With this as his programme Prince Carl appeared off Revel on May 2 with a force of twenty battleships and six heavy frigates as against ten battleships, one heavy frigate and a number of smaller craft, all moored in three lines with the eleven heavy ships in the outermost. The odds in his favour were 2 to 1, and if the attack had been made in accordance with his, or rather Nordenskjöld's plan, which involved doubling on each Russian ship, boarding and anchoring, there can be little doubt that the Russians would have been overwhelmed, as the French were at the Nile. Unfortunately there was too much wind for such refinements and Prince Carl attacked without waiting for more favourable weather; all that was possible was for each ship in succession to close in, run along the Russian line and turn away again. This was what the French had done at St. Kitts in 1782 and was even less successful, since it resulted in the loss of two ships, one captured because she was too much damaged to get away and the other wrecked on the way out. The Russians were practically unhurt.

Two days later the division of the Russian flotilla which had wintered at Fredrikshamn was attacked by a much superior force of Swedes. Nearly half its vessels were captured or destroyed, but the remainder were able to hold off a second attack for long enough to let reinforcements reach the garrison and make the place reasonably secure. After this, leaving Fredrikshamn untaken in their rear, the Swedes went on eastward, crossed Viborg Bay and took up a position in Björkö-sund, to await the result of the coming encounter between their sailing fleet and the Russians from Kronstadt.

This took place on May 23 and 24 some twenty-five miles west of Kronstadt. Kruse had seventeen ships in his line against Prince Carl's twenty-four, but five of the Russians were 100-gun ships and two of the Swedes frigates, so that there was actually little difference in their strength. In the morning of the 23rd the wind was easterly and the Russians to windward, but for the other two actions, later in that day and on the next, the positions were reversed. Tactically speaking the series of actions was quite indecisive, but from the Russian point of view that was enough, since the arrival on the scene of Tchitchagov's ships from Revel would soon make them distinctly the stronger side.

As had happened after the battle of Hogland in 1788, Trevenen felt at first that his services had not been sufficiently recognized. He complained that Kruse had failed to mention him in his despatches and wrote claiming to have done more than others whose names had been included. Kruse, however, assured him that no slight had been intended and that the Empress would put matters right. This proved to be the case; Trevenen received a second honour and one superior to that given to the officer whose performance he had gone out of his way to compare with his own.

Within a few hours of the end of the last skirmish, for it was little more, the Swedes were in touch with Tchitchagov's fleet. He might, indeed, have brought them to action, but made no attempt to do so, and when he first sighted Kruse's fleet on the 26th, he took them for the Swedes and actually anchored to await an attack, thinking, as Trevenen says, that his success at

Revel had proved that a fleet at anchor was invincible. By then, though, the Swedes were thinking no longer of attack, but of defence; they were on their way towards Viborg Bay 'to protect the flotilla'. According to some accounts, Captain Sidney Smith, who then held an ill-defined position as adviser to the Swedish King without being officially in his service, brought orders to this effect, but actually he seems to have been already on board Prince Carl's flagship and he certainly claimed later that the idea of entering Viborg Bay was his and was enthusiastically accepted by the Prince.

Wisely or unwisely, by the King's order or thanks to Sidney Smith's sudden inspiration, the Swedish fleet took up a position across the mouth of Viborg Bay and the Russians slowly followed, to anchor in their turn well out of gunshot. Had it not been for one thing, the Swedes would have been well placed, especially when opposed by a commander who believed, as Tchitchagov seems to have done, in the impossibility of overcoming a fleet anchored in line. The difficulty lay in the fact that the shores of Viborg Bay were entirely in Russian hands, so that the Swedes were cut off from all supplies, even of water. Trevenen thought an attack both desirable and feasible, but Tchitchagov preferred to wait for his enemy to make a move, and in this he was justified by events.

The author of the Memoir, writing as a biographer rather than a historian and basing his account almost entirely on Trevenen's own journal and letters, naturally tended to overlook the important part played by the rowing fleets in this year's operations. When the two sailing fleets took up their positions facing one another, the main Swedish flotilla was in Björkö-sund on the east side of Viborg Bay, while what might have been a considerable reinforcement was still to the westward and out of reach. The Russians were in three bodies, some at Fredrikshamn, some at Viborg and thus behind the Swedes, some assembling at Kronstadt. These last were under the direct command of Nassau Siegen, who was again to be Commander-in-Chief of the Russian flotilla.

The Russian gunboats from Fredrikshamn joined Tchitchagov on June 8, but the westernmost Swedes, who should have intercepted them, but only followed ten days later, were held back by a few frigates and cutters stationed by Tchitchagov some ten miles to the west of his main fleet. Meanwhile the Swedes from Björkö-sund, with the King in command and Smith taking an active part, had tried in vain to force the approaches to Viborg. On June 18 Nassau Siegen anchored just south of Björkö-sund and the Russian concentration was practically complete.

It may be that Tchitchagov would at last have felt bound to take the offensive, but his enemy soon saved him from having to make up his mind. Directly after their repulse from Viborg they had decided that the only course open to them was for both sailing fleet and flotilla to break through the Russian blockade at all costs. All they needed was a favourable wind and it was probably no more than a coincidence that their dash for freedom began within a few hours after Nassau Siegen had fought his way through Björkö-sund and taken them in the rear.

Viborg Bay has three navigable approaches, the easternmost through Björkö-sund, the next between Björkö and the large shoal of Salvör-grund and the third between this shoal and other shallows off the promontory of Krysserort. The middle passage is the widest and it was there that the bulk of the Swedish fleet lay, while four of their battleships were anchored in the Krysserort channel faced by five Russians under Rear Admiral Povalishin, Trevenen's *Netron menya* being one of these. It was through this passage that the Swedes made their escape in the morning of June 22 and in doing so their leading ships caused far more damage than they received. The *Netron menya* suffered badly and both Trevenen and his second-in-command, Aiken, were seriously wounded, Trevenen mortally.

He knew that his condition was hopeless, but hoped to live long enough to see his wife and child, since Povalishin promised that the *Netron menya* should be sent back to Kronstadt at once; but this promise was useless, because Tchitchagov's approval could not be obtained until it was too late. When at last, on June 28, his ship was ordered to proceed, Trevenen was on the point of death, if not already dead.

Before he died he would have heard that the battle, which must have looked at first like a successful attempt by the Swedes to escape, had ended disastrously for them. Half of their fleet passed the Russian line in safety, Tchitchagov was slow to make a move and there seemed little to prevent the escape of the rest; but at this moment a Swedish fireship meaning to attack the Russians off Krysserort ran aboard one of her own battleships, which collided in turn with a frigate; the three ships blew up together and the explosion added to the normal smoke of an action made visibility so bad that another four battleships, two frigates and some smaller craft went hard aground and were captured. The rest got away safely for the moment, but two more battleships were overhauled and taken before they could reach safety at Sveaborg. The Swedish sailing fleet had lost one third of its strength.

The flotilla was more fortunate, though it lost several vessels in passing the Russian detachment to the west. The King himself might well have been taken prisoner if a signal from Tchitchagov had not recalled Crown's *Venus* at the wrong moment. As it was, the Swedes were able to reach Svensksund, south of Fredrikshamn, and join the vessels already there, a force more than enough to make up for their losses.

Here Nassau Siegen with the whole strength of the Russian rowing fleet attacked them on June 28. He hoped to mark the anniversary of the Empress's accession by a resounding victory, but actually suffered a severe defeat, losing nearly half his flotilla, largely on account of his own foolishness in attacking in unfavourable weather, as the Swedes had done at Revel earlier in the year.

Sweden had lost, or at least failed to win, every battle save the last, but that final victory did much to secure far more favourable terms of peace than could have been expected a few days before. It was not, however, the only factor in Sweden's favour. Austria, with whom Russia had been allied against the Turks, was now faced by a revolt in the Netherlands and unable to continue her support. This left Catharine to fight two enemies single-handed and she decided to come to terms with Sweden on the basis of re-establishing the position in Finland as it had been before Gustaf III made his foolish and unprovoked attack. One thing could not be restored; the Swedish fleet never recovered from its losses and was never again strong enough to face the Russian with any hope of success.

Chapter 1

ST. PETERSBURG AND KRONSTADT

[Trevenen left England for Russia on June 2, 1787, sailing from Harwich in the Helvoetsluys packet. He had a 'very tedious' passage lasting three days and was very sea-sick at first; but that, as he wrote, helped to keep his mind off his sorrow in parting from his family and friends at home to take up a new life in an unknown country. From Helvoetsluys to the Hague he was accompanied by 'an old Hessian officer, the Duke of Brunswick's cook and one other person' and from there to Berlin, a week's journey, by 'his Russian companion', of whom we hear remarkably little. The journey was uncomfortable, for the roads were bad and the gauge of his carriage differed from that of the local vehicles and the ruts they had made. Spending only one night in Berlin he left again on June 22 and passed through the eastern part of Germany without incident; only to suffer a serious accident a day or two later.]

This accident, the evils of which were not confined to the pain and distress immediately incurred by it, but the delay which it occasioned, was perhaps the cause of his original plan being frustrated, and of course led to the subsequent chain of events.

[On the way down a steep hill near a small village in Courland called Tadaikin, with the postillion leading one pair of horses and Trevenen the other, the weight of the coach caused the horses to break into a gallop. Trevenen's boat-cloak caught in some part of the harness and threw him to the ground in front of the coach, so that first one wheel and then another passed over his leg. He was carried to the village and a surgeon was sent for, but at first only his apprentice arrived and did nothing, and even when the surgeon himself appeared, it was only to declare that no bones were broken, though Trevenen was convinced that they were and had made an attempt to set the limb himself. Some days later he was in a high fever and it was necessary to call in a physician, who at once recognized a fracture and set it, though by then the damage was done and it was impossible to get the leg really straight. Delirium followed and recovery was very slow, so slow that Trevenen had to remain in 'the worst inn's worst room' for nearly two months before he could be moved.

In the meantime the Baron de Sass, 'the Lord of the Village of Tadaikin and of the neighbouring territory', who lived some 10 miles away, had heard of the accident and had at once brought his whole family to stay in the village and look after the unfortunate English traveller. From them he received every possible attention, and when, on August 22, he was at length fit to be moved, they took him to their home, to spend another three weeks as a convalescent before resuming his journey to Mittau and thence to Petersburg.]

This history affords many lessons on the uncertainty of human hopes and expectations. James, accompanied by his kind friends, had not travelled above five miles when he met a Russian Major from Petersburg, who informed him that four ships, which he had before heard were fitting out at Kronstadt to go on discoveries, were already sailed for England, where they were to pass the winter. He had naturally expected from the Empress's answer and the hurry of the Ambassador for his proceeding, that he should gave gone out in those ships, in which case he would have wintered in England, but as he still had expectations of being despatched after them, he hoped to arrive at Petersburg time enough to sail in some English vessel.[1]

[Trevenen went on to Mittau and thence to Riga, where he stayed for eight days with his leg gradually getting better. He wrote from there on September 23 and 27.]

Here also he first learnt with certainty that the Turks had declared war against the Russians,[2] and his expectation of the chief command in the ships bound on discoveries was much damped by finding that their present commander was a man of much interest, being a natural son of the Minister of Marine.

Having purchased a carriage and hired horses to take him all the way to Petersburg, a journey of 420 miles, he left Riga on September 27 or 28. The journey was not surmounted under twelve days,[3] but no particulars are mentioned till he arrived within twelve miles of Petersburg, when in the middle of the night the carriage broke down and the poor invalid was obliged to move up and down the road on his crutches, till at last a dung-cart

[1] This expedition had been planned and its commander, Mulovskii, appointed in December 1786, some weeks before the presentation of Trevenen's 'Plan', but its objects were primarily discovery and annexation, not trade. The ships which were to take part had left Archangel at the end of June 1787 and reached Kronstadt at the end of August or early in September. They had certainly not yet sailed for England and in fact never did so, since the outbreak of war with Turkey made it necessary to take their crews for the main fleet.

[2] The Turkish declaration of war, which took the form of imprisoning the Russian Ambassador in Constantinople was made on August 5th. The Russian counter-declaration did not follow until September 9th.

[3] *Author's note:* I take this expression of the number of days from one of James's letters, but there must be an error somewhere, as his last letter from Riga is dated September 27th, and he arrived at Petersburg on Sunday night, October 7th.

was procured, in which vehicle drawn by his own horses he made his entrée into the superb city about 2 o'clock in the morning. And he remarks in a letter to his mother: 'So you see nothing but misfortunes has happened to me from my first entering the dominions of the Great Autocratrix. Whether they are to last, time will determine.' In another place he says: 'An entry by no means triumphal. What will the sortie be?'

The following morning, upon sending to the houses where he expected letters to be addressed to him, he had the mortification to hear that none awaited him after his toils and dangers. This disappointment he laments in the strongest manner of his energetic pen.

He despatched a messenger for Novikov, a name which does not before occur in my materials, but I find him to be his fellow-traveller from England to Tadaiken. This gentleman immediately attended him and a consultation was held respecting the best manner of proceeding. Novikov dined with our traveller and after dinner made the tour of the magnificent city in a carriage. Petersburg has been so often described as to become as well known in England as a description can make it. I shall therefore (for the present at least), omit all accounts that occur in my researches after the more interesting history of the subject of these memoirs.

He had been furnished with a great many letters of recommendation and introduction to the ministers, grandees and merchants, but his instructions and advice upon the method of delivery, both from Count Vorontsov and others, had made him cautious how he went to work. An Englishman has little idea of the guard necessary to be held over his words and actions, when he first enters the regions of despotism and intrigue.

Count Vorontsov repeats in his letters: 'I above all advise you to place confidence in the Count Bezborodko, Admiral Greig and my brother'; and his letters to other great men were not to be delivered without Count Bezborodko's permission, Vorontsov no doubt fearing that a letter delivered to a man who may have become one of an opposite party might be as fatal as a visit to the Duke of Lerma after his disgrace.

Novikov attended his friend to the Secretary of the Prime Minister[1] and after enduring the pains and penalties of a great man's antichamber for a tedious time he had at last the honour of delivering Count Vorontsov's letter, was graciously received and desired to return on the Thursday morning, the Count meanwhile promising to speak to the Empress.

After this important transaction he waited on Messrs. Shairp and Yeldam, English merchants. He dined with the former and met a Dr. Guthrie, to whom he had a letter and commission from his friend Pictet. The

[1] Count Bezborodko.

knowledge gained this day was the necessity of patience in attending on the great and that it was the custom at a dinner visit to keep your carriage waiting and to go away very soon after dinner without tea or coffee.

It was known as a certainty that the projected voyage round the world must be postponed till the war against the Turks should be concluded, as so many choice seamen could not be spared.[1] Indeed the Court of Russia appears not to have foreseen so sudden an explosion and to have been illy[2] prepared for it.

Having waited on Count Bezborodko at the time appointed and attended an hour and [a] half in the antichamber, James was at last desired to call again on the Sunday, as Admiral Greig would be then in Petersburg. These attendances and delays were deeply felt by the high spirit of my friend and it required all his fortitude to summon patience to bear this new mode of life.

The appointed Sunday came and after some time spent at the Minister's levée our expectant traveller was informed that his affair was this day to be debated in Council and a note to Admiral Greig presented to him. He had, however, an opportunity of asking the Count's nephew whether he might deliver Count Vorontsov's letters to the Counts Tchernyshev and Osterman and was answered in the affirmative. But the delay of presenting these letters was unfortunate, as these noblemen being of the Council, their being previously interested personally in his favour might have had a useful effect.

The next day after calling in the morning on Admiral Greig he found that he was arrived in Petersburg, but was not at home. Hearing that the evening was the most likely time to meet the Admiral he called again and had the satisfaction of finding him at home. I will give the account of this interview in the words of the journal.

'At half past seven waited on Admiral Greig and luckily found him at home. He received me with great goodness and politeness and we soon began to talk on business. He said that Count Bezborodko had desired him to speak to me on the subject of entering into the Russian service. That the voyage being laid aside for which I was more particularly destined, the Empress and Count expected that I should enter into their marine service to serve in the present war with Turkey and he desired to know my determination on that head; adding that they would be very willing to give me the rank of *first* Captain, had there been a precedent for it, but there not being one, they desired to know whether I would be contented with that of *second*, in which I should not remain longer than three or four years; this rank to

[1] Orders to this effect were issued on October 29th.
[2] *Sic* in MS.

be dated backwards, so as to make it superior to that of Billings.[1] I answered that I was contented with this for myself, but spoke of Hergest and wished to know what would be done for him. Admiral Greig said he would also speak upon that subject. He did not say positively that the expedition to those seas was laid aside, but seemed almost certain of it. He told me the pay of 2nd Captain was so inconsiderable as 400 roubles per ann., but that the Empress was inclined to give me appointments that might be more considerable and handsome. He asked if I had waited upon Admiral Senyavin and upon my answering in the negative and saying that I had a letter from Count Vorontsov to him, he said that if he could possibly find him tomorrow after the Court, he would call upon me and take me to him. He said my accident was an unlucky one, for that most likely, if I had arrived so early as without my accident I should have done, I should most likely have been ere this sailed for England. I told him that I had always regretted my accident more on account of the time in which it had so inconveniently occurred than of myself and my sufferings. We had a good deal of conversation more and I came away much pleased with him.'

It was not until October 30 that any further progress appears to have been made in business. On that day Admiral Greig called with information that the Council had come to a resolution to grant our adventurer double pay and satisfaction for his expenses.

The Admiral recommended to him to take up his residence at Kronstadt, to be out of the way of extravagance, and to keep quiet till leave to enter into the Russian service, which had been applied for, should arrive. The rank of 2nd Captain answers to that of Lieut.-Colonel in the army and to this offer he had no objection, as there was no precedent of higher rank being given to a person of similar rank to his in the British service. But the pay, when doubled, amounted to no more than £150 per ann., a very trifle considering the state necessary to be kept up in that country and seems more especially diminutive from a recollection of the magnificent, though vague, promises in the letter from the Empress to Count Vorontsov and from the ardour with which he was pressed into the service. . . .

However, it appears that all the English in Petersburg thought the offer as handsome as could be expected and that he could not in decency ask more for the present.

Waiting for leave from the Admiralty at home and doubting whether

[1] Joseph Billings, who had been in the *Resolution* with Trevenen as A.B., had joined the Russian Navy as Midshipman in 1783. Two years later he was appointed to the command of an expedition to the eastern parts of Siberia, travelling thither by land. Starting as Captain Lieutenant he was authorized to assume the rank of 2nd Captain at a stage in his journey which he actually reached in June 1787. Trevenen's rank was back-dated to December 1786, to allow him to remain his senior.

he was justified in entering into a foreign service for purposes so different from those projected kept his mind in a state of great agitation, which was not a little heightened by continual disappointment on every post day of letters from Cornwall, on which subject he expresses himself with great warmth both in his journal and letters. . . .

November 1. On this day, James, in company with Capt. and Mrs. Dennison,[1] set out from Petersburg to proceed to Kronstadt, where they arrived the following day having crossed the river in Capt. Dennison's barge. The party slept at Oranienbaum in their way and the accommodations and impositions at that place are spoken of in terms of high disapprobation. Our traveller remained till the 4th, frequently seeing Admiral Greig and many of the officers with whom he was afterwards destined to serve. Admiral Greig was very attentive, and he also seemed pleased with Admiral Kruze and received a good deal of information from Capt. Elphinston,[2] whose account of the Russian service was by no means satisfactory. Admiral Kruze was captain of Admiral Spiridov's ship when she was blown up in the memorable engagement between the Russians and Turks in the Mediterranean.[3]

At Admiral Greig's levée on the morning of the 4th he was informed that the Empress had granted him 500 ducats to pay his expenses and that he (the Admiral) would keep one of the new 60-gun ships open for him to command in the projected expedition to the Archipelago and promised him also an English Lieutenant who spoke Russ, till he was master of that language, which however he soon became from the strength of his abilities and facility of acquiring languages.

Passing in Admiral Greig's barge to Oranienbaum he returned on the same day to Petersburg.

Very shortly after this little trip to Kronstadt Admiral Greig came again to Petersburg and at an interview informed our expectant and anxious friend that Count Bezborodko had forgot his promise of waiting till permission from the British Admiralty arrived and had got the Empress to sign the order for his admission into her service,[4] that the Russian Admiralty

[1] Francis Dennison appears first in 1777, when he was promoted from Lieutenant to Capt.-Lieutenant. He was now a Captain of the First Class and had recently brought a ship from Archangel to Kronstadt.

[2] Samuel Elphinston, son of John Elphinston, who had commanded part of the Russian Mediterranean fleet as a Rear-Admiral in 1769–70. The son entered Russian service at the same time as a Midshipman and followed his father's example by resigning in 1771. He became a Lieutenant R.N. in 1778, but returned to Russia in 1783 as Captain.

[3] The battle of Tchesma in 1770. Kruse is sometimes said to have been English or Scottish, but had been born in Moscow, in 1726. His father, also a Russian naval officer, appears to have been of Danish origin.

[4] The order for Trevenen's admission to the Russian service as 2nd Captain was issued on October 27th. He was given seniority of December 1st, 1786.

would, of course, send for him and that it was now hardly possible for him to avoid entering immediately into the service.

No transaction ever came before my notice more evidently meriting the charge of trepanning than this. I feel indignation that such a man as Admiral Greig should have had a share in it. . . .

Behold, then, our friend become Second Captain in the Russian Navy and appointed to the command of the *Yaroslav* in the second division of the fleet under the command of Admiral Tchitchagov, who seems to have received the Captain with the most mortifying coldness.

I do not find that there was much hesitation in accepting the offered commission, but a very powerful motive, which led to this easy acceptance before the answer from England arrived, was the thought of having accepted the Empress's money in England and the difficulty of retracting after having so far advanced. The force of this argument does not strike me, as the terms were not complied with on the part of the Empress and the *plan* of the proposed enterprize was of more worth to her Majesty than a thousand times the sum advanced.

From this time Capt. Trevenen was busy in procuring all things necessary to appear in the Russian naval uniform.

On the 20th he received a message to attend at the proper office to receive his 500 ducats, but some further delays took place before he got possession of this trifling sum, which was at last paid in paper, there being no ducats in the Treasury.

On the 25th Capt. Trevenen was presented to the Grand Duke[1] by Admiral Senyavin and by the Duke to the Empress, which being a ceremony of some consequence, I shall detail it, partly from the rough journal, partly from letters.

About 10 in the forenoon he set out in a carriage to call on Admiral Senyavin, but by some means or other could not find his house and at last had the good fortune to see him pass on his way to the palace, where he followed him, but losing sight of him in the crowd had great difficulty in finding the Grand Duke's apartments from ignorance of the language. After waiting an hour in a richly furnished hall, he followed the Admiral into a small apartment and was presented to the Grand Duke, who graciously kissed his cheek, preventing him at the same time from bending the knee to kiss his hand. Several questions of no moment were put and the presentment to the Grand Duchess took place and he had the honour of kissing her hand.

The Grand Duke desired the Captain to wait in another apartment till the Empress returned from Mass, which she did in about an hour, preceded by the proper officers and followed by the Grand Duke and Duchess and

[1] Afterwards the Emperor Paul I.

the maids of honour. Here the Grand Duke presented him and he had the honour of kissing the Royal hand and bowing his knee before the Great Autocratrix of the North. His rank was not high enough to admit of his being spoken to and this important affair over he retired. . . .

I should have mentioned that on the 23rd our traveller at last received letters from England. . . . At the same time he mentions passing a very pleasant afternoon the preceding day at Miss Farquharson's, which I mention as being the first time the name of that lady, since so highly interesting to the readers of these pages, occurs. The journal of the day is this: 'Yesterday I dined at Mr. Tooke's and spent a pleasant evening at Miss Farquharson's in spite of my headache'.

[The next three pages are occupied by a long extract from the journal in which Trevenen 'unburdened his mind by giving his thoughts vent on paper'. These thoughts were mainly concerned with the problems of existence in general and his own in particular. The final paragraph begins: 'Why was I born? Thou alone, O God, canst resolve the question'.]

In returning to my narrative, the next occurrence to notice is the refusal of the British Admiralty to his request of leave to enter into the Russian service. I have not been able to find the official letter from Mr. Stephens (then Secretary to the Board of Admiralty) on the subject; and as no precedent for this refusal could then be found, both the applicant and his friends were surprised at it. A letter from Count Vorontsov in my possession affords, however, the true sense and I will translate the part relative to the case, as being more plain than I could otherwise make it.

'I have had the honour of seeing Lord Howe[1] on the subject of the leave of absence which you have requested and he has communicated to me the answer which the Board of Admiralty have sent to you. The refusal which it contains is in consequence of an order of his Britannic Majesty, which, in consequence of the troubles which the Emperor's pretensions to the Scheldt have occasioned in Holland, forbids any of his Naval Officers to enter into any foreign service. This order being positive, Lord Howe, notwithstanding my solicitations, could not make an exception in your favour, but I dare flatter myself that you will be well recompensed by the service into which you have entered for that which you have quitted.'

I rather think that the Count in the latter part of this extract *dares flatter himself* a *great deal*, and with this idea about him I cannot fancy him soliciting very warmly with Lord Howe.

In the remainder of the letter the Count encourages the Captain in the hopes that peace with the Turks will soon enable him to proceed in his projected expedition.

[1] Then First Lord of the Admiralty.

It appeared now to Capt. T. that he had no other alternative but to renounce the Russian Navy, which, having entered into it at the commencement of a war, he thought himself bound in honour not to do, and with this to give up the pursuit of his plan of discovery, which he was very unwilling to do; or else to relinquish for ever his connection with the British Navy, in which his chance of promotion, but from his merit, was very trifling. At the same time it must be considered that his high value was not known to the British Admiralty and, if known, high birth and borough interest are too often found to carry more weight than the most intrinsic worth.[1] The latter choice was what he adopted, certainly with an unwilling and heavy heart, but with the most firm rectitude of principle, whatever may have been the error of judgement. He enclosed his commission in a letter to Mr. Stephens. This letter I have been fortunate enough to procure and, of course, hold it my duty to insert.

Petersburg,
December 24, 1787

'SIR,—I received your letter of the 13th of last month in answer to mine requesting leave from my Lords Commissioners of the Admiralty to enter into the service of the Empress of all the Russias, and announcing to me the very mortifying and unexpected intelligence that their Lordships do not think fit to permit any of the Officers of the Royal Navy to enter into the service of any foreign Prince or State. Their Lordships will do me the justice to perceive that I could not have been aware of this from any like circumstance having hitherto happened to any Officer of the Navy that has found himself in a similar situation with respect to this country either at a more remote or later period, or imagine that I should have been the first in this singular case. This I take notice of only to endeavour by it to justify myself in their eyes for the steps I have already taken and those that I fear I am farther put under the necessity of taking in consequence of their Lordships' refusal of my request. Not expecting this refusal I had made no hesitation in consenting to accept the offers made me here for entering into the service of her Imperial Majesty, which held forth to me the rank of Second Captain with the command of a line-of-battle ship and double pay and a future prospect of being employed in the same line in which I was engaged under the late Captain Cook. Their Lordships will easily perceive that I could not balance whilst I expected to gain their consent to accept

[1] *Author's note:* It must be allowed that the perusal of the plan offered to the Russian Government would have at once convinced any enlightened man of the enlarged views and great capacity of the writer of it. On this subject my friend and I had many arguments and I always insisted on the propriety of its being shown to our Ministers for their previous adoption as far as the situation of Great Britain rendered it useful.

their offers; and even now that I may perhaps be driven to the necessity of choosing between the two services, when I reflect that almost all the Captains, under whom I served in the British Navy and whose esteem I flattered myself with having gained, are dead, that I am therefore quite unconnected in the service, utterly without patronage in it and consequently without any founded hopes of promotion, there appears to be still the same balance of interest to determine me to remain where I am, and even, if necessary, reluctantly to resign the more satisfactory service of my own Country and a commission for which it was endeavoured to qualify me by a most expensive education at the Royal Academy at Portsmouth and which I afterwards purchased by very severe service in a most memorable expedition at a period prolonged by the unusual length of the very voyage that procured it and which itself precluded the possibility of an earlier and more profitable promotion that might else have been expected, as having fallen to the lot of hundreds who were only in the same degree of pretension with myself.

Their Lordships are, however, judges of what is right and necessary, and to their decision I shall submit with humility.

Whatever it may be, I cannot help flattering myself that in forming their opinion of my conduct they will have some regard to the very peculiar concurrence of circumstances that have directed it and that however they may think fit to discourage the proceeding, they will not, yet, disapprove of the motive that leads a young man to prefer an immediate and honourable employment, though in a foreign country, to the prospect of[1] inactivity and idleness, even in his own.

I am then compelled, Sir, if their Lordships insist on the hard necessity of the condition, to beg leave to resign my commission as Lieutenant in the British Navy and do accordingly pray you to communicate this my request to their Lordships.

It only remains that I beg pardon of you, Sir, for having so long trespassed on your patience, that I beseech you to believe that the wish alone of justifying myself as much as possible to their Lordships has made my letter so troublesome, and that I subscribe myself with great truth and respect, Sir, Your most obedient and most humble servant, JAMES TREVENEN.

Philip Stephens, Esq.'

This letter with the enclosed commission he transmitted to Mr. Wood, who prudently consulted with Mr. John King (brother to the late Capt. King and Under Secretary of State) and the result was that the giving in the

[1] MS. has 'to'.

commission was worse than useless, as it was an irritating measure, and if the British Admiralty took no notice of his entering into the service of Russia, his friends should undoubtedly be silent on the subject.

At the same time with the commission he dispatched letters to Count Vorontsov and Mr. King giving reasons for the resignation of his British commission. In his letter to the Count, which is in French, he expresses himself under obligation to him for procuring him some seniority of rank as well as some indemnification for his expenses, which he states at 500 ducats. But what appears to me singular is the following expression, which shows that the Ambassador was better acquainted with the intentions of the Admiralty than he himself was and accounts in some measure for his having asked leave to visit foreign countries instead of entering into foreign service. Speaking of the refusal of leave he says: 'Votre Excellence m'ayant averti que ce serait le cas avant que je suis parti d'Angleterre, je n'en ai êté surpris'.

Yet in his letters to his friends as well as that to Mr. Stephens the refusal is stated to have been unexpected, and though he found the Ambassador right at last, I have no idea that he ever thought so before.

After this time he appears to have made Kronstadt his home for the winter, and I shall now proceed to collect as many circumstances attending that period as possible. His first step was to begin the study of the language of his new companions, and although this was so different from the others he had made himself master of as not to admit of their being of any use towards its acquirement, yet a long habit of application made even this easy to him and in the course of the winter he had become a tolerable proficient.

He lodged at the house of an Irish Captain in the Russian service and speaks highly of the kindness of his host and hostess; but, his great object now being retirement to pursue his studies, 'a silent room and a sea-coal fire' were the great objects of his desire. But in his present situation he was annoyed by the squalling of 'beaten brats' in a language he did not understand and was mastering all his fortitude to endeavour to reconcile himself to his situation. To the Irish gentleman above mentioned, but whose name I have not heard, he had been introduced by Mr. Forster, Governor of the Russian Company, and he speaks of this gentleman as having rendered him more essential service than any other of the numerous personages to whom he had been recommended.

Soon after his arrival in Kronstadt he dined with Admiral Greig, where he met two very interesting personages—'Prince Nassau, who went round the world with Bougainville, projected the attack upon Jersey, commanded the floating batteries against Gibraltar and is now going to join the Russian army[1]—and Count Orlov, who commanded the Russian fleet up the Archipelago, when they burnt the Turkish fleet in Tchesma Bay, and has been concerned in several other great events relative to this country.[2] The The former seems a sort of madman and the latter is above six feet high, *ergo* unquestionably a great man.'

Captain T. makes very many complaints of the severity of the winter, which he says, 'though not so severe as I expected in general, there are days of cold misery that make one quite agree with the Scotch preacher, who told his flock that a certain place of punishment was colder than their ideas could represent, thinking that, if he told them it was a hot place, they would be all for going there. I suffer very much from the cold and constitutionally, for the numbness of my fingers in great cold recalls to my memory the times when my dear mother used to rub her child's white fingers between her own, to recall the blood that had left them'.

This and the foregoing extract are taken from a letter to his mother of January 1, 1788.

The only professional duty which appears to have fallen to his share during his winter stay at Kronstadt was a weekly guard taken in rotation by the captains. The Captain of the Guard resided for the week at the guard-house, which is separated from the town of Kronstadt, standing on the south mole that runs round the haven for the ships of war. The charge consisted in preventing the approach of improper persons and to guard the ships from accidents by fire. As no one resides on board the ships when laid up for the winter, the risk of the latter calamity in such a climate does not seem great.

It was not surprising that he soon found himself most thoroughly hated by all the Russian officers over whose heads he had been promoted. Merit generally draws the envy and ill-will of the ignorant on the possessor; but when that merit gains reward and attention to the detriment of the undeserving, their weak minds cannot forgive and they keep labouring to find defects, instead of endeavouring to copy excellence. It does indeed appear a hard

[1] Prince Charles of Nassau-Siegen served as a Volunteer with Bougainville in 1766–9. As a French Colonel he was in command of the abortive attempt against Jersey in 1779 and as a Spanish Major General commanded the floating batteries in the unsuccessful attack on Gibraltar in 1781. Going to Russia in 1786 he accompanied the Empress on her journey to the Crimea in 1787 and was given command of the Russian flotilla acting against the Turks in the following year with the rank of Rear Admiral. Promoted after the destruction of part of the Turkish fleet, he was transferred to the Baltic in the same capacity. There he won a somewhat unsatisfactory victory at Svensksund in 1789 and was badly beaten at the same place in 1790. Trevenen's impression seems to have been not far from the truth.

[2] Count Alexis Orlov had been Commander-in-chief of the Russian expedition to the Mediterranean in 1770. Though without previous experience at sea he was forced to take direct command of the fleet as the only way of reconciling the claims of Spiridov and Elphinston, the commanders of its two divisions. Greig had then been his Flag Captain.

case, that a stranger should at once be put into a situation which very many have been for years struggling to attain; but nations emerging from barbarism must consider themselves as scholars, who, when one master leaves them, have another put over them, whom perhaps they never saw or heard of; but, had one of the boys been promoted to the vacancy, all would have remained in ignorance.

To show his little expectation of comfort from any society with his Brother Officers I need only give a short extract of a letter dated in April 1788, when he had seen a little more of them. After complaining of the hatred borne him on account of his elevation he says: 'If their good opinion were worth much, I think I might gain it by attention, but it is by no means so. They are in general people whose minds are degraded beneath the capability of our liberal or honourable sentiment, whose conversation breathes envy and detraction and whose society affords no other recreation than that of gambling'.

This spring was rendered memorable to the British officers in the Russian service by the admission of Paul Jones into the Navy of the Empress.[1]

The insult of barely admitting such a rascal in the same service was full enough to raise the indignation of every man of honour; but that this piratical vagabond should have been elevated above the rank of all the English in the Imperial service, except the veteran Admiral Greig, and vast numbers of old native officers was certainly a stretch of power to which Russians might submit, but certainly not those who have the free feelings of Britons. The Russians bore the yoke imposed upon them like the feudal vassals of a tyrannic lord, but the British united on a remonstrance and a resolution of quitting the service, should it be contaminated by the entrance of Paul Jones into it. It was with much difficulty that the cautious Admiral Greig could be persuaded to put his hand to this paper, and still more difficult to get a Russian to translate what to the utter astonishment of the natives appeared to suggest that the hand of the Empress had signed an order not perfectly consistent with the fullness of wisdom and justice.

But this plan was frustrated by its being fully known before perfectly executed. Admiral Greig was given to understand that, the Empress having already signed the order for the admission of Paul Jones, his character must of course be good; her infallibility must not be doubted and the officers must hold their tongues. Admiral Greig, who had been merely pushed into any concern in the matter, stopped at the very first instance of Royal

[1] Jones was first invited to enter Russian service in December 1787. He reached Petersburg on April 23, 1788 and left for the Black Sea on May 7, to take command of the sailing ships there, while Nassau-Siegen commanded the flotilla. The order from the Empress for his appointment as Captain-Commodore was dated February 15 and another of April 4 had provided for his promotion to Rear Admiral on taking over his command.

displeasure. There was a universal astonishment that a body of officers should deem a Royal order anything less than a compound of law, reason and justice; and Admiral Greig was thanked by the Grand Duke for stopping by his coolness so very precipitate and improper a measure.[1]

Public proceeding in their affair being thus ended, Capt. Trevenen had to take care of himself and waited on the Grand Duke with a suitable address. But his Highness so earnestly pressed him not to deliver the paper which he held in his hand (the contents of which he knew by a letter from Admiral Greig, which Capt. T. had presented for that purpose) and so requested him to continue in the service, with many fair promises and professions, that he at last prevailed on the indignant warrior to renounce his resolutions. But he never could have succeeded in his point but by a nearly positive assurance that Paul Jones should never be appointed to serve either with or over him.

Although neither the memorial of the officers nor the private remonstrance or address of Capt. Trevenen were delivered as intended, yet their contents are of a nature which will interest the reader, and I therefore insert them both.

'The British officers in the fleet of her Imperial Majesty, alarmed at finding that the notorious John Paul, commonly known by the name of Paul Jones, is received into the naval service of Russia and conceiving that such a step can have only taken place from the grossest misrepresentation of the real character of the man, think themselves bound by their duty to her Majesty and by their respect and zeal for her service, to make public and present to her the annexed sketch of his history, as taken from the information of Lieut. MacDonald[2] of her Imperial Majesty's navy, who will vouch for the truth of what he has there advanced.

'The British officers apprehend that a person possessing such a character as is therein manifested is unworthy to be admitted into the service of any Prince or State, because he has already proved guilty of treason towards his own Prince and Native Country.

'That he is unworthy of commanding officers and seamen in the service of any Prince from having already proved guilty of cruelty, inhumanity and murder towards those under his command, whilst in the service of merchants.

'That he is unworthy to rank with the officers of her Imperial Majesty's fleet, many of whom have served in her Navy for a great number of years and many of whom have likewise borne commissions in the service of his

[1] *Author's note:* I cannot but surmise that Admiral Greig had given information to the Grand Duke of the intended memorial and by that means saved himself the risk of delivering it and the Government the dilemma it must have occasioned them.

[2] John Macdonald had joined the Russian navy as a Midshipman in 1783 and had been promoted to Lieutenant in 1784.

Britannic Majesty, and all with approved fidelity and reputation; because he has never borne any commission under any Prince, but only under the standard of rebellion and treason; and because he has no reputation, except for deeds of desperation, which very deeds have in the eyes of all Europe branded his name with the stamp of infamy.

'That he is unworthy to bear a commission, because he dares not avow his real name.

'And, lastly, that he who has violated every principle of honour and honesty and the laws of God and man, not only cannot be worthy of trust, but must bring disgrace and contempt upon any Corps of Officers or service into which he may be admitted.

'The British Officers therefore pray not to be so degraded in the eyes of Europe and not to be put in a situation in which they will be ashamed to meet the looks of their countrymen.

'They anxiously pray to be saved from the shame and grief they must feel on turning their eyes upon themselves, whenever they shall be obliged to acknowledge an abhorred criminal of their own country for their brother officer.

'They pray that the respectable pride of the military character may not be destroyed in them by their degradation to the level of Paul Jones.

'They pray that honour, which in all ages has been the chief need of officers, may not be annihilated for them by his admission amongst them.

'They pray, by the memory of past services, by their ardour for the future and by the glory of her Imperial Majesty, to be saved from the scorn and sneers of the world, from mortification, reproach, contempt and dishonour.

'Lieutenant MacDonald of her Imperial Majesty's Navy, who was himself born in the County of Dumfries in Scotland, will make oath:

'That the surname of the father of the person calling himself Paul Jones is Paul.

'That he was formerly a peasant in the family of Lord Selkirk in the County of Dumfries in Scotland (to the best of his knowledge acting as his gardener) and that he was lately in the same capacity with Mr. Douglas Hamilton of Arbigland in the same county, who has since changed his name by Act of Parliament to Craig.[1]

'That the real name of the person calling himself Paul Jones is John Paul and that he was born somewhere in the County of Dumfries.

'That he sometime commanded the brig *John* in the service of Messrs. Ross and Kirkpatrick of Whitehaven.[2]

[1] All other accounts spell the name Craik.

[2] Other accounts give the name of the owners as Currie, Beck & Co. This firm was dissolved in 1771 and the *John* sold. Ross and Kirkpatrick may have been her later owners.

'And that (Mr. MacDonald being then in the *Berwick*'s tender on the coast of Scotland) the said John Paul, *alias* Paul Jones, landed at Lord Selkirk's house in Dumfries and plundered it of plate and furniture and destroyed what he could not carry off.

'Lieutenant MacDonald will farther advance upon oath: That it was always universally understood over the county that Lord Selkirk had taken the said John Paul, *alias* Paul Jones, under his protection in his youth.

'That he had it by verbal information from Mr. Lawson, a gentleman on board the said brig at the time and since a Lieutenant in the Royal Navy of England, that on a voyage to Grenada the said John Paul, *alias* Paul Jones, murdered his Carpenter by a violent blow of a handspike; and that he also caused a boy of the same vessel to be so severely flogged that he shortly after died of the injuries he received in that punishment.[1]'

Thus far Mr. MacDonald's Evidence.

'It farther appears by the public papers of the times and has been universally received by the world that after these actions he fled from his country to America, to avoid the justice done to his crimes, and being there known for a desperate person he obtained the command of a privateer, in which he committed many pilfering robberies on the coasts of Great Britain.

'Much stress has been laid on his having attacked and taken a frigate of 44 guns and an armed ship of 20 guns of his Britannic Majesty's and his desperation has been considered as a sufficient substitute for every other quality necessary to form the officer; but it should at the same time be remembered, not only that his own force, consisting of a 50-gun ship[2] and two stout frigates, was greatly superior to that of his enemy, but that, had he then been taken by him, his own head and those of most of his crew, which was chiefly composed of persons like himself, were forfeit to the justice of the country. Therefore these actions, which appear most bold and daring, seem to have a very probable origin in despair and in the fear of punishment, which presented death by the fire of their enemies as preferable to the only alternative left them, if they submitted, that of perishing by the hands of the Common Hangman in England.

'His Britannic Majesty, called on by the general voice of his Kingdom, found the behaviour of his officer, who so well resisted the greatly superior force of Paul Jones and sank his ship, so meritorious that he instantly

[1] The facts, as far as they can be ascertained, seem to be that Jones had a man flogged in 1770 and that this man died after shipping in another vessel. At a later date, 1773, Jones did actually kill a mutineer. In the first case he was completely exonerated; in the second he offered to surrender to justice, but was urged by his friends not to do so. See De Koven, *Life . . . of John Paul Jones*, Vol. I, pp. 14, 21, 25–7.

[2] The *Bonhomme Richard* actually carried forty-two guns.

knighted him and held up his conduct as a noble example of persevering valour to the officers of his Navy.

'The world has talked so loudly of many others of his enormities that they do not need to be mentioned; but if any doubt still remain in[1] the mind of any person, such incontrovertible evidence may in a short time be had from the proper Magistrates in England as cannot fail to convince the most incredulous and confirm his infamy in the most glaring and public manner.[2]

'Having entered into the service of her Imperial Majesty with assurances that I should never have reason to repent quitting that of my own country I gave up there the prospect of substantial advantages which are no longer within my reach: But I did it cheerfully, because hopes were held out to me from hence of an employment that would have compensated for the sacrifices I had made.

'The circumstances of the times having removed those hopes, I was obliged to submit to my fortune, and the object of my pursuit in England being now disposed of to another, rather than trail my wounded body to disappointment at home, I still chose to accept the satisfactory and honourable offers made me by her Imperial Majesty's Ministers for entering into her naval service and taking part in the war against the Turks; and prepared to do my duty with alacrity, although of a nature entirely different from that I had immediately in view on quitting the service of my own country for that of Russia.

'Possessing the highest respect and veneration for both services, I could not see without the greatest concern the admission of a notorious traitor to his country into that of her Imperial Majesty, and the sudden advancement of the miserable commander of a privateer over the heads of veteran officers, who had long been accustomed to place their pride and happiness in the honour of serving in the navies of Russia and England and bearing the commissions of their Imperial and Royal Majesties.

'As I find it impossible, after the most mature and deliberate consideration, to reconcile my mind to the possibility of ever coming under the command of such a man, I think it necessary to declare in the most unequivocal and positive terms that I never will in any case submit to his authority. And therefore I have to request that, if a contrary conduct is, or ever will be, expected of me, I may now be permitted to resign my commission in the service of her Imperial Majesty, whilst that of England is still open to admit me to my former station (though not to my former prospects) in order that

[1] MS. has 'on'.

[2] Apparently the general manifesto of the British officers extends thus far and is followed by part of Trevenen's own letter, but this is not made clear.

I may never expose myself to such a possibility, wherein not only my own character but the service of her Imperial Majesty might suffer.

'If it were permitted me to exhibit the man in his true colours, the motives of my conduct must appear to be right and reasonable.

'And I apprehend that it would not be wondered at that I should desire to quit the service of Russia, although in so doing I forego every inclination I had conceived for the proposed employment of the fleet I belong to and every prospect of interest, advantage and honour that a season so peculiarly favourable to the exertions of the military professions holds out to officers.'

The settlement of this matter did not take place till late in the spring, but after the introduction of the name of Paul Jones I thought it better to include everything respecting him before I proceeded in my narrative.

The dispute was of more probable consequence to the Captain and his friends than we may be at first aware of; for so firmly resolved was he to quit the service of Russia, unless he was morally certain that Paul Jones and he should never serve together, that he delayed writing home for some weeks in the expectation of being able to say that he should soon follow his letter in person. Indeed, though now bound by the strong tie of honour to the Russian service, unless the bond was loosened by the powers above him, so little inclination did he feel for it that he confesses he almost felt disappointment at the issue of his conference with the Grand Duke.

He had indeed a plea for leaving the service at this time, which myself and others of his friends urged him to make use of. This was the King's proclamation ordering all British officers who were abroad to return home in expectation of a war with France. But the idea that his honour was now engaged prevented any effect either from the proclamation or our instances.

Count Vorontsov continued to write to his protégé frequently and appears to have formed a much higher idea of the comfort and satisfaction attending his situation than I can form from any documents that have fallen in my way. In a letter dated March 4, 1788, written to introduce to Capt. T's notice a son of Admiral Senyavin who was also brother-in-law to the Count, he says: 'I have heard with infinite satisfaction from my friends at Petersburg that you are pleased with our service and with the treatment you receive, and that all are pleased with you. I have no doubt but that the longer you remain in our country the more you will be attached to it and the less you will regret your own.'

Not having the least doubt of the Count's sincerity or of his attachment to the interests of my friend, I give him full credit for the truth of his expressions, but it reads very strange to a Briton.

The whole of the season at Kronstadt appears to have been passed in a state of great anxiety, though relieved at intervals by the cheerful society of Petersburg, of which favourable mention is always made.

Towards the latter end of May, however, the fleet had been equipped and proceeded into the road before Kronstadt[1] and the following extract from a letter dated June 20 O.S. will give a better account of his situation as a Russian Captain than anything I could present of my own.

'I have before said that I was very careless about what might happen to myself when I carried my memorial on the subject of Paul Jones to the Grand Duke; and I was so, because, as C. Penrose rightly supposed, I meet with a great many very disagreeable circumstances in this service. Some, relating to the dislike of the officers, I have already mentioned. There are many others. There is no society worth seeking in Kronstadt, a reason why I should never think of establishing myself here. Again, a Captain of a man-of-war is a very different being here and in England and everything is in favour of the latter. Whilst here he is made a child of. He can do nothing whilst within reach of the Admiralty, but that will partly cease as soon as we sail. A great concern is the difference of the officers under him here and in England. There a man may rely on them in all cases of whatever moment or danger. Here a man has no one to rely on but himself, no capable Lieutenants, no such comfortable person as the Master to attend to his anchors and cables and nobody above a Boatswain's Mate to attend to his rigging. He must be all in all himself. He is answerable for everything and for every officer, even for their morals, of which they have none, and if any misfortune happens to him, he has the comfortable reflection that not only all his brother officers among the natives exult in his fall and will not fail to verify the fable of the sick lion, but that even his own officers will join in the cry and desert and accuse him for what probably only happened from their own unconquerable ignorance and supineness. For my own part I am as well off with respect to my officers as almost anybody; and my Captain-Lieutenant is very much of a gentleman, having served in England for some time, where the seeds of principle and honour seem to have taken such strong root in his mind as to withstand all the pestilential blasts of poisonous vapour that attack and destroy every sprout of morality and honesty that chance to show their heads in the degrading climate of despotism. He is, however, fastidious and peevish, somewhat like myself, and does not agree with the other officers. If I could descend to the little policy of dividing the two parties, I might always have one on my side; but it is a policy I despise, and if I cannot carry all through the strong hand of power and rectitude of intention, why e'en let all run riot.'[2]

[1] The bulk of the fleet, including Trevenen's ship, assembled in the roads on May 27.

[2] *Author's note:* There is no post-mark on this letter, but by what private hand it came is not said.

This is not a very pleasing picture of the fruits of command and would justify a common idea that a man ambitious of command sets aside all the disagreeable parts of service for the selfish pleasure of gratifying a ruling passion. The subject of these memoirs was a man of the most lively ambition: let us then see what he says of the sweets of command in an extract from the same letter which has just before shown us the reverse of the picture.

'With all these disagreeable circumstances there are sweets in authority which I taste with gust[1]: there is exultation in command and even in command in danger, that repays one's anxiety; and in command one may enjoy the pleasure of doing good and of being actively serviceable. In keeping peace amongst officers and in making them know their own true interests. In endeavouring to distribute impartiality and inflexible justice, and in lifting up the desponding heads of the poor miserable Russian recruits, who come upon a new element from their peaceful habitations in the depths of the wilderness to what they imagine a certainty of death and of living in misery till they are relieved by it. The lives of men are beyond imagination valueless here and deaths so common as to excite no observation. There are 24,000 persons in the small town of Kronstadt; and in the sea-hospitals from the beginning of spring hardly less than 20 have in any day departed for the other world. The rest are so dispirited that they die from no other cause, like the Swiss soldiers, who sing melancholily of the charms of their native mountains and die in regretting them. *Domum, Domum, Dulce Domum.*'

[1] *Sic* in MS.

Chapter 2

THE WAR WITH SWEDEN: 1788

In relating the subsequent events I shall not be able to regulate the dates of facts with so much accuracy as I could wish owing to some letters and papers being dated according to the *old*, others to the *new* style, but the consequence is not great.

The ship now commanded by Capt. Trevenen does not appear to be the same to which he was first commissioned, but the *Rodislav*[1] of 64 guns.

Before the Russian fleet under Admiral Greig were quite ready for sea, news of a most unexpected nature arrived and once more changed all the individual hopes of my friend and caused a total subversion of all the warlike schemes of the Empress. This was the sailing of a Swedish fleet, which was said to be cruising in the Gulf of Finland and seemed to threaten to dispute the passage of the Russians down the Baltic.[2] Doubts had been before entertained whether the Spaniards would quietly admit the Russian fleet to enter the Mediterranean, but this new obstacle was wholly unexpected, either to the warriors or politicians of her Imperial Majesty.

Three Russian ships of the line had already proceeded safely to Copenhagen. The Russian frigates had reconnoitred the Swedish fleet without molestation and their pacific intentions were still hoped by some. But the indignation of the great Autocratrix was roused by the insult and she is reported to have said that, should the Swedes attempt the smallest hostility, she would make a losing peace with the Turks and turning her whole force against Sweden leave nothing in that country but rocks and barrenness. We are hence to conclude that her having suffered Sweden to retain its former proportion of population and cultivation was more owing to want of power than any sensation approaching mercy or mildness in this elevated woman.

The Russian fleet sailed on June 23, still with the intention of proceeding to the Mediterranean, and the ships had on board troops, flat-bottomed boats and other preparations for the campaign in the Archipelago.

The apparent amicable disposition of the Swedes did not, however, last long. Accounts were received of their commencing hostilities and on the

[1] MS. has *Radisloff*. This is a phonetic spelling, but that given above is a more correct transliteration. She was a ship of sixty-six guns.

[2] The Swedes left Karlskrona on May 29/June 9.

27th the captains were called by signal on board the ship of the Commander-in-chief and informed of the war being declared against Sweden and furnished with the usual orders to sink, burn and destroy.

The Russians, having no foreign settlements and scarcely any trade either foreign or coastways carried on under their own flag and being also 5 months every year confined by the ice within their ports in the most supine idleness, have no possible means of possessing a body of experienced seamen; and this deficiency can be but miserably compensated for by crowding their ships with peasants torn from their native spots in regions far from the sea and almost without the knowledge of the existence of such an element. Dragged from their friends and exposed to a violent change of life to them replete with horrors, their spirits sink into perfect dejection and they welcome death as the best relief from miseries so completely dreadful to their feelings.

The Russian officers were well aware of this state of their crews, but hoped that in the length of the voyage to and up the Mediterranean time and attention would reconcile them to their situation, harden their constitutions and make these poor wretches, torn from their milk and vegetables, eat the vilest rye-bread and bad meat with an idea beyond that of merely prolonging a miserable existence. The fineness of the climate and probability of a good passage rendered their expectations probable as well as natural. But it was a terrible baulk to these expectations, instead of a long and pleasant voyage of preparation and at the end of it to meet an enemy to whom they thought themselves decidedly superior, to find that on the instant almost they had to engage a veteran enemy, used to manoeuvring and to be constantly at sea. But this sentiment was chiefly confined to the Russians, for Capt. T. says: 'To me it was exactly the same and I was rather pleased that something was to be done so soon'.

After leaving Kronstadt the Russian fleet encountered a foul wind for ten days, which was so far fortunate that they were enabled to exercise their men five times at the great guns.

The wind at length came fair and the fleet stood down the Baltic to the westward and in the morning of July 6 the enemy's fleet were seen to leeward formed in a good line of battle.

I find many notes of the events of this day, but so short as merely to serve as hints to assist the memory of the writer to draw up a detail on a future occasion. I shall insert the only journal of this day which I can find, and then reduce any other materials into as good a narrative as I can.

'*July 6th*] At ½ past 12 (noon) discovered the Swedish fleet, 33 large sail or thereabouts. Ours 17 sail of the line. Know not yet how many of theirs.

1 p.m. Bearing down upon their line in tolerable order.

3 p.m. Within an hour of engaging. My people keep a tolerable countenance, but want exercise. If anything happen to me, Adieu my mother, relatives and friends. JAMES TREVENEN.'

The Swedish fleet, commanded by the Duke of Sudermania (brother to the King of Sweden) consisted of sixteen sail of the line and ten stout frigates, which latter were all placed in the intervals of the line to leeward and by this means enabled to annoy the Russians with their fire.[1]

Admiral Greig approached his foe with all the dispatch the manoeuvres of the latter admitted of, but the Russian line was never regular.

The Swedes permitted their enemy to approach their line within a quarter of a mile, when their van opened a heavy fire, which soon spread to their centre and rear and was kept up with great spirit for some time.

As this was beginning to fire too soon, I understand it has been a disputed point which fleet began the engagement. About 5 p.m. Admiral Greig made the signal to Rear Admiral Kozlyaninov[2] to bear down and engage the enemy, which signal the Rear Admiral repeated with a gun *shotted*, but not with the intention of engaging till closer. The Swedes, however, immediately opened their fire and the van and centre of the Russians immediately returned it. Admiral Greig had at this time only made the signal to the fleet to near the enemy and engage, but not to engage till nearer. This rapid return of the enemy's fire argues great want of coolness and discipline on the part of the Russians.

The first fire of the Swedes was so brisk and effectual that the poor Boors of Siberia, who now for the first time heard the whistling of a shot and saw their comrades fall dead by their side, were quite confounded, but being 'encouraged to do their duty for the glory of Russia and the love of the Virgin Mary, they fell to with a continued spirit and alacrity worthy of British veterans. Nothing could be better, their want of knowledge excepted, and even in that respect the most poor, stupid, miserable creatures among them became for the time intelligent, strong and healthy men'. In consequence of this energy it appears that the Russian fire gradually improved, while that of the Swedes as gradually slackened.

It is a fashion among the Russian officers, when going into battle, to take leave of each other. Trevenen had on board his ship as a volunteer a young Prince Dolgoruki, whom he describes as an amiable young man and who had been appointed to command the soldiers on the quarter deck. In compliance with custom he had just embraced his commander, when one

[1] The Swedish line consisted of fifteen battleships and five heavy frigates; there were five other frigates present.

[2] MS. Koslynoff here and elsewhere. He was in command of the Rear squadron, but the Russian fleet was now in reversed order and he was actually leading the line.

of the first shot from the Swedes struck him into his arms and broke Trevenen's sword and the spying glass in his hands. The wounds were evidently mortal, but this being no time for pity or condolence, he could only order his afrighted soldiers to carry the dying youth below and attend himself to the properly placing his ship in the line.

During the battle, which raged nearly six hours, the crew of the *Rodislav* made frequent enquiries after the safety of their commander and if they did not see him for some time would run to the quarter deck to ask if he were well; and finding it was so, 'then all is well', they would cry, 'fight away'. An apology is made for such a circumstance being mentioned, which rebounds so much to the honour of the narrator; but he assigns as a reason for their personal attachment, that the Russian Captains, who are also *Pursers*, make money by distressing and cheating their men, but as his honour and liberality of course prevented his participating in this crime, his crew idolized him for his justice and generosity.

The action having lasted, as above mentioned, near six hours, at half past ten the Admiral made the signal to cease firing, the Swedes having borne away and left the Russians masters of the field of battle and in possession of their Vice Admiral, Count Wachtmeister, a fine fellow, who had served some years in the French navy. His ship had been engaged for a long time by Capt. Elphinston, whose ship being quite disabled and the Swede indeed rendered incapable of running away with his companions, Admiral Greig came up and obliged him to strike after another combat of 3/4 of an hour. This gentleman seems to have made a most vigorous defence and had 132 men *killed* before he struck his colours.[1]

The rear of the Russian fleet had engaged at an awful distance and several ships did not do their duty, for which their captains were superseded. The weight of the action appears to have fallen on about seven ships, of which the *Rodislav* was one. Considering the state of the contending powers in a maritime point of view it is surprising to find the Russians victors in this battle, yet it is not difficult to discover the cause of this victory, so unexpected, and most particularly so to the Swedes, who had laid their account in the capture of the Russian fleet. There can indeed be no doubt, but that the British Admiral and Captains in the fleet gained the victory for the Russians, which, had five or six individuals only out of the many thousands in the fleet been changed, would have declared for the Swedes or the battle never have been fought. There seem some proofs somewhat beyond conjecture on this point. For, when a show of pursuit was made after the Swedes, who retired in good order, only four Russian ships kept

[1] Wachtmeister's ship, the *Prins Gustaf*, actually had thirty-three killed and 115 wounded.

their heads towards the enemy, three of which had British commanders, viz. Admiral Greig, Captains Dennison and Trevenen. The fourth was captain Mulovskii (who had been intended for the expedition round the world). Captain Elphinston had been disabled in his gallant contest with the Swedish Vice Admiral. And afterwards, when honours were distributed to the officers, out of seven orders of Knighthood the British received four.

Admiral Greig received the order of St. Andrew, the most honourable in Russia. Rear Admiral Kozlyaninov, who commanded the van, had the 3rd order of St. George, or of Merit, and his captain Makarov, Mulovskii, Dennison, Trevenen and Elphinston the 4th order of the same. The insignia of this Order of Merit is a black[1] and orange striped ribband with a white enamelled cross pendant to it, worn between the second and third button-hole on the left side. St. George killing the Dragon is exhibited on one side and the other bears his cypher. Some priviledges are annexed to this order, one of which places the holder of it more immediately under the protection of the Empress as head of the Order and prevents him from being tried by a Court Martial without her permission or till she has taken away the cross. A pension is occasionally annexed to the honour, but a very small one, being not more than £15 per annum. The Elders of this class have always this pension.

I now return to relate some further particulars of the battle of the 6th.

On board the *Rodislav* 24 men were killed and 27 badly wounded. Seven of the former fell on the first broadside.

The loss of the Swedes in killed was allowed to be 700 and that of the Russians from four to five hundred[2]; a most remarkable slaughter considering the number of ships engaged, but the smooth water of the Baltic must always make a sea-fight there a scene of great carnage. The loss of ships was equal on both sides, as the rear ship of the Centre dropped into the Swedish fleet in a way not very easy to be accounted for and was captured.

The desperate resolution of one of the soldiers of the *Rodislav* in the action merits insertion. He was mortally wounded and knew it. To quit his pain and sorrow quickly he begged an officer to dispatch him outright; but being of course refused, he drew his own sword and put a final issue to his bodily sufferings.

The Russian fleet continued on the scene of action for some days, and then returned nearer to Kronstadt in order to meet a reinforcement of ships

[1] MS. has 'dark'.

[2] The Swedes actually had 127 killed and 290 badly wounded among their naval personnel, while fifty-nine soldiers were either killed or mortally wounded. The Russian loss was 326 killed and 742 wounded. These figures do not include casualties in the ships captured.

in lieu of those that had been disabled and had returned into port. The fleet anchored off Seskär in the Gulf of Finland, but did not return into port.

Rear Admiral Fondezin[1] was disgusted at not receiving any honorary reward for his services and three captains were superseded for not doing their duty. The famous Admiral Spiridov even seems to have been a long time before he got into his station, and indeed very little resolution or enterprise seems to have been evinced by any Russian except Mulovskii.

In the action that has now been detailed it does not appear that Capt. Trevenen had any opportunity of signalizing himself particularly any farther than in being one of the very few who received marks of the Empress's favour. He regrets this want of opportunity in his journal, but adds: 'Upon recollection of this whole affair I have nothing to reproach myself with, no false step, no omission. I know myself better than I did and am more satisfied. I do not at all know that I could have done better than I have done.'

This is a most satisfactory piece of self examination and I doubt not but that he had honestly probed all the depths of his conduct.

In a letter to John King I find mention that he received a slight wound in the hand at the time his sword and glass were broken.

The fleet remained at anchor till July 18 and returning to their former station found four Swedish ships of the line and two frigates at anchor on the scene of the late action. It was at dawn of day they were discerned at some distance, and had it not been for an unfortunate delay by one of the Russian ships getting aground, they would at that time have been close to them and the Swedes would have paid dear for their vaunt of taking possession of the field of battle. The Swedes immediately cut their cables and made sail for a port about 4 leagues distant, where the remainder of their fleet lay at anchor. Near the entrance of the port one of the Swedish squadron, a fine new ship of 64 guns,[2] ran ashore and struck her colours to the Russians, who took her crew prisoners and at their leisure set her on fire and she blew up. The Swedes, though just within the port[3] and able to have come out, chose to put up with this insult and every other their enemy could devize, some of which they must have felt, as their provision-ships were taken by the Russian cruisers almost within gun-shot.

Having cruised here for some time want of water obliged Admiral Greig to repair with his fleet to Revel and it was whilst lying in this port that the orders of merit, which I somewhat prematurely mentioned before, were conferred on the officers supposed to merit them. But this affair had not proceeded very amicably. In the first letter from the Empress only Admiral

[1] MS. Vondysen. The name was originally Von Dessen, but was always written Fondezin in Russian.

[2] The *Prins Gustaf Adolf* 62, built in 1782. She was taken on July 26.

[3] *Author's note:* Helsingfors.

Greig, Rear Admiral Kozlyaninov, Captains Makarov and Elphinston had their respective orders sent them, with the Empress's thanks to all the others except those who were disgraced. Trevenen and Dennison, who were conscious of having done much more in the action than only to deserve thanks in common with the herd who had not been disgraced, fired at this treatment and Trevenen in a very spirited letter to Mulovskii (who was a natural son to Count Tchernyshev) caused his ire also, and the trio waited on Admiral Greig, to whom they complained in no very moderate terms. The Admiral assured them that he had mentioned their names in the highest degree of approbation[1] and made some excuses for the Court as being afraid to do too much and in consequence having done too little. Mulovskii sent Trevenen's letter and another from Dennison to the Count, his father, but I cannot exactly determine whether these gentlemen got their well-merited honours in consequence of their representations or by the Empress having discovered her error. I hope the latter.

About this time I find a character of Admiral Greig, which, being written in the plenitude of this gentleman's power, I think well worth inserting.

'My favour with Admiral Greig is by no means great, nor have I ever since entering into the service received the least marks of it. Yet I am much deceived if it might not be gained, but that must be by stooping much lower than I can submit to. He is of a character to suppose, and he has lived long enough to confirm it, that every man about him is selfish and interested. If admitted to confidence most people might acquire an ascendancy over him and possibly abuse it. Conscious of this and devoid of penetration he has chosen to wrap himself up in a political honesty and, doing his best and firmly supported by the Empress, to depend on his own efforts. In plain matters of fact common sense will carry people through, if not in the best, at least in the usual way.' I think this an admirable character of him.

The fleet did not remain long at Revel, but returned, August 13, to cruise off the Swedish ports.

Upon August 13 Captain Trevenen received orders to proceed to Hangö-udd, a port in Swedish Finland, having under his command three sail of the line and several smaller vessels, to take possession of it and to maintain it as a post.[2]

The above mentioned force I take from a letter which announces this honourable command, but it appears that, when he left Admiral Greig, he had only two frigates besides his own ship and the intention at first was probably only to intercept a flotilla of small vessels navigating among the rocks along shore. I extract the following account of the general nature of

[1] Greig's despatch of July 11 actually mentioned both Rear Admirals and all save one of the Captains of the Van and Centre in identical terms.

[2] *Author's note:* His force varied occasionally during his stay at Hangö-udd.

the command from a letter to his mother, dated Hangö-udd, August 26, O.S., 1788.

'I have been here these ten days, the commander of a squadron of 3 sail of line-of-battle ships and 4 frigates blocking up a fleet of Swedish galleys and frigates not far off. The mark of Admiral Greig's confidence I am most anxious to merit and am only sorry that my situation will not suffer me to act offensively except as to blocking up the fleet. I hoist a broad pendant and have a right to call myself Commodore, but that does not lie so near my heart as the wish to do something.'

The selection of Captain Trevenen out of the long list of commanders under Admiral Greig's orders does equal credit to the discrimination of the one and the abilities of the other, which had now begun to be acknowledged. The honour of the trust will be seen by the importance of the post, which I shall endeavour to describe, and the wisdom of the choice will appear by the steady resolution with which the station was preserved.

I select the following account of the situation and importance of Hangö-udd from various papers, chiefly in French, and which appear to be rough copies or rather notes of the information sent by him to the Admiral and some of the members of the Government.

Hangö-udd is a town and port in Swedish Finland situated in that part of it where the land trends away to the northward and forms the east shore of the Gulf of Bothnia and also to the eastward forming the north shore of the Gulf of Finland. By this situation it is of great importance to either the Swedes or Russians, when they are at war; particularly as the islands and rocks, which shelter the port to the south and west, leave a passage within them deep enough for the largest vessels and thus affords[1] a free communication along the coast of Finland without danger of interruption from the enemy. A narrow neck of land runs out to the S.W. and protects the port from the North and West winds and its only exposure is towards the S.E., but these winds are seldom violent in the Baltic.

But the great importance of the place was its affording an easy passage for the Swedes to convoy provisions from Stockholm and the country round the Gulf of Bothnia, particularly Åbo, to the ports in Finland where the fleets and armies were collected and the seat of war lay. Although this advantage appears to be sufficiently evident to have attracted the attention of any commander, yet it seems to have been entirely overlooked by the King of Sweden and his brother. Admiral Greig taking advantage of this neglect, appointed Commodore Trevenen to seize this valuable post and maintain it as long as the season permitted.

Near Hangö-udd is another port named Tverminne,[2] where at this time

[1] *Sic* in MS. [2] MS. Zweermunde.

lay a great number of Swedish frigates, sloops of war, gunboats and galleys, intended no doubt to protect the victuallers from the Russian cruisers and convoy them to Helsingfors, a principal port of Finland situated farther to the eastward. Their number of guns and men greatly exceeded the force under the Commodore, but his ships were of a larger size. By this judicious position of the Russian ships, however, the Swedish squadron remained blocked up and useless during the remainder of the season.

On his first arrival on his station he found the peasants and fishermen well disposed towards the Russians, and the magistrates for forty versts round sent to claim his protection. Even some of the Swedish noblesse sent their peasants with provisions and refreshments for sale, and their situation, except to him who had the cares of command, appeared almost as tranquil as if they had been in a friendly port. But the arrival of some military, at first about 100 dragoons and afterwards some infantry and additional cavalry, put an end to this friendly intercourse and in some degree changed the scene. For although the force collected could not do much in acts of violence, they easily prevented the former acts of courtesy and rendered strict guard and precaution necessary.

But, when I speak of the establishment of a friendly intercourse, it was only between the Commodore himself and the inhabitants of the shore. The conduct of the Russians, Captains, officers and men, was for some time shameful in the extreme and no hordes of savages from the forests of America could have shown fewer marks of civilization than did these savages of the North, and the Commodore was obliged to recur to the full power of his station to repress their enormities, although backed by manifestoes from the Empress herself and the positive commands of Admiral Greig. I will extract an instance or two from the rough journal, by which my readers will judge how much his cares of command must have been increased by such conduct in the officers and crews.

In a letter to Admiral Greig dated August 25 he says: 'I had all the good intentions in the world to comply with your Excellency's orders relative to the treatment of the peasants, etc., and immediately on my arrival here I gave out orders to that purpose. But not a peasant was to be seen and all the villages around us were abandoned.[1]

'It was still in our power, however, not to do any mischief, but I am sorry to say it was not in the inclination of some amongst us and that a day or two after my arrival I was surprised to see two villages near us on fire. I endeavoured in vain to find out who had been concerned in it and gave

[1] *Author's note:* These abandoned villages were immediately contiguous to the shore. There was frequent intercourse with villages at a little distance with flags of truce, etc.—particularly one where the Swedish troops were stationed.

written orders to the captains of the squadron to find out the offenders, that they might be severely punished. I can answer for my own ship having had no hand in this affair.'

The fact is that the captains themselves were concerned, for in a journal of this time I find the following. 'In the evening I was astonished to perceive by the smokes rising around us that the two villages were burning, one on the island near the passage and to the westward, the other farther up the country. Seeing two boats come off from the former I sent to learn what officers were in them. I cannot say I was astonished to find all my captains there, although I had not expected they would have gone such lengths.' The Commodore did not fail to issue proper orders respecting such conduct in future and to reprimand for the present; but at the rather humble request of the captains he did not immediately complain of them to the Admiral, but stated the facts in general terms. Again the journal states:

'I gave out Admiral Greig's order against plundering the peasants, but there were no longer any to plunder; therefore I permitted our people to take off some small kegs of salt fish, etc. and what live stock they could find. I would infinitely have preferred to have lived in peace and amity with the peasants, who would doubtless have better supplied our wants at a moderate price, but the savageness of the Russian officers and men had delighted in doing all the mischief possible, never reflecting for a moment that they could be acting against their own interests. Wherever there is anything to be got they are capital, plundering affording them great delight. They are a sort of grown children, as indeed are most savages, for this cause that reason has been very little cultivated amongst them. This was evident in the conduct of a party I sent to a larger village about 3 miles off, where were some tolerable houses; the breaking the windows of which and destroying the furniture afforded great delight, not only to the miserable men, but also to the officers. These were not amongst those who had behaved best in our action. And so it almost always happens. The brave man is compassionate and exerts not his courage upon objects unworthy of him. The miserable wretch, who trembles in the day of action, struts the hero, when there is a decided superiority, and thinks he shows his bravery by his cruelty.'

These extracts I thought necessary to show the kind of men with whom Trevenen had to deal. He had, however, under his command several foreign officers and volunteers, German, English and Dutch, most of whom accorded more with him in sentiment than the natives of Russia.

It will easily be imagined that this command, however honourable, must have been anxious and irksome in the extreme. The enemy near at hand without a possibility to attack them and the blockading force liable to an attack from the Swedish fleet from without. This to an ardent mind is the most wearying life possible. The longing to attack the enemy constantly baulked and the mind constantly engaged in keeping up the defensive system. For this purpose a boom was placed across the principal channel of entrance and the frigates lay without, to give an early alarm. Beyond this a few foraging parties and flags of truce about prisoners and other trifling occurrences was all that happened to mark one day from another. For, although this place was of much consequence, yet it afforded but small scope for the active mind of the Commodore, always longing to act on the offensive and ill brooking its confinement to the tedious delays of a blockade. Many plans did he form to draw the enemy to action or to find a possible means of attacking them in their port; but the former object of course depended on the enemy themselves and the latter was impracticable from the strength of their position. He frequently in his boat, went close to them in the night and in the morning was obliged to fly from their boats pursuing them.[1] But these attempts were by no means useless bravadoes, for by their means he contrived to form a chart of the coast, which, although in sight of all the trade to and from Petersburg, was still utterly unknown. In all his labours of this kind he appears to have been assiduously and ably assisted by Mr. Opperman of the Engineers and he also speaks very favourably of a Mr. Casal of the Artillery.

I shall fill up this barren void of the blockade with some extracts from letters from Admiral Greig, both as being interesting from the high name that gentleman has gained in the north of Europe and from the evidence they afford of the confidence he reposed in his correspondent.

Extract of a letter from Admiral Greig, dated Revel, August 21, 1788

'I beg you will inform me of what has passed with you since I left you and what movements you have observed amongst the enemy's flotilla, or if you have been able to pick up any news amongst the inhabitants. I have only to recommend you to behave with civility to the innocent inhabitants who are not in arms, and, if you can procure any fresh provisions or vegetables, to pay ready money and a reasonable price for it. Tomorrow I shall send Capt. Pellisier with such a vessel as the *Sv. Mark* to join you.[2] He will have on board 80 land-soldiers which you may send on board the *Pamyat Evstafia* to strengthen her crew, which is very weakly. If you think you will have occasion for any further reinforcements to maintain your post, be so good as to let me know. Here enclosed is a present from Countess Tcherny-

[1] *Sic* in MS.

[2] Pellisier's ship *Provornyi* and the *Sv. Mark* of Trevenen's original force were both 'rowing frigates'.

shev for you. Believe me ever, Dear Sir, Your most obedient servant, SAML GREIG.

P.S. I have sent you Capt. Lieut. Korobka for your own ship and make no doubt but you will be pleased with him.'

This letter impresses the reader with very favourable sentiments of the writer. It will be proper now to attend to the answer to it, a rough copy of which I fortunately possess. I have already given an extract in page [138] and proceed to insert nearly the whole of the remainder. We have already seen ample specimens of the Commodore's abilities in domestic and friendly correspondence and we shall now see his talent exercised in military detail.[1]

Letter to Admiral Greig, dated Hangö-udd in Finland, August 25, 1788.

'SIR,—I am this day honoured with your Excellency's letter of the 21st instant and in obedience to your order shall tomorrow send Capt. Bodisko in the *Nadezhda Blagopolutchia* to join your Excellency at Revel. I proceed to relate what has happened during our stay here.

Just before our arrival I perceived to the eastward among the rocks a part of the enemy's flotilla bearing down before the wind and we made ready to receive them, if they should attempt to pass during the night. But we saw nothing of them till next day, when we perceived over the land to the eastward the masts of a frigate lying at anchor and at some distance within her, I suppose about half a verst,[2] the flotilla of galleys, row-boats, etc. They lay all together, so that we could not number them, and we could not see their hulls.

Your Excellency knows that the *Slava* frigate had been here before and had made prisoners some of the inhabitants, who had come aboard supposing her to be a Swedish frigate.[3]

Soon after my arrival a letter was brought me from a Mr. Kisinger styling himself *Conseiller des Mines* and *Chevalier de l'Ordre de Vasa* begging the restitution of 3 men of his, who going aboard the *Slava* frigate while under Swedish colours had been made prisoners. His demand was founded on the Empress's declaration, published on the frontiers, *that she had no reason to be dissatisfied with the Swedish nation and had given orders to all her subjects not to molest such as did not bear arms.*

I returned for answer, that it was very true that her Imperial Majesty had given such orders, and therefore I imagined that, when his three men

[1] *Author's note:* When I made the extract just mentioned, I had not intended to insert the whole of this letter, but on a reperusal I thought it would afford the reader a very good account of the situation of affairs at the beginning of this command.
[2] *Author's note:* A verst is 3,500 feet English measure.
[3] *Author's note:* Here follows the extract given in page [138].

should be returned to him, they would not complain of their treatment during the time of their imprisonment. I assured him that they should be set at liberty before I left this port, but that at present I had reasons for detaining them, which your Excellency will presently see.[1]

I took this opportunity of telling him, that if the peasants had remained quietly in their houses, they would not have been molested, and that, if they would now return and supply us with what we might want, they should be justly paid; and added that, if they refused to let us have what we wanted for our money, they could not take it ill if we endeavoured to supply ourselves with so essential and indispensable an article as fresh provisions. At the same time I disavowed the few excesses that had been committed by our people as being entirely contrary to my own inclinations and to the orders I had received from your Excellency.

I have as yet heard no more of him, but soon afterwards I received two different petitions, apparently from the Magistrature of the country round, expressing their peaceable disposition and claiming protection. I returned for answer a sort of manifest to the same purpose as my answer to Mr. Kisinger and I have since heard by private intelligence that the magistrates wished to have this read in all their churches, but were prevented by the interference of the military, and it is now under penalty of death that the peasants are forbidden to supply us with the least thing.

This interference of the military, it may be reasonably supposed, is the reason why we have lately seen no person except one man, who comes about twice a week at night and brings with him about enough vegetables to supply one ship with that refreshment. As he runs the risk of his head, he expects to be well paid, and as he gives us intelligence, I do not like to discourage him. I suspect him to be the gardener of the Baroness Taube, a lady who lives not far off and is the wife of a Major in the Army. He comes as from himself, but with notes and presents from her, which must also be well paid for.

We meet with berries on the numerous islands, though in no very great abundance, and sometimes pick up a few abandoned sheep, with which we have the opportunity now and then of giving a fresh meal to the people. I imagine your Excellency cannot disapprove of this, as it is of absolute necessity to keep the scurvy from appearing.

Early after coming into this port I drew a couple of hawsers across the

[1] *Author's note:* Both the request of Mr. Kisinger and the Commodore's reply appear to have been marked with great courtesy. The prisoners were detained at present merely to have an excuse at some proper time to send them to the village where the Swedish troops were stationed with a flag of truce, in order that the escort might make as many useful observations as possible. Mr. K's letter was attended by a present of melons, apples, etc.

fairway to the eastward and made these a sort of slight boom, because, lying in sight of an enemy on his own coast, I thought it possible that, if he were enterprising, he might with his galleys and row-boats attempt to burn us during the night by surprise. As, however, he attempted no such thing, I began to reflect whether we might not possibly attack him in our boats. But the distance of 3 German miles[1] is so great, the want of pilots and our ignorance of his situation and force rendered such a step unadvisable. It was, however, in prosecution of the same design that I engaged one of the Swedish prisoners to go as a spy to the eastward and endeavour to gain the intelligence we wanted. The man was knowing enough for the purpose and to all appearance entered heartily into the scheme and left his wife and baggage as a pledge of his return. However, he did not return and we have since heard that he was seized on and imprisoned on suspicion.[2] After this the scheme of attacking them with the few boats we had was not to be thought of and within this day or two another frigate has joined the former off Tverminne. But being ourselves joined by a greater force I mean to reconnoitre them by our boats in the night.

From the man who brings us the vegetables we learnt that in two villages about 15 versts from here are quartered 100 Dragoons commanded by a Capt. Lomberg, who are daily expecting to be relieved by 300 foot-soldiers, and these keep the country from supplying us. Some few patrols have once been seen by some of our officers. I was much pressed by Mr. Casal and Opperman to suffer them to take 100 soldiers and surprise these dragoons, but the weakness of our ships, which would have been thus deprived of their best defence against a night attack, and the unimportance of the object have hitherto prevented me from listening to this proposal, although I have wished most heartily to do something with that part of your Excellency's fleet which you have done me the honour to entrust to me. I am very sorry to have only to inform your Excellency of what we have not done, but at the same time I imagine that even in our inaction here we render a service not unimportant to Russia in distressing greatly the enemy by entirely putting an end to all their coasting trade and by the very object for which your Excellency sent me here. I mean that of stopping the flotilla to the eastward.

Through the same channel I also learn that 3000 men have been ordered from Helsingfors to Stockholm and that one detachment has already passed through the country in their way to Åbo, a city which your Excellency will

[1] *Author's note:* A German mile is nearly 3 English miles.

[2] *Author's note:* All wars furnish a large supply of examples to justify this measure as far as general practice goes. But, as a military man, I cannot pass this fact without stating it as my opinion that no situation, no number of examples however great or from whatever source derived, can justify the attempt to make a man a traitor.

easily discover in the chart. They are there to take shipping across the Gulf of Bothnia. Perhaps it will appear to your Excellency most probable that these 3000 men were embarked on board the very fleet which we now stop and that it is only from the impossibility of going by sea that they are driven to the necessity of passing by land to Åbo. At the same time your Excellency will pardon the liberty I take in remarking that the [———][1] appears to be always good and clear, though sometimes narrow, and that, if we had a small fleet of galleys or row-boats to employ now in these coasts if Fonland, we might still more effectually stop the enemy's operations to the westward, whilst his fleets are blockaded to the east.

Only two or three small vessels have appeared to the westward, all of which the *Sv. Mark* frigate chased, and the *Panteleimon* took one in coming in this afternoon, which I now send to your Excellency.

Most probably Capt. Perskii[2] of the *Sv. Mark* will have informed your Excellency that in consequence of having observed great quantities of wood both for firing and construction lying on different parts of the coast and supposing these magazines to be intended for the supply of Helsingfors, I thought it my duty to destroy them and accordingly sent him with the boats of the squadron for that purpose, a piece of service which he executed very effectually.

Since we have been in this harbour Mr. Opperman of the Engineers has been most indefatigably employed in making a plan of it and the numerous islands in the environs.

I enclose to your Excellency the progress he has already made and shall only add that it is laid down scientifically by angles taken from measured bases. The possible utility and future importance of this port have been the spurs to animate his endeavours and he still unremittingly pursues his object. It is to be regretted that good water is not in plenty here. The inhabitants of the village in the bay evidently make use of rain water. There is a small but insignificant spring in the bay: However, on the island where stands the land-mark[3] is a large natural cistern of water collected in the rocky hollows, from whence we get enough to supply our present needs and in case of necessity to lay in a quantity of it.

Wood is in great plenty all round the bay: Indeed we find it ready cut to our hands. Your Excellency will perceive by the plan of the bay that behind the spit of mainland there is no water for shipping, but also that the rocks

[1] *Author's note:* A word occurs here which I can by no means make out. From the context I conclude it to mean the passage between the small islands and rocks, which are everywhere scattered on this coast, and the mainland. By these passages the coasting trade is carried on. N.B.—From a word that occurs afterwards I believe the hiatus may be filled up with *Fair-water*, for which the above description answers.

[2] MS. Purko.

[3] Presumably Rusarö, 2½ miles S. of the present town of Hangö.

form a small harbour to the westward through the passage, where a ship might bring up in case of riding heavy in a S.E. gale in the bay.

The rock marked with 7 fathom on it contributes to spoil the inner port. We brought up there at first in 19 fathom and having veered 40 fathom of cable found only seven.

The disposition of our ships in an angle opposite the east fairwater was intended to cover both that passage and the entrance from the sea.

The country is so very rocky that it would be very difficult to raise batteries against us.

As to the disposition of my force: When the two small frigates arrive, I mean to keep two frigates constantly cruising, as the vessels bound for Helsingfors generally make the land here. As yet we have seen but three, which the *Sv. Mark* chased, and though frightened from her prey by our other frigates appearing, yet she drove them into their hands. The *Panteleimon* took the one yesterday which I sent to your Excellency. Captain Lotyrev let slip another bound to Helsingfors with wine and apples, which I would not have done in his place. He said something from your Excellency about keeping one ship cruising, which does not agree with what your Excellency has written to me. If we are to stop the Swedish ships from proceeding to the westward, it will be necessary to keep more than one ship cruising. I beg your Excellency's orders relative to that business.

A few days ago we perceived three pretty large vessels to the N.W. among the islands at a great distance, perhaps employed in transporting the detachment of which I have spoken to your Excellency.

If the two small frigates could get that way, we might do something. Indeed it is never enough to be regretted that we have not perfect charts of the place, but as it is, we are in perfect darkness as to all about us.

I beg your Excellency to believe that I am fully sensible of the honour done me in entrusting so considerable a force to me, and that I wish for nothing so much as to prove myself worthy of it.[1] This mark of your Excellency's confidence will always remain engraven on my mind as long as I shall possess the power of acknowledging myself Your Excellency's obliged and obedient humble servant, J. TREVENEN.

P.S. As the greens we are able to procure are not more than sufficient for one ship, and as our means of procuring fresh provisions seems to be nearly exhausted, perhaps your Excellency will think it proper to send us some from Revel.'

[1] *Author's note:* I have constantly regretted that I cannot find any list of this force or of the officers employed under Commodore Trevenen in this service.

[Trevenen's original force consisted of the *Rodislav* 66, *Premislav* 36, *Slava* 32 and *Sv. Mark* 20. He was joined at various times by the *Pamyat Evstafia* 66, *Panteleimon* 66, *Podrazhislav* 32, *Nadezha Blagopolutchia* 32 and *Provornyi* 20, but had usually only six or seven ships on the spot.]

Some parts of the preceding letter not being intelligible without the plan of the port and neighbourhood might perhaps have been omitted, but I have been induced to insert the whole that my readers may see how comprehensive the views of the Commodore were, who, although new to a command of this nature, seems at once to have embraced all the great political consequences of his station without forgetting the smallest items of the detail.

In all his letters about this time he complains much of the officers employed under him, of their ignorance, indolence and inattention to orders. The former might naturally arise from want of experience; the second there is no excuse for; and the last seems in many instances to be ventured upon from the idea that a foreigner either would not choose to enforce his authority with exactitude, or that they could form some excuse on the score of difference of language.

I find a note on one occasion, after Lieut. Perskii of the *Sv. Mark* had been sent to burn the wood mentioned in the foregoing letter: 'I learnt some time afterwards that this officer had not confined himself to burning the wood, but had also set fire to a village of the peasants.'

I must also insert a remark of the Commodore on this occasion, before he heard of the Excesses committed by his officer. 'At the same time I could not help fearing that this wood might be the property of some country gentleman or farmer. These things cannot be helped, and as I would wish to avoid needless mischief, so I must be careful to destroy everything that appears to be the property of the public'.

The *Nadezhda Blagopolutchia*, Captain Bodisko, received his orders to sail on the 26th,[1] but by the copy of a letter dated the 28th I find he has still delayed executing his orders. I translate parts of the letter.

'SIR,—Why will you oblige me to say harsh things to you? How far do you think my complaisance will carry me? Certainly not to the neglect of my duty; and my duty presses me to send you as quick as possible to Revel, to give Admiral Greig the information he has demanded of me and which it is important he should know. You should have been there before the accident which happened to your ship yesterday, and that accident even would not have happened, had you been on the spot.'

The Commodore proceeds to give this negligent officer some directions how to put to sea and ends thus:

'Part quickly, that Admiral Greig may not surprise us and demand the reason why his orders have not been complied with. The reasons I shall be forced to give him exactly as they are—etc., etc.'

For the whole of the month of September I cannot find that anything

[1] Presumably to take the letter given above.

material occurred. The letter of Admiral Greig in answer to those of the Commodore give the most clear insight into the transactions and I insert them pretty nearly entire, both on that account and also for their intrinsic interest on the score of the writer and his high situation. Indeed they include many circumstances of which I cannot elsewhere find the least notice.

'Revel, September 3, 1788

DEAR SIR,—I have received your reports of the 25th, 26th and 27th of August and I am perfectly satisfied with all you have done since your taking possession of the port of Hangö-udd.[1] It is certainly a post of great consequence, since it entirely cuts off the communication between Stockholm and the Swedish fleet and armies in Finland, at least for their small craft and victuallers, and if I could spare you a more considerable No. of frigates to cruise between your post and Stockholm, every one of their victuallers might be stopped.

The two Swedish men of war and one frigate which have taken post behind the *skärs* off Porkala,[2] might have been intended to attack your post, but I am rather inclined to think that they have taken post there to observe the motions of our fleet and for that purpose have established signals the whole way from thence to Sveaborg. They might also have in view the cutting off of our cruisers, which cruise off Sveaborg to observe the motions of their fleet—etc., etc. Your post, however, is of such importance to them that I make no doubt but that they will risk a good deal to drive you from it. I had even some hopes that it might lead to a general action ....

On Thursday, 17th inst., the King of Sweden left Helsingfors and set out for Åbo on his return to Stockholm, where the defection that began amongst the Finland regiments has already spread and by all accounts become very serious. As the King's presence alone in Stockholm without the support of the military and the principal officers attached to his person, I am apt to think, will rather irritate than appease the tumults of the people, dissatisfied with a war begun by the King's caprice and prosecuted without the success he had made them expect, and which in probability may end in limiting his power to the old Constitution. It is therefore of the utmost importance to prevent as much as possible the return of the troops to Stockholm....

I shall be glad that you can cultivate a good understanding with the natives in your neighbourhood, as it is quite agreeable to our present plan to make them dissatisfied with the conduct and person of their King and

[1] *Author's note:* This port is spelt in at least twenty different ways in the different documents before me. [Here it is 'Ganghoud'.]

[2] MS. Skairs off Porkeland. *Skär* in Swedish means a rock or small island, usually close to the mainland. Porkala is another promontory between Hangö and Helsingfors.

L

give them all possible encouragement to restore their ancient limited form of government.[1]

The Duke of Sudermanland left Helsingfors the day after the King and he set out to take command of the army on our positions at Hogfors, which the King had been obliged to leave. All the officers of the fleet assembled and dragged his coach through the streets of Helsingfors. This mock pageantry I take to be the last effort of his party to support his credit. Had he been popular, the tars would never have given up that honour to their officers.

I superseded Perskii, who abandoned you,[2] and have given the command of the *Sv. Mark* to Lvov,[3] who is now recovered and has eight live bullocks for your squadron. I have only to counsel you to be upon your guard against any surprise from the eastward, and you may be assured that I shall take all possible care that you shall not be overpowered by a superior force from the south entry. However, you'll take the necessary precautions in case of an attack from that quarter, as you know there is a possibility of their escaping our vigilance from the uncertainty of wind and weather. If the enemy should afford you an opportunity, I'm persuaded you will both do honour to yourself and to me in the choice of a person proper to maintain that important post.

There is no cessation of arms, but only with the Finland regiments, who have absolutely refused the King to serve against Russia and demanded the King to assemble a Diet of the States, which he absolutely refused before he went away. They then sent a deputation to the Swedish army at Hogfors inviting them to accede to the confederacy and oblige the King to assemble the States. But I have not yet heard if they have agreed to it, but at any rate they seem not willing to fight and I imagine the general infection has reached the fleet also. . . .

If Casal's project had taken place[4] and the King had fallen into his hands, it would have been a glorious prize. . . .

I have the utmost confidence in your unremitting diligence and attention to every object that regards your post—and am ever, Dear Sir, Your most obedient servant, SAML GREIG.'

Nothing can evince higher confidence than is expressed in this letter. Bad weather, however, prevented its being dispatched and it was

[1] *Author's note:* This is singular language from a subject of Russia and we can guess how pure the motives which led to this benevolent wish for the Swedes.

[2] *Author's note:* I find no mention of this circumstance elsewhere and from the employment the *Sv. Mark* has had I cannot guess when this defection can have taken place.

[3] This gentleman's name generally appears spelt Swoff or Lwoff and I think was Capt. Lieu. of the *Rodislav* in the late action with the Swedes.

[4] *Author's note:* This is all I can find of Mr. Casal's project.

accompanied by another of September 20 of which the following are extracts.

'DEAR SIR,— . . . I now herewith send you the frigate *Nadezhda Blagopolutchia*, the *Sv. Mark* and an English transport with provisions for the squadron under your command. . . .

I received your dispatches[1] by the *Slava* and am glad to find that all is well with you and that you maintain your post properly. I yesterday received dispatches from her Imperial Majesty, where amongst other things she strongly recommends the maintaining of the post of Hangö-udd to my particular attention, and nothing can be a stronger demonstration of its importance to the enemy than the proposition made by the Duke of Sudermania to Count Musin-Pushkin for our leaving it, of which I here enclose you a copy, as also extracts from her Majesty's dispatches as far as regards your station, from which you will observe the falsity of what your corresponder[2] Cuzinger wrote you relative to the Empress's having given orders not to act against the Swedes in Finland.'

The remainder of the letter is an uninteresting detail of service. It concludes:

'I need say nothing to excite your vigilance and attention after what you see in the extracts of her Majesty's dispatches. Believe me ever sincerely, Dear Sir, Your obedient servant, S. GREIG.

P.S. You'll observe that the post at Hangö must be maintained as late as possible in the season by the Empress's commands. So you'll arrange yourself accordingly.

You'll herewith receive a chart of the Gulf of Finland sent you in a present by Count Vorontsov from London being lately published there. The Count sends you many kind compliments. All our English friends at Petersburg are much pleased to hear that you have the post at Hangö which now appears of such consequence.'

Here follows a translation of the letter from the Duke of Sudermania to General Musin-Pushkin.

'If I can receive a positive assurance that the fleet of her Imperial Majesty shall evacuate the port of Hangö and quit that station and not return to it during the year, I will cause the troops which under my orders occupy the village of Hogfors [to withdraw] within the limits of the King my brother, with the flattering hopes that this pacific step will prove my good will to accelerate a truce so much wished for by both nations.'

[1] *Author's note:* A second letter, of which I have merely a rough memorandum.
[2] *Sic.* in MS.

Louisa, September 8 [N.S. ?], 1788
(The original is signed thus) Charles
Duc de Sudermanie (L.S.).

The extract from the Empress's dispatches mentioned in Admiral Greig's letter is in English as follows:

'The above mentioned General having forwarded this letter to his court, her Majesty has written to Admiral Greig to direct him to attend carefully to the preservation of the post of Hangö-udd, which appears so important to the Swedes, and charges him to exert his vigilance to maintain it and to cut off the communications between Stockholm and Helsingfors.'

It may be proper to mention that the letters from Admiral Greig to the Commodore are in English and in his own hand-writing. I shall now make some extracts from the latest dated letter in my possession and which does not long precede the death of the writer.

'*Rostislav*,
September 19, 1788

DEAR SIR,—I should have been glad to see you, but the wind being directly upon the shore, could not bear up so far to the leeward with the fleet.

Pray let me know if you have learnt anything of the strength or number of men in those vessels and if a descent of 2000 or 3000 men would not be the best method to dislodge them. I have now both the bomb-ketches with me, in case the wind would have permitted to try whether they could have been used to advantage.

You'll observe that it is the Empress's orders that you maintain the post at Hangö-udd as late as the season will permit, it being of the utmost consequence to the enemy to have a free communication by water for their small craft and galleys between Sweden and Finland. The squadron under your command must therefore winter either at Revel or at Baltic Port,[1] though I rather fancy it must be the latter, as ten ships of the line only can be placed in the harbour of Revel and Baltic Port is always later of freezing and earlier open than Revel harbour. . . . I cannot remain here long at present, but, as soon as I see a favourable opportunity, I shall endeavour to come and see you and talk with you. . . . I wish you all health and happiness and a successful campaign and am ever, Dear Sir, your most obedient servant, S. GREIG.'

This correspondence of the worthy Commander-in-chief strongly shows his high esteem for the character of the Commodore, who seems clearly intended by him as the commander of the advanced guard of the fleet.

In the rough copy of the answer to parts of the latters of Admiral Greig

[1] *Author's note:* A harbour a little to the west of Revel.

very little information is to be gained. I make some extracts such as elucidate either the character or situation of the writer.

'I was very happy by your Excellency's expressing your satisfaction at what has hitherto been done here. Nothing in my power shall be wanting to prevent the enemy from passing us, or to give them a good reception, if they think proper to attack us.

September 13th. The Baron Pahlen[1] went ashore with a party of men to examine the environs and will have the honour of making his reports to your Excellency himself. It will be a great satisfaction to me to have a post established here on the shore, as it will be a better means of our knowing whether they intend to attack us from that quarter and give us an opportunity to annoy them in their work; whereas else they may mask their batteries till they open upon us, and to prevent which we are from time to time obliged to send parties on shore.

September 14th. . . . All the day was foggy, and the 15th we perceived the enemy's fleet to the eastward increased by the addition of 4 large vessels, of which 3 are much larger than the others.[2] Capt. Grevens, who arrived this morning, thinks them all frigates.[3] I set out in company with the Baron Pahlen to reconnoitre them, but the fresh wind prevented us from approaching near them.

With regard to throwing bombs among them I can as yet say no more than I have already reported to your Excellency, that till within 4 versts of them there is always water for a line-of-battle ship, i.e. never less than four fathoms, but two of the passages are not more than 30 fathoms wide. They are, however, short. Within 4 versts of them I know not how it is, but I mean to take the Swedish steersman, who is still on board my ship, and endeavour to gain some further information, as soon as ever the weather will permit. This information I hope to have ready against your Excellency's visit, when I will pledge myself to undertake whatever your Excellency will plan. . . . .'

One of the many vexatious circumstances likely to occur to a British officer serving another government occurred here about this time. This was the detaining an English vessel bound to Helsingfors with provisions for the Swedes. This was a necessary measure, but I must fancy it very irksome in the execution.

[1] *Author's note:* This gentleman had lately joined the Commodore. He was Major of Engineers with a rank of Lieut.-Colonel, superior to that of the Commodore. This is bad management in the Admiralty, but their several duties could not interfere, unless they were acting on shore.

[2] *Sic* in MS.

[3] According to Swedish accounts the new arrivals were four *turumas*, which were sailing and rowing vessels of twenty-six guns rather larger than the two Russian 'rowing frigates'.

When the Baron Stedingk and the other officers made their appearance near the ships, it was easy for an enemy to conjecture that the visit was not merely compliment, although it was endeavoured to make it appear as much so as possible. The Baron insinuated that a truce was about to take place, expressed the highest esteem for the Commodore and repeatedly assured Mr. Casal that he was convinced that every outrage that had taken place was entirely contrary to his orders and wishes. He proceeded to request that parties from the hostile squadrons might meet in an amicable way to dine on some of the neighbouring islands and added as much complimentary matter as the length of time permitted. I find a copy of a note to the Baron in French, which I conclude was sent on shore to answer his compliments, etc., etc. I insert a translation, as it requests the Baron to depart in as civil a way as I have met with.

'Permit me, Sir, to say that the expressions you have used in my favour give me sincere pleasure, as the marks of esteem from a brave and respectable enemy ought always to do. But in the mean time I must add that I cannot suffer so near me an enemy so strong as you appear to be and therefore I must beg you to retire. I need make no excuse for this conduct, as all military men understand it well.

As soon as I hear news of the truce being made, I shall not fail to give you notice, and it is then that I shall have great pleasure in making your acquaintance and to assure you of all the esteem and consideration, with which I have the honour to be very sincerely, etc., etc., etc., J. TREVENEN.

A Mons. le Baron de Stedingk, Capitaine de haut bord, Chevalier des Ordres de Franc . . . etc.'

Thus anxiously and uninterestingly passed away the month of September, the active mind of the Commodore constantly at work to devize some mode of making his command distinguished in a way superior to what could result from the mere act of defence.

Early in October he had in some degree his desires realized by being able to take offensive measures against the enemy. His position had rendered it very difficult for the Swedes in Tverminne, Helsingfors and indeed all the south coast of Finland, to get supplies of provisions; and it became at last absolutely necessary that an attempt should be made to relieve both the fleet and army as well as the inhabitants from their distress.

From the Russian squadron they had observed near the neck of land several times small laden vessels make for the little island and rocks and there conceal themselves. From this the Commodore concluded that they landed their provisions by night at the village of Hangö-udd, which lies a little to the northward of the neck of land and thence carried it[1] over the isthmus to Tverminne, whence the passage to Helsingfors was open.[2] He formed plans for seizing these vessels, but they were all postponed by a storm of 15 days continuance, at the end of which 15 sail were seen at once pushing for the inlets. By steady assistance from Mr. Opperman a chart of the channel had been by this time constructed and it was found that by it their frigates might be piloted between the rocks. A calm now fortunately occurred and on October 4 Mr. Opperman undertook the pilotage of the *Sv. Mark*, which ship was reinforced by 30 additional hands and attended by several armed boats from the squadron. On the 5th a short storm of wind prevented any progress, but a fog at the same time had prevented the attempt from being discovered. Early on the 6th, the wind being very light, the *Sv. Mark* by dint of rowing had advanced so far as to send the boats to the attack of the merchant vessels, which now dispersed in all directions, but with so little wind that they made little progress and none of them seem to have been calculated to make use of oars. It must be remarked that the obstacles to this attack were so great, that with every exertion the *Sv. Mark* had only advanced eight miles.

Upon the morning of the 6th also the Commodore, observing the Swedish flotilla appearing in perfect quiet, proceeded in his barge to the scene of action, where he found everything going on to his satisfaction. Captain Lvov had before daylight dispatched his armed boats and some of the provision vessels were already in their possession, but which they were obliged to burn in order to proceed in chase of others. Flattering hopes were now entertained that the whole would have been taken and Finland starved. The Commodore, however, was very soon recalled by a signal from the *Rodislav*, which was instantly complied with and his anxiety to know the occasion was very great.

Upon his return he found all the Swedish flotilla in motion, several sailing and rowing gun-boats pushing out to sea, while two xebecks warping and rowing amongst the skerries showed an intention to attack the *Nedezhda Blagopolutchia*, which ship was stationed without the others, to prevent the passage of the enemy's small craft. The captain of this ship, Bodisko, appears to have thought that he was the sole object of this movement of the Swedes, but the Commodore soon perceived that this latter was merely a feint and that the principal object of the enemy was to pass with their gun-boats

[1] *Sic* in MS.

[2] The 'neck of land' must be between the present town of Hangö and the point of Hangö-udd. The village in that case would be what is now known as Hangöby, almost directly north of the town. It would have been impossible for the Russians to see what was going on in the direction of Djupvik, where Peter the Great had tried to take his galleys overland in 1714.

without the rocks and fall upon the *Sv. Mark* and the boats with her. In pursuance of his fears Bodisko stood in to join the main body of the squadron, but before the Commodore's return to his ship the commanding officer had very properly made the frigate's signal to chase the gun-boats and the *Panteleimon* of 66 guns, Captain Lotyrev, to warp out, which seems to have been done as quickly as possible. The Commodore, having repeated the signal to Bodisko, went himself on board the frigate and in bolder hands she was soon turned to the assistance of the *Sv. Mark* and had some ineffectual cannonading with the gun-boats. The light breeze prevented their stopping the progress of these vessels and seven rowed past to attack the *Sv. Mark*, while all those under sail returned to Tverminne. The Commodore advanced towards the *Sv. Mark* in order to render her assistance in case of attack from the gun-boats and also, and I believe principally, to offer another point of rendezvous to his own armed boats, which were much scattered in the pursuit. But on board this frigate he had neither pilot who knew the passage nor a man capable of heaving the lead to show the depth of water as they advanced. The Commodore, however, succeeded in taking her through the narrow passage in spite of the obstacles I have mentioned, aided by a dark night, but almost as soon as she was clear of the narrows ran her upon a sandbank, where however she fully answered the second object of his intentions. Meanwhile the *Sv. Mark*, having collected as many boats as she could, was returning towards the Commodore, when she was attacked by the seven gun-boats above mentioned and maintained a smart contest with them for 3/4 of an hour within two gun shot of the Commodore, who was prevented from moving to her assistance.

The light airs at last wafted the *Sv. Mark* past her opponents, whose heavy metal in perfectly smooth water rendered them much superior to the broadside of the little frigate. The Swedes either were not well skilled in the art of attack or had had as much fighting for the day as they thought convenient; for, although the wind continued so light that succours could not speedily arrive and the *Sv. Mark* had run upon the same bank of sand as the *Nadezhda Blagopolutchia*, where the gun-boats without much risk might have seriously annoyed them, they returned also quietly into port and the two frigates soon after hauled off into deep water without damage.

In the morning the Commodore had also the satisfaction of seeing all the boats, which had been scattered twenty miles in the pursuit, return safe after having captured 14 sail of vessels laden with provisions of various kinds, all of which however they were obliged to burn, some during the attack of the Swedes, others owing to their striking upon rocks or shoals. On the part of the Russians no loss whatever was sustained. That of the Swedes from the report of a deserter was the loss of two of their gun-boats, which they were obliged to run ashore, and eight men killed. On the next night many lights were observed at the place of the attack, which appeared to confirm the truth of the report, as it was imagined the Swedes were employed recovering the cannon from the gunboats.

On the whole this seems a very satisfactory affair. The plain of attack on the part of the Commodore was ably laid and well executed through many difficulties; and the counter-action of the Swedes also seems to have much merit and called forth the exertions of the Commodore for fresh arrangements to overset it.[1]

On the part of Capt. Lvov there seems much credit due both for assiduity and zeal in advancing at first and repelling the strong attack made on him afterwards. The conduct of the officers and crews of the boats seems also to deserve much commendation, and Capt. Lvov and all the officers were recommended to the Commander-in-Chief. Mr. Opperman appears to have been a most valuable officer and added to the indefatigable exertions he had used to gain a knowledge of the archipelago of rocks and shoals on this coast, he seems to have taken an active part in the pursuit of the Swedish vessels. Most of these were from 60 to 100 tons burthen, the others small sloops.[2]

I have now laid before my reader all the details I have been able to procure respecting this first separate command of the subject of these memoirs. For soon after this action he was recalled by order from Admiral Kozlyaninov, which mortified him in some degree, as being sorry to leave a place where he had been of signal use to the service he was engaged in, although he had not been fortunate enough to meet an opportunity of achieving such great actions as would redound to his fame amongst those who only judge from sounding names and the numbers engaged, killed and wounded. From Admiral Greig's letters and the instructions of the Empress it appears that the port of Hangö-udd was to be held as late as possible in the season, and as it appears that at the time of this recall the Admiral was on his death-bed, it seems likely that a little Russian envy might have been the cause of it, as it was to the infinite mortification of the native officers that a Captain who was a foreigner should have the command of a force which hitherto had only been bestowed on Admirals.

With his orders to return he received many cautions to put himself on his guard against the Swedish fleet, which was expected to be at sea; and

[1] The Swedish version of this affair is as follows: 'At last on the 6th of October Ankarsvärd went with 1 hemmema, 1 turuma, 6 gunboats and 2 gun-barges to attack an enemy frigate and 1 xebec which lay outside Hangö beacon. The frigate retired towards a battleship nearby; the xebec, which at first tried to resist the gunboats, soon had to do the same; when the frigate turned to help her, she went aground. Darkness prevented any advantage from being taken of this.' Mankell, *Svenska Skärgärds-Flottans Historia*, p. 64.

[2] MS. chaloops.

therefore, immediately on receiving his orders, every expedition was used to embark everything from the posts formed on the shore and small islands; and on October 14 the Commodore and his squadron sailed from Hangö-udd and were two days on their voyage to Revel.

Upon the night of his arrival at that place he heard of the death of his patron and friend Admiral Greig, which, however, was not announced to the public till the next day, October 17.[1] I shall here insert an extract from a letter to his friend Riou written some weeks subsequent to this event, as affording a lively specimen of the talents of the writer in expressing his feelings and delineating character.

'Revel

MY DEAR FELLOW,—Many and curious occurrences have taken place since I left off writing, and if I had time, I would relate them to you, but to go on in equal detail would perhaps be voted a great bore. We remained in the same situation at Hangö-udd till the 14th of October by which time the weather had become much colder than we had it in our voyage round the world and we suffered from it excessively. However, had not my third tutelar genius, my household god, my successor to Cook and King died, we should have been there much longer and till the complete closing of the ice had firmly locked up the Duke of Sudermania and all his command. But for the happiness of Sweden Admiral Greig had long been unused to putting confidence in anybody and thence had nobody on board his ship who had the wish or ability to assist him in his multifarious business. In the one constant line of affairs at Kronstadt matters had gone on very well, but when he came to the complicated troubles of a naval war in such a sea as the Gulf of Finland, he bitterly felt the want of some friend on whose shoulders to lean for the few moments that nature required rest from continued watchings and anxiety. He had no such person with him, but [was] obliged to be in his own person Admiral of the fleet, Captain of his ship and Lieutenant of his watch. In short, I am decidedly of the opinion that he fell a victim to the incapacity of everyone about him and to the honesty of his intentions and zeal for the service of the Empress. In the delirium of his last illness his ravings turned on the Swedish fleet, his fear of their escaping him and his disapprobation of the conduct of several officers on whom he was obliged to place dependence. In the character which I wrote John King of him[2] I was right in many parts, but with regard to his honesty, which I then pronounced *political*, it is necessary I should retract my opinion. For he has gone through the fiery ordeal of temptation and not a spark of dishonour

[1] Greig died in the evening of October 15.

[2] *Author's note:* See p. [136].

has branded him with a stain. He has been seven times tried in the fire and is proved pure. The touchstone of virtue has been applied to him and his character remains unchanged and unspotted. In short, after having had the disposal of immense sums of money, which in going through the hands of Russians would have melted like the baseless fabric[1]—After having had the implicit confidence of his Sovereign for near fifteen years, which to them would have been only an unmeasured liberty of abusing it, after having had all possible means of becoming immensely rich he has died poor and his wife and children are left in dependence. Alas, they are left so still and the pension of Imperial munificence is merely proportioned to the poor character of the wife and not at all to the meritorious services of the husband. Oh magnificent Catherine! Can thy wonted liberality, which showered plenty and independence upon the minutiae of merit; which, like the full hand of Nature, poured out unbounded benevolence with undistinguishing prodigality upon the probabilities of merit, can that channel be now dried up on so notorious and so glorious an occasion and cease to flow there, where thy tears have flowed on the first impulse of generous affliction for this loss of thy friend, thy tried and faithful servant, thy defender and protector, the champion who fought thy battles and was such a corner-stone to the foundations of thy glory? Nay then; let opinion run loose; let it throw off the trappings of slavish respect, break through the glass of Royalty and pronouncing boldly on the qualities and virtues of Sovereigns proclaim to the world that thou wast never capable of any sentiments but the offerings of vanity; that the great Catherine was never the protector of virtue, but the slave of miserable vanity! . . . I have done.—This one circumstance of his poverty will no doubt prove to you, as it has done to me, that his character was all unity and that the unfashionable ungain[li]ness of his appearance and manner, and which I always took for an awkward hypocrisy, took its rise only in those feelings, in that consciousness, which he alone in the whole circle possessed, whilst everyone around him was wrapped up in the well fitting armour of impudence and dissimulation.'

The strong language of this character, written at Petersburg,[2] somewhat surprised me, considering the strict care which is often stated to be necessary with regard to what it trusted in a letter. But I am inclined to think that this letter was never dispatched,[3] but remained in the writer's portfolio, probably on account of this very extract, which appeared on reperusal not very safe

[1] *Sic* in MS.

[2] It was actually headed 'Revel'.

[3] *Author's note:* This opinion I find confirmed by a paragraph in a letter to Riou dated January 3, 1789, in which he says the reason his friend had not heard from him was his unwillingness to send mutilated accounts of his proceedings and he was now going to try to write what might be sent to the post with safety and without offence to the ruling powers of the North.

to trust abroad. It has no mark of having been folded up, nor is the letter concluded, but I do not recollect how it came into my possession.

From part of this extract it appears that the pension assigned to the widow and family of Admiral Greig was but scanty. However, as the Empress had loaded Greig with favours during his life, upon hearing of his death she immediately gave orders respecting his funeral and directed that all honours should be paid to his remains and declared his widow and family to be under her immediate protection.

Trevenen, now again descended to the rank of Captain, assisted at the funeral as one of the bearers.

In one of the rough journal books in my possession I find some anecdotes of the life of Admiral Greig, which I conclude will not be unacceptable to my readers.

'The fleet was quickly after hauled into port and I shall take the opportunity of its inaction to speak something of the character of Admiral Greig, who had so brilliantly commanded it, and who, risen from a low origin by his own merit and a concurrence of favourable circumstances, has cut so considerable a figure in the relations of the present times and who will yet do so in the annals of posterity.

He was born in Scotland in the Lowlands[1] and the close reserved character of the Lowlanders seems to be inherent in him. I do not know whether he first began his career in the British navy or in the merchant service, but I rather think the latter from the predilections he had for that mode and the choice he intended to make of it for his own children.[2] How he got his Lieutenancy in the British Navy I know not, nor when, but he was long with Keppel in the *Torbay*, in Hawke's engagement with Conflans and afterwards at the taking of Belleisle, which latter event was his hobby horse, of which he mostly delighted to talk, as I have heard from others.[3] It was at the close of that war (1763) that he entered into the Russian service. He came in as 2nd Captain with some other English Lieutenants, but having studied the lunar observations and shown their use here he was quickly promoted to the rank of Colonel or 1st Captain.[4] The part he acted in the Turkish war at the destruction of the fleet at Tchesma is well known to the world; and all who are acquainted with the circumstances of the affair are agreed that

[1] At Inverkeithing in Fife. He was born in 1735.

[2] He first went to sea in merchantmen, probably those belonging to his father, a shipowner. His eldest son is said to have been made a Midshipman at birth (1775) and two other sons were also Midshipmen.

[3] According to the *D.N.B.* he 'entered the R.N. as Master's mate in the *Firedrake* bomb' and was in her at Goree in 1758; then served in the *Royal George* in 1759 and was acting Lieutenant of the *Albemarle* armed ship in 1761, but was not confirmed in that rank. The two accounts are not easy to reconcile.

[4] The first mention of Greig in 'Materials for the History of the Russian Fleet' records his appointment on June 18 (O.S.), 1764 as First Captain with seniority of March 20.

it was all his. Admiral Elphinston first taught the Russians to fight at sea, but disagreeing with Spiridov, so that they thwarted each other in all their notions, Count Orlov perceived that it was absolutely necessary to take the command of the fleet upon himself, which he did, and then depended totally upon the counsels of Greig, who was Captain of his ship. This is a known fact to all that were there and nobody disputes it, so that whatever naval transactions passed in that war belong to Greig.

He had afterwards a command in the Mediterranean and it was on board his ship that Count Orlov decoyed the unfortunate woman supposed to be a daughter of Elizabeth by Count Razumovski (to whom she was legally, though privately, married) who before lived in poverty and obscurity at Rome. Greig has been censured by many for the part he took in that affair, but as far as it relates to the ship it is without cause. If Count Orlov, having decoyed the woman on board, put her into his charge as his prisoner, he could not do otherwise than carry her to Petersburg or wherever else his superior might direct him. But if it be true, as I have heard asserted, that he sent for his wife from Russia for the express purpose of serving as the decoy duck; and if he entered as a principal into the matter, it becomes an affair of treachery in which I should have been very much ashamed to have borne a part.[1]

Orlov's friendship was of the greatest service to Greig in bringing him into notice. I do not know that he got any other step out of the usual line,

[1] *Author's note:* The whole of the transaction respecting the Princess Tarrakonov is marked with peculiar infamy and sinks the Empress and Orlov to the level of the most detestable of mankind. The French author of the memoirs of Catherine asserts that Mrs. Greig was at Leghorn and assisting at the horrid transaction. But the English translator of that work knew that this lady was then at Petersburg and I am led to hope that Admiral Greig was not deeply implicated, though I do not know how fully to acquit him.

[The story as given in Hunter's translation of Castéra's *History of Catherine II*, may be summarized as follows: Princess Tarrakanov, daughter of the former Empress Elizabeth, had been taken away from Russia by Prince Radzivil and left in Rome under the care of a governess; the idea being that she might, as a possible claimant to the throne, be of use to him in his efforts for the freedom of Poland. Orlov was given the task of securing her return to Russia. He went to Rome, made love to the young Princess and actually pretended to marry her before taking her to Pisa and thence to Leghorn, where 'the division of the Russian squadron under the command of Rear Admiral Greig had just returned'. The Princess stayed in the house of the English Consul and his wife and Greig's became her constant attendants. She expressed a wish to visit the Russian ships and was ceremoniously taken on board, but only to be made a prisoner. 'They carry her down to the bottom of the hold. Next day the vessel sails for Russia'. On reaching Petersburg she was imprisoned and finally drowned in prison by a flood six years later.

Tooke's translation follows the same lines, but names neither the Consul's wife nor Greig's, merely speaking of 'several ladies'. Nothing is said as to Mrs. Greig's having been in Petersburg at the time. In a footnote the flood in which the Princess was drowned is said to have taken place in 1777 and the kidnapping is thus put in 1771, when, according to another footnote, she would have been only sixteen years old.

Actually it took place in 1775 and is mentioned in some detail in the account of Russian movements in that year in 'Materials for the History of the Russian Fleet', but promotion was then very rapid. The affair of Elizabeth's daughter[1] made him particularly known to the Empress and she favoured him ever afterwards. The Government of Kronstadt was a consequence of that favour, as well as the principal direction of naval affairs, which he enjoyed ever afterwards and which made Count Tchernyshev, the Minister of Marine, and all the senior Admirals his enemies, though they always carried a good countenance towards him, not daring to do any other. He never lost the Empress's good will and she supported him through everything, even once when the Grand Duke seemed to become his enemy. I have heard it asserted that Greig's conduct in that affair wanted manliness and that he was too much affected by the displeasure of the Grand Duke, though he carried his point by the assistance of her Majesty. I do not recollect what the dispute was.

His person was rather large and excessively awkward. His legs very large; his belly and breast rather sunken; his shoulders round and his head stooping forward. In his winter dress at Kronstadt nothing could look more like an old Scotch wife well wrapped up in cold weather. His dress, when not in uniform, was plain, almost to an affectation of plainness, only that I believe (though it was not always my opinion) that he had not a spark of affectation of any sort in him. The features of his face were large and marked, but as for character there was nothing observable but much seriousness and reflection and perhaps somewhat of profundity. When he was not speaking there was a heaviness, almost dullness, marked in it, but his countenance brightened much in conversation. He was in general very silent, but sometimes, in particular companies, he knew how to make himself entertaining by producing with much good nature and pleasantness some of that inexhaustible fund of knowledge and information that he had acquired by constant application in the latter years of his life; for in his early stages his education had been evidently much neglected. His remarks were always judicious, for he was capable of observing and reflecting as well as of application to gain the ideas of others. With all this he was certainly slow and heavy from nature. In affairs of writing, however, method supplied all

Vol. 12, p. 311. Greig was then in command of a squadron sent out from Russia at the end of 1773 and now on the way home again. He had reached Leghorn from the Archipelago in November 1774. The following is a rough summary.

On February 12 (O.S.) at 4.30 Count Orlov came on board the *Isidor* (Greig's flagship) and with him one lady with one servant and Messrs. Domonskii and Tchernovskii with five servants. On their arrival every ship saluted with thirteen guns. One ship then exercised with great guns and another with small arms. At 6 o'clock the Count left for Leghorn and by his orders the persons mentioned and their servants were put under arrest. On February 13 the male prisoners were transferred to other ships and on the following day the squadron put to sea. It reached Kronstadt on May 24 and the prisoners were sent to Petersburg in a yacht two days later.]

[1] *Author's note:* Princess Tarrakanov.

quickness of parts and in the active business of a fleet he threw off that part of his character and was busy, energetic and decided.

It was a very marked feature in his character that he never put off anyone who came upon business, but always gave an answer immediately. This is very conspicuous and particularly in this country.'

This character seems to end abruptly and some blank pages after it augur that more was intended.

During the former winter Admiral Greig had taken so little notice of Capt. Trevenen that he felt himself neglected, nor did the summer seem to draw them together. In the letter from which I extracted the first inserted character of Admiral Greig he complains of not having his confidence. But that it appeared thus to his feeling mind must have been owing to the reserve which had become habitual to the Admiral from having served so long with men unworthy of his confidence; and it is evident that he must have seen the merit of his countryman in the late action and during the summer campaign, as he appointed him to the important command of Hangö-udd after only two months' service together in preference to so many officers whom he had long known.

The confidence reposed in Capt. T. by his Commander-in-Chief became known to him on a sudden, for having delayed a letter from Revel of about August 10 or 12 he added a cover to it from Hangö-udd dated August 27, to announce his new command and to express his sense of the trust reposed in him.

A similar instance occurs at this time. In a letter of October 25 after speaking of Admiral Greig's death amongst other causes he laments him as he had become his peculiar patron and had honoured him with his confidence. He expresses his fears that his reports from Hangö-udd will now be suppressed and his actions and conduct misrepresented. The whole letter is written in a style of despondence from a dread of his rise in the service being checked by the loss of his patron, into whose ship he had entertained hopes of being removed before the next campaign, where he would have been able to obtain a more enlarged view of the character of the war, an opportunity of inspecting at a less distance the springs of action and the secret of the *primum mobile*.

Luckily, this letter had not been dispatched and it was hastily concluded on the 27th with higher hopes and in spirits much improved.

'Having kept this letter in waiting a post, in order that I might have a chance of an answer from Petersburg to my request for leave of absence I have been agreeably surprised in the meanwhile to find that the fears of losing the reward of my services were vain and that on the contrary her

Majesty has in the most gracious manner and entirely of herself promoted me to the rank of Colonel,[1] a step by which I leap over the heads of about 15 and approach within 20 of the list of Admirals. A step which puts it in my power to receive more commands; a step by which the envy I mentioned to exist among by brother officers is very much increased, but which makes it hide its head more than before; a step of importance, by which I am bound with endless gratitude to her Imperial Majesty; a step by which the only melancholy reflection excited is that it removes me farther from my own service in putting within my prospect rank and command that I could never hope to acquire at home. It has, however, . . . a melancholy in others that borders nearly upon . . .[2] and is an indirect proof of the so much decried maxim of Rouchefoucault, "we find something that does not displease us even in the misfortune of our best friends". Sitting at home in the evening with my best friend here[3] he could not refrain from repining at his unlucky fate, that during 15 years that he has served here has never helped him forward out of the common road of promotion, whilst he saw other people revel on[4] the most unaccountable good luck. This must naturally have hurt me and I pitied him, but at the same time I could not help reflecting on the rareness of that stubborn and principled virtue that I rejoice to find in all my brothers, in Ward, in Riou and in Hergest. It is the growth of another soil.'

Another day's delay allows a second postscript to this letter still more encouraging to the ardent spirit of the writer. This is dated October 29.

'I have an answer to my petition that orders me directly to Petersburg. This is doubtless to give an account of my late post, etc., etc. I am at all events glad to be delivered from hence. Why have I not now, whilst my good star seems to prevail, a little more seniority? I should then have no doubt of receiving a more considerable command next year.'

It is pleasing to recount such instances of merit bursting through obstacles. They serve to show those who deserve well that they ought not to despair of their due reward, as those who act so as to merit success can never know how near its arrival may be, whether they see it or not. The genuine ambition and ardent spirit of the subject of these sheets is also highly portrayed in the foregoing extracts from his letters.

It appears that the rank of Colonel was conferred on Capt. T. before there was any intention of summoning him to Petersburg. The latter resolution seems to have been taken on the Empress's reading a long letter to Count Tchernyshev containing a very full detail of all the occurrences that took place at Hangö-udd and also showing all its local advantages,

[1] Trevenen's promotion to First Captain was on October 23.
[2] *Author's note:* The missing words are torn out with the seal.
[3] It seems probable that this refers to Dennison. [4] *Sic* in MS.

modes of defence, etc., etc. The two following translations of letters will eludidate these matters.

'St. Petersburg,
October 23, 1788

SIR,—It is with very great satisfaction that I have the pleasure to inform you that her Imperial Majesty has made you Captain of the first rank. Your handsome conduct in the battle as well as your constant perseverance in guarding the post entrusted to you has procured you this mark of her goodness.

I have great pleasure in announcing this to you as well as to assure you of the sentiments of esteem with which I have the honour to remain, Your obedient humble servant, I. G. TCHERNYSHEV.'[1]

The other letter is as follows, dated October 28, 1788:

'SIR,—In reply to the letter which you did me the pleasure of writing the 22nd of this month I have that of informing you that I have had the honour of receiving the orders of her Imperial Majesty, to whom I had that of presenting your letter. She has directed me to cause you to come here for some days only that I may have some conversation with you. I have written in consequence to Admiral Kozlyaninov, to whom you are to address yourself, not only for leave of absence, but also money for the expense of post-horses.

It will give me pleasure to see you as soon as possible with all the papers mentioned in your letter and to assure you in the meantime of the very particular esteem with which I am and shall always be, Sir, your most obedient humble servant, TCHERNYSHEV.

Mr. le Capt. Trevenen

It is impossible to avoid remarking in this last letter how naturally the courtier rises in his style of conclusion as the Empress's favour to his correspondent increases.

I have a paper which I take to be the heads of the letter to the Count containing nearly the account of Hangö-udd I have given, and the papers mentioned must have been the nautical remarks and plans of fortifications with descriptions of the different passages to the eastward of which I see some marginal notes.

About this time also, Capt. T. received a congratulatory letter from Count Vorontsov mentioning the favourable accounts he had received of his conduct in the late battle and the high estimation in which he was held at Petersburg, as the Count's letters from that city informed him.

[1] MS. Czernichew here and below.

A Mr. de Lvov also writes about this time with much apparent earnestness and friendship pressing him to come to his house as soon as he can get leave of absence from Revel. I find no prior mention made of this gentleman than that of being one of the persons to whom Count Vorontsov had given recommendatory letters on J.T. leaving London.[1]

It is with much regret that I find myself destitute of materials for the next two interesting months, as I have only one letter from the last date to January 10, 1789, nor any notice in any way of the journey from Revel to Petersburg, which however we may take for granted to have taken place without delay.[2]

The reception, however, which Capt. Trevenen met with at Court was highly flattering and he had the honour of an audience with her Imperial Majesty. At the public dinner of the Order of St. George she often addressed herself to him and sent him with her own hands a plate of grapes. And at a subsequent levée she enquired particularly about his health and assured him it was of material consequence to her. Indeed, by this time her Majesty's penetration had enabled her to discover the treasure fortune had thrown in her way, and she used to speak of him in public as 'her own Captain', 'her gallant Englishman', etc., etc.

I conclude that it must have been at the audience above mentioned that her Majesty directed Capt. Trevenen to form a plan for the ensuing naval campaign, to be laid before her. Nothing can more strongly evince the very high opinion entertained of his abilities by her Majesty than a demand for a plan of an important and extensive campaign from a stranger whose rank was only that of a captain of a ship of war.

The plan was forwarded in an enclosure to the Prime Minister on December 16th. In the letter to the minister some apologies are made for deviating from the exact bounds of a campaign for a year and pointing out some defects in the usual management of the Russian fleet.

The plan being long, the remarks in it local and intermixed with proper names of places and technical terms, etc., not easy to reduce well into English, I have thought it best only to give my readers the general tendency.

The Russian fleet had been laid up this winter in three divisions, at Kronstadt, Revel and Copenhagen; the impolicy of which measure struck the English officer, although it had been deemed a wise measure by the Court. The Swedish fleet were all together at Karlskrona. The plan first

[1] *Author's note:* From some subsequent documents I find this gentleman to have been in office under Count Bezborodko, the Prime Minister.

[2] *Author's note:* Feb. 18, 1806. My pen has been idle for some weeks in consequence of information that some further documents had been found. I have only opened them this day and find that nothing in them relates to the present or any future part of these memoirs. What relates to prior events will be noticed in the proper place.

suggests the weakness of the port of Revel, the improper position of the batteries, and states the destruction of the ships there as a very easy enterprise to an enemy of any degree of military daring. Subsequent events will show that the Swedes were not unaware of this advantage, but that they were not equal to make proper use of it. So apparent was the weakness of Revel that Capt. T. recommends a wooden pier with a heavy battery be constructed in haste, to serve till one of masonry could be properly executed. The Swedish fleet at Karlskrona could sail earlier in the year than that from Revel on account of the ice, which opens sooner at the former port, and from this circumstance would be in the way to attack either of the Russian squadrons on their way to join the others and gain a great advantage. Or they might be ready to make an attack on Revel the very first moment military enterprises were practicable.

The Swedes from being first at sea were able to insult the Russians in the Gulf of Finland, knowing that they were superior to those ships to the east as well as the others to the west. This situation he advises to prevent by every possible energy. The ice was to be broken so as to allow the ships to come out of the harbour and moor in a curved line of battle in the road, so as to be able to withstand an attack of a superior force, till favourable opportunities occurred to allow either the squadron from Kronstadt with an easterly wind or from Copenhagen with a westerly wind to join them. Every energy was to be used to proceed with the united squadrons off Karlskrona to blockade the Swedes in port and to keep them there all the summer. Then the Russians would have to cruise in the Gulf of Bothnia instead of that of Finland, where in comparison they would be in perfect safety. The enemy would be removed at a distance and the superior number of ships of war possessed by the Russians would admit of their sending some to cruise in the entrance of the British Channel to capture the numerous and valuable merchant ships of Sweden. But parts of this plan required British seamen to execute as well as a British head to propose, and we shall see by the narrative how far it was followed. At the same time that the request for a plan of operations for the ensuing year was honourable, it must have been far from pleasing in other respects. If the plan was followed and from the ignorance or wilfulness of those concerned happened to fail, 'There stands the audacious foreigner who presumes to be wiser than all of us', and if thrown by or neglected, mortification must of course be the consequence.

In the early part of the winter Capt. T. had apartments in the house of Count Tchernyshev, the minister of marine, who appeared his warm admirer and zealous friend; but the rooms were large beyond the power of the stoves to warm and he suffered so much from the cold that after being obliged to keep his bed two days he removed to humbler but warmer lodgings. This winter, however, proved a most interesting period in the life of the subject of these memoirs and witnessed a very sudden and important change in all his wishes and expectations.

On February 9, 1789 he married Miss Elizabeth Farquharson, daughter of John Farquharson, Esq., of the very ancient and respectable family of that name, the family seat of which is Invercauld in Aberdeenshire.

A sister of this lady was the wife of Capt. Dennison, whose name has already appeared in these pages; and at this gentleman's house in Kronstadt Capt. Trevenen remained some little time during the former winter while looking out for a house for himself. At Capt. Dennison's my friend had the opportunity of discovering the value of Miss Farquharson and her society proved a brilliant relief to the otherwise sombre mode of life at Kronstadt.

A letter dated January 10, 1789 to his mother contains the earliest intelligence of the surrender of his heart and affections and requesting her consent to his union, which at this time it was his intention to await. But unexpected orders[1] from Court directed him to be in Revel early in March, which, of course, was long before his mother's consent could reach him; and as waiting for it would postpone his happiness at least till after the ensuing campaign, he with difficulty persuaded his amiable friend to make him happy without delay and proceeded with him to Revel, where the fitting out his ship would occupy some time. The delicacy of Miss F. made her strongly urge the propriety of awaiting his mother's consent, but his own eloquence backed by the persuasions of her father and sister, who had been induced by the peculiarity of the case to second the captain's wishes, at last prevailed.

I shall never forget the pleasure with which I read the letter announcing this happy event, which seemed at once to gratify every wish of every member of the family by the delightful prospect it afforded of having our beloved friend restored to us in possession of his heart's choice and fixed in the service of his native country.

I insert the whole of the letter to his mother stating his reasons for not awaiting her consent.

Petersburg,
February 12, 1789

MY BELOVED MOTHER,—I wrote you about 3 weeks ago to beg your consent to be married. What will you think of me now that I write to say I am married? Will you accuse me of undutifulness in not waiting for the sanction of your consent? I hope not, and when I shall have explained the matter to you, I trust not. At that time I supposed that more than two months might

[1] *Author's note:* Probably these orders were occasioned by the plan we have just been noticing.

elapse before I should be ordered to join my ship at Revel and it was also possible that I might have got a new ship at Kronstadt, where I should have been always at hand to have heard from you directly and to have taken my measures the same as if remaining constantly at Petersburg. On a sudden we are told that we must all be at Revel by the 1st of March, to superintend the fitting out of our ships, which is to be done with all possible expedition. Now, my dear Mother, if I had gone from hence without being married, I must inevitably have waited till next year. At the same time God knows what the summer's campaign may produce. If, therefore, I had waited your consent, most likely I should not have been married this year. Now, as you can have no other ground for forming your opinion than what I give you, and as I think that my happiness being so essentially and so entirely concerned, you will consent to rely upon my judgement and not withhold your consent upon an uncertainty. I have presumed upon it and am a married man of 3 days old. Oh, my dear Mother, consider that I am not of a cold character and then reflect whether it were possible for me to put off till next year a matter in which my happiness is the principal object and on which you could never have any other information to give your consent upon than what I myself should give you. Consider whether in a service of such danger as ours I am not right to grasp at happiness whilst I may, and whether the hope of leaving behind me someone to be remembered by in the world may not fairly come in for a share of weight in the argument. These at least have seemed so convincing to me that I could not have two opinions on the matter; but my wife was more difficult of persuasion and the whole force of father, brother and sister was necessary to make her give up her ideas of duty to mine of temporary necessity. Sweet creature, she is all duty, delicacy and love. If you have any regard for my comfort, my dear Mother, you will be glad to hear that I am married. For my own mind has gained peace, happiness and tranquility and my health also cannot fail of profiting by the ease of my soul. It seems to me that the hodge-podge of my life is now about to take some sort of consistence and that the vagabond insignificance of it will meliorate into some sort of consequence to myself and the world. As for anything else, my beloved Mother, I am by no means a bit more bound to this country by this even than before. For it is the constantly expressed wish of my wife's heart to live in England and I only pray that it might be true that their Lordships of the Admiralty have expressed an intention of recalling and providing for me. I am told so from London, but the thing is improbable. By being married I am much more likely than before to give up all sort of romantic schemes and to prefer solid domestic happiness to the visionary bubbles of Fame and Danger. On being married I begin immediately to sigh after Old England. For myself it was of little consequence where I lived. But for a family. . . . Whatever may be the case with the first English mastiff transplanted into a foreign country, his descendants at least are sure of dwindling into curs, and there are instances enough of it here to make me dread the prospect. The beginning of March, then, my Dear Mother, we shall set off from hence to go to Revel, 300 miles. We shall be two or three months in fitting out there and whether my wife will remain there or return here must depend on circumstances.

I am now obliged to finish, but will write soon with more circumstantial detail, although I have not been happy in hearing from Cornwall for about 2 months.

My wife sends her duty and every proper sentiment and I can assure you all that she is worthy to form a part of your worthy society. Without the partiality of a lover or the fondness of a young husband I may safely say that there does not exist a better heart on earth.

Adieu, adieu, adieu, my beloved Mother. Your dutiful son, J. TREVENEN.' Her age is 28.'

The journey to Revel seems to have been delayed somewhat longer than could have been expected, as I find a letter to Mrs. C. Penrose dated at Petersburg March 24.

Soon after the date of this letter, Capt. Trevenen and his lady went to Revel, in which port the Russian fleet continued locked up in ice till near the end of April. The fleet was busily fitting for sea, but owing to the *Rodislav's* masts having been amongst the last examined and repaired she was one of the last ships ready.

I have no account of either of Captain Trevenen's journeys to or from Revel.

Before he left Petersburg Capt. T. received a letter from his mother with her full approbation of his marriage and I shall now insert extracts from his interesting answer from Revel. It however has no date. It explains the remarkable expressions in the end of the last inserted letter and accounts for so little mention having been made of Mrs. Trevenen till so near the time in which she took that name. My business being to exhibit the character as well as to narrate the actions of my friend I must trust much to that excellent lady's indulgence in this part of the work for the insertion of letters which dwell so much on herself; but my labours would be imperfect without them.

'MY DEAREST MOTHER,—I am resolved to write, although every minute of my time is subject to interruptions. Wonder not, therefore, if my letter is incoherent. I have been long intending to answer your last blessed letter, in which you consent to and approve of my marriage. I received it a day or two before I left Petersburg, where I had been kept waiting more than a month beyond my expected time of departure. I need not say it added very much to my happiness. It completed my felicity as well as that of my beloved little wife. It has struck me since my marriage that you must have thought it very strange that I should never have mentioned so important an affair to any of you till so lately. The fact is that it was very late before I could bring myself to relinquish all the prospects with which I had hitherto fed myself and all the projects which had hitherto employed all the past and still were marked out for the employment of my future life. I had never yet resolved to change my object and substitute domestic tranquility in the place of anxious but glittering turbulence. I had not yet perceived the true road to happiness, and even when I got a glimpse of it, I had a foolish shame in abandoning what I had always been the advocate of and what had got such strong hold of me as nearly to tear away my reason in its departure. It was a change I could by no means resolve on, yet was I most heartily ashamed of myself and infinitely too much so to disclose to any one of you, to any soul alive or even to myself, that I loved this sweet creature with the most violent affection. It was a miserable state. Will you be affronted with me for yourself or will you despise me for her, when I say that it was principally to drive such thoughts out of my head that I took the strange resolution of asking leave to go to England in the beginning of last winter. Strange! from its being in the time of war and from the length of the journey and the short leave I could have had. However, that did not hinder the desire of seeing my mother from being a powerful motive. Admire the ways of Providence!, for when I consider all things, I cannot attribute my present state to chance. Instead of having leave to go to England I was ordered to Petersburg.

Here I soon had more frequent occasions of being convinced that all that had charmed me was not only a lovely, winning, feminine appearance, but real, delightful, exalted virtue; that in her severe principles were softened by the truest tenderness; that her good sense was directed aright and capable of a right affection; that the knowledge of the world had not impaired the purity of her mind and that her character was all unity and sincerity. It was impossible to resist. My heart against my consent had betrayed its emotions and all the world perceived long before myself that I was hastening to a crisis. It was indeed a violent one. But my eyes were opened to sense, to reason and to nature. I became as decided on one side as I had before been on the other, and I instantly threw myself at her feet. No consideration was then capable of delaying me a single moment. A refusal might have destroyed my heart, but my pride would not have been affected; and, as far as it was possible, I should have gloried in my misfortune and have thought myself the worthier man for the attempt. It was a tribute due at all events to such irresistible virtue and at least no emotion of shame could have resulted to me from my repulse. By the favour of Heaven I was accepted and my happiness is ensured beyond the power of man to change it. Think, my dear Mother, on what slender threads it hung. We were in England together without knowing each other. My ridiculous rambling ideas led me to Russia. Family affairs sent her there at the same time. My broken leg probably hindered me from going round the world immediately on my arrival. The war breaking out afterwards set aside totally the expedition. We were bound next to the Archipelago. I parted from her with a breaking heart, but without saying a word. I was gone quite. The Swedish fleet brought us round up and sent us back again. I wanted to go to England and asked leave for that purpose, and was called to Petersburg and married her. Heaven be praised! My first object is now my own and I am easy and tranquil about all the rest. No more repining or bewailing at Fortune. The attainment of my ambitious prospects is become a secondary object, that in their failure affect me but lightly, for my happiness is not interested in them. In their success they give me a joy doubled and trebled by communication. What right have I to such a wife and such happiness! . . .'[1]

Here we observe the same energetic feelings which pervaded every action of the writer; and above all I am led to admire the intrepid honesty which made him search out himself and the lay the result before his friends. He was consciously bold in integrity.

[1] *Author's note:* I find from expressions in other places that this letter must have been written the 26th or 27th of April, 1789.

Chapter 3

THE WAR WITH SWEDEN: 1789

The first movement of the Russian navy this year (1789) was the sailing of a detachment under Capt. Trevenen, April 28,[1] to reconnoitre his former post of Hangö-udd having a frigate and two cutters under his command. The frigate was commanded by Capt. Sivers, of whom Capt. T. speaks as an excellent officer, and one of the cutters by Lieut. Scott.[2] Nothing being left to his own discretion, he soon fulfilled the object of his cruise and found that the Swedes had become so fully sensible of the importance of the post, that during the winter they had erected five batteries for its defence. He returned to Revel on May 17.

A favourable opportunity having offered while out on this service, it was embraced to exercise the men at the guns, which in a calm were heard at a great distance and made the Commander-in-Chief, Admiral Tchitchagov, shake in his shoes, and he appears to have been not a little frightened and angry. I have not yet found one good trait of this Admiral and I shall insert some extracts of letters relative to him written at this period.

The following is an extract of a letter to Mr. Farquharson of May 23.

'We exercised and manoeuvred: the noise of our guns put the Admiral in a fright and made him get up in the night, which he complains of sadly, and will I perceive never forgive me. He is fit for nothing but a bum-boat woman, and yet I think not even for that, for he would never sell his gin or gingerbread for fear of not getting enough money for them. His whole object is the hindering his captains from making money by their command and his economy exerts itself in saving powder from the exercise and the ropes and sails from being worn out in manoeuvring. It was only yesterday he could muster energy enough to loose his topsails, though he has been a fortnight in the road. He is the stupidest old jackass that ever was inspired by the breath of nonsense. I shall make a plan of Revel and of the disposition of our fleet, in order to have it in my power to damn him at any time. He used to be friendly formerly, especially when frightened, but now, when it

[1] This date must be wrong. The ice did not allow the Revel squadron to leave harbour until May 2 and the ships of the detachment are all included in a list of ships in the roads on May 5. Two of its vessels are recorded as putting to sea on the 9th and that was probably the date of Trevenen's sailing also. A possible explanation is that Penrose made allowance for Old Style in quoting from a document already dated by that method.

[2] The detachment consisted of the *Rodislav* 66, *Premislav* 36, *Letutchii* and *Pospyeshnyi*.

seems as if the Swedes did not mean to come out, he takes it in his head to blame me for exercising at sea, and for that he is the laughing-stock of Revel.'

After Capt. Trevenen's return from reconnoitering Hangö-udd he recommended to the Admiral to look out for some other station which might be seized upon to answer the same purpose and proposed Porkala-udd and Tverminne. The Admiral immediately sent another to examine these places and to take post at Porkala,[1] a measure which excited the proposer's indignation, as he thought himself entitled to the honour of putting his own schemes into execution. In another letter to Mr. F. he says: 'I wish much for another battle to expose the insufficiency of this stupid old monkey, who besides other discouragements to officers abuses the captains behind their backs to their officers and does not speak to them himself.'

About this time I find he was employed in procuring from London sets of Hawksworth's and Cook's voyages for the Russian Academy and its memorable President, the Princess Dashkov. His friends in London took pains to procure the best impressions and to have them handsomely bound.

After so long a continuance of the war an Englishman will be surprised to hear that the Russian navy continued to be most execrably manned, nor will he be less surprised after considering this circumstance at the fleet doing so well as we find them doing in many trying circumstances.

The following extract on the subject is from a letter of June 6 to Mr. Farquharson. In a former letter in April I find that the recruits were beginning to sicken fast.

'The Kronstadt fleet arrived here the 26th of last month happily, but in such distress for want of good sailors that it is found necessary to make a division of those we had the trouble of teaching last year. My only reason for keeping my old ship, or rather for not asking for another, which I had a great right to do, arose from my desire to keep the people whom I knew and who knew me and who had been already in action. So that, when they take my people, I shall beg them to take my ship too; for the promotions among the seamen last year and the battle have already taken away most of the old and good sailors I had. Heaven send us fine weather.'

Wishing to lay everything before my readers which may give them amusement I make another extract from the same letter relative to an honest Englishman and his wife in the Russian service; for after reading the extract it will not be thought fair to exclude the lady from a fair share of whatever honour may accrue from that situation.

'You mention a brig of ours blocked up in Bornholm. That is our friend

[1] This detachment sailed on May 15 or 16. It seems that Trevenen must have returned by the 15th at latest.

Crown's vessel.[1] I have a letter from him today from that place, or I may rather say from his wife, who apologises for her husband's not being able to write from multiplicity of business. For the singularity of the thing I think it worth while to transcribe her words:

'We were sent from the fleet on the 28th of April to reconnoitre Karlskrona. With much difficulty in getting through the ice we arrived on our station the 8th instant and observed in Karlskrona 15 sail of pennants. The 14th we were chased by two frigates and a cutter, and indeed so we have been ever since, but from foggy weather have lost sight of them for a day or two. Yesterday in endeavouring to regain our station we met them again and were obliged to put in here. On the 11th we captured a cutter mounting 12 guns and were so fortunate as to receive no damage but having some of our rigging shot away. I am of opinion that some very heavy blows will be struck this campaign. God preserve you and all our friends in this service. I am your most obedient humble servant—MARTHA CROWN.'[2]

This lady would have been in high request at the court of Thalestris.[3] Capt. Trevenen speaks highly of the energy and activity of Lieut. Crown and styles him an excellent officer.

About this time Capt. T. received a letter from Count Vorontsov from London evincing so much good sense and friendship for his correspondent that I am tempted to translate it. I have reason to believe that some very confidential subjects passed in letters between him and the Count, but such correspondence required to be very carefully managed in Russia.

'London,
April 22 (N.S.), 1789

SIR,—I should not have delayed so long to answer your friendly letter dated November 28th, 1788, but for want of certain opportunity. Mr. Halliday, who is returning into Russia, offers one and I have charged him to deliver this personally, if possible. I shall be much flattered if you will afford him your countenance. He is a young man to whom I am much attached and who has conducted himself perfectly well during a long and active service in the Royal Navy.

I regret much, Sir, that I cannot enter particularly into all the interesting matters which your letter contains. I have only leisure to enter upon that topic which interests me most, I mean yourself.

It is with a true satisfaction that I hear from all my friends and relations

[1] Crown's ship, the *Merkurii* 24, was classed as a cutter, but was very probably rigged as a brig. She had been bought in England and had joined the Russian squadron at Copenhagen.

[2] The dates in this letter are in New Style.

[3] Queen of the Amazons.

that your merit becomes more and more known; that her Imperial Majesty knows it and surely will employ and recompense it.

There remains nothing on your part, permit me to say, but a little patience to overcome certain unpleasant circumstances inseparable from all situations, but particularly in a foreign service, where envy generally attaches itself where emulation should arise; but with perseverance you will triumph over these obstacles. It is not to flatter you, Sir, that I assure you that a brilliant career is open to you, which you may pursue almost without a rival. Your merit assures you the situation of Admiral Greig, of that man who will be immortalized in Russia. You will one day replace him and you will replace him worthily and partake of his glory. Think, Sir, when you feel any disgust, what great things you may do, being sure of the friendship and support of all which is estimable among us. I sincerely wish you a brilliant fortune and it would be with pain that I should see it in danger.

Without criticizing the British navy, you will observe upon reflection that it is not without its unpleasant circumstances. A change of Administration often confounds the most favourable hopes and suffers the most eminent merit to remain in perfect inactivity.

When you did me the honour to write to me, you were full of ideas which promised you an unpleasant campaign. Now (and I am in earnest in congratulating you) that you are become a happy husband, probably you will see matters through a less unfavourable medium. I heard of your marriage with the daughter of one of my oldest friends, for whom I have a great esteem, with sincere pleasure and I wish you all imaginable happiness. I will not conclude without recalling to your recollection my brother-in-law Senyavin[1] and recommending him to your friendship. All that you show him I shall take personally to myself.

You will oblige me on your part by furnishing me with occasions to prove my attachment and the perfect consideration with which I have the honour to be, Sir, Your obedient humble servant, J. C. VORONTSOV.'

This letter seems written in earnest and with much good sense. I dare say his correspondent had spoken with perfect freedom on the subject of his situation and opinion of affairs in Russia.

I have one other letter to his mother, written before the fleet sailed from Revel. It is dated June 26 and I insert an extract or two relative to his present Commander-in-Chief and the amount of his income in this Imperial service.

'I am now descended from my dignity of Commodore into the rank of private Captain and perhaps I am likely to remain there some time, for our present commander-in-chief is remarkable for nothing so much as for his

[1] Probably Grigorii Senyavin at this time in command of the bomb-vessel *Perun* with the rank of Captain-Lieutenant.

violent aversion to foreigners, and I cannot say I have any desire to serve under a man who betrays everyone who has any dealings with him. I had experience of it, as far as was possible, during our late cruise.[1] However, I have no other reason to think I shall be set aside from command, as I had flattering attentions paid to me at Petersburg by the great and my advice was asked, given at length, received with great approbation and has hitherto been followed with regard to the method of carrying on the war in the Baltic. I know too that the Empress recommended me to our Admiral, that he should give me any command that might offer; but by that I only gain from him a grudged civility and he has hitherto given no proofs of his intention of complying with her request. In short, the death of Admiral Greig has left the English without a protector in Russia, and although it was currently reported at Petersburg that I was to have an immediate and rapid advancement and although a sort of apology was made to me when it was dropped, that they were afraid of disgusting the other captains—although I received a further mark of the Empress's confidence in having a young man, whom she has caused to be educated, a sort of foundling, put under my care —yet all this is no assurance but that I may be utterly forgot, especially if our Admiral takes care to keep me back and should be otherwise successful, which his great force, but not his abilities, seems to promise. However, these things do not affect me now as formerly. My wife, my first object, is always my own.'

The following extract I insert to show the small encouragement given in Russia with regard to emolument.

'MY DEAR MOTHER,—These new prospects of a family bring always with them new cares as well as new pleasures and oblige me to think very seriously on economy. Unluckily in this country there is very little money and officers are obliged to be contented for their services with rank and honours. What little we receive is paid in paper, which bears a discount of 20 per cent against specie, and even that is debased. Not very long ago the exchange with England was 52 pence for the Rouble and now it is only 30. Owing to this debasement, notwithstanding the scarcity of cash, everything is excessively dear, much more so than in England (except indeed meat), so that I have never been able to save any money in this country, although last year the profits of my ship with my pay amounted to about £400. Considering the things I have had from England I fancy my emoluments in this country have not hitherto kept me. Wood has sent me many things and some that I would not have ordered had I known I was going to be married, and yet I am not £100 before hand here, notwithstanding that on my arrival I had a

[1] This must refer to Trevenen's visit to Hangö-udd. There had been no cruise by the fleet.

present of about £250 made me. As a single man I cared not for money and having last year a command above my rank my expenses also were above it. Now I shall be more economical and it is the more necessary as my gains will not be like those of last year, for our present commander, having no military merit, is resolved to make up for it by the civil one of economy and his chief care is to cut off from his captains all the advantages they enjoyed under Admiral Greig; so that at the instant my expenses increase my gains diminish. My Mother, I will not stay in this country to ruin myself. I am likely to tell the same story as Gil Blas to his patron: "Whilst I am overwhelmed with goodness I have nothing to eat".'

I do not know the exact date of the Russian fleet sailing from Revel, but it must have been early in July or the last day of June.[1] The great object was to form a junction with the squadron which had wintered at Copenhagen and was under the command of Kozlyaninov, who was at least suspected of being very far from a brave man.

On July 14, however, and before the intended junction the Swedish fleet made its appearance to windward and preparations were made for battle.

The Russian fleet consisted of twenty sail of the line, in which number were three ships of 100 guns. The Swedes amounted to twenty-one sail of the line, the largest of which was of 74 guns, but they were strengthened by eight large frigates with heavy metal. These were all brought into the line of battle; and as the Admirals on each side seemed to have an aversion to close action, their heavy guns rendered them very effectual. Several manoeuvres took place on both sides, but the day passed without any engagement. It lay, however, wholly with the Swedes so far to choose their time and distance, though towards evening the Russians might have perhaps closed with the rear of the enemy by going on the other tack.

In the morning of the 15th the manoeuvres on both sides recommenced. In the night the Swedes had increased their distance to windward a little and after forming their line bore down slowly towards their opponents. Meanwhile, the wind being somewhat variable, Tchitchagov took great pains in reforming his line upon every change of wind, all which occasioned his edging away from the enemy, so as at times to bear the appearance of a flight. The Admiral himself and part of the van appear to have made sail from the enemy at one time, when the wind by no means furnished them with an excuse. By 8 o'clock the Swedes had approached within three gunshots, but it was not till ¼ before two that they thought themselves near enough to try their distance by firing a shot.

The Swedes made their approach in such a way that their van approached

[1] The fleet sailed on July 2.

much nearer to the van of the Russian fleet than their opponents, but the closest part of the lines was at a very awful distance.

The instant the Swedes had fired the experimental shot, the Russian ships opened their fire, although no signal was made for that purpose and the distance so great. The *Rodislav* took the infection and about three broadsides were discharged before her commander could reduce her to silence. This he did as soon as possible, though those astern of him at a still greater distance continued their roar. When the smoke cleared away, Trevenen perceived not only that the Russian shot fell not more than half way towards the enemy, but that the signal was flying on board the Admiral's ship for the centre and rear to cease firing. Capt. T. had afterwards the thanks of the old Admiral for the good example he had set. The battle continued between the rear and centres of the fleets an hour or more, but did not cease between the vans till past 7 o'clock. After Capt. T. had reduced the guns of his ship to silence he had sufficient leisure to look on and it does not appear from his observations that the shot of the Russians had made any impression at all upon the enemy. The Swedes were much better gunners and understood the art of pointing their guns well at an elevation and of this the Russians appear to have been ignorant. Not a hole could even be perceived in the sails of the Swedish fleet and the Duke of Sudermania appeared very averse to coming too near the 100-gun ship in which the flag of the present Commander-in-Chief was flying, perhaps from the recollection of the drubbing he received from her last year whilst under the more skilful and gallant conduct of Admiral Greig.

After about two hours' action the *Deris* of 64 guns commanded by an English Lieutenant (Preston), being the second ship from the Russian van, bore up and towed out of the line. It was afterwards found that four of her lower-deck guns had burst, killed 120 men[1] and forced part of the lower deck into the hold. A sufficient reason for leaving the line.

The van ship, the *Mstislav*, soon followed with the loss of her fore top-mast, but the occasion of her leaving the line was the death of Mulovskii, who had signalized himself in the action of last year and has been more than once mentioned in these memoirs. On board the *Mstislav* four men are said to have been killed and I cannot hear of any other damage being done on either side except on board the ship commanded by Capt. Dennison, though the battle between the vans must have continued near six hours.

As the Swedes had brought on the action, they also departed from it by hauling their wind at the time before mentioned.

I have been favoured with a letter from Capt. Dennison[2] to Mr.

[1] The *Deris* actually had fifteen killed and ninety-two wounded.
[2] Of the *Sv. Petr*.

Farquharson giving an account of this affair and I insert part of it, as he was one of the few within reach of the enemy's fleet.

'To give you an account of the scuffle we have had with the Swedes would be needless, as Trevenen has done it already. Suffice it to say, that it was the most wretched affair on both sides that ever was, and that if there be any man more incapable than our Commander-in-Chief it must be him that commanded the Swedish fleet on the 15th and 16th of July. They bore down on us on the 15th, engaged us partially: the few of us that had any part in the action were only within random shot. I happened to be one of those engaged and had 5 men killed and 22 wounded. Preston had 5 of his guns burst, which obliged him to make the signal of distress and run out of the line. The headmost ship, Mulovskii, had his top-mast shot away and 4 men killed, of whom he himself, poor fellow! was one. His death put that ship in confusion and it bore out of the line with the other.[1] Notwithstanding all this, together with our Admiral's continually bearing away, the Swedes took no advantage, but withdrew after firing a great deal of powder and shot in vain. I believe some of our van fired away from each ship 3000 shot without having a man killed or wounded. The next day they chased us and we ran lustily! The day after again. They bore away in the night for their own port.'

I admire this concise and lively description of the battle. The remainder of the cruise is so well detailed in a letter from Capt. Trevenen to his mother, dated July 25 at sea, that I give it in his own words.

'The Duke of Sudermania lay opposite our Admiral, who was in Admiral Greig's 100-gun ship that gave him such a dressing last year, and I verily believe he did not like to have anything more to say to her. He certainly does not possess a soul great enough to seize the important stake that lay within his grasp. He lost his opportunity and could no more regain it. The next day, the Swedes having still the wind, our Admiral (it seems) did not like to engage any more and therefore he ran away, but in a line of battle, and the Swedes pursued us in ditto. Towards evening they came up very near us and it then became necessary to offer them battle, but it was now too late, and so we lay by all night looking at each other. The next day light winds and manoeuvring delayed and kept us at a distance. After having twice lost the wind by his ignorance a sudden change at last decided it in our Admiral's favour and he had his choice of the distance to engage at. But it seems he had a safer game to play and chose to wait till the fleet from Copenhagen should appear according to their orders. To say the truth, the

[1] *Author's note:* This circumstance must strike an English reader particularly. Mulovskii dies and his ship retires in confusion. Nelson dies and neither the vastness of his loss nor the poignancy of grief at that loss occasions a moment's delay or confusion in the operations of a vast fleet.

Swedes did not seem over eager to engage, till they saw we would not, and then they chased us again. But night and the wind separated us. And thus we remained near a week, surely the most uncomfortable that ever was spent. In hourly expectation of fighting, all the while without rest, nourishment or any conveniences, I might say necessaries, of life. At night we dressed what was absolutely necessary for the morrow's food. Most heartily we all wished to decide the business at once and not remain in a disagreeable suspense. The Swedes were, however, frightened with the apprehension of our other fleet appearing. The 5th day they withdrew towards their own port leaving us a free passage. The 6th we had sight of our other squadron and the 7th joined. The Swedes were by this time safe in their harbour.'

Remaining a few days off Karlskrona with the united fleets amounting to thirty-one sail of the line, many of them capital ships,[1] to show them to the Swedes, satisfied the Russian Admiral for the cruise and he made sail for Revel, at which port the *Rodislav* arrived the 16th of August.[2]

I have a pretty full journal of the events of the few days that the hostile fleets were in sight of each other; but the remarks are merely nautical, to show the various tiresome and timid movements on both sides and to point out the various blunders.

Nothing indeed appears more unofficerlike than all the conduct of old Tchitchagov on this occasion, and I cannot guess how such glaring misconduct escaped punishment from his severe and penetrating mistress.

It was currently reported and believed on good foundation, that after having formed a junction with the squadron from Copenhagen he was to have gone with the whole fleet to that place, to water and refit; then return to cruise off Karlskrona, leaving a squadron off Gothenburg. A mean and erroneous idea of economy led the whole fleet back to Revel, where ignorance and indolence together prevented the ships from even beginning to complete their water till a courier was sent to Petersburg and returned. Indeed, till the return of the courier the fleet remained in the road, and then received orders to go into the harbour.

The return of the fleet to Revel had not been foreseen by anyone and therefore Mrs. Trevenen had embraced a favourable opportunity of returning to Petersburg immediately after its sailing; a measure which the captain very sincerely regretted. He wrote a letter to his mother as soon as possible after anchoring in the road of Revel, for fear the same reports should reach her as had found their way to his wife. By the time these reports had reached her they had arisen so far as to state that his ship had been

[1] Here 'capital ship' is evidently used in what was then an old-fashioned sense as meaning a three-decker.

[2] The fleet had been at anchor in the Gulf of Revel since the 9th.

sunk and both his legs shot off. How barbarous and infamous are the propagators of such rumours!

Upon August 16 the long-expected courier arrived and brought orders for the fleet to put into Revel and at the same time that seven ships of the line and three frigates were to be put under the command of Capt. Trevenen for detached service as a flying squadron. Before I enter upon the narrative of its operations, however, I cannot resist from inserting the following letter to his sister, as it exhibits a fine specimen of the epistolary powers of the writer.

[A very long letter begun on July 10 and continued on August 16 largely devoted to praise of his wife. It contains the following reference to his new appointment.]

'We have no less than six Admirals in a fleet of 30 sail of the line and as many Brigadiers, i.e. Commodores. Yet I, a simple Captain, am by the express orders of her Majesty appointed to a separate command of seven ships of the line and a proportion of frigates. Think of a poor foreigner in the situation; what envy, hatred and malice must it give rise to! This is easily conceived, but it is not the worst. I do not know my destination; nor, if I did, must I tell you. But it may be conjectured a service of danger and complicated operations, of which the difficulties must be necessarily so much increased by the nature of the Baltic Sea (to which the Flemish banks are a trifle) and by the approaching tempestuous season of the year, that they make me look forward sometimes with the most serious apprehensions; not on account of the enemy, but of the rocks, shoals, gales of wind and the ignorance and incapacity of the tools I have to work with.'

Including frigates, chebecs and other smaller vessels of war the squadron put under the command of Capt. Trevenen amounted to twenty-five sail.[1] A very evident and flattering mark of the high confidence reposed in his zeal and abilities, when so large and important a command was given to a captain, whilst six Admirals and as many Commodores were already in the fleet. From several documents it appears that the Russian government attached great consequence to the success of the enterprise.

In a letter to his friend Samwell about this time, he mentions his labouring under severe indisposition and suffered[2] much from a pain in his breast and on the setting out of the expedition he feared that he should be obliged to retire from the service before the completion of his orders, but with his usual zeal and ardour he expressed his hopes of first performing some brilliant service with the respectable force under his command.

[1] It does not seem that Trevenen had quite so many ships under his orders at any one time.

[2] *Sic* in MS.

His instructions, which were kept a profound secret, were first to attack his old station of Hangö-udd, which the Swedes had taken much pains to fortify after the evacuation of it by the Russians last year. It will be remembered that the reconnoitering that port was the first service performed by Capt. T. in the present year and the opening of the campaign. He had then an opportunity of observing the means adopted by the enemy for its defence and he now formed a plan of attack from which he had sanguine hopes of success. Having taken Hangö-udd he was to proceed to Barö-sund and drive [off] or destroy the Swedish gunboats in that port. From thence the operations were to extend towards the coast of Sweden and cut off the communication between that and Finland, penetrating, if possible as far as Åbo. He was also to make a descent on the island of Åland, for which service a battalion of Livonian chasseurs were embarked.[1] 'Here was enough service pointed out for a whole campaign and only the month of September and part of October remained. However, I resolved to do as much as I could.' This remark occurs at the end of the sketch of the instructions I have given above.

Not only the time allotted was wholly inadequate to put into execution the service pointed out, but the means were not well adapted to the effect required. Many difficulties occurred in the equipment and most of these I conceive were occasioned by the orders passing through the hands of old Tchitchagov, who seems to have possessed to the full the faculty of doing everything wrong. The elevation of Capt. T. to the honour of this command, though I believe without any additional emolument, drew on him the envy of the whole Russian navy; and the old Admiral, whose dislike of foreigners amounted to antipathy, had his full share; so much so, indeed, that in all probability it overset his patriotism altogether.

But, whilst the preparations for the departure of this detachment were proceeding as fast as the unremitting exertions of its commander could accomplish them, news arrived that an attack was meditated by the Swedes on the port of Porkala-udd, where a small squadron of Russian ships were stationed. The Admiral, instead of forming another detachment from his large fleet of thirty sail, thought proper to detach Trevenen to support or relieve it and thus wasted the time which would have been spent on the first and grand object of attack and took him away from completing the fitting-out of the ships which had been put under his command.

This was in itself a matter of serious consequence, as Tchitchagov, either from malice or ignorance, took especial care not to expedite any and even to keep some back altogether.

[1] These orders follow very closely those sent by the Empress to Tchitchagov on August 12 with the proviso that Trevenen was to be in charge.

With his usual alacrity on service, however, Trevenen sailed[1] and arrived in good time to save Porkala-udd, as a Swedish squadron came and reconnoitred them, but not liking their force, though still inferior to their own, made sail and departed. In working into this dangerous place the *Rodislav* struck upon a rock, but got off without damage, though not without imminent risk.

Two Russian ships, the *Evropa* and *Iannuarii*, were stationed in Porkala-udd to prevent supplies of provisions being carried along the coast by the Swedes, but it soon appeared to Commodore Trevenen that this station was utterly unimportant, as there was an excellent water-communication by a lake a few miles inland.[2] Dispatches were instantly sent over to the Admiral with a description of the place and information of the strength and apparent destination of the Swedish squadron. The latter he promised to follow, but on sailing *unfortunately* took a different direction from that they were known to have taken.[3]

In all the scraps of journal I meet with relative to the naval service of Russia the conduct of the officers appears more like that of great blubbering schoolboys than of men: constantly making complaints and telling tales upon each other. The two captains, Glyebov and Sukin, who commanded the ships found at Porkala-udd, were in this situation. One, Sukin, had been attacked by the Swedish gunboats and lost one man in the action.[4] He complained that Glyebov did not come or send to his assistance, and Glyebov says that Sukin made mountains out of mole-hills and that the attack was nothing. Both made many attempts to persuade the Commodore that it was necessary for their ships to go to Revel for repairs, but both were ordered to remain where they were.

The Commodore remained in or near Porkala-udd till the beginning of September, and the nature of the service he was on rendering it necessary to keep his ships frequently under sail, his fatigue and anxiety must have been very great. A reference to a good map of the coast of Finland and a knowledge that this service was carried on inside those innumerable little rocks and islets which are scattered along that broken coast can alone give an idea

[1] The *Rodislav* left Revel on August 23. At Porkala Trevenen found the battleships *Iannuarii* and *Evropa*, the frigate *Sv. Mark* and the cutter *Letutchii*.

[2] This is not the case, but the chart suggests the possibility of a very short portage.

[3] A Swedish squadron of three battleships, three heavy frigates and three small craft left Karlskrona on August 14 (O.S.), passed Hangö on the 23rd and reached Barö-sund, some fifteen miles west of Porkala, on the 25th. Trevenen had arrived at Porkala on the 23rd and Tchitchagov left Revel with his whole fleet on the 27th. By then the Swedes were out of reach; having seen Russian vessels both off Porkala and out at sea, they had retreated after only one night's stay. Tchitchagov cruised in the Gulf of Finland till October 11, but never went far to the westward.

[4] This was probably on August 15.

of the difficulties and dangers to be surmounted. A seaman only can truly appreciate them.

But many more difficulties than appear at first sight attended the situation of the Commodore. He was to make descents on the Swedish coasts and had not a Swedish interpreter. He was to make signals and issue orders to a large squadron and had neither secretary nor signal officer who spoke French or English. These things had all been represented without effect to the wretched Tchitchagov.

The remaining occurrences of this campaign and its unfortunate conclusion are summed up in so masterly a way in a letter to his mother, that I insert it entire in this place and shall afterwards more particularly detail some of the events recorded in it.

Revel, October 27, 1789
November 7, New Style

'It is now about two months since I have written to you, my beloved Mother, but in the mean time I charged my better half to supply the place of the worse, and if she have not done it, I will not fail to scold her, as soon as I arrive at Petersburg, where she now is. In that space of time many momentous events have befallen me, and instead of saying with Tom 'in the midst of life I am in death', I may rather say 'in the midst of death I am alive'. I told you I had the command of 7 ships given me. Afterwards that command was changed to 4 ships and a number of small vessels amounting in all at last to 25. With these I was sent amongst the Swedish rocks, and after surmounting infinite difficulties in that advanced season of the year I at last arrived before the destined place of attack. I dare say you will have seen the account of that affair in the gazette. Therefore I shall only say that I only wanted proper vessels to have gained a very complete victory and to have entirely destroyed the enemy's fleet of galleys and small vessels. As it was, we took two batteries, destroyed two vessels and defeated the rest; but not being able to pursue them among the rocks with my frigates, I was obliged to content myself with this and keeping possession for 5 weeks of a post which entirely interrupted all the commerce of Finland. By the stupidity of one of my captains one of my ships ran on a rock and was lost, but we saved everything from her. After this the enemy attacked us several times and with various success. They took a post we had established on shore, but we chased them from it again. They were gradually reinforced and the King himself came to look at us. At last we were obliged to confine ourselves to our ships, they having on shore 4000 men to our 600. They built bomb-batteries and bombarded us, but from want of resolution never came near enough to us, and I did not quit my post till the lateness of the season compelled me. During the time of my being among those frightful rocks all my ships and frigates and cutters got on shore one after another, but we were lucky enough to haul them all off again, though sometimes under the fire of the enemy. We had a great many skirmishes and I was obliged to be everywhere; but as the Swedes kept generally at a great distance and from the nature of the place and their vessels had the choice of doing so, we had not many men killed. One day they erected a battery on shore against our advanced frigate and as I went on board her to reconnoitre it they fired a shot which I watched[1] and saw coming right towards me. The pleasant spectacle went about a yard over my head through an ensign. You may well guess that during the whole five weeks that I stayed there I had not much rest. Night and day we were in constant alarm and fears of bombs and fire-ships and all sorts of infernal instruments. I may say I scarcely ever pulled off my clothes the whole time. At last the joyful day of departure came, but my pains were not finished. I had the same dangerous navigation to go over again for the space of ten leagues and in doing it had frights enough from sunken rocks, sandbanks and cross winds and currents setting us on them. However, only one of my frigates struck in going out and she came off without harm. At last I got out in the open sea. Heavens! what a load was removed from off my breast! I saw before me no more dangers: I had a fair wind for my port: I was relieved from the thousand anxieties that had disturbed me for so long before and I was going home to a winter of ease and delight, to the bosom of my dearly beloved and tender wife, whose anxieties had been no less than my own and in the relieving of which I foresaw more pleasure than all the rest. I was going home, too, with flying colours triumphant, carrying with me the spoils of the enemy and expecting to receive the thanks and rewards of a liberal Sovereign whom I had served with heart and soul and with effect. What a delightful prospect after so much trouble and danger! I gave all the rest to futurity, however, and only revelled in the hope of soon clasping to my bosom the dear creature that so fully occupies it. I was to comfort her tender distresses, to uphold her against an approaching momentous occasion and to employ myself in the delightful occupation of making her happy. My satisfaction was complete; it wanted nothing and I was all exultation. In an instant I found my ship on shore. Was it not too bad? In the entrance of our own port, in a known place and frequented every day my pilot mistook his marks and ran me on a bank of sand and rocks. Several others of my squadron stuck fast beside me and in an instant all my brilliant and pleasing hopes were dashed to atoms and the most disagreeable prospects before me. It was impossible not to ask one's self on such an occasion: Is this the hand of Providence? or is all this ruin

[1] *Author's note:* If the eye chance to see a shot after it is discharged from the gun, it is easy afterwards to trace its progress.

and blindness in the common course of events and due only to the imperfection of our senses and negligence? Let those who will decide. I am only sure that I wanted no lesson of Providence to damp my too aspiring hopes, to curb my ambition or to teach me to bear misfortune. I have had enough already to temper my spirit, nor would the height of the vain prosperities of this world elevate me to one presumptuous idea of self-forgetfulness, nor destroy the mental humility that is the happiest attainment man can acquire in it. Be that as it may, my first business was to get my squadron off and I flatter myself I set about it with all the sang froid imaginable. I could have little right to say Prosperity should not elevate me, if I suffered adversity to depress me; and except the pangs that now and then occurred to me from the thoughts of my wife and some little leaven of dashed ambition I soon reconciled myself to my situation and thought myself best worthy the name of a man, when I could laugh at the cruel trick Dame Fortune had played me. I got off all the other vessels, but my old *Rodislav* remained a sacrifice and the wind increasing she quickly filled and broke. The weather was cruelly cold and the wind blew hard and we were nearly in the open sea; yet we worked hard for four days and got out all her guns and nearly all her stores. And the 5th and 6th the wind increased to a storm and saved us an infinite deal of trouble by knocking her to pieces so completely that her place was no more to be found.

I am now waiting here a few days till I get leave to go to Petersburg, where I shall quickly forget my ill fortune in the society of the dear little creature that anxiously expects me, You must know, my dear Mother, that in this country it is a terrible thing to lose a ship and one cannot justify oneself as in England. No man is here permitted to be unfortunate. So that I do not know how this may be taken among the great in Petersburg, although I know I have done enough for them to qualify their ill-humour. This I know, that if they offer me the least affront, I quit instantly their service, and in so doing shall, I fancy, comply with the wishes of my mother and my wife as well as all my friends. It is a great pleasure to feel always independent. If I had fixed my heart upon the rank and honours that people destined me upon the occasion of my victory, I had been perhaps disappointed. But these are so little object with me in comparison with the happiness that is within my power, that they give me no uneasy thought. It is true that the idea of having raised myself to the rank of Rear Admiral, which I might almost have expected, before the age of 30 and without the assistance of any soul on earth now and then flattered my ambition a little. But I have always kept such a strict rein on my imagination that I never permitted myself to build in such a sandy foundation any loftier ideas than those proper to an English Lieutenant.

As to money matters: my command, so far from being advantageous, put me on the contrary to a great expense for my table without a farthing's gain, which joined to the loss of my ship-furniture, which amounts to near £100, has almost ruined me. As we are not this year, as last, pursers of our ships, my pay will scarce amount to £200. For this I have commanded a squadron of 25 vessels and rendered mickle service. I have been Commodore and Captain of my own ship and pilot in a new and dangerous navigation without any one of the aids that usually accompany commanders. I am a stranger and yet imperfect in the language and I have had my equals in rank to command, natives of the country particularly jealous of foreigners.

Whether rewarded or not, I find that I have acted a great part in the world, and whilst I have my health, my limbs and my wife, I care for nothing.

Adieu! my tender and beloved Mother! J. TREVENEN.'

The account of the emoluments in the Russian service is not very encouraging. It must be remarked, however, that Trevenen received some sums of money from the Empress at different times, knowing that his pay could not maintain him or enable him to support that style of life she herself would wish to see him in. I know not the amount of the Empress's presents, but have no reason to think them either frequent or large.

During the latter end of August the ships and vessels which were to compose the squadron gradually collected and the Commodore made his arrangements and issued his orders relative to the intended attack of Barö-sund, to which place he had to make his way good through dangerous channels utterly unknown to himself and those under his command. They were through these difficulties to find a way to attack an enemy strongly posted and prepared with mortars, red-hot shot, galleys, gun-boats etc. In short, the enemy appears to have had the most proper tools that could be procured to perform the service required, whilst the Commodore had hardly one part of his force calculated to work with the best effect. In the midst of these obstacles a heavy gale of wind came on on the 1st of September and lasted two days, putting the squadron into great danger and causing considerable delay.

After having with considerable pains drawn up a narrative of the attack of Barö-sund from the different letters in my possession I have been fortunate enough to find among papers which came afterwards into my possession a copy in French of the Commodore's account of the transactions to Admiral Kruze, who at that time commanded the squadron of reserve in the Gulf of Finland. From particular circumstances I conclude this letter to have been dated at Barö-sund Sept. 10th, but no date appears upon the rough copy, of which the following is a translation.[1]

'Having received the orders of her Majesty through Admiral Tchitchagov to proceed to the attack of the port of Barö-sund and to endeavour to destroy the enemy's vessels I might find there, and the *Aleksandr Nevskii* having joined me on the 31st of August with the greatest part of the battalion of Estland chasseurs, I lost not a moment's time in causing the squadron to move out of Porkala-udd by every favourable occasion and hasted to put it in condition to fulfill my orders as soon as the opportunity offered.

By the 4th of Sept. the ships were all out and on the 5th we sailed with a fair wind at S.E., 4 ships of the line, 2 frigates, 1 bomb-vessel and 4 vessels of smaller size.

We were piloted by Lieut. Lally of the *Stchastlivyi* cutter, who had already explored the passage, and the *Sv. Mark* frigate, which from her small draught of water ran safely through these passages. We passed this dangerous navigation without accident and anchored the same evening in the passage of Barö-sund about 3 versts from the enemy's batteries.

I lost not a moment in reconnoitering the position of the enemy during the day and in taking soundings in the night, and assisted by the advice of Lieut. Keyser of the Engineers, a very skilful and experienced officer, I concerted the plan of attack and resolved to put it into immediate execution.

The entrance into Barö-sund is not more than half cannon shot across and on each side are great numbers of small islands and rocks.

On an advanced point on the south side was a barbette battery of six guns, 12-pounders, and farther within the bay on the north side another battery constructed with embrasures and mounted with four 30-pounders. These, as well as a frigate and chebec placed between them, commanded the entrance and enfiladed the whole length.

Advanced without the batteries and flanking the passage a cutter of 20 guns, about 12 galleys and a great number of cantilibuses,[2] gunboats, etc. were dispersed amongst the rocks and so concealed by them that they presented no other object but the muzzles of their guns and were discovered only by their fire. We saw on the batteries fires constantly burning and

[1] The full despatch, dated September 10, is given (in Russian) in 'Materials for the History of the Russian Fleet', Vol. 13, pp. 604–10. This has been used to correct names, etc. The variations are no more than would be expected between a first draft and a fair copy, if one allows for translation in each case.

[2] In the Russian version this word appears as 'kantchebas', this being the singular. Veselago's 'List of Russian Ships' includes thirty-three vessels of this type, but spelt 'kontchebas', as built on the Dnieper in 1736. They were evidently small craft of some kind. Swedish accounts put the highest strength of their force in this neighbourhood as one frigate, one turuma (evidently called a chebec by Trevenen), seven galleys and a few gun-boats.

from the mode of fighting that the Swedes have lately adopted we concluded, and rightly, that they were preparing red-hot shot. Add to these the imperfect knowledge which we had been able to acquire in the space of only one day and [a] half, and the soundings taken principally in the night, and I think it will be allowed that appearances were formidable and discouraging.

Nevertheless, having received her Majesty's orders to attack this post, having been informed of its importance and now convinced by my own observation of a great number of transports which were constantly passing from east to west amongst the rocks and before the batteries, and fearing they might soon return laden with provisions for the army on the frontiers, I judged that it was absolutely nesessary to make the attack, whatever risk the ships entrusted to me by her Majesty might run.

The Swedish steersman that had deserted and was retaken said that this was the key of the skerries.[1]

As the southern battery was more advanced than the other and as our soundings had not extended farther than it, my plan was to attack this battery and the vessels which were on that side close with half my force, whilst the other half kept up a more distant fire on the battery and vessels to the north, and to endeavour to drive or destroy the galleys, gunboats, etc. in aid of our principal attack. It was also resolved to make a descent with the troops during the night and at dawn of day they were to attempt the battery by assault, whilst we attacked it from the sea.

For this purpose the battalion of chasseurs, with the marines, forming a corps of 600 men under the command of Lieut. Colonel Shiling and a corps of volunteers under Lieut. Keyser of the Engineers were assembled on board my ship at midnight Sept. 6th. They were to proceed from thence in the boats and on board the *Sv. Mark* frigate and two cutters[2] under the command of Capt. Lieut. Tutolmin, who was ordered to escort them ashore and cover their landing.

It is certain that, if this design had been put into execution, all the enemy's troops posted in the south battery would have fallen into our power. But unfortunately it was prevented by a strong gale at S.E., which brought in so heavy a sea that I judged it impracticable to disembark the troops on an unknown and rocky beach during such a night. With the most poignant grief I was obliged to abandon my plan for the time and wait a more favourable opportunity.

[1] *Author's note:* Small islands and rocks, within which the Swedes could navigate in safety from the enemy's cruisers, but the situation of Barö-sund was such that all must then come to one point; and of course its capture would put an end to the whole of that navigation. At Porkala-udd and other places the channels appear to be numerous.

[2] *Stchastlivyi* and *Letutchii.*

On the following afternoon the wind lulled, and although I feared that it was then late and also that the troops would be too much exposed in landing under the fire of the enemy in the day-time, yet reflecting on the dangers of delay and looking round at my situation in a narrow and bad roadstead with a considerable squadron and where one ship had already struck on a sharp rock which had escaped all our researches; the bad season also approaching, when a change of wind might have put it out of my power to make the attack for a long time and would have given the enemy an opportunity of sending fireships against us with effect. Considering all these things I saw myself under an absolute necessity to render myself master of the place without delay and hastily arranging the troops in the boats I made the signal for the attack.

The *Panteleimon* was the first a-weigh, my ship quickly followed and the *Aleksandr Nevskii* was also soon under sail. The troops rowed towards the land, and when we were within long gun-shot the enemy opened his fire on all sides. Nevertheless, this was not equally formidable throughout. The frigate and chebec soon cut their cables and escaped through a narrow passage to the west, where we could not follow without pilots.

When our fire opened against the batteries, their fire slackened, and after some rounds of red-hot shot, by which the *Panteleimon* was five times set on fire, the enemy abandoned the southern battery after having spiked some of their guns.

Colonel Shiling, however, was close at their heels and so near that he found two guns not only without spikes, but loaded, primed and well pointed against our troops. They saw the last man of the enemy, who threw down his musket and saved himself by swimming to another small island.

The northern battery was also abandoned and before we anchored the enemy began to fly on all sides, the gunboats only prolonging the affair; and these did us the principal damage by hiding amongst the rocks and firing from places where they could not be seen. However, as soon as our ships were anchored and the guns were better directed, these also fled leaving us complete masters of the field of battle and of the important post of Barö-sund. The battle continued about an hour and [a] half and at the commencement was well maintained by a lively fire from the enemy, but this diminished considerably after some time.

I cannot exactly ascertain the loss of the enemy. One galley, not being able to escape, was burnt by her own crew. We secured her flag, which I send to you, and I hope to recover her cannons. Another escaped with the loss of her mainmast and lying upon one side and one of the gunboats had all her oars on one side shot away. During this time Lieut. Col.

Shiling had passed over to the north and taken possession of the battery there, which he found evacuated. All the guns were spiked, two of them dismounted and marks of blood on the platform. Both the batteries were furnished with all things necessary for heating shot and we found a considerable quantity in the fire. One had fallen on the platform of the south battery and set it on fire, but it was extinguished by our people. We found a considerable quantity of powder and shot.

Hitherto all went on well and I am much mortified to interrupt the narrative of so fortunate an event by that of a considerable misfortune which befell us.

Observing that 5 or 6 galleys had taken shelter in a bay not far from us and conceiving that it might be with the intention of keeping close till night in the hopes of making their escape in the dark, I directed the *Syevernyi Orel* to change her situation a little and place herself so as to command the entrance. There was little wind and the steersman was sent to take soundings. But notwithstanding this precaution, such are the dangers of the place, that she struck upon a sharp sunken rock, so small that it had not been discovered, and in spite of all our efforts remained there till the next day, when unfortunately the wind increased considerably and blew from the only point of the compass to which this place is exposed. She then began to strike upon the rock with such violence that being before a weak and leaky ship owing to her having been aground and amongst the ice all the last winter at Copenhagen, the water gained upon the pumps and she lies at present in such a situation as leaves us very little hope of getting her off.

The *Bryatcheslav* frigate also struck upon a rock, but is gone off without any damage.

When looking round on all that nature has done towards fortifying this place, the considerable force that defended it and the dangers that surround it, whilst I exceedingly regret the loss of the *Syevernyi Orel*, I cannot help being rejoiced that I have not suffered greater losses. I must attribute this to the panic which seized the enemy and which prevented their making the most of the means of defence in their power; and in part to the good fortune which conducted us amidst many rocks which we have since found, but which had before escaped our most diligent searches. The rocks rise to a point sharp and steep (and that in the midst of the best places for anchorage) so that the lead may long search them in vain.

The enemy's batteries, according to the report of Lieut. Keyser, are built with a solidity and care which may assure their duration for ages and their position renders them capable of a most destructive effect on an attacking enemy. Yet we suffered more from the gunboats than from the batteries or galleys; and being in considerable numbers in a narrow place and raking in all directions, it might be expected that we suffered severely.

Near the batteries they had begun to build huts and other dwellings for the troops destined to occupy this post.

As soon as Lieut. Keyser has finished a plan of this place, I shall forward it to you and you will then judge of the force of the enemy and how formidable it was.

List of the killed and wounded:

Rodislav	2 killed	1 wounded
Panteleimon	– ,,	7 ,,
Bryatcheslav	1 ,,	1 ,,

All the damages done the hulls, masts and rigging are of a nature which we can soon repair ourselves.[1]

I cannot sufficiently praise the conduct of Captain Lotyrev of the *Panteleimon* during all the time he has been under my orders. When taking the soundings to discover the entrance into this port I had his personal assistance night and day and I reaped the most essential benefit from it. The bravery with which he attacked the galleys and batteries demands my warmest thanks and his active services in the dangerous employ of trying to save the *Syevernyi Orel* during the bad weather which prevailed all give the right to say that he has served his country ably, zealously and with good effect. I must not omit that, when he had furnished his quota for the descent, only 254 men remained on board his ship. I also owe my thanks to Capt. Lieut. Lomen for his conduct in this affair.

Capt. Lieut. Tutolmin conducted the landing of the troops with great resolution and good conduct under the fire of the enemy and he praises Lieuts. Lally, Ogilvie and Fondezin, who commanded the boats on this service.

Of the officers of my own ship I beg leave to recommend particularly Capt. Lieut. Aiken for the assistance he rendered me on this occasion.

My Lieuts. Shelting, Kushelev, Varrer and Golostenov set an excellent example to their men. The midshipmen Velikii, Odintsov and Moisyeev merit my praise. My Steersman and the greatest part of my officers and crew behaved well and I am satisfied with them.[2]

The good countenance and spirit of the troops under Lieut. Colonel Shiling whilst they advanced to the shore under the enemy's fire demand

[1] In the Russian version this paragraph comes at the end and includes three wounded in the *Syevernyi Orel.*

[2] *Author's note:* These names are written with Russ letters interspersed with the English, so that I can make little hand of them. [Kushelev and Varrer appear as Keymenilt and Suppet.]

my warmest praises and certainly contributed not a little to make the enemy so soon abandon the south battery.

The Lieut. Col. bestows particular praises on the Captains of his corps, Anton Weideman, Joachim Huck, Lieut. Peter Prande, Second Lieut. Boris von Wrangel, Franks Wiechtort, Gregory Embrachton. He praises also particularly the midshipman of the *Syevernyi Orel*, Andrei Polozov, for his resolution and good conduct in taking the troops ashore.

The conspicuous merit of Lieut. Keyser of the Engineers entitles me to say that his science, experience and resolution would do honour to a higher rank in his profession.[1]

As much merit as can be derived from misfortune is due to Capt. Palitsyn[2] of the *Syevernyi Orel* for his good disposition and activity in endeavouring to save his ship. . . .' [3]

It is not possible to read the detail in this admirable narrative without adjudging to the writer in an eminent degree all the great requisites of an able commander. Foresight, judgement, valour and perseverance unite with an active mind which seizes all advantages and obviates all difficulties. The plan of attack evinces great ability and promised full success, which however the Swedes should have caused to have been more dearly purchased. I am glad that the custom of the Russian navy required so minute a detail to be given of such an event. Till I found this letter I was much at a loss for many connecting circumstances.

It may not be amiss here to insert the list of the ships employed at the attack of Barö-sund as I find them named at the bottom of the plan of the attack, and where they are more distinctly written than I have found them elsewhere.

Russian Force

Ships of the line	Guns	Frigates	Guns	Cutters
Rodislav	66	*Bryatcheslav*	40	*Stchastlivyi*
Aleksandr Nevskii	74	*Nadezhda*	30	*Letutchii*
Panteleimon	66	*Sv. Mark*	22	*Yastreb*
Syevernyi Orel	66	*Pobyeditel*	bomb	*Sokol*

Swedish Force

A battery of twelve guns, 12-pounders.
A Battery of four guns, 30-pounders.
A frigate and chebec.
About fifteen galleys, five gunboats, a great number of armed boats and a cutter of 22 guns.

[1] These two paragraphs do not appear in the Russian version as printed. Names of military officers are given as written in the MS.

[2] *Author's note:* I cannot make out the name [blank in MS.], but it differs from that which will shortly appear in the list of the ships of the squadron.

[3] In the Russian version mention is made of 'the officers' instead of the Captain.

In another place I have a complete list of the squadron under the orders of Commodore Trevenen and I insert it here as showing the large force entrusted to him and the names of many of the officers serving with him.

	Guns			Cutters	Guns		
Rodislav	64	Trevenen	Commodore	*Baklan*	16	Grant	Lieut.
		Aiken	Capt. Lieut.	*Stchastlivyi*	12	Lally	do.
Syevernyi Orel	64	Palitsyn	2nd rank	*Letutchii*	16	Ogilvie	do.
				Lebed	16	Davydov[1]	do.
Aleksandr Nevskii	74	Zhochov	do.	*Gagara*	16	Brown	do.
				Sokol	10	——	
Panteleimon	64	Lotyrev	do.	*Yastreb*	10	Dunn	do.
Bryatcheslav	40	Lomen	Capt. Lieut.	*Kretchet*	10	Gamalyei	do.
Patrikii	30	Nefedyev	do.	*Neva*	10	Fondezin	do.
Gavriil	40	Pustoshkin	do.	*Olen*		Kashintsov	do.
Nadezhda	30	Smirnov	do.	(New Plan)			
Sv. Mark	20	Fondezin	Lieut.				
Pobyeditel	bomb	Tutolmin	do.		Transport		
Strashnyi	do.	Babaev	do.	*Anna Margarita*			

Porkala-udd Squadron—			
Iannuarii	64	Glyebov	1st rank
Evropa	64	Sukin	2nd do.
Volk cutter	12		

N.B. The squadron of attack is copied from the plan of attack; the whole squadron from a rough sketch of the Commodore's own writing.

By the following letters it appears that Velikii had been dispatched with the news of the capture of Barö-sund and I have thought it best to insert the congratulations from two such great men as Bezborodko and Tchernyshev immediately after the narrative of the event.

'Petersburg,
September 16, 1789

Sir,—The Empress in entrusting you with the command of one of her squadrons has given you a striking mark of her favour and of the value she attaches to your talents and zeal for her service.

Her Imperial Majesty sees with satisfaction that you have justified the choice she had made. You know her last orders through Vice Admiral Kruze and you will agree yourself, Sir, that the advanced season and the

[1] MS. has Deviedoff. Russian lists for this year give Ovsyannikov. There were several officers called Davydov. All names, both of ships and officers have been corrected, but all were quite recognizable.

want of the necessary means will not permit you at present to extend your operations. We shall be perfectly satisfied if you succeed in preserving the post you have occupied until the time comes for returning into our own ports, and in the mean time to endeavour to destroy their flotilla and to spread the alarm along the Swedish coast. The remainder must be reserved for the next campaign. We then intend to give you three other ships of the line, two or three large frigates, two frigates proper for the skerries, four chebecs, twelve gunboats which they have begun to build at Fredriskhamn, some boats for landing troops . . . .

The number of troops will be augmented and enterprizes of moment may be undertaken.

I remain with sentiments of the most distinguished consideration, Your very humble and very obedient servant, A. CTE. DE BESBORODKA.'

I have not been able to give the whole of his Excellency's letter as exact as I could wish, as he deals in French words which my dictionaries or vocabularies do not admit, and there are some other vessels named of which I can find no interpretation. The letter, however, is a convincing document of the sense the Empress and her Minister entertained of our Commodore.

Count Tchernyshev had been very attentive in forwarding letters during Commodore Trevenen's absence and they were always accompanied by polite and friendly notes. I translate the following, as it contains somewhat more than compliment.

'Petersburg,
September 18, 1789

SIR,—The Midshipman Velikii arrived yesterday and brought us the news of the capture of Barö-sund. I offer you my lively and sincere congratulations and feel on the occasion as a subject and a friend ought to feel.

As M. Velikii after leaving Court went directly to the Grand Duke at Gatchina, which would have delayed the delivery of your letter to Mrs. Trevenen, I took it and forwarded it immediately to relieve her from suspense and uneasiness. She has just sent me her answer by my old friend Mr. Farquharson and it accompanies this. There is nothing to add to the orders you will receive, unless to tell you that the loss of the *Syevernyi Orel* is in no way attributable to you. It remains only for me to offer my wishes for your perfect satisfaction and full success in all you shall undertake for the good of the service and to beg you to believe me with very particular esteem and consideration, Sir, your very humble and obedient servant, CZERNICHEW.

P.S. We have no news from Admiral Tchitchagov. The Prince de Nassau is here. The campaign is nearly finished with the galleys. There remains only one strong squadron near Fredrikshman, near the mouth of the Kymene. We have nothing to announce to you from the land side, but we are expecting great news from Moldavia with the Turks.'

Soon after the despatching of the letter to Admiral Kruze lately inserted the Commodore sent Lieut. Colonel Shiling on a reconnoitering part, when they surprised a village and in a skirmish with some troops killed about twenty of the enemy and burnt their barracks with the loss of only one killed and two wounded. Some more exact information was procured with respect to the situation of the flotilla, which had been driven from Barö-sund, but for want of galleys and gun-boats it was found only practicable to continue the blockade. All the remaining transactions at Barö-sund will be found in the following copy of a letter to Admiral Kruze.

No date, but near the end of September[1]

'In my last dispatches to your Excellency I had the honour to inform you of Lieut. Colonel Shiling's having surprised the enemy at the village not far from us and of my having heard that their frigate was aground near the land. I sent Lieut. Barrer of the Navy to discover whether this was true or not. He returned the same night with intelligence that the frigate was afloat and lying at her anchors with her topgallant masts struck, to all appearance to prevent her being seen over the hills. The village was abandoned by its inhabitants and occupied only by a few of the military, among whom there appeared no stir or unusual bustle. However, having been reinforced from the mainland, they made an attack on our post on shore a little before daybreak the same night[2] conducted by a corporal of the Esthonian chasseurs, who had deserted to them. They surprised and made prisoners our advanced picket and the second had hardly time to give the alarm before they were attacked and driven back to our batteries.

This[3] was first attacked by a number of armed peasants, who were quickly dispersed by the fire of our people, when the whole regiment of Dahl appearing surrounded the battery and poured in a very brisk fire from musketry and 3 field-pieces. The battery was defended by a double abbatis with chevaux de frise between them, by two pieces of cannon, 12-pounders, and two falconets; 200 soldiers under the command of Capt. Weideman of the chasseurs and 6 artillery men with a 2nd Lieut. to command them. It was also under the guns of the two ships,[4] particularly those of the *Aleksandr Nevskii,* which was at no more than 2 cables length from it and soon

[1] Parts of this despatch are printed in 'Materials for the History of the Russian Fleet,' Vol. 13, pp. 616–18. Its date was September 27.
[2] The 19th.
[3] *Sic* in MS.
[4] The Russian version has 'three ships'.

after the alarm began firing upon the enemy with round and grape. A reserve of 40 men from each ship was also ordered to be in constant readiness to reinforce the battery and accordingly attempted to push on shore, but from the suddenness of the alarm the enemy had time to post themselves at the landing place in such numbers as to prevent our troops landing. My own ship also quickly began firing to the left of the battery and we had the pleasure of seeing with great effect. The battery, thus surrounded by an infinitely greater number of men, was defended with the greatest resolution by Capt. Weideman, nor given up till stormed and carried after a most obstinate resistance in which about half his people were killed or wounded and he himself had received several wounds. Our people, when thus forced from their post, retired to the water's edge and found shelter under a rock from the fire of the Swedes. However, the latter kept not long possession of the battery, for the fire of our ships, no longer restrained by the fear of hurting our own people, now played upon them with great effect. They persisted to remain in it no longer than to carry off part of their killed and wounded, and then retired leaving everything in the situation in which they found it together with some stands of arms, swords, etc., etc.

Our boats quickly pushed ashore and again took possession of the post. The ships continued their fire as long as it might be supposed to have effect in the woods.

Of our people 27 were killed outright and of the many wounded several are since dead. Among the wounded are 3 officers, viz. Capt. Weideman, Lieut. Myakinin of Marines and the 2nd Lieut. of Sea Artillery [Maltsov]. Lieut. Myakinin is since dead of his wounds. Captain Weideman, though much wounded, will I hope recover. The bravery with which he defended the post entrusted to his charge cannot enough be praised. He quitted it not till wounded in several places and carried off by force by his own people; and if the enemy prevailed against him at last by their superior numbers, there is reason to think that by his brave defence their loss was much greater than ours. On the battery 15 of the enemy were found dead and one wounded, but likely to recover. A little further in the wood two more were found, and a sergeant who had been made prisoner and escaped about 2 versts from the battery found 15 men dead on the road at different distances. Among the dead at the battery was one officer; and a person who appeared to be the commanding officer was seen carried off by his own people after being struck down by a cannon ball. From the first of the affair to the last, which was about an hour and [a] half, the Swedes were observed carrying off their killed and wounded.

From the report of the prisoners this regiment of Dahl was on its road to reinforce the army and passing by was called in to make this attack on us.

Joined to the rest of the troops here they compose a body of between 2 and 3000 men and this whole regiment of 1300 together with a large body of armed peasants or chasseurs were employed at the attack of our battery. Immediately after our again taking possession I ordered it to be reinforced with more cannon and troops, but since, on account of the great superiority of the enemy in our neighbourhood, I have taken our troops and cannon on board and destroyed the works. However, we keep a picket on shore, that we may be informed of the enemy's motions.

On the [23rd] they opened a bomb-battery from a high hill commanding the passage to the north bay where the galleys lie, and threw many bombs among our frigates and cutters employed in blocking them up. Some of them I ordered to remove to a greater distance and towards evening the enemy ceased their fire, apparently from some accident that happened to them, as we perceived an explosion, after which they fired no more.

On the —— Lieut. Brown arrived in the *Gagara* cutter with your Excellency's orders.

As I am in expectation of fresh orders from your Excellency with regard to my remaining here or putting to sea, I beg leave to remark that ever since I came here on the 6th the wind has held so constantly to the east that I never could have got to sea with my squadron and it was with difficulty that the cutter which carried you my account of the capture of this place was able to make good her passage through the rocks. Now, the northerly winds making smooth water here and the passage out very narrow, it might be dangerous to keep the squadron here too long, as the coming on of an after easterly wind might keep us in for the winter, which must necessarily bring on the loss of the whole squadron.

I remain your Excellency's, etc. etc.'

I have no particulars of events during the remainder of the stay of the squadron in Barö-sund, but it appears that part of the Prince of Nassau's squadron or flotilla must have put in and been supplied with provisions,[1] of which the Commodore's ships began to find a want in early October. About the 5th or 6th of that month a Concilium of staff officers was called and it was unanimously agreed 'that on account of the lateness of the season and the dangers of this place it is necessary to withdraw the squadron and proceed to Revel with the first favourable wind and weather.'

On what day this resolution was put into effect I cannot find, but it appears that having according to the wishes of the Empress remained as long in possession of his post as the season permitted he got his squadron out of port in safety and proceeded towards Revel and in his way on

[1] This does not appear to have been the case.

Oct. 16th[1] met with that unfortunate accident of which I shall have occasion to speak at large in the sequel, but which has been already so well narrated in his letter to his mother of Nov. 7th.

But before I entirely take leave of Barö-sund I must insert two little detached sentences elucidating the character and describing the situation of the Commodore at the time of writing them. The first was written the 7th Sept. 1789, when in consequence of the reasons given in his letter to Admiral Kruze he had determined to make the attack by daylight.

'Resolved to begin the attack. Occupied in preparation for that purpose. Oh! my sweet wife and beloved friends! May the God of Heaven bless you! My conscience does not reproach me much and I have always considered the Almighty as more merciful than severe to judge.'

In the midst of such full occupation as the writer must have had at this time, how amiable, how admirable does the mind appear which snatched a moment to pen such a sentence!

The other is dated Sept. 15th.

'The exultation of triumph had restored my breast for some time, but now again that I become a prey to doubt and anxiety it begins to pain me severely. It is the business of a commander to overcome difficulties and this is so strongly impressed on my mind that I cannot easily yield to the impossibility of attacking the galleys; although, if it succeed, I am sure it must be with the loss of men on our side disproportionate to the object; and, if we fail, we hazard our small vessels upon rocks and banks from whence there would be no retreating and where they would be torn to pieces'.

The particulars of the loss of the *Rodislav* near Revel will appear when I come to give an account of the Court-Martial which was the consequence of that loss, but that did not take place for some months and I shall reserve it for its proper date. The following letter, however, to Admiral Tchitchagov, written while endeavours were using to save the old ship, is a good specimen of the clear and decisive way of informing a Commander in Chief that he neglects his duty.

'Sir,

My last report I sent by the *Slava* frigate. It was delayed some time by contrary winds. In it I have answered to what you ask me in your dispatch of the —— and as to the chance of saving the ship I have told you that it depends on your sending us pumps from the shore, as I tried in vain to get them from the *Vseslav*, Brigadier Makarov. I have before said that I believe the ship to be broke but as that is not absolutely certain it is

[1] Trevenen left Barö-sund on the 14th and was wrecked on the 15th.

necessary that I should make an effort to determine it. If we can diminish the water, there is yet a possibility of bringing her into Revel. But for this purpose I must tell your Excellency that expedition is absolutely necessary, for if there comes a strong wind from the north, the ship will certainly be altogether lost. I cannot help expressing my surprise that being so near such a port as Revel where there is an established Admiralty I have yet received no assistance from thence. I have not a single warp[1] in the ship and if we lighten her I must have warps. Our lower-deck ports are partly under water and although caulked yet the water has washed out the oakum and my few carpenters and caulkers are insufficient to stop them, nor have we here planks, nails or oakum. A ship-builder can better judge of the state of the ship than my Carpenter or myself and if she should be floated to judge better her leaks and deficiencies. And in all cases like this which I have ever seen before no time was lost in sending from the nearest port all sorts of officers, men and stores that might in any way assist in saving the ship or getting out her stores, if she was lost. Yet I have not received the least possible assistance, and whose-ever fault it may be getting the ship ashore, there is yet another fault will lie elsewhere. I mean the want of proper assistance to save her.

By the time you will have sent us the pumps, everything will be got out of the ship that can be without cutting up the decks. If we find the ship entirely lost, it remains with your Excellency how long the people shall remain fishing up the things in her hold, principally the 25 guns which are there, and how many men. For my own part, neither will my health permit a much longer attendance, nor do I think it at all decent that after having for so long a time commanded a considerable squadron with the approbation of her Majesty, I all at once through the fault of my steersman find myself degraded to the employment of fishing up two or three casks of salt beef from the hold of a sunken wreck.

I must further tell your Excellency that the season of the year renders it highly dangerous to keep vessels in this riding much longer. My people are also constantly exposed to imminent danger. The frigates do not lie within 3 versts of the ship, so that I cannot send them backwards and forwards every day, as half the time would be lost by that means. Therefore I am obliged to keep them on board the small vessels that lie near the ship and there they are huddled together without any convenience to the detriment of their healths, and as these are changed every day they cannot have their bedding or clothes with them. Add to this that our boats having served the whole compaign and having been exposed here to much weather

[1] *Author's note:* Hawsers or small cables for removing the ship from one place to another.

are all leaky and there is no safety in them when it blows any wind. Now, am I to risk my people in them in such an uncovered place, or my officers, or myself ——? —— —— ——.'

We have here a lively picture of the situation of the Captain and crew of the *Rodislav* and of the head and heart of old Tchitchagov. I can hardly despise that man enough to prevent my abusing him.

The *Rodislav*, however, was fated to remain on the shoal where her ignorant pilots had placed her and I know no further particulars of the time employed in saving her stores etc. or when the Commodore arrived at Revel.

Just as the *Rodislav* ran ashore Trevenen wrote a few lines to Capt. Dennison, thinking that he was at Revel. That officer, however, only received this note at Kronstadt and wrote instantly to Mr. Farquharson. He ends his letter thus: 'Thesiger's ship is also lost: I know no further particulars. It is Providence only that saves ships in the country. The whole squadron escaped by good fortune'.[1]

[The next few pages are mainly occupied by the author's somewhat fulsome praise of Trevenen and abuse of Tchitchagov and of the Russian service in general. A few portions are more worth including.]

It will be easily imagined that the Commodore, now indeed again only Capt. Trevenen, was eager to proceed to Petersburg, but I know not when he was able to do so. There is a note from Count Tchernyshev dated Oct. 29th which appears to reply to his request for leave and says: 'You have only some days longer to wait with patience'.

The first date I observe from Petersburg is Dec. 21st and I have now to lament great paucity of materials respecting the events of this winter, but I conclude that the Court Martial took up some time and I fear that neither his health nor spirits were good during that period. . . . He was much dissatisfied with his reception at Petersburg and very justly thought that his services merited more solid marks of approbation than a present of a gold sword, which the Empress made him about this time.

I have no letter or other document to connect my subject between the end of Dec. 1789 and Feb. 1790. On the 16th of this latter month Capt. Trevenen wrote to his mother to announce the joyful event of the birth of a daughter and the safety of the mother.

How far the proceedings of the Court Martial for the loss of the *Rodislav* broke in upon his time or comforts I cannot say, but I conclude

[1] Thesiger's ship, the *Vysheslav* 66, was one of eight ships which left Revel on October 18 for Kronstadt. Thick weather forced them to anchor near Rödskär, S.W. of Hogland. The rest of the division were able to continue their voyage next day, but the *Vysheslav* was driven ashore and lost.

that it took place at Kronstadt in the middle of January[1] and I shall here insert all the particulars that I have been able to collect. These consist of two or three written documents, the first a rough copy in English of the narrative of the loss of the ship, which is always given in by the Captain upon such an occasion in the British service and the truth of the narrative he is to substantiate in evidence. I conclude the following to be the narrative given to the Court Martial on the present occasion.

'The 16th of Oct.[2] in the morning was a very thick fog, as may be seen in the journal. As soon as it cleared away a little, I got under weigh from the coast of Finland and stood over towards Revel. The wind being at first light, I wished to go in between Nargen and Wolf, that the squadron might get in before night to a place of safety, as the weather looked threatening and stormy. I therefore asked my steersman if he could take me in that way. He answered in the affirmative. Having never been in that way myself nor reconnoitred the appearance of the land, I should not have thought of carrying the squadron through that way, if I had not had in the persons of my steersmen pilots on whom I thought I could depend, but should have gone between Nargen and Surop.[3] Having made Nargen and the Nova Mel[4] we stood on till we thought ourselves half-way between them and then shaped our course right over for the island of Wolf, which course would have carried us clear of the shoals, and then we intended to have hauled up in the large channel for Revel Road to the eastward of the two Red Flags. The wind at this time had freshened to a strong breeze and we went very fast through the water. Though there was no longer a fog, there remained after it a haze that overspread the land on both sides. We were however, going very well over to Wolf, when the steersman discovered a white flag a little on the starboard bow, which he said was the Wolf Flag. I told him it could not be, for that the Wolf Flag must be seen to the left hand of Wolf and this was to the right or nearly on with it. He answered me that the land I saw was not Wolf but land to the S.E., which ran farther out that way. I must take notice again that I had never been in this way, so as to be able to recognise the appearance of the land and judge for myself; and I was given to understand that the Wolf Flag was laid down much farther out to the N.W. than the chart showed it. Upon my objecting that this Flag could not be the Wolf from

[1] *Author's note:* But it will be found that the sentence was very long before produced.
[2] This date must be wrong. Tchitchagov wrote on the 15th having already heard from Trevenen of his misfortune. Apparently the stranding took place in the afternoon of the 15th, which would be counted as the 16th in the ship's log, the nautical day running from noon to noon.
[3] The point on the mainland S.W. from Nargen.
[4] This should be 'Novaya Mel', New Bank. A shoal about 4½ miles N.N.E. from Nargen.

its being so far off from it, my first Lieutenant said that it was a long way off from Wolf. I then asked the Steersman, where was the Nargen White Flag, if this was the Wolf. He answered that the Nargen flag must have been knocked down by the *Simeon* frigate, when she ran aground.[1] Thus my remarks which tended to show the true course of the ship, were rendered of no effect by those in whom I placed my chief reliance. The haze after the fog I have mentioned rendered the land so obscure that no judgement could be formed of distances, for Wolf appeared at least as near as Nargen. In the meantime we were running so quick that after seeing the flag we were soon up with it. There was not time for deliberation or for verifying our position by the compass. What remained for me to do? I had made my objections: I had pointed out the errors we were making: and was overruled by those who had often been here before and consequently must know better than I could. If I had any confidence in the chart, I should not have been overruled; but the error of a point in the compass and the supposed errors of the chart would have made all the difference of the bearings of the two flags. The steersman supported his opinion by pointing out the two Red flags to the right of the White flag and this was what led him into the error.

As I have said before, there was no time to deliberate and we hauled up to go to windward of the flag and ran aground upon the point of the Nargen shoal about a verst from the flag and according to several bearings not on [a] shoal by [the] chart.

I must take notice that the haze was the original cause of this mistake by rendering it impossible to judge of distances and thereby carrying us nearer Nargen than we ought to have gone. This is proved by our seeing two Red flags to the right of the White flag.

Had we been on coming in with Nargen really, as we judged we were, half way between Nargen and the Nova Mel, we should have been in no danger, for we should have had a clear run over to Wolf without the Nargen flag coming at all in our way and should have made the two red flags properly to the left of the Nargen flag and have hauled round them in safety.

The haze then in deceiving us as to the distance from Nargen was the original cause of the mistake and loss of the ship; to which circumstances I beg the Court's particular attention.

For my own part, what could I do more than I did? In the English service the Master has altogether the charge of the ship in pilot-water and I had two steersmen of Officers' rank on board the ship whom I supposed, and had a right to suppose, acquainted with the places and given me on that

[1] The *Simeon* went aground on September 21, but this was on the Novaya Mel, which they had already passed.

very account and to do the exact duty of our Masters. Could it then enter into my head or is it reasonable that any regulation should require of me to take charge of the ship in a place I have never seen before? Had I imagined it, I never would have accepted of a command in the service, for I defy any man to be a good pilot for places he has never seen. It is absolutely necessary to be acquainted with the appearances of the land. Yet I pointed out to the steersman his errors and it will, I imagine, appear that, if I had conceived myself to have the charge of the ship, I should have carried her through safe by the bearings of the land. But, if I have the charge of the ship, why have a steersman? If I am to depend on their knowledge, how am I responsible for the consequences? Or, if I am not to depend upon their knowledge, why have I them? Whatever their use I never conceived myself to have the charge of the ship in pilot-water; nor can I, nor ever shall I conceive it consistent that, having two steersmen, officers, whose duty it is to know the place and its appearances, the ship can be supposed to depend upon one who has never seen the place. Had I had no pilots, the ship had been safe.

On the Swedish coast, where I had no reason to depend upon my steersmen, I carried a numerous squadron in safety through much more dangerous places than the entrance of Revel Bay, except the *Syevernyi Orel*, which was lost in battle. There I looked upon myself as answerable for the squadron, because my Pilots could have no knowledge. In pilot-water I never did, nor ever can think it consistent with justice. January 22, 1790, JAMES TREVENEN.'

The next and most material paper is a copy of Captain Trevenen's defence, by which it appears that the 1st Lieut. and pilots had made an attempt to throw the blame of the loss of the ship on the Captain. The Defence is in French and the following is a translation.

'Reply of James Trevenen, knight and Captain of the highest Rank, to the accusation of Lieutenant Shelting and of the Pilots Yani Vran and Yanikov.[1]

1st. It is asserted by these officers that I had before passed several times between the Nargen and Wolf, that I had seen the flags and therefore ought to know the passages.

I beg the Court, however, to remark that it is not said that I had come from the sea into the Bay of Revel. I had only gone from thence to sea; and I must add that between Nargen and Nova Mel I had neither passed in nor

[1] These names are written as Jani Vrana and Janikoff. The first is mentioned in Materials for the History of the Russian Fleet', but the second is not.

out. Of course I could not know the least of the passage in debate. For it does not suffice to have seen at a distance the flags of Nova Mel, of which I never doubted but that the colour was Red or White as marked in the charts, but it is necessary to have seen from that side the appearance of the land, which alone could supply the necessary knowledge to assist the judgement of the person coming in.

When I have entered the Bay of Revel, it was *within* the Wolf Island,[1] and it will be granted that to have seen a piece of land on one side does not at all inform you what is its appearance on the other.

On leaving a bay in the entrance of which there are dangers, we are more occupied in avoiding those that are before than in paying attention to the shores that are passed (except when it is only by the bearing of those shores that those dangers are to be avoided). Also, the few times which I have come out of the Bay were in time of war and either in company with a numerous fleet or being myself commander of a squadron, under which circumstances attention is to be paid to signals and many other points of duty and either a captain of a ship or commander of a squadron is generally far otherwise occupied than to think of becoming Pilot.

But I must repeat that even in going out of the Bay of Revel it was always by the side of the Wolf. On the other side, near Nargen, I never either went in or out, and if any importance can be attached to the knowledge of the Flags, I can say that I never in my life saw the Flag near Nargen, where my ship was lost.

2nd. Lieutenant Shelting asserts that, suspecting the danger, I was able to have gone back to sea.

It is only unfortunate for me that this idea has struck him so late; and for him that it was his own counsel joined to that of my pilots which lulled the doubts I had conceived and that without him and without them we should have been in safety. For the Court has seen that the *Rodislav* was steering a very proper course towards the Wolf island and that there was neither danger nor cause to suspect danger but at the moment in which we approached the Flag of Nargen, which the Pilot insisted to be that of the Wolf.

The Court will have also seen by the account I have already given of the remarks I made to the Pilots, that if at this moment I had followed my own judgement, I should have gone past the Flag in continuing my course towards Wolf and no danger would have existed. But it was entirely the confidence of my Pilots and of Lieut. Shelting—all three used to the passage

[1] In spite of the emphasis laid on this statement it must be pronounced impossible. Trevenen must mean 'close to', but even then he could not have seen the other side of the island. He also contradicts his previous statement that he had never sailed *into* the bay, but only out. In any case, he had entered Revel from the sea at the end of the operations of 1788.

—which led them to combat my ideas, lulled my fears, which would have put my ship in safety. It was, I say, this confidence on their part which has lost the ship. And this appears to me a full answer to this insinuation.

But this is not all. My Captain-Lieutenant Aiken said to the pilot, in approaching the danger, that if he had the smallest doubt, he had better put out to sea. The Pilot was confident in himself and neglected this good counsel.

See what a misplaced compassion for these men (whom the remains of the fog had so unfortunately deceived) had led me to pass over in silence. Their accusations, altogether ill-placed, oblige me to say everything and to insist strongly on this part of my defence.

3rd. If I did not ask the advice of Lieut. Shelting upon the passage, it was that in reading the tenth article of the Pilots' instructions I saw that in the places where the Officers were not acquainted and the Pilot was, that he alone was responsible for the ship.

Now, not knowing the passage, I asked the Pilot if he knew it and he answered 'Yes'. I concluded then that he was entirely answerable and after all I have seen of service during 17 years that I have been at sea I am entirely of opinion that one man can only well perform one duty and that it is that of the officer of the watch to take care of the masts and sails and, under orders, of manoeuvres. But, if he apprehended danger, it was his duty to have informed me of it. Is an officer justifiable in having neglected his duty from pique or a point of ceremony?

But notwithstanding this and although Lieut. Shelting would insinuate that his advice was not asked, it is no less true that unfortunately for me he gave it. This so important advice was given on the side of the Pilot: he combated my opinions and believed that it was the Flag of the Wolf which we saw. I could easily doubt the truth of a chart which I have found full of errors and of my compasses which never agreed within a point of each other.[1] These three persons, that is to say my Lieut. Shelting and the Pilots Vran and Yanikov, were used to the passage. Of course I yielded and it is thus that the unfortunate advice of Lieut. Shelting contributed to lay aside my doubts and to lose my ship.

4th. Here is an accusation very useless and very malicious which is not part of the duty of a pilot, which could not exculpate anyone, if true, and which could only serve to throw blame needlessly upon me. It is, that I neglected the means of getting my ship off the shoal.

Nevertheless it is easy for me to reply. When I saw the *Aleskandr Nevskii*, a ship of the line, the *Gavriil* frigate and the *Lebed* cutter had fallen into the

[1] *Author's note:* Some particular errors of the chart are mentioned which I cannot make out.

same misfortune as my own ship, I thought it my duty as commander of the squadron to seek for the best means of saving all these vessels; and even if I had found it for the good of her Imperial Majesty's service to combine our efforts to save one, even by abandoning all the others, I should have taken that part without considering whether it was my own ship or another. I do not see the merit of seeking individual benefit at the expense of her Majesty's service. If I am to blame, as they say, I can only say in my excuse that it is the effect of my education and that unfortunately I have not yet lost the idea it has inspired me with.

For this time, however, it happens that the means which were used to save the *Gavriil* frigate were also the best that could be devized to get my own ship out of danger also.

I hope to prove this and I assert, whatever these officers may say, that my ship was much more firmly fixed on the shoal than the others. Also she was nearer the middle of the bank to leeward: the others were only on the point of the bank and to windward.

If the stern of my ship was not so fixed as the fore part, this was principally owing to her situation which turned her stern towards the wind in such a way that the sea, which ran very high, beat over her with great force, lifted that part and caused it to strike violently against the bottom. These officers ought to have remarked that there was in no part water enough for the ship to float in. As far as I recollect, forwards there were about 17 feet of water on the starboard side, 19 feet on the larboard side and abaft 19. The ship required 19 ft. and $\frac{1}{2}$ to float her. These things considered, I maintain that the means which I used were the best possible, as well for the general good as for that of my own ship in particular, from the following reasons. 1st: Because the *Gavriil* frigate was to windward and nearly in the direction by which it was necessary that the ship should be got off and was more easily and quickly removed from danger than my ship, which had double the distance to make.

2ndly. Because I had but two warps,[1] of which I think one was of 25 pood, the other 13. These might easily haul off the frigate, though they could do nothing for my ship.

3rdly. Because the frigate, being got off the shoal, could not only have let go her anchor and sent me the end of her cable, which was the only efficacious means of saving my ship, but also she might have assisted me with all her warps.

[1] *Author's note:* I translate the word Verp to be Warp, a small kind of cable, but the word is not French, as far as I know. There are throughout this Defence some Russian technical terms of which I have given the English judging of their meaning by the context. They are described as of so many *pood*, i.e. a certain number of feet of one cable weighed 25 pood, the same length of the smaller weighed only 13 pood. A pood is 40 lb. English Apothecaries' weight.

4thly. Because Mr. Pustoshkin having carried away a stream cable[1] and demanded assistance from me, I saw that, if no one assisted him, neither he nor I could have got our ship off and both had been lost.

I therefore determined first to get off the frigate, which was lighter, more to windward and less firmly fixed. Add to this that it was better worth to save this new and fine frigate than my old and rotten ship.

I therefore sent my stream cable to the frigate and it is that which saved her. But the wind was so strong that being off the shoal three warps could hardly hold her and she dared not attempt to haul farther off for fear of their breaking and of the ship again driving on the bank.

Is it to be believed, then, that my warp only could have saved me? Or rather is it not clear that in sending to the *Gavriil* I saved that frigate and that this was also the best means of saving my own ship? The frigate not daring to heave further ahead she could not let go her anchor, when she was in danger of striking upon it, and indeed there it would not have been of service. The anchor of the *Panteleimon* was also lost, although there was a very experienced officer in the boat, and left me without resource.

My small warp of 13 pood not being of any service to me, I sent it to the *Lebed* and I believe it was that which got her off the shoal. Not being able to do any more for myself I sent my boats to assist the *Aleksandr Nevskii.* As to Lieut. Shelting and the Pilot Yanikov I do not recollect, but I aver that Vran said 'we ought to save ourselves first'. Also at that moment I knew well that these were words thrown out on purpose and were those of a man who cared not for her Majesty's service, but for himself.

At last the ship broke. We worked severely and incessantly to save all that it was possible to save, and on the 9th day, as well as I recollect, a storm took her completely away.'

It appears to me from the above defence that the Court Martial would have been a thing of course, as it is in England on the occasion of the loss of a ship of war, and that the Lieutenant and Pilots above-mentioned, finding that blame very justly attached to them and must appear so to the Court, had worked up a charge against their Captain in hopes of giving the affair a different turn.

The result of the Court was:

The Captain and Captain-Lieutenant are entirely acquitted:
The Pilots to lose rank for a year:
The Lieutenant to lose his promotion for a year:[2]

Unless they get good certificates.

[1] *Author's note:* A rope larger than a warp, but smaller than the cable by which the ship generally rides at anchor.

[2] He was promoted in 1792, having been in command of small craft in the interval.

Now it appears to me that in England the charges would have been declared both frivolous and malicious and utterly unfounded. The Lieut. would have been put at the bottom of the list and the Pilots made over to the Marshalsea for a year to recollect themselves.

I have before mentioned that the Court Martial took place at Kronstadt in the middle of January, but by the date of the following memorandum, which I was truly sorry to see inserted in one of the manuscript books, it will appear that the sentence was long delayed.[1] In the mean time Capt. Trevenen had been appointed to the command of the *Netron menya*,[2] of the same force as the *Rodislav*, I believe.

Everything that has as yet appeared of Count Tchernyshev has been so perfectly friendly and to all appearances warmly and zealously so, that it gives me pain to insert the following conversation. But as Capt. T. thought it of importance enough to minute it in his Journal, it would be improper in me to omit it.

'*March* 21*st*. I called upon Count Tchernyshev and told him I could not think of fitting out the ship I was appointed to, whilst a Court Martial was sitting on me for the loss of the other. He told me the Court Martial would soon be finished. I answered, there was no appearance of it. I had been told 3 or 4 times already that it was finished and I was convinced it had been finished and that at those times everybody was satisfied, but that going home to their closets and possessing the wish of finding out something against me as a foreigner, they constantly returned from thence with some fresh charge and therefore I saw no probable end of those tricks. "*A propos*", says he, "I have great reason to complain of you. You know I have always been your friend and am so still. Why, then, did you not come to me frankly and tell me how matters went, that I might have assisted you? I might have spared you some uneasy nights".

I did not choose to say that, imagining there could be no influence in the case, I trusted myself alone to the justice of my cause, but said I did not think it depended upon his Excellency, but merely upon the Court Martial. "Ah", says he, "I beg your pardon. I could have saved you a great deal". Again, thought I to myself, "Why then did you not, since you are so much my friend?" But I said: "Then all your Excellency can complain of is that I have been wanting to my own interests". "It is very true", says he, "that you have". I then told him that my reason for not caring about the matter was the total indifference I had for the Russian service, in which I saw nothing but toil and trouble, misery and envy,

[1] A report of the Court Martial, but not its findings, was entered in the Admiralty Journal for April 25.

[2] *Author's note:* In English *Touch me not.*

without any advantages. He differed as to the advantage, for though, says he, "our pay is small, yet in the manner in which you are regarded here you might have found the highest hopes of future advantage. You are esteemed by the Empress and all that ranks in Russia. Your misfortunes even have done you credit; for, having in your memoir on the subject foreseen them, predicted them and yet offered yourself to encounter them; when they really happened to you, everybody agreed in exculpating you and even in doing honour to you".

I told him I only wished to quit the service in peace, though I had the Empress's promise in writing that quitting that of England should have been much to my advantage. He was hurt at this and said that doubtless I might do as I pleased, yet he would advise me to stay and apply myself to their language and service. He could mean nothing but the intrigues of the service and upon the whole I plainly saw that his object had been to reduce me to a dependence upon him by interesting himself for me and doing me some service on this occasion; and, as I had not courted him, he was vexed at having missed his aim and therefore, I suppose, might have even encouraged the virulence of others against me.'

[The next three pages contain a letter to Penrose himself dated April 12th, partly concerned with family matters and partly with repeating his views on the Russian service. The following is a characteristic extract.]

'And this has been the peculiar harshness of my situation ever since I have been in Russia, to have had such commands as admitted not so much of brilliant as of solid advantage to the country; because my tools alone of all the officers employed were unfit for the business. You will immediately except this from the general vulgar proverb, when I explain that I had to act among rocks with ships, while others either had galleys among rocks or ships in the open sea. In such a situation it was impossible to have success without some misfortune. My last year's business was dreadful from these situations, and when I had overcome all the difficulties that opposed themselves to my possibilities and when the last and capital stroke was rendered easy, my hand was withheld in its descent and I was robbed of my due honour and reward. I mean when I had forced the Swedish post, taken their batteries and their galleys were retired in confusion into shoal water, I, alas, had nothing to follow them with and they remained blocked up till the autumn. However, for the business of taking their post and stopping their commerce I expected to have had my order a button-hole higher, as you express it, and I have it not.'

Chapter 4

THE BATTLE OF VIBORG

The season for action now approached and the first of it seems to have been seized by the Swedes to make an attack upon one part of the Russian navy before a junction could be formed with the other. Admiral Tchitchagov commanded the part laid up at Revel: Admiral Kruze at Kronstadt. The *Netron menya* was in this last part and in the division commanded by Povalishin. The Kronstadt fleet consisted of eighteen or twenty sail of the line.

Capt. Trevenen's health was at this time in a very indifferent state and such as would fully have justified his retiring from the service, but his gallant spirit could not brook this measure at the opening of a campaign likely to be a very busy one.

In letters dated May 4th and 10th to Count Bezborodko and Mr. Lvov, Capt. T. was under the necessity of stating how totally inadequate his pay was to the support of his rank even with the greatest economy. His two separate commands had led him to great expenses in keeping a hospitable table, particularly on account of the Land Officers embarked with him, some of whom were put on board without the time to make any provision for themselves. A great disappointment also had happened, as the unexpected attack of the Swedes had put aside all thoughts of the separate command which had been promised, which we must naturally conclude would have led to promotion.

In consequence of the letters above mentioned he received a present of 1000 Ducats,[1] which was announced to him by the following letter from Count Bezborodko.

'May 13, 1790

SIR,—The Empress thinks always of your services and is ready to seize all the occasions in her power to give you proofs of her munificence. Her Imperial Majesty has directed me to send you 1000 Ducats for the use of the campaign and of your house. Her Majesty hopes that your state of convalescence will soon permit you to employ your zeal at a time when a rencontre with the enemy is certain; but she begs you to husband your

[1] *Author's note:* I believe the value of Russian money has varied at different times. In a table of Russian money a ducat is said to be equal to two roubles—a rouble worth 4*s.* 6*d.*

health and take care of it. As to Mr. Velikii, the Empress thinks he may be embarked on board another ship in case you are not able to go on board yourself. I am with every sentiment of esteem and attachment, Sir, your very humble and obedient servant, A. C. DE BESBORODKA.

This letter would have come with a much better grace had it not been for the two others I have mentioned. The campaign opened by a daring, though irregular attack made by the Swedes on the Revel squadron,[1] and so badly was it disposed by Tchitchagov that if the Duke de Sudermania had possessed a tolerable share of nautical skill, he might have made a serious impression. As it was, he made a precipitate retreat with the loss of one line-of-battle ship.

It appears that his Royal Highness had chosen rashness for his order of the day; for no sooner had he received this disgraceful check at Revel than he sailed with all expedition up the Gulf of Finland and appeared off Kronstadt before the fleet under Admiral Kruze was well under weigh.

This was a most interesting moment; for Capt. Trevenen's health was at this time in a very indifferent state and the enemy close at hand. His ship, I believe, sailed out of port before he joined, but he quickly followed in a yacht which was ordered to attend him, and joined in good time before his services were wanted. I know not the exact day, but it must have been after the 13th of May, as the letter of which the following is a translation is dated on that day.

[A few lines omitted.]

The letter is to Count Bezborodko.

Petersburg,
May 13, 1790

MONSIEUR LE COMTE,—The moment that Count Tchernyshev informed me that our fleet was to proceed immediately to sea I sent to my physician earnestly pressing him to allow me to depart as soon as possible, stating to him the probability of an approaching battle.

His answer, which your Excellency has probably seen, I sent to Count Tchernyshev. It forbids me to set out and I am obliged to submit to his direction, particularly as he farther told me that in going aboard in my present state I should expose myself to the risk, not only of being useless in the fleet at present, but also for all the remainder of the campaign.

The properest measure I can pursue is to continue to nurse myself for two days, when, if the contrary wind continues (which I cannot help

[1] *Author's note:* Trevenen had always pointed out the possibility of an attack on the fleet at Revel. Had we commenced hostilities against Russia at this time, as was once expected, Revel would have been soon in our power. It was reconnoitred by an English officer at this time preparatory to its being attacked.

praying may be the case), I shall still find our fleet at Kronstadt. If it is sailed, I will, with permission, get on board some cutter or boat to endeavour to join it. In the meanwhile my bed, provisions, clothes, etc. are all embarked and I have only to follow in person. If after all I am not in time to be useful in one way, I shall be in another, and it is a matter of indifference to me in what place I am of use. I hope in spite of this sickness that I shall not pass an idle summer.

I have received the money which you were so good as to send me on the part of her Imperial Majesty. This new proof of her munificence penetrated me with gratitude and attachment, and no less so does your Excellency's letter, so full of kindness. I never doubted either of one or the other, but knowing the important concerns in which your Excellency is engaged I was not willing to trouble you with my wants till they were pressing, as I had the honour to say to your Excellency. At present I am at my ease to think of matters different from domestic concerns.

Meanwhile (with submission) I cannot bring myself to believe that the Duke de Sudermania will dare to hazard an engagement which must eventually prove to his disadvantage, perhaps to his destruction, which is well within the chapter of accidents, considering the proximity of the Revel fleet and the force of our ships in general. Further, I beg your Excellency to be assured that I have nothing so near at heart as to be aboard the fleet and to believe in the respectful attachment with which I have the honour to be—etc. etc.

P.S. I should not have been surprised if the Duke of Sudermania had attempted another attack on our fleet at Revel, but that he should attempt the one at Kronstadt surprises me much. I have recommended Mr. Velikii to the care of my Capt. Lieutenant till I can embark myself.'

We shall soon see that the opinions entertained in this letter respecting the fleets were founded on a most sound judgement.

In a very few days after the date of the above letter Capt. Trevenen joined his ship, and I have reason to believe that, if the Russian fleet had sailed at all from Kronstadt, it must have anchored again close by.[1]

On the 23rd of May the fleet under Admiral Alexander von Kruze[2] had hardly got under sail when the fleet of the enemy was seen at a great distance.[3] This was very eminently a situation to show the character of a commander and Kruze showed himself worthy of the charge he sustained. Having the weather gage he gallantly resolved upon an immediate attack,

[1] The fleet had left Kronstadt on May 12, but had gone no farther than Styrsudden, some twenty-five miles to the west.

[2] *Author's note:* This gentleman had served seven years in the British fleet.

[3] The Swedes were actually sighted on the 21st, but no action took place till the 23rd.

although the Swedes had 22 ships of the line and 8 large frigates, whilst his force amounted to only 16 sail of the line and 9 frigates.[1] But Kruze knew that this was not the time to count the number of guns and weight of metal, and about 4 in the morning, he engaged and totally defeated them, but owing to the backwardness or unskilfulness of some of the Russian captains, the blow was not followed up. This ignorance or hesitation gave confidence to the beaten enemy, who taking advantage of a change of wind in the afternoon of the same day made an undecisive[2] attack upon the Russians.

On the 24th the Swedes, still retaining the weather gage, made another attack, but with no better success. Admiral Kruze appears by all accounts to have done his duty in these rencounters and evinced both judgement and resolution. By this time, however, the Swedes were convinced that Tchitchagov and the Revel Fleet must be near at hand, and to avoid the apprehended evil of being placed between the two fleets, rashly and most foolishly entered Viborg Bay, the whole coast of which was in possession of Russian troops and from whence their escape was morally impossible, if the Russian commander after the junction of their whole force had acted with common prudence or spirit. Many papers relating to this event I shall find occasion to insert in an appendix, but I have judged it right to break very little in upon the narrative during the remaining part of the memoirs.

Some little misunderstanding took place between Admiral Kruze and Capt. Trevenen owing to the former having neglected to mention him in his public dispatches in the way in which he judged himself to be entitled, and Trevenen wrote to Bezborodko as well as the Admiral himself on the subject. Kruze, who appears to have been a man of habitual indolence of disposition, did all he could to make amends and assured Trevenen that he had since written in such a way as would be more satisfactory to him than if he had been more particularly mentioned in the first despatches.[3] The Empress, however, had such a sense of his services that she distinguished him with the 3rd order of St. Vladimir and Capt. Lieut. Aiken was promoted to 2nd Captain.

It was with very much pleasure that I found a letter dated soon after this new mark of distinction from Count Tchernyshev written with all the warmth of apparent friendship and indeed evincing great solicitude and well-timed recollection; so that I hope the conversation inserted in page [208] had no future consequences.

[1] The Swedes had twenty-two battleships and two heavy frigates in the line, the Russians seventeen battleships, five of them 100-gun ships.

[2] *Sic* in MS.

[3] *Author's note:* More of this will appear in the Appendix No. 3.

It should be remarked here that the three last actions were so near Kronstadt that the guns were distinctly heard at that place and even at Petersburg. We must easily judge the great degree of anxiety suffered by the friends of those who were fighting their battles at their very doors.

The present position of the two fleets was at a very short distance from Petersburg and hostile navies have seldom been placed in a more interesting situation. The Swedes had retreated into a port near the great naval arsenal of Russia and the capital city and were very soon straitened for supplies of all sorts of provisions. Their fleet in this bay might perhaps have been so arranged as to have made an attack upon it a very hazardous measure on the part of the Russians; yet with a superior force and such an advantage of situation from a ready supply of bombs, fireships, gun-boats etc. an enterprising Admiral could not have hesitated to adopt that measure.

But old Tchitchagov, calculating that want of supplies would soon oblige the Swedes to force their way out, conceived that he had a surer part to act, not doubting but that he could effectually destroy them when driven to their last resource.

The Russian officers at this moment thought themselves sure of their prey and the Russian Government made no doubt of a brilliant and decisive victory. But Greig did not now command the Russian fleet and Tchitchagov did. Happy had it been for Russia if the Revel fleet had sailed without their Admiral.

Tchernyshev expresses the highest surprise at the step the Swedes had taken and Brigadier Dennison in a letter at this time writes: 'We have at last the Swedish fleet blocked up and so situated that no one ship can escape, if it be not our own faults'. He proceeds to say that their situation was such that the victory would be obtained without personal risk to the conquerors. 'Trevenen is quite well and you may assure his wife that he is pretty safe now, as we are two to one against them.'

During this time, however, Capt. T. continued to have severe returns of a sore throat and fever, sometimes to such a degree as almost to induce him to return to Petersburg for cure; but the hopes of seeing an end to this singular position of affairs made him persevere.

[Here the author mentions a letter from Trevenen to Farquharson, and apparently lost, but in his Appendix 4 he explains that the letter has been found and gives the whole of it, as follows.]

'To Mr. Farquharson

DEAR SIR,—You accuse me of being resolved not to write you, whereas every letter I have written to my wife has been marked on the back *to either*, that whichever got it first might reap the benefit of all the intelligence it contained, and my illness has never permitted me to be much of a penman since I have been on board. It could not well be otherwise than that the enormous fatigues I underwent after leaving you should have brought on another attack of my sore throat and fever; and this I foresaw so plainly that I resolved to be prepared for it by the greatest care in eating and drinking. I never pulled off my clothes after leaving you, but once at Kronstadt, till we had got the Swedes fast locked up in Viborg Sound, except also that I once or twice shifted myself in part on account of having got wet through. I have now got rid a second time of all sore throat and fever, but my strength and appetite are far from being yet returned. I have been only twice out on deck and I do not think yet of quitting my ship. I am, however, rejoiced that according to all appearances I shall be able to assist at the coup de grace, that it will be in our power to give the Swedish fleet as soon as ever the Prince[1] joins us. You ask me why the Swedes were not beat instead of being blocked, a question Admiral Tchitchagov alone can answer. Ten thousand reports are circulated in the fleet, as that he saw us engaging, but was too prudent to bear down till the thing was decided. This is certain, that they heard us engaging and a council was held thereupon, where only one captain was of opinion that they should endeavour to join us as soon as possible. Of whom exactly this council consisted I do not know, but that Captain was Sivers (not Dennison's) a Livonian.[2] The rest was of opinion that it was better to wait the event, so they came to an anchor between Hogland and Seskär. Traitors to their country and unworthy of the rewards they got at Revel, where they all agree only 4 Swedes engaged them properly. Thus the Swedes, by favour of a fog and calm which succeeded, and the assistance of their flotilla were permitted to retire towards Viborg, where we followed them as slowly as you please, but with so little other necessary precaution that in the finest weather in the world two of our ships grounded and it required six hours of the same fine weather to get them off again. Thank God, the fine weather did last long enough.

Were I to dwell upon every folly we have committed, or rather every necessary thing we have left undone since we came here, I should never have done, and moreover it would be indiscreet. It is much more agreeable to praise than to blame. Admiral Kruze showed much resolution, coolness and intrepidity in the conduct of his fleet, which was rendered the more difficult to him by his having been unprepared with the necessary signals

[1] Prince Nassau-Siegen, commander of the Russian galley fleet.

[2] Iochim von Sivers was captain of the *Izyaslav* in the Revel squadron. Dennison was at this time in commmand of the rowing-frigates and Georgii von Sivers was probably one of his officers.

for such a command and thereby obliged to deliver out many of his orders by sending boats, a method equally tedious and insufficient. I understand from others, for I have seen him but once since the action, that he does me the honour to consider me as the one captain that best seconded him, notwithstanding which he was going to forget me in his first despatches. I wrote him an angry letter about it, as soon as I understood the business, but I have now reason to be perfectly satisfied with his intentions and we are the best friends in the world by messages. Were he to command a fleet again, I should much like to be his signal-captain, in which place I think I could be more useful than as commander of a single ship, that department having been exceedingly defective with him. As to his hot fiery character, I think I could manage that with as much ease as you would do a fiery horse. He has an honesty and sincerity about him that is much preferable to the civil dissimulation of the old monkey.

I have written to both Counts, but much more particularly to Bezborodko, and have told him everything we have to do. I have asserted the certainty of our destroying the Swedes by a proper mode of attack? which I have offered to project and lead to execution, as soon as we are brought near enough to reconnoitre more particularly the enemy's situation. I should be quite sure of succeeding if I were seconded well; and I should esteem it as a very great piece of military good fortune. But it cannot be. They cannot give me the command, nor would old Tchitchagov consent to be taught what he does not know, though I would be content without any more of the honour than her Majesty's being acquainted with the part I had in it. Because he beat the Swedes at an anchor, he imagines every fleet at an anchor to be invincible; whereas, unless both wings be so secured as not to be attacked separately, such a position is good for nothing. Now I only require the assistance of our galley fleet to keep theirs employed and a battery upon the land to keep the wing of the Swedes which extends to it at a distance from it, and then, besides sending different machines to carry fire and confusion amongst them, I would fall upon that wing with a much superior force and should have no doubt of beating it, after which the rest would fall of course. The misfortune of being at an anchor in such a case would prevent them from seconding each other and plainly prove the folly of imagining all situations at anchor alike. It would be just as much to the purpose to swear that all the wigs in the world were alike. So much for those who prove one thing by another that has no resemblance to it. I have desired the Count, if he does not disapprove of my ideas, just to signify as much to me, as at present I am labouring with great zeal without knowing all the time whether I am not drawing on myself the imputation of presumption. Of the certainty of my plan I am fully convinced and that it would be attended with little loss. But you must take care, my dear Sir, not to mention this to our dear Betsy, as she would not only be frightened, but quarrel with me for it. You give me great pleasure by praising my little girl; I long to see her. Mr. Morris's packet contained only newspapers giving an account of the *Guardian* and the noble conduct of my friend Riou who commanded her. He is one of the finest, handsomest, best made, strongest, honestest, cleverest and noblest fellows that ever old England produced, and the whole of his conduct exhibits the very man such as I have known him from a child.

I return to the Swedes. A day or two past 40 deserters from one of their watering parties were brought on board by our Cossacks, amongst them a sort of officer who asserts they are in a miserable condition; the King on board the galleys and the Prince on board the fleet. The latter never shows himself of late. Poor wretches! They were before short of provisions and now are reduced to half allowance. Water also little and bad, and they are afraid of sending for more, lest their people should all desert. The officers, he says, exert themselves wonderfully to keep up the people's spirits, to which end they tell them ten thousand lies. They had 15 or 20 killed in many ships during the actions and were so fatigued that the people dropped dead from their guns. Well they might, for whilst we contented ourselves with looking at them they kept up a constant roar the whole day at such a distance sometimes that not one shot in ten reached.[1] If you come down here at the time we engage them, I shall refuse you entrance, I believe, unless you will consent to go down in the cockpit in case of coming to action, for I should not like the trouble of taking care of any of your broken limbs, nor what my wife would say to me on the subject. So make up your mind before you come. I will be much obliged to you to be very discreet as to many parts of this letter and cautious of showing it to any but those on whom you can depend. If you come or send by any good opportunity, I shall be much obliged to you for different articles of which I am much in want. I thought I had taken with me paper enough for a long while, but it is nearly done already, as I have many borrowers about me, besides the great use I make of it myself. 2 or 3 pounds of the same portable soup you gave me would be very acceptable. It is much better than Miss Frazer's, takes up little room and eats nothing. The servant who buys it can also get me 10 pounds of sago, an article I am in great want of and have not. Some good English, Dutch or Holstein butter would be very acceptable.

Adieu my dear Sir. Dennison is ordered to Kronstadt and has already

[1] Kruse reported that the Swedes fired blank to a great extent. Tevenen says the same in his journal (see below).

loosed his topsails. I must write my wife by him. If you should have any opportunity of being kind to Capt. Marshall, a young man, Lieut. in our service and son of one of the most respectable officers in it, you will oblige me much. His father is now a Commissioner of the Navy, he who fought the *Belle Poule* in the beginning of last war before Keppel's action, where he commanded the *Arethusa*. The son is a young man of genius, but excentric, and has left England against his father's consent. I know the father well. Adieu, my dear Sir, yours affectionately and sincerely, J. TREVENEN.

On board the *Netron menya*[1] off Viborg Sound, June 6th, 1790.

[The author goes on to say that 'all regretted that Kruze had not the command' and to wonder why the Empress 'did not remove this man (Tchitchagov) from standing between her arms and victory'. He then continues his narrative.]

As soon as the situation of the Swedes was known, the Russian fleet anchored, but occasionally got under sail and approached the enemy, as proper passages could be found amongst the rocks and shoals. Various movements were made on both sides between the 29th of May and 22nd of June in order to strengthen the relative positions of the two fleets and much good advice on the part of Capt. Trevenen was thrown away on his Commander-in-Chief.

Admiral Povalishin with a division of five ships had the charge of defending the passage out of Viborg Bay, which is rendered very narrow by a bank which lay between the two fleets. The *Netron menya* was the advanced ship of this division and in her post of honour could not fail of receiving the first and hottest fire of every Swedish ship as she attempted to come out. This squadron appears to have been judiciously placed.

On the 22nd of June about six in the morning the Swedes began to break ground and evinced a determination to force a passage, the Duke of Sudermania being driven by necessity to this decided and vigorous measure.[2]

[Appendix 5, which is printed here, is taken from Trevenen's Journal and covers the period May 24th to June 22nd, ending just before Trevenen's ship was engaged.]

'*May 24th, 1790*. This is a cruel situation: so ill and weak as I am, to be obliged night and day to attend to the duty of my ship, and in such an anxious moment as the present, when we are before the enemy, who now

[1] MS. has 'Hemporel'.
[2] *Author's note:* See Appendix No. 5 for the particular detail of operations during the time of the blockade.

seem bearing down to attack us. My head aches and my blood is hot, and it seems to me that it is only by absolute starvation I preserve myself from a new fever and sore throat. At another time I might trust to my officers. In the present I must see everything with my own eyes.

'*June 7th*. This was written before the last action on the *24th of May* when the Swedes bore down and attacked us. Their rear came down on our van with great apparent resolution, or rather it was only their Rear Admiral, for the ships ahead of him kept at a great distance to windward in spite of the number of guns he fired (I suppose to put them in mind of their duty) and his seconds astern behaved very little better.

'This officer is said to be Rear Admiral Modée. He chose a strong part of our fleet to attack and where we were best formed. He came down on my ship, but only fired on Admiral Kruze, who was the second astern of me. Between us was the *Knyaz Vladimir*, another 100-gun ship, and ahead of me was a 64. These four ships were very closely formed and all opened upon him at once, but too soon, Admiral Kruze making the signal for battle when he was at the distance of point blank, whereas had he suffered him to approach nearer, which he seemed well inclined to do, we must certainly have had him, from his being unsupported by any seconds to partake of our fire. As it was, he hauled his wind again immediately on our opening and kept up a good fire, but as we were laying to and he kept his wind, he was soon out of distance and did not seem to have suffered from our fire, although I saw numbers of shot fall close to him and he has since been without a main topgallant mast. The fire continued for some time at a great distance, almost without effect, and Admiral Kruze, perceiving the enemy's intention to fall on our rear with greater numbers, sent his boat to me and some others, to quit our places in the van and go to support the rear. I instantly obeyed, wore round and stood towards the rear followed by the *Iannuarii*.

'Admiral Kruze soon afterwards made the signal for wearing and endeavoured to form on the other tack, for which he had no sort of signal. I took a place in the rear, which however the enemy had very feebly attacked. God knows why however; I found several of our ships bearing up and amongst them Rear Admiral Povalishin, deceived I fancy by the ambiguity of the Admiral's signal, which seemed to indicate as if he meant to keep before the wind; this was soon rectified.[1] One of the ships, the van, and I think Chomutov,[2] was however left a long while alone engaging, but at so great a distance that no harm could come of it. Our distance throughout the line was at this time a long random shot and the action continued a long time without any effect; on our side very few shots were

[1] Punctuation as in MS. [2] In the *Sv. Petr*. MS. has Kermootof.

fired, but a great many on that of the Swedes, or rather, as was remarked by a great many in the fleet, powder without shot, the end of which is difficult to conceive, unless to hide a poverty, which could have been better hid by not firing at all. About six in the evening we observed three small vessels bearing down from to windward with signals flying, which I made no doubt were to indicate to the Swedish Admiral that Tchitchagov's fleet were approaching. The wind freshening, the signal was made for tacking one after another, and when about, our van ship looked up for the rear of the enemy and so well to windward that I think, had we kept our wind and chased, we might have fetched them, which I think on all accounts we ought to have done; first, because we had reason to presume that the Revel squadron was not far off; secondly, because the enemy declined the engagement, which is seldom done (especially by the party that had before sought eagerly to engage) without some very good reason on his part, and that is a sufficient one for his adversary to seek it, and still stronger when he has himself no reason to avoid it, which was altogether our case.

'We had heard several guns fired from the westward, which must have been from the Revel fleet.

'*25th.* In the morning about four o'clock saw several sail to windward, about 12 or 13, which answered very well to the number of the Revel squadron. The enemy seen at the same time. We made the signal to the Admiral; that for chasing to the windward was made a little after. The wind continuing westerly. A fog and very little wind came on soon afterwards, which hindered is from seeing the enemy at times. Only one of our fleet was able to get near the enemy (the *Sv. Petr*, Chomutov)[1] and he backed his main topsail and lay to for the rest. We lost sight altogether of the strange sails seen to the westward, but heard many guns fired from that quarter. The wind dying away and every ship going ahead of my old dung barge, I resolved to change my measures, to have at least a chance of coming up with the enemy, and finding I must necessarily be among the last upon this tack, I put about on the other and stood over to the southward in hopes that, if the wind should veer to that quarter, I might find myself to windward of the whole fleet and have the best chance of gaining the enemy. If it came to the northward, I could not be worse off than I was. My scheme this time answered perfectly, but it had no consequences. By favourable light winds I neared our van ships all day and in the morning of the *26th*, the breeze freshening and coming to the southward and eastward, I found myself up with the headmost.

'We early saw a fleet to leeward and began to form for engaging and

[1] MS. this time has Homoolof.

soon discovered it to be our own Revel squadron, to our great disappointment; for where then can be the enemy was the question which each man put to his neighbour, and old Tchitchagov asked us why we had let them escape and supposed they might be gone to Kronstadt, like an old fool without judgement. Being obliged, however, to suppose them somewhere, we were under the necessity of imagining they might have hazarded a passage to the northward of the shoals north of Hogland, and as the wind today became fair (that is easterly) for them, they might in that case be already past them and in so fair a way of reaching Helsingfors that we could no way prevent them.

'Mutual recriminations passed about letting the Swedes escape, but nothing could be plainer than that we had done our best to detain them, and that if there was any fault it must lie with Tchitchagov, who had been directly in their way and had come to an anchor to wait for them instead of cruising. The old fellow, because the Swedes failed in their attack of him in Revel bay, imagines every fleet at anchor to be impregnable, and he is not the only one that gives in to this ridiculous idea.'

[Here follows a part of the journal removed from its context and copied as Appendix 3. See above, p. 213.]

'In the meantime whilst we were laying to I went on board of Kruze who seemed very glad to see me and caressed me much, but said: "I have to beg your pardon Captain Trevenen for not having recommended you to the Empress in my first despatches. I had intended it, as also Capt. Thesiger,[1] but it slipped out of my memory in the multiplicity of business I had at that time", and I understand that having now given up the command he no longer corresponded with the Empress, but intended writing her secretary Turchaninov and begging him to clear up the mistake. At this time, not imagining that, if he had forgot me, he had remembered anybody else of my rank, I did not care much about it, although a little discontented with him for having forgot me, who certainly paid more attention to his signals than anyone else, at least in my part of the line. By way of precaution, however, I instantly borrowed a piece of paper and sat down and wrote a few lines to Count Bezborodko, stating the matter simply as I have related it here and throwing myself upon his friendship, that this unmerited neglect should not hurt me in the opinion of her Majesty. After dinner I carried Dennison on board his frigate in my boat and in the way he told me that Kruze had recommended Borisov, Senyavin[2] and his own captain and that forgetting the arduous situation he had just been in he took the reasons of this conduct from other circumstances than those of the present battle, as that Borisov ought to have had the cross

[1] Of the *Prins Gustaf*.

[2] Of the *Vseslav* and *Pobyedoslav*.

before for Ad. Greig's battle. Senyavin was an old friend; Preston was his own captain etc. Now 'tis true these Captains had behaved among the best, but that he should have recommended them before me and Thesiger filled me with the highest indignation.

'Dennison had pointed out to him the injustice of the thing, remarking that we were the only two which had made no fault, whilst all the rest at one time or another had made a great many. Kruze with his natural idleness was going to let the matter rest, notwithstanding; therefore, as soon as I got aboard, I wrote him a very angry letter, in which I told him the plain truth, both with regard to myself and the behaviour of some of the other captains, whom he had not forgot and whose behaviour I had an opportunity of remarking; however, not to offend him, I added what I might with great justice that however I might be offended I was ready to do justice to his conduct in the action and acknowledging the intrepidity he had shown; (however Dennison assured me that he had found him a little tipsy on going aboard after one of the actions). To this letter I had some days afterwards a very polite message expressing his sorrow for the neglect and assuring me he had written in such a manner to Turchaninov as would make his recommendation of Thesiger and me much more remarkable than if it had been sent at first. Thus ended this affair, but it appeared afterwards that my note to Bezborodko had weighed more than his amends.'

[Here the author inserts 'the rough copy of the letter to Admiral Kruze'.]

'Sir,—In quitting Petersburg so soon after my illness in order to serve on board the fleet under your orders it was a pleasure to me in addition to that of doing my duty that I was to be commanded by an officer for whom I had a high personal esteem and to whom my father-in-law had an attachment from his youth. It was not therefore without the highest surprise and grief that I learnt yesterday from Brigadier Dennison, after quitting your ship, the wrong you had done me. As long as I had conceived that in not recommending me you had likewise not recommended any but of a superior rank, I was content, but now that I hear that several captains have been preferred to me, I cannot conceal my astonishment at the ill return you have made for my zeal in your service. If really anything to except against my conduct, upon my honour I desire nothing but the strictest justice, but if, as your Excellency expressed yourself, you were quite satisfied with me, what reason can possibly have induced you to do me the most cruel injury that my greatest enemy could have imagined. I understand that Captain Senyavin amongst others is recommended in preference to me. Now I have a great regard for him, but in this case I must do myself justice, at least to your Excellency. How he might have bore[1] down at first I know not, but I know that towards the latter end of the action there was but one of the vanguard near the enemy and that (I believe) was Odintsov.[2] When Brigadier Dennison bore down to support the van and wore round again upon the larboard tack, he passed to leeward of all the van and weathered my ship.

'Let me ask your Excellency what afterwards became of the vanguard when the wind shifted and the enemy bore down upon us and for a little while after us. The vanguard all ran to leeward of me and Capt. Senyavin himself hailed me in passage and said he thought things went ill with us. I brought up the rear and had all the fire of the enemy, which it is true did me no great harm, because they were at too great a distance—that is, that of random shot. Who then paid any attention to your Excellency's signal to form the line as we could? Everyone tried to get as far to leeward as possibly they could and I was the last ship in the fleet, which was remarked by your own signal officer to Mr. Velikii, when he went on board of you. My officers even desired me to make more sail along with the rest, not to be the last, but I refused, and the ships that had formed the enemy's van bearing into their rear had all their shots at me. After this, when your Excellency first made the signal for the line on the starboard tack and hove to, then wore and made the signal for the line on the larboard tack and hove to yourself, who followed you? For the starboard I waited to get into your wake, but you wore to the larboard and I then hove to immediately, astern of Admiral Suchotin's ship[3] and in a line with you, whereas everybody else ran to leeward. Where was then the vanguard and where Capt. Senyavin's ship? Before I can be satisfied of his right to a preference I must be satisfied about this. Two ships afterwards luffed between me and Admiral Suchotin, which were Lotyrev's and (I believe) Glyebov's,[4] and the *Knyaz Vladimir*[5] brought to leeward and between your Excellency and myself. The rest of the van was then to leeward of the fleet. What passed afterwards I leave to your Excellency's recollection and to that of the Line and the Frigates. But I must just recall to mind that except the one combat on the starboard tack, when Admiral Povalishin led the van and our rear was feebly attacked, I was in every combat that was given, and your Excellency knows that in the last I was both in the van and rear. I hope your Excellency will excuse me when I say that as the honour of an officer is the dearest thing in the world to him, and as mine must be affected if any captain in the fleet is preferred before me on this occasion, I shall desire a Court-martial to be held upon me. I flatter myself, however, that,

[1] *Sic* in MS. [2] In the *Ioann Bogoslov*. [3] The *Dvyenadtsat Apostolov*.
[4] The *Aleksandr Nevskii* and *Iannuarii*. [5] Kiryeevskii.

although your Excellency has already done me an essential injury with her Majesty, yet, as you were kind enough to acknowledge, it was without intention; your acquaintance with and consideration for the character of an officer upon such an occasion will lead you to take every step that may make me what amends are yet in your power. With regard to what I have said of Captain Senyavin it is merely to put my pretensions to at least a right to an equality of recommendation in a clear light to your Excellency. I have too much regard for himself and his relations to be envious of his good fortune or to open my lips to anyone on the subject.

'In conclusion I cannot help calling to your Excellency's attention that in coming on board the fleet in my present ill state of health I ran a much greater risk than from the enemy's fire; that it's hard to have one's zeal thus recompensed; that I am at this moment very ill, and that the idea of what her Majesty may think on not seeing my name on the list of recommendations is poorly calculated to make me better. However, my reliance is upon your Excellency's justice and consideration for the character of an officer; and whatever reason I may have to complain in particular, I am ever ready to acknowledge the greatness and intrepidity of your Excellency's conduct, and subscribe myself with every sentiment of esteem and respect. *Netron menya*, May 27th, 1790. J. TREVENEN.'

Rear Ad:l. Kruze.[1]

[Here it is necessary to return to Appendix 5 for the continuation of the Journal.]

'To return to my journal—Dennison and I went afterwards on board Tchitchagov and by this time the Swedish fleet was seen, to our great astonishment, sheltering itself among the skerries to the north-east of us; so that we saw it had not escaped out of our hands. The old boy received me in the most cordial manner, and though I know that he wishes me ill with all his heart, yet he came up and kissed me with great demonstrations of good will. In other countries such dissimulation is only the growth of the court. In Russia it is the natural product of every man's heart, or, to speak justly, of the slavery their education inculcates into them. Of Dennison he by no means took so much notice and I was well aware of the cause of so much distinction towards me. It springs from my having once been recommended by Bezborodko to him and from his knowledge of my correspondence with him. What was to be done with regard to the Swedish fleet came upon the carpet and I quickly perceived the old boy was afraid to do anything and equally afraid of doing nothing. The

[1] Kruze had been a Vice Admiral since 1783.

consequence was natural—irresolution, delay, loss of opportunity. Not having yet a good idea of their situation, I could only answer him that it must depend upon that. Afterwards Dennison and myself tried every method to engage him to follow them, but all to no purpose, and he called a council of Flag Officers.

'At this time Crown having chased inshore with his frigate[1] and a cutter[2] was firing at some of the enemy's Flotilla, who returned his fire, and Tchitchagov frightened out of his wits not only called him back by signal, but sent Dennison and all his frigates to help him. Upon which I went on board my ship. Crown, when he came back, told him that, if he had not recalled him, he would have prevented that part of the enemy's flotilla from joining, upon which the old fellow acknowledged himself faulty.

'Instead of following the enemy we did nothing but stand off and on about Nerva,[3] looking at them sheltering themselves behind the rocks, whereas, had we pursued them, they must have precipitated their flight and probably might have run some of their vessels aground, in which case they must have infallibly abandoned them to us.

'My sore throat and fever attacked me again today and with such symptoms that I feared much my being obliged to return to Petersburg to get myself cured. I was obliged to take to my bed.

'*27th.* We came to an anchor in the afternoon for a little while, afterwards got under weigh, and in the evening came again to an anchor about 12 versts from the enemy, who we perceived had taken a position behind the island of Rondö.[4] Heaven only knows why we do not go nearer to them. The wind being fair and little of it.

'*28th.* A fair wind and little of it, but we did nothing but look at the enemy.

'*29th.* About noon we weighed and stood towards the enemy, the wind fair and light. This we might as well have done on the 26th, there not being a shadow of a reason more for it than before. As it was, we went about it as stupidly as possible. All the world knows our charts are very little to be depended on for this part, yet instead of sending small vessels before us to the sound and following them one after another, we went in a line abreast, as if to sweep for the shoals, without any other precaution than keeping our boats ahead sounding. We passed the little island Halli[5] and

[1] The *Venus*.
[2] The *Merkurii* in which Crown had captured the *Venus* in 1789.
[3] This is probably another name for Seiskär.
[4] Rondö lies in the middle of the wider (eastern) entrance to Viborg Bay. Its distance from Biskopsö or Peisari on the east is about 2½ miles and from Krysserort on the N.W. about 5½. Much of this latter distance is taken up by shoals, but there is a narrow deep-water passage near Krysserort.
[5] About 7 miles W.S.W. from Rondö.

stood to the north-east, where some ships had come to an anchor before us.

'I thought I could run no risk in steering for the ship that was next me in the line, i.e. the last of the centre, but just as I came a cable's length ahead of her, I found 7 fathoms and a boat ahead of me called out 4. I let go my anchor and immediately a 100-gun ship next me stuck fast aground. Luckily the weather continued fair and the wind light, otherwise she would have been lost as well as another ship in another part of the line that likewise ran aground. In sounding about the ship we found nowhere on the bank less than four fathoms. It is not marked in the charts.

'Having deep water to our place in the line I weighed and stood on to my station and came again to an anchor at about one-and-a-half cables' length from the bank. Here we lay at about five versts distance from the Swedish fleet, which was ranged in a line extending from the island Peisari to the great bank S.W. of Krysserort: 20 ships and several frigates N.W. of the bank and between that and Krysserort lay 3 ships and a frigate to defend the small passage there.[1] The little island Rondö lay exactly between our fleet and theirs at a long gun shot from each. Under it lay several Swedish gunboats and cutters, and I made no more doubt of their fortifying it than of our undertaking to drive them from it. I was deceived in both my suppositions, but it [is] surely astounding that nobody should have perceived the importance of this island, commanding the only passage by which it is probable that either we can attack the enemy or that they can come out, if they choose to try to push through us.

'I think the enemy should not have chosen their present position, but should have kept nearer the island Rondö, so as to have protected it, after having fortified it with red-hot shot batteries. Their line should have extended from the great bank to Rondö, thence to the other bank and islands S.E. of it, which would have protected them much better than they are now protected by extending their line to Peisari, for as that island is ours and our troops may soon take possession of it, our batteries from thence will easily drive them to the distance of 3 versts from it, by which they will find that wing altogether exposed to be doubled and their situation at an anchor will turn very much to their disadvantage instead of an advantage to them. It is true they would have more openings to defend if they had adopted my position, but that their flotilla might have done for them; and their line would have been unattackable had it extended from

[1] There must be mistakes of copying here. The 'great bank' lies S.E. from Krysserort, not S.W. Apparently the punctuation should be altered also and the sentence should read: 'from the island Peisari to the great bank S.E. of Krysserort 20 ships and several frigates; N.W. of the bank and between that and Krysserort lay 3 ships and a frigate'. This would at least correspond with the actual disposition of the Swedish fleet.

the great bank to Rondö, a little behind it, and thence to the 4 fathom bank Hoika[1]; their frigates and a ship or two might have defended the small passages and Rondö would have been worth several ships to them.

'From this time to the 7th of June, when I take up the journal again, we did nothing but look at the enemy. My sore throat attacked me again immediately after our junction with the Revel fleet, a natural consequence of the fatigues I had undergone, never having pulled off my clothes from Petersburg till we came to an anchor off Halli.

'I had a great mind to return to Petersburg to get cured, but the desire of seeing this affair brought to an end detained me here from day to day, till at last I got better again. In the meantime I wrote to the Counts Bezborodko and Tchernyshev my sentiments on the state of things in the letters of these dates and Turchaninov coming down here I sent to him that I should be glad to see him to talk about the state of things. He promised he would come on board, but apparently he had no time. I had before written my ideas to Tchitchagov, which I now suppressed, thinking to take Turchaninov's advice about it. As he did not come, I let the business drop.

'I had forgot to mention in its proper place that I had received the order of St. Vladimir of the third class in consequence of our battle. Fedorov and Dennison, brigadiers, received the same. Borisov, Thesiger, Chomutov and Lomen, captains of the second rank, received golden swords[2] and Preston, Admiral Kruze's captain of the first rank, and Obolyaninov, Povalishin's captain, also of the first rank, received the order of St. George of the fourth class. Myasoyedov, Admiral Kruze's Capt. Lieut. for the signals, the Admiral's son and Aiken, my Capt. Lieut. were advanced to the rank of Captains. Count Golovkin and young Elphinstone, both on board the Admiral's ship, from Lieutenants to be Capt. Lieutenants. Count Ivelitch to be Colonel in the army from Lieut. Colonel, and Knobel, the Artillery Officer on board Kruze got also a golden sword.

'I wrote a second letter of thanks to Bezborodko and to tell him what we ought to do.

'*June 7th, 1790.* Having recovered somewhat from my second illness I undertake the journal of events. We now lie in the entrance of Viborg sound, blocking up the Swedish fleet, which is placed in a line between the Isle of Peisari and the large bank to the S.W. of Krysserort.[3] We on one side the little island Rondö, they on the other. We have not done the

[1] About 1½ miles S.E. from Rondö and 1¼ from Peisari. MS. has Gouka.
[2] Trevenen omits Senyavin, who received the same honour.
[3] Again the MS. has S.W. where it should be S.E.

least thing yet to get a better knowledge of the coast, though we perceive the chart to be entirely faulty. The day before yesterday, however, the *Boleslav* was sent towards the island Rondö with a frigate, and the Swedish vessels that lay near it, viz. two cutters, immediately got under weigh and joined their fleet, which as well as ours lies out of gun shot of it.

'It seems to me strange that the possession of this island should be so indifferent to us both, lying as it does in the mid channel between us and commanding it. I look upon it as a great fault in the Swedes not to have taken possession of it and a still greater in us not to have done the same immediately on coming here. However, our mistake becomes now of little consequence as they did not fortify it. We may, when we please, and if we persist to block them up, we should.

'This morning a village to the northward of us seemingly on the island Roskil[1] was set on fire and burnt, apparently by the enemy, and if so, very foolishly; for they are now in a position to fear a reprisal on their persons for any ill behaviour, for surely they never can escape from us.

'In the morning arrived from Revel 2 bomb vessels, 2 fireships, 2 hospital ships and 3 cutters.

'*Saturday 8th.* The wind still westerly, a fine breeze, just such as I attacked Barösund with.

'We had yesterday an order from the Admiral to keep ourselves in all readiness for attacking the enemy and warning us, when that shall happen, to be careful in sounding and sending our boats before us also for that purpose. Instead of which he should now make it his business to sound, even under the enemy's guns, but he attempts nothing.

'More houses burning in the same place as yesterday. In the afternoon a signal for Lieutenants and an order for sending the steersmen to sound the passages previous to a new disposition of our force, by which it appears that the Admiral's design is not to attack, but to block up the Swedes. My ship is appointed one under the Rear Admiral Povalishin to block up the N.W. passage and I am to be the leading ship, and the extreme one on that side next the land. Our distance from the enemy to be exactly beyond gun shot. Today arrived Slisov's squadron of gunboats from Fredrikshamn, in No. 49.—The wind in the evening shifting to the north.

'*Sunday 9th.* The Admiral loosed his topsails and got under weigh in order to take his place according to the new disposition. The Swedes immediately veered on their springs, but were quickly removed from their apprehensions by seeing him come to an anchor again yet a long way from them. We sent our boats sounding towards Krysserort, where we found clear ground.

[1] MS. Rogel.

'Captain Crown having been sent yesterday to chase a Swedish brig along with several of our small vessels cut her off this morning from getting to the westward and I see her in flames. I suppose her own crew will have deserted her.

10th, 11th, 12th. 'Hindered by the weather from getting exactly in our place. In the meantime Capt. Crown returned with 4 small prizes laden with provisions for the Swedish fleet. They were under convoy of the brig burnt. She was a King's vessel. Everything of this sort is a great stop to them, if we may believe the report of about 40 of their men, deserters from a watering party of theirs, who say they are in great want of provisions and already reduced to half allowance. This was the cause of their desertion. They added that in the action most of their ships had 15 or 20 men killed, which I don't believe. The *12th* nearly in our place, i.e. about 2 versts from the enemy, very good random shots. They began the battle of the 22nd at a much better distance. In the evenings they row guard and come very near us. We do nothing.

13th. Thursday. 'Povalishin made the signal for all Captains. Not being able to go myself I sent my 2nd Captain Aiken (promoted from Captain Lieutenant on account of our late battle), who assisted at a Council called to consider the propriety or possibility of attacking the enemy on this side, which was recommended to Admiral Povalishin by Admiral Tchitchagov in so curious a letter that I could not help taking a copy of it. The Council decided that the measure was unadvisable in itself and impracticable in the manner Admiral Tchitchagov proposed as the only proper one, that is, that of approaching them altogether sideways—unadvisable because of the narrowness and dangers of the passage. I could not be of the Council, but as soon as I understood the purport of it, I sent my opinion in writing, agreeing with the opinions of the Council, with my reasons for so doing and recommending and offering to lead an attack on the other side, i.e. in the large passage. Where the enemy could be attacked to greater advantage, as we might fall with a great force upon a small part of his, only taking the necessary measures. And adding that a necessary consequence of the success of this attack would be the surrender of their four ships[1] without a blow. Admiral Povalishin sent me back his thanks for my communication, saying he looked upon it to be so right and of so much consequence that he should send it immediately to Admiral Tchitchagov.

'At midnight, or rather at 12 o'clock, for we have no night now, the Swedish frigate, being the westernmost and most weatherly of the squadron got under weigh and stood towards the body of their fleet. The rest of the

[1] Those in the N.W. passage.

squadron making the like motions and the Commodore actually getting under weigh. It seemed evidently that the Swedes were going to abandon this passage in order to fortify the body of their fleet. Lotyrev in the *Panteleimon* with his usual bullying presumption immediately loosed his topsails before the Admiral, who however soon loosed his also, and the squadron in consequence. I expected an order to get under weigh every minute and was all clear for action, but the Swedish Commodore seeing this and apparently something preventing the other two ships from following him, he came to again immediately, not having gone above a quarter of a cable out of the line. The frigate also hove to, but a long way to leeward. Our Admiral soon sent me an order not to get under weigh, but observe his motions; upon which I went very quietly. Some officers abused him for loosing his topsails, which certainly hindered the Swedes from quitting their post, as they feared from our being so near that we should be amongst them before the other two ships had cleared the channel, whereas, had we left them to themselves, they certainly had abandoned the post. But this is judging from events only and unsoundly. It is certainly a good general maxim to do everything that may precipitate the retreat of an enemy; therefore Admiral Tchitchagov was right in loosing his topsails. And again, if it be really that which hindered them from abandoning the post (as I really believe it was) yet I do not see that we have lost anything by having prevented them from putting their design in execution; for if they had such a design, we may reasonably suppose they planned it upon good and necessary grounds; consequently their being prevented from putting it in execution is unfavourable to them and it is a general maxim in war to will just the contrary of what your enemy wills. I have but one reflection to make upon such events, that it is necessary for a commander to have resolved every possible one in his mind beforehand, that he may be prepared for it against it happens and not be surprised or found off his guard, which leads to unsound and precipitate measures.

'The only use we could make of this passage other than the present one of blocking it will be to send a squadron through it in order to double the line of the enemy and put him between two fires, when Admiral Tchitchagov shall attack him at the same time from the other side. If that should be resolved on, we can do it at any time. As to attacking it separately, it can possibly be of no use to us.

'The three Swedish ships kept their ground and we furled our sails again, only the frigate joined the body of the fleet and was relieved by another.

'*Friday the 14th* passed without anything worthy notice, except that in consequence of its blowing pretty fresh one of our fire-ships of Brigadier

Lezhnev's squadron drifted down on the enemy and was taken possession of by their boats. There seemed something very incomprehensible in the manner of the thing. The men did not seem to be taken out, yet the vessel made no sail nor any effort to escape or run on shore. Or, if the crew had deserted her, they might have set her on fire and she would have drifted right down on the enemy's fleet. The only solution I can imagine for so much nonsense is the commander of her being a young blockhead who knew not at any time what to do with his vessel and still less when the enemy began to fire at him. The Russian colours were quickly hauled down and the Swedish hoisted in their stead. The vessel was brought to an anchor under the Prince of Sudermania's stern.[1] Several heavy guns fired inshore towards the opening between Torsari and Peisari; we expect daily the Prince of Nassau that way. In the night it blew so hard that we struck topgallant yards and masts and let go another anchor, having no room to drift.

Saturday 15th. 'Moderate breeze from the westward. A flag of truce rowed up from the enemy's fleet to Admiral Tchitchagov's ship. I suppose to send back the Midshipman taken in the fireship, as the Swedes, having but little provisions, would rather have his room than his company, and at the same time appear vastly polite and humane.

Sunday 16th. 'In the morning Admiral Povalishin sent for me, or if I were sick, to say he would come to see me. I went to him and our conversation was about my letter to him on the subject of the attack of the Swedish fleet. He said he had received a reprimand from Tchitchagov for not joining his own opinion to mine on that subject; but, he said, "I had not time". Admiral Tchitchagov ordered him to thank me for the good will I showed, but supposed I did not know the dangers of the ground. He asked me in what manner I meant to attack them; I said it was a very serious matter and not lightly to be undertaken; that it would require a great many precautions and that I would begin by building fire stages upon the island Rondö.[2] He flew out upon this and said that was a thing sooner said than done; that it was vain to propose what was impossible and raised so many difficulties that I saw it was useless to say anything more on that subject. We then talked of a blockade, for which purpose I said it was absolutely necessary to fortify Rondö and Krysserort. Here he flew out again. Where were we to get guns? How did we know through which passage they would come out? and a thousand other ridiculous articles that quickly silenced me; for to hear an Admiral demand where

[1] Russian accounts put this incident on the 15th. The discrepancy may be caused by the use in the ships' logs of the nautical day beginning at noon, but it is also possible that Trevenen made a mistake, as he seems to have done later (see below).

[2] MS. has Potegz, but Rondö seems the only possibility.

we were to get guns for a couple of shore batteries was a question I did not expect to hear in a fleet of 30 line-of-battle ships, nearly as many frigates and a still greater number of gunboats. I was instantly convinced I might as well hold my peace, which I did after telling him that the man who attempted nothing was sure of doing nothing. He said our first object was to place our fleet in the best possible manner for intercepting them. I agreed to this, said it was quickly done and did not at all interfere with the other business. After some heat we said no more and were very good friends as to anything else. I dined with him and learnt that the fireship we lost passed under the stern of Brigadier Lezhnev and asked him if he should run her on shore. Now the wind was by no means too great for him to work to windward till he could get supplied with other anchors, but this did not enter into the thick head of the Brigadier, who told him not to run her on shore, but he would send the boats to take the people off and then he might abandon her. This was done, only one man wounded by a shot from the enemy was left behind. The flag of truce of yesterday came from the Prince of Södermanland[1] to bring the baggage of this officer. In the boat came Captain Smith of the English navy, who sent from the cutter, which was sent down to them, to say that not being in the Swedish service, but only a companion of the Prince's, he hoped to be indulged with being admitted on board the Russian fleet. I don't think his reason for hoping so was at all good, but at the same time there was no reason why he should not see the Russian fleet, if the Admiral thought proper, as our ships are in good condition and our situation may be discovered from their fleet as well as from ours. The Admiral did not think it proper and Capt. Smith was sent back without his errand.

'I learnt also that four men having deserted from one of their parties on shore were so warmly pursued that 3 were killed; the 4th escaped to our posts. He brought intelligence that the Swedes have no water but that from alongside and only 15 days provisions. The vessel we saw the other day grounded off Torsari was the *Chvat*[2] (snap up), one of our transports going to Kronstadt with sick men; these were taken off by the *Mstislavets* frigate, but a long-boat being sent from her afterwards to get out some stores, without an officer, the vessel was surrounded by 6 of the enemy's gunboats and this long-boat with 20 men were taken.

'In the night the wind came round to the north-east and blew strong with rain and foggy weather all night. I expected the enemy would have taken the opportunity of running out, for we should not have been able

[1] MS. Sunderman-Land.

[2] MS. Qvaff. There was a Russian ship called *Chvat* at a later date and the meaning agrees with Trevenen's translation.

to lay on our springs, and as he must run some risk to get out from hence at any rate, as well now as at another time. I therefore kept my people at quarters all night, but covered from the wet. The Swedes lay fast; what they will do with their galley fleet when they go out I am at a loss to know. But I suppose force all together.

Monday the 17th of June. 'I had a visit from Crown, who related more circumstantially the affair of the flag of trace. Capt. Smith came as interpreter to the officer who brought back the baggage of the commander of our fireship. This officer brought a letter from the Duke of Södermanland to the Admiral, signifying that having taken the baggage of an officer and the war not being carried on with any ungenerous animosity, he had sent it back again by a flag of truce. However, I heard that only a uniform was sent back, whereas the officer lost several trunks. Without any proof we know very well that the Duke only made use of this pretext to send Capt. Smith to see what he could see and learn what he could learn. Besides this letter Capt. Smith said he had another for the Admiral, which he was to deliver into no hands but his own. It was the Admiral's son who went on board Scott's cutter to receive the flag of truce, and he told Capt. Smith that his father could not admit him on board his ship and that at all events it would be useless, as he neither wrote nor spoke any language but his own; therefore, says he, if you give it him yourself I must still translate it for him. However Capt. Smith persisted in not giving it into any hands but the Admiral's and therefore kept it himself. The negociations finished thus. But Capt. Smith put a great number of questions to Scott, against which he was much upon his guard. He asked if there were many English officers on board the fleet, was answered, yes, and added "indeed we see with our glasses that it is an English and not a Russian fleet that we have to contend with". He asked about me; whether I was in the fleet; whether I had a flag; whether I did not command this squadron, i.e. Povalishin's. Scott answered him very drily that I was in the fleet, and he asked no more.

'He said he was authorised to declare that all the English officers who would go home would be provided for (another account said they would gain a rank) and that Mr. Whitworth at St. Petersburg would say the same, to whom Scott might use his name. Scott answered that he was certain the English officers in the service of her Imperial Majesty were so well satisfied with it that not one would quit it on any consideration till they obtained her every honourable satisfaction.

'He asked Scott how he came to have so small a vessel; his answer was that he only kept her till he got a beautiful Swedish frigate he had set his heart on, and which in a little time he expected to have the honour of commanding. He said he thought the manoeuvre in coming here resembled either that of Lord Howe in relieving Gibraltar or Lord Hood at St. Christopher's (accounts vary as to which). Scott said, not the least Sir. You came in here against your wills, so did we, who were never here before, nor ever wished to be here, and you have not now a door to get out of. Upon the whole Scott seems to have been very fearful and pompous at first, but more collected afterwards, and certainly Smith's last idea was a ridiculous fanfaronade.

'Scott asserts that he saw him lately at Revel disguised in a Flushing packet, that although he recollected perfectly the having seen him lately, he could not think where, and that, if he had recollected it at the time, he would have told him he was acting a part very unbecoming a British officer. However, in this he may very likely be mistaken.

'Captain Smith said that he was not at all in the Swedish service, but merely a volunteer companion and adviser of the Prince's, that he lived upon a footing of perfect intimacy with him and with the King (both of whom he praises very much) and with whom he dined alternately, for the King is here with his galley fleet. It is said that he was at an attack the Swedes lately made upon our troops on shore, in which being worsted he was obliged to throw away his coat and waistcoat of English uniform, which were found by our soldiers; this is said by Count Saltykov. Captain Smith told Scott that he was lately in great danger on shore in an attack.

'I learnt also that Admiral Spiridov is again come down to the fleet by the Empress's order, which some say must be as certain a sign of peace as the swallow is of summer.

'Had some dispute with Crown about the best manner of attacking the Swedes, in which it appeared to me that he looks no farther than to trifling objects and judges without consideration.

18th. 'Had a letter from Admiral Povalishin desiring me to go asounding with him—set off for that purpose, but the wind was too fresh from the westward. His object is to place me farther inshore in order to cut off more effectually all possibility of a passage that way for the enemy, for besides his fear that the enemy, if ever he attempts to force out, will choose that way (whereas I think he will go out in the straight road) he is fearful lest 12 of the enemy's gunboats seen to windward should push through, i.e. through 4 frigates exactly in the way, past 40 gunboats of ours lying ready close to the passage and within gun shot of our 5 ships. Today Admiral Spiridov hoisted his flag on board the *Sv. Nikolai*, 100-gun ship. The captain being known for a coward I can only compare their conjunction to the addition of two minus quantities in algebra and the addition will make a negative quantity considerable enough to destroy utterly the value of a hundred guns.

'However, poor Spiridov is a good-natured little fellow and I wish him better luck. Heaven knows how he reconciles it to himself that Kruze, on board whom he was, is rewarded as well as the captain of the ship with orders, while he alone is left neglected. I should think there was something too positive in this to bear.

'Orders today to send our sick on shore and build a tent for them, likewise to send for water; sent accordingly.

'About midnight a small Swedish schooner worked up within point blank shot of our squadron. Nobody took any measures to drive her away till Lotyrev began firing at her, although she was nearer the Admiral than him. He also manned his boat and sent towards her, but she had already bore[1] away. Some of his shot reached in richochet the nearest Swedish ships. The Admiral sent Lotyrev a reprimand "for needlessly alarming the whole fleet".

Wednesday 19th. 'Wind still westerly, as constant as a Trade and like it freshening as the sun rises and moderating as it sets.

'Captain Crown having again chased to windward with another frigate and some cutters appeared to have got fast aground upon a bank to the westward; however, he got off again in the evening and there was some firing between him and the gunboats I have mentioned. When it was about half over, our gunboats also chased to windward and one of the new-built frigates, but the latter seemed by backing all at once to be likewise near the ground and came afterwards to an anchor. However, drawing only 10 feet water they are much better adapted for chasing among the rocks than the *Venus*, which draws 18 feet. Nevertheless our Admiral with his usual inconsistency keeps the 2 of them which he has with him lying here like guardships and Crown always chasing in this miserable place.

'Received an order today from the Admiral to be much on my guard against one of the enemy's frigates which they had turned into a fire-ship, but kept still disguised with wooden guns and wooden men.

'In the afternoon a Swedish small boat turned up on this side Cape Krysserort[2] and Lotyrev, who it seems was on board the Admiral at the time, went in his boat armed to try to cut her off. She was, however, too much upon her guard.

21st. 'The Swedes after a night battle with our galley fleet all getting under weigh with an apparent intention to force their way out. Indeed, pressed as they are for provisions, they have now nothing else to do, and I have no doubt of their taking the present opportunity. It will now be

[1] *Sic* in MS.

[2] MS. Capt. Krieserost.

seen that my advice should have been taken of fortifying the island Rondö.

7 & $\frac{1}{4}$ in the morning.'[1]

The wind was N.E., right out of the bay. As the Swedish ships got under weigh they formed a line of battle and approached Povalishin's squadron, of which the *Netron menya* was the advanced ship, under easy sail. The Swedes were led in the most gallant manner by Admiral Modée[2] and received with steadiness and returned with vigour the Russian fire, each ship pressing sail as soon as she passed the advanced squadron. Too much praise cannot be given this Swedish Admiral for his gallantry and address on this occasion.

From the situation of the *Netron menya* she had to receive the first and of course the hottest fire from the Swedish line in passing, yet did our gallant friend escape unhurt till nearly the close of the battle and till every flattering appearance promised a glorious termination. The *Netron menya* had borne the fire of the whole Swedish fleet and made them feel severely the weight of her shot in passing her, when, about 10 o'clock, the wind freshening and coming more to the eastward, the second Captain (Aiken), who commanded the guns below, found a change of position necessary in order to use them with full effect and came upon deck to mention it to the Captain. A change in the position of the ship was accordingly made[3] and before returning to his quarters below Capt. Aiken remained a short time congratulating his commander on the glorious prospect of complete victory before them.

At this moment Capt. Trevenen, perceiving an opportunity of annoying one of the enemy's ships which was handling them rather roughly, advanced to the fore part of the quarter deck (Aiken attending him) to give directions for pointing the fire upon her.

At the instant he was giving these orders a fatal shot, which from its descending direction was apparently almost spent, first took off the head of the Quartermaster, stripped the flesh of Trevenen's thigh from the hipbone half-way down and afterwards struck off Aiken's foot.

The confusion which ensued on this dreadful catastrophe is not to be described. The crew of the ship, perceiving the fall of that commander who was equally loved for his goodness to them and revered for his gallant

[1] This entry is repeated elsewhere with the difference that the time is given as 7½. The author notes that the date appears to be wrong, since 'every other account' puts the action (rightly) on the 22nd.

[2] The leading Swedish ships were *Dristigheten* 64, *Camilla* 42, *Rättvisan* 64 and *Adolf Frederik* 70; Modée was in the last of these. The line was actually led by Lt.-Col. Puke.

[3] *Author's note:* In a paper of the Appendix it is said that the *Netron menya slipped* her cable, but this was not the case. The cable was *veered away* only and perhaps the position of the ship changed by a *spring*.

conduct, made a general exclamation of grief and were crowding round him. He assured them his wound was of no consequence, reassumed his sword, which had fallen when he received it, and causing himself to be covered with his cloak where he lay upon the deck encouraged his men to fight courageously, and he would continue to command them. The loss of blood, however, soon obliged him to be taken below, but there unfortunately was no surgeon to attend to the wound and I understand that both Capt. T. and Aiken remained several hours without proper assistance.[1]

I have heard different opinions given respecting the wound our noble Trevenen had received and the probable issue if skilful chirurgical assistance could have been timely administered. Upon the whole I am led to believe that it was of a nature not admitting of much hope, had all the advantages of care and science been used immediately. He had a pretty large key in a side breeches pocket which being struck by the shot considerably extended the wound and by mangling the flesh rendered a cure much more difficult. Add to this that the blood after being heated in action and after a long series of keen anxiety is in a state much against the chance of recovery from a wound of this nature. I have dealt somewhat more on this subject than I at first intended, as my mind was relieved, when I found that my gallant friend was lost to us by the inevitable stroke of his destiny under the unerring hand of Providence and not from the want of human assistance, and I concluded that his other friends would feel a similar ray of consolation in the same persuasion. Capt. Aiken says in a letter to me: 'From every report of the faculty the cavity was too large for any human means to save his life'. The idea that such a valuable life was lost for want of proper assistance is so dreadful that I have always derived a degree of satisfaction from knowing that it was not the case and we have only to lament the lengthened sufferings of the man and have not to attribute his death to the absence of the surgeon. I conclude from Capt. Aiken's letter that their proper surgeon attended them in two or three hours' time and the following day Brigadier Dennison had an opportunity of visiting his friend and left with him his own surgeon, Mr. McDugal, and a Mr. Zeddleman, a nephew of Mr. Farquharson, to assist in paying all the attentions possible. The wounded hero was also attended by the son of the Baron de Sass, at whose house he had been so kindly entertained after his accident in Courland. Capt. Trevenen had exerted himself as much as

[1] *Author's note:* Some tents for the sick had been pitched on shore and each ship was to send her surgeon in turn to take charge of them. Unfortunately it was the turn of the surgeon of the *Netron menya* to be at this time on that duty. Capt. Aiken positively says they were without assistance, in which case there could not have been any assistant surgeons or surgeon's mates on board.

possible by the most friendly attentions to this young man, to endeavour to repay the assiduous kindness of his family.

It was so long after the period of which I am writing before I began to collect the materials for this narrative, that very many interesting particulars were forgotten and of those I have received some circumstances clash with others in such a way that I am careful as to what to insert. Capt. Aiken's accounts, as far as they extend, are no doubt accurate, but he is not so minute as I would have wished. Some others I received from Mr. Farquharson, which he had endeavoured to procure for me; and I have a transcript of the journal of Otto de Sass which is by far the most full and entirely consistent with the others, except in stating that the *Netron menya* got under sail some time between the [beginning of] the action and the catastrophe I am adverting to. I have from these several documents arranged the remaining part of these memoirs.

While the surgeon was attending to the wound and, I understand, evinced by his manner that he dreaded the consequences, the gallant sufferer called for pen, ink and paper and wrote a few lines to his beloved wife, which he entrusted to the care of Otto de Sass, at the same time giving that young man his watch as a testimony of his esteem.

The following day Rear Admiral Povalishin called on him and promised that the ship should be instantly ordered for Kronstadt, a promise which greatly soothed his mind, as there he would be sure of receiving all those attentions which might contribute to his recovery, if that was possible or at least enjoy the melancholy satisfaction of dying in the midst of his friends, and perhaps have taken a last farewell of his dearest treasures. . . .

But even this soothing promise was not performed, and there does not appear the smallest plea of necessity of service which needed to prevent it. Whither could the ship with so much propriety have been ordered as where her destination could have given ease to the mind of the hero who had gained them the victory[1] and was expiring in their cause. His friends and attendants, who saw how chagrined he was at the delay of the order which he expected in consequence of Povalishin's promise, endeavoured at last to persuade him that the order was come, although it had then been known that counter-orders had been given. But, suspecting the truth of his friends' account, he ordered a compass to be brought before him on the couch on which he lay, and this he anxiously watched from time to time, to see whether the ship was under sail and steering the course his heart was so much bent on. Superior as the Russian fleet was then to any enemy, it fills me with astonishment and indignation that either the *Netron menya* or one of the frigates was not instantly ordered to take Trevenen and

[1] *Author's note:* See Appendix No. 7—Swedish officer's letter.

Aiken to Kronstadt. Till this mystery is cleared up and the blame attached to the right person, I can but most deeply regret that in addition to his other misfortunes my friend arrived at their climax amongst men who must have been strangers to the best feelings of humanity. I can hardly think that Povalishin would have made the promise, had he not believed he should be able to see it performed; and therefore this refined and cruel tyranny (it deserves no better name) must most likely lie at the door of Tchitchagov.

Be that as it may, no excuse can be offered, and it certainly contributed to irritate and embitter the last days of poor Trevenen. From the moment that he received his wound he never flattered himself with any hopes of recovery, as he often assured the friends who attended him and who would willingly have indulged the belief of so desirable an event and endeavoured sometimes to persuade their patient to join them.

Had he been gratified in the particular instance of going to Kronstadt, beyond a doubt all his hours after his wound would have been passed in that serenity which his great faculties would have enabled him to assume. As it was, his feelings were frequently irritated at the disappointment he met with in his last earthly hopes, and for which his reason could not furnish him with the smallest excuse. . . .

In this state he lingered, not in very severe pain, but gradually becoming weaker, till the 28th of June, O.S., when he expired at six in the morning in the presence of De Sass, Zeddleman and McDugal. . . .

Immediately after his death the body was embalmed and a few days after the *Topaslowe* frigate was ordered to take the corpse with Capt. Aiken, De Sass and Zeddleman to Kronstadt, to which place they had a long passage owing to calm weather.[1]

On the fourth of July the body was interred with all military honours in the British burying ground at Kronstadt. The solemn ceremony was attended by several Admirals and all the military of high rank, his father-in-law[2] and many other sorrowing friends.

[A very long peroration, in which at one point the author likens Trevenen to Wolfe and Nelson, ends with the following paragraph.]

[1] There was no ship in the Russian fleet with a name even suggestive of that given; while Povalishin's report of June 28th ends as follows: 'At this moment, on account of Trevenen's dangerous condition and at his earnest request, I have sent the *Netron menya* to Kronstadt with him'.

[2] *Author's note:* This worthy gentleman had to suffer severely in this war. On the same day on which Trevenen died Brigadier Dennison was shot through the head in a desperate action with the Swedish frigates and galleys, when as usual his gallantry had been most conspicuous.

Thus did ambition, of a tendency the most virtuous, but vast in its scope, tear from home and from happiness a dutiful son, an affectionate brother and firm friend; and who in addition to these endearing ties had latterly been allowed a little season to show himself an affectionate husband and fond parent, and he has left me ever to regret his loss the more feelingly that, as in war he was to establish his fame and end his days, his services were not exerted in the defence of his own country and his life ended in her cause.

FINIS.

APPENDIX

[Penrose's Appendices Nos. 3, 4 and 5 have been included in the text. No. 6 is a letter from Trevenen to his wife, to be delivered in the event of his death. The author of the Memoir writes as follows.]

I understand the original to be dated 'June 21st 1790, on the Swedish coast'. This letter is copied from what was inserted in the newspapers, and as it had found its way there (I understand) in a clandestine manner, however admirable it may appear I conclude it does not do justice to the original.

[In a final unnumbered Appendix dated 1809 he gives 'a correct copy of the original'. It is dated July 19th, 1789, and has a continuation dated July 18th.][1]

[Appendix No. 7 is mainly concerned with a letter from a Professor Pictet of Geneva together with a copy of an obituary notice inserted by him in the Journal of Geneva. This includes the following.]

'Extract of a letter from an officer in the Swedish service to his friend in London. Svensksund, July 18th 1790.

You will have doubtless heard of our defeat on the 3rd and 4th inst. and subsequent victory on the 9th and 10th. We, however, consider the former as more than equivalent to the latter, as in that engagement our old Portsmouth contemporary Trevenen, the very soul of the Russian fleet, received a wound, which in a few days at the age of about thirty put a period to as bright a career of glory as ever adorned the annals of naval history. Poor fellow! I ever admired his character and revered his abilities, though my junior in age and naval rank. He had formed himself on the character of old Saunders and it is here generally allowed that his intrepidity of attack, his coolness in action and activity in pursuit have been the great bulwark to Russia, through which we never could penetrate, nor would the King, whose character and conduct are here adored, have thought of attacking the enemy again so soon but for Trevenen's wound, as he has been heard to say that there was no eluding his vigilance. On the 3rd inst. we should have escaped with very little loss, had he not concluded

[1] The discrepancy of dates is obvious at once. Probably the last written, July 18, is correct and July 19 a mistake for 17. The letter begins by saying: 'Tomorrow it is likely we shall again meet our enemy', and that would be reasonable on that date, when there was a prospect of a renewal of the Battle of Öland. The date given in the printed version was evidently added in the knowledge that Trevenen was killed in an action taking place on June 22, 1790.

what we are about and slipped his cable in which he was followed by 4 or 5 others, your old friend Dennison among them, whilst the remainder coldly stayed to weigh their anchors; whereas, had he been properly supported, we should none of us have escaped. We are told here that he received his wound from the last shot fired from our ships. It was in his thigh and not at first thought dangerous, but his weak state of body brought on a fever which carried him off. Thank God! the shot came not from my ship. Hitherto I have escaped free; how long I may continue so God only knows.'[1]

[This appendix ends with a short account of the Orders of St. George and St. Vladimir introduced by the following paragraphs.]

My readers may not be displeased at my here inserting some account of orders of merit which were conferred on Capt. Trevenen by the Empress.

His address from the public characters was latterly thus:

A Monsieur
Monsieur de Trevenen
Capitain de haut bord du premier rang au service de
S.M.I. de toutes les Russies
Chevalier de St. George and de St. Vladimir
Sur le vaisseau
Netron menya

His address therefore in English would have been:

To
Sir James Trevenen
Post Captain of the highest rank
in the service of H.I.M. of all the Russias
Knight of St. George and St. Vladimir
on board the ship of the line
Netron menya

As my friend did not survive to get the permission of his proper Sovereign to adopt his well-earned titles, I have, of course, in my narrative omitted them.

[1] At first sight this letter seems likely to have been written by Sidney Smith, but he was younger than Trevenen and does not seem to have been educated at Portsmouth. In any case it is not altogether accurate. There is a conflict of evidence as to whether the *Netron menya* did or did not slip her cable, but it is certain that Dennison was not one of those who followed her supposed example. He was not in the sailing fleet, but in command of the rowing frigates of Nassau Siegen's flotilla and was killed in the battle of Svensksund on June 28/July 9. One would have expected the writer to have known this, since Dennison's ship was one of those captured.

INDEX

For names of Ships, see separate SHIP Index.

INDEX OF SHIPS

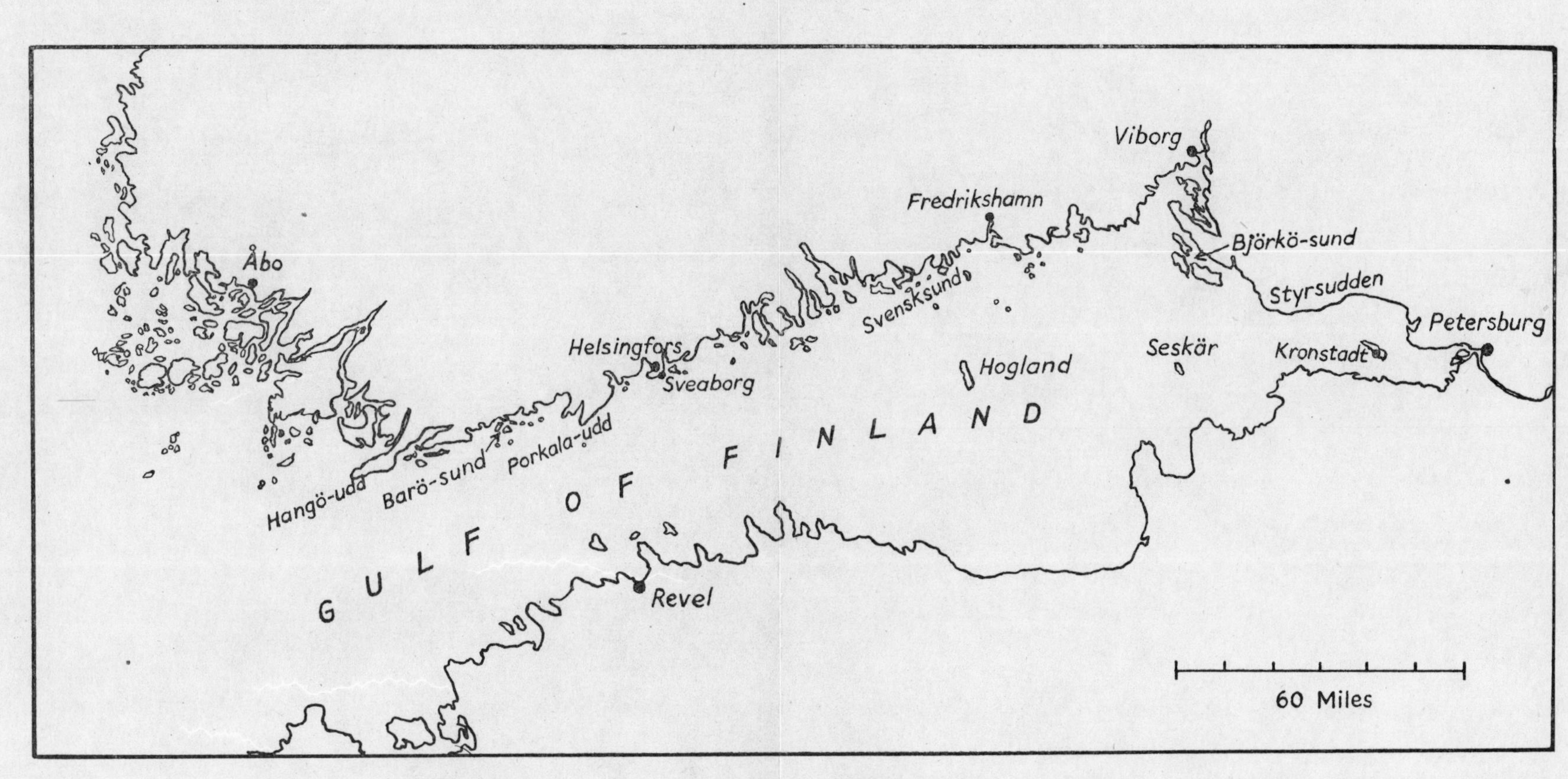

THE GULF OF FINLAND

Navy Records Society

(FOUNDED 1893)

THE Navy Records Society was established for the purpose of printing rare or unpublished works of naval interest. The Society is open to all who are interested in naval history and any person wishing to become a member should apply to the Hon. Secretary, Royal Naval College, Greenwich, London, S.E. 10. The annual subscription is two guineas, the payment of which entitles the member to receive one copy of each work issued by the Society for that year.

The annual subscription for members under thirty years of age is one guinea.

MEMBERS or NON-MEMBERS requiring copies of any volume should apply to the Hon. Secretary.

The price of volumes published before 1950 (*i.e.* Vols. I–LXXXVII inclusive) is 21/– to members and 25/– to non-members. Volumes published after that date are available at 42/– to members and 45/– to non-members.

The Society has already issued:—

Vols. I. and II. *State Papers relating to the Defeat of the Spanish Armada, Anno* 1588. Edited by Professor J. K. Laughton. (Vol. I. and II. *Out of Print.*)

Vol. III. *Letters of Lord Hood*, 1781–82. Edited by Mr. David Hannay. (*Out of Print.*)

Vol. IV. *Index to James's Naval History*, by Mr. C. G. Toogood. Edited by the Hon. T. A. Brassey. (*Out of Print.*)

Vol. V. *Life of Captain Stephen Martin*, 1666–1740. Edited by Sir Clements R. Markham. (*Out of Print.*)

Vol. VI. *Journal of Rear-Admiral Bartholomew James*, 1752–1828. Edited by Professor J. K. Laughton and Commander J. Y. F. Sulivan.

Vol. VII. *Hollond's Discourses of the Navy*, 1638 and 1658. Edited by J. R. Tanner.

Vol. VIII. *Naval Accounts and Inventories in the Reign of Henry VII.* Edited by Mr. M. Oppenheim.

Vol. IX. *Journal of Sir George Rooke*. Edited by Mr. Oscar Browning. (*Out of print.*)

Vol. X. *Letters and Papers relating to the War with France*, 1512–13. Edited by M. Alfred Spont.

Vol. XI. *Papers relating to the Spanish War*, 1585–87. Edited by Mr. Julian S. Corbett.

Vol. XII. *Journals and Letters of Admiral of the Fleet Sir Thomas Byam Martin*, 1773–1854 (Vol. II.). Edited by Admiral Sir R. Vesey Hamilton. (*See* XXIV.)

Vol. XIII. *Papers relating to the First Dutch War*, 1652–43 (Vol. I.). Edited by Dr. S. R. Gardiner.

Vol. XIV. *Papers relating to the Blockade of Brest*, 1803–5 (Vol. I.). Edited by Mr. J. Leyland. (*Out of Print.*)

Vol. XV. *History of the Russian Fleet during the Reign of Peter the Great. By a Contemporary Englishman.* Edited by Admiral Sir Cyprian Bridge.

Vol. XVI. *Logs of the Great Sea Fights*, 1794–1805 (Vol. I). Edited by Vice-Admiral Sir T. Sturges Jackson. (*Out of print.*)

Vol. XVII. *Papers relating to the First Dutch War*, 1652–54 (Vol. II.). Edited by Dr. S. R. Gardiner.

Vol. XVIII. *Logs of the Great Sea Fights* (Vol. II.). Edited by Vice-Admiral Sir T. Sturges Jackson. (*Out of Print.*)

Vol. XIX. *Journals and Letters of Sir T. Byam Martin* (Vol. III.). Edited by Admiral Sir R. Vesey-Hamilton. (*See* XXIV.)

Vol. XX. *The Naval Miscellany* (Vol. I.). Edited by Professor J. K. Laughton.

Vol. XXI. *Papers relating to the Blockade of Brest*, 1803–5 (Vol. II.). Edited by Mr. John Leyland. (*Out of Print.*)

Vols. XXII. and XXIII. *The Naval Tracts of Sir William Monson* (Vols. I and II.). Edited by Mr. M. Oppenheim. (*Out of Print.*)

Vol. XXIV. *Journals and Letters of Sir T. Byam Martin* (Vol. I.). Edited by Admiral Sir R. Vesey Hamilton.

Vol. XXV. *Nelson and the Neapolitan Jacobins.* Edited by Mr. H. C. Gutteridge.

Vol. XXVI. *A Descriptive Catalogue of the Naval MSS. in the Pepysian Library* (Vol. I.). Edited by Mr. J. R. Tanner.

Vol. XXVII. *A Descriptive Catalogue of the Naval MSS. in the Pepysian Library* (Vol. II.). Edited by Mr. J. R. Tanner.

Vol. XXVIII. *The Correspondence of Admiral John Markham*, 1801–7. Edited by Sir Clements R. Markham.

Vol. XXIX. *Fighting Instructions*, 1530–1816. Edited by Mr. Julian S. Corbett. (*Out of Print.*)

Vol. XXX. *Papers relating to the First Dutch War*, 1652–54 (Vol. III.). Edited by Dr. S. R. Gardiner and Mr. C. T. Atkinson.

Vol. XXXI. *The Recollections of Commander James Anthony Gardner*, 1775–1814. Edited by Admiral Sir R. Vesey Hamilton and Professor J. K. Laughton. (*Out of Print.*)

Vol. XXXII. *Letters and Papers of Charles, Lord Barham*, 1758–1813 (Vol. I). Edited by Sir J. K. Laughton.

Vol. XXXIII. *Naval Songs and Ballads.* Edited by Professor C. H. Firth.

Vol. XXXIV. *Views of the Battles of the Third Dutch War.* Edited by Mr. Julian S. Corbett. (*Out of Print.*)

Vol. XXXV. *Signals and Instructions*, 1776–94. Edited by Mr. Julian S. Corbett. (*Out of Print.*)

Vol. XXXVI. *A Descriptive Catalogue of the Naval MSS. in the Pepysian Library* (Vol. III.). Edited by Dr. J. R. Tanner.

Vol. XXXVII. *Papers relating to the First Dutch War*, 1652–1654 (Vol. IV.). Edited by Mr. C. T. Atkinson.

Vol. XXXVIII. *Letters and Papers of Charles, Lord Barham*, 1758–1813 (Vol. II.). Edited by Sir J. K. Laughton.

Vol. XXXIX. *Letters and Papers of Charles, Lord Barham*, 1758–1813 (Vol. III.). Edited by Sir J. K. Laughton.

Vol. XL. *The Naval Miscellany* (Vol. II.). Edited by Sir J. K. Laughton. (RE-BINDING.)

Vol. XLI. *Papers relating to the First Dutch War*, 1652–54 (Vol. V.). Edited by Mr. C. T. Atkinson.

Vol. XLII. *Papers relating to the Loss of Minorca in* 1756. Edited by Capt. H. W. Richmond, R.N.

Vol. XLIII. *The Naval Tracts of Sir William Monson* (Vol. III.). Edited by Mr. M. Oppenheim.

Vol. XLIV. *The Old Scots Navy*, 1689–1710. Edited by Mr. James Grant.

Vol. XLV. *The Naval Tracts of Sir William Monson* (Vol. IV.). Edited by Mr. M. Oppenheim.

Vol. XLVI. *The Private Papers of George, second Earl Spencer* (Vol. I.). Edited by Mr. Julian S. Corbett.

Vol. XLVII. *The Naval Tracts of Sir William Monson* (Vol. V.). Edited by Mr. M. Oppenheim.

Vol. XLVIII. *The Private Papers of George, second Earl Spencer* (Vol. II.). Edited by Mr. Julian S. Corbett.

Vol. XLIX. *Documents relating to Law and Custom of the Sea* (Vol. I.). Edited by Mr. R. G. Marsden.

Vol. L. *Documents relating to Law and Custom of the Sea* (Vol. II.). Edited by Mr. R. G. Marsden.

Vol. LI. *Autobiography of Phineas Pett*. Edited by Mr. W. G. Perrin.

Vol. LII. *The Life of Admiral Sir John Leake* (Vol. I.). Edited by Mr. G. A. R. Callender.

Vol. LIII. *The Life of Admiral Sir John Leake* (Vol. II.). Edited by Mr. G. A. R. Callender.

Vol. LIV. *The Life and Works of Sir Henry Mainwaring* (Vol. I.). Edited by Mr. G. E. Manwaring.

Vol. LV. *The Letters of Lord St. Vincent*, 1801–1804 (Vol. I.). Edited by Mr. D. B. Smith.

Vol. LVI. *The Life and Works of Sir Henry Mainwaring* (Vol. II.). Edited by Mr. G. E. Manwaring and Mr. W. G. Perrin.

Vol. LVII. *A Descriptive Catalogue of the Naval MSS. in the Pepysian Library* (Vol. IV.). Edited by Dr. J. R. Tanner.

Vol. LVIII. *The Private Papers of George, second Earl Spencer* (Vol. III.). Edited by Rear-Admiral H. W. Richmond.

Vol. LIX. *The Private Papers of George, second Earl Spencer* (Vol. IV.). Edited by Rear-Admiral H. W. Richmond.

Vol. LX. *Samuel Pepys's Naval Minutes*. Edited by Dr. J. R. Tanner.

Vol. LXI. *The Letters of Lord St. Vincent*, 1801–1804 (Vol. II.). Edited by Mr. D. B. Smith.

Vol. LXII. *Letters and Papers of Admiral Viscount Keith* (Vol. I.). Edited by Mr. W. G. Perrin.

Vol. LXIII. *The Naval Miscellany* (Vol. III.). Edited by Mr. W. G. Perrin. (RE-BINDING.)

Vol. LXIV. *The Journal of the First Earl of Sandwich*. Edited by Mr. R. C. Anderson.

Vol. LXV. *Boteler's Dialogues*. Edited by Mr. W. G. Perrin.

Vol. LXVI. *Papers relating to the First Dutch War*, 1652–54 (Vol. VI.; with index). Edited by Mr. C. T. Atkinson.

Vol. LXVII. *The Byng Papers* (Vol. I.). Edited by Mr. W. C. B. Tunstall.

Vol. LXVIII. *The Byng Papers* (Vol. II.). Edited by Mr. W. C. B. Tunstall.

Vol. LXIX. *The Private Papers of John, Earl of Sandwich* (Vol. I.). Edited by Mr. G. R. Barnes and Lieut.-Commander J. H. Owen, R.N.

Corrigenda to *Papers relating to the First Dutch War*, 1652–54 (Vols. I. to VI.). Edited by Captain A. C. Dewar, R.N.

Vol. LXX. *The Byng Papers* (Vol. III.). Edited by Mr. W. C. B. Tunstall.

Vol. LXXI. *The Private Papers of John, Earl of Sandwich* (Vol. II.). Edited by G. R. Barnes and Lieut-Commander J. H. Owen, R.N.

Vol. LXXII. *Piracy in the Levant*, 1827–8. Edited by Lieut.-Commander C. G. Pitcairn Jones, R.N.

Vol. LXXIII. *The Tangier Papers of Samuel Pepys*. Edited by Mr. Edwin Chappell. (*Out of print.*)

Vol. LXXIV. *The Tomlinson Papers*. Edited by Mr. J. G. Bullocke.

Vol. LXXV. *The Private Papers of John, Earl of Sandwich* (Vol. III.). Edited by Mr. G. R. Barnes and Commander J. H. Owen, R.N.

Vol. LXXVI. *The Letters of Robert Blake*. Edited by the Rev. J. R. Powell.

Vol. LXXVII. *Letters and Papers of Admiral the Hon. Samuel Barrington* (Vol. I.). Edited by Mr. D. Bonner-Smith.

Vol. LXXVIII. *The Private Papers of John, Earl of Sandwich* (Vol. IV.). Edited by Mr. G. R. Barnes and Commander J. H. Owen, R.N.

Vol. LXXIX. *The Journals of Sir Thomas Allin*, 1660–1678 (Vol. I. 1660–66). Edited by Mr. R. C. Anderson.

Vol. LXXX. *The Journals of Sir Thomas Allin*, 1660–1678 (Vol. II. 1667–78). Edited by Mr. R. C. Anderson.

Vol. LXXXI. *Letters and Papers of Admiral the Hon. Samuel Barrington* (Vol. II.). Edited by Mr. D. Bonner-Smith.

Vol. LXXXII. *Captain Boteler's Recollections* (1808 to 1830). Edited by Mr. D. Bonner-Smith. (*Out of Print.*)

Vol. LXXXIII. *Russian War*, 1854. *Baltic and Black Sea: Official Correspondence*. Edited by Mr. D. Bonner-Smith and Captain A. C. Dewar, R.N.

Vol. LXXXIV. *Russian War*, 1855. *Baltic: Official Correspondence*. Edited by Mr. D. Bonner-Smith.

Vol. LXXXV. *Russian War*, 1855. *Black Sea: Official Correspondence*. Edited by Captain A. C. Dewar, R.N.

Vol. LXXXVI. *Journals and Narratives of the Third Dutch War*. Edited by Mr. R. C. Anderson.

Vol. LXXXVII. *The Naval Brigades in the Indian Mutiny*, 1857–58. Edited by Commander W. B. Rowbotham, R.N.

Vol. LXXXVIII. *Pattee Byng's Journal*. Edited by Mr. J. L. Cranmer-Byng.

Vol. LXXXIX. *The Sergison Papers*. Edited by Commander R. D. Merriman, R.I.N.

Vol. XC. *The Keith Papers* (Vol. II.). Edited by Mr. C. C. Lloyd.

Vol. XCI. *Five Naval Journals*, 1789–1817. Edited by Rear-Admiral H. G. Thursfield.

Vol. XCII. *The Naval Miscellany* (Vol. IV.). Edited by Mr. C. C. Lloyd.

Vol. XCIII. *Sir William Dillon's Narrative of Professional Adventures* (*1790–1839*) (Vol. I. 1790–1802). Edited by Professor Michael A. Lewis.

Vol. XCIV (additional volume for 1953). *The Walker Expedition to Quebec, 1711*. Edited by Professor Gerald S. Graham.

Vol. XCV. *The Second China War*, 1856–60. Edited by Mr. D. Bonner-Smith and Mr. E. W. R. Lumby.

Vol. XCVI. *The Keith Papers*, 1803–1815 (Vol. III.). Edited by Professor C. C. Lloyd.

Vol. XCVII. *Sir William Dillon's Narrative of Professional Adventures* (1790–1839) (Vol. II. 1802–1839). Edited by Professor Michael A. Lewis.

Vol. XCVIII. *The Private Correspondence of Admiral Lord Collingwood*. Edited by Professor Edward Hughes.

Vol. XCIX. *The Vernon Papers*. Edited by Mr. B. McL. Ranft.

Vol. C. *Nelson's Letters to his Wife and Other Documents*. Edited by Lieut.-Commander G. P. B. Naish, R.N.V.R.

Vol. CI. *A Memoir of James Trevenen*. Edited by Mr. C. C. Lloyd and Dr. R. C. Anderson.

Navy Records Society

LIST OF MEMBERS

1959

Allan, Lieutenant John F., R.N., Calderside House, Shotts, Lanarkshire.
Allen, Lieutenant (S.) A. E., R.N., Tudor House, 61 Grant Road, Farlington, Portsmouth, Hants.
Allenby, R. F. H., Esq., The Beacon, Shanklin, Isle of Wight.
Ampthill, Captain The Lord, C.B.E., R.N., 6 Springfield Road, St. Johns Wood, London, N.W. 8.
Anderson, R. C., Esq., Litt.D., F.S.A., 32 Dartmouth Row, London, S.E. 10.
Andrewes, Vice-Admiral Sir William, K.B.E., C.B., D.S.O., Sparkford House, St. Cross Road, Winchester.
Armytage, Captain R. W., A.M., R.N., Foxlease, Limpley Stoke, nr. Bath.
Arrowsmith, Lieutenant H. C., R.N.V.R., Moorings, Grove Road, Southlands, Stone, Staffs.
Artingstall, Dr. D. C., M.R.C.S., L.R.C.P., "Hendra", 1 Wash Lane, Yardley, Birmingham, 25.
Atkinson, C. T., Esq., 16 Chadlington Road, Oxford.
Austin, E. D., Esq., 17 Earls Court Road, Penylan, Cardiff.

Baddeley, Sir Vincent W., K.C.B., 60 Harley House, Marylebone Road, London, N.W. 1.
Bailey, Lieutenant N., R.N., Ravensthorpe, Northampton.
Barlow, Captain T. E., D.S.C., R.N., Boswells, Wendover, Bucks.
Barnard, Vice-Admiral Sir Geoffrey, K.C.B., Bramdean Lodge, Bramdean, nr. Alresford, Hants.
Barnes, Lieutenant-Commander H. J., R.N., Office of Flag Officer, Reserve Aircraft, R.N. Air Station, Arbroath, Angus.
Barnes, Sir George R., The Clock House, Keele, Staffs.
Barton, D. F., Esq., Henslow Close, Fyfield, Abingdon, Berks.
Bateman, C. J. L., Esq., Caixa Postal 416, Santos, Brazil.
Baugh, D. A., 34 Hinton Way, Great Shelford, Cambs.
Bax, Allan E., Esq., Union Building, 8–14 Bond Street, Sydney, Australia.
Beale, Commander P. S., R.N., Lane End, Green Lane, Lee-on-Solent, Hants.
Beard, D. R., Esq., Southlow Cottage, Wetley Rocks, Stoke-on-Trent.
Beattie, Captain S. H., V.C., R.N., A.C.R. Department, Queen Anne's Mansions, London, S.W. 1.
Beeston, P. S., Esq., c/o National Bank of Australasia Ltd., 308 Queen Street, Brisbane, Australia.
Begg, Captain M. M. I., R.E., c/o Glyn, Mills & Co., 22 Whitehall, London, S.W. 1.

Bell, Captain L. H., C.B.E., R.N., c/o The Admiralty, London, S.W. 1.
Bellairs, Rear-Admiral Roger M., C.B., C.M.G., Wyvenhoe, Farnham Royal, Bucks.
Benbow, Colin H., Esq., B.A., 33 Heathfield Gardens, London, N.W. 11.
Bennett, Captain G. M., D.S.C., R.N., c/o National Provincial Bank Ltd., The Hard, Portsmouth, Hants.
Besford, C. H., Esq., 4 Vine Cottages, Grove Footpath, Surbiton, Surrey.
Besnard, Lieutenant P., R.N.N., c/o Marine Post Kantoor, Amsterdam, Holland.
Bing, M. S., Esq., 3 East View, Hitchmead Road, Biggleswade, Beds.
Blair, Arthur W., Esq., 22 Thorn Drive, Bearsden, Glasgow.
Blake, Vice-Admiral Sir Geoffrey, K.C.B., D.S.O., 34 Sloane Court West, London, S.W. 3.
Blundell, Captain G. C., O.B.E., R.N., Goldicote House, nr. Stratford-on-Avon, Warwicks.
Booth, Lieutenant Norleigh, R.N.V.R., Stanner's Close, Corbridge-on-Tyne.
Boultbee, Lieutenant-Colonel W. R. P., R.M., 38 Priestfields, Rochester, Kent.
Boyer, Francis L., Esq., Box 1459, Corpus Christi, Texas, U.S.A.
Boysen, Asmus, Buchhandlung, Hamburg, 1, Hermannstrasse 8, Germany.
Bright, Captain B. N. F., B.Hist., 16 Deva Terrace, Chester, Cheshire.
Brock, Rear-Admiral P. W., R.N., c/o Bank of Montreal, 47 Threadneedle Street, London, E.C. 2.
Brockman, Captain (S.) W. E., c/o Admiralty, (D.W.S.C.), Queen Anne's Mansions, London, S.W. 1.
Bromley, John S., Esq., M.A., Keble College, Oxford.
Brooke, Mrs. Cecil, Hampton Court Palace, Middx.
Brooks, Lieutenant-Commander C. E., R.C.N., Residence 197, H.M.C. Dockyard, Esquimalt, B.C., Canada.
Brown, Thomas W. F., Esq., D.Sc., Dumbreck, Wylam, Northumberland.
Buckland, J. V., Esq., Honer House, South Mundham, nr. Chichester, Sussex.
Buckle, F. A., Esq., The County Secondary School, Midhurst, Sussex.
Bulley, Lieutenant H. C. E., R.N., St. Edmund's School, Hindhead, Surrey.
Bullocke, Professor J. G., 5 Dartmouth Grove, Greenwich, London, S.E. 10.
Burden, Lieutenant (S.) H. S., R.N.V.R., 63 Eastfield Road, Waltham Cross, Herts.
Burnford, J. M. W., Esq., Borough Farm, Pulborough, Sussex.
Burns, Lieutenant-Commander George, R.N.V.R., 201 Bath Street (2nd Floor), Glasgow, C. 1.
Burrough, Admiral Sir Harold M., K.C.B., K.B.E., D.S.O., c/o Westminster Bank Ltd., 21 Clarendon Road, Southsea, Hants.
Burton, Commander E. A. Angerstein-, R.N., The Old Rectory, West Lexham, King's Lynn, Norfolk.
Butler, Professor J. R. Montagu, O.B.E., M.V.O., M.A., Cabinet Offices, Great George Street, London, S.W. 1.
Butler-Bowden, Captain M. E., O.B.E., R.N., Dapsland, Mayfield, Sussex.

Calvin, C. C., c/o Fasken Robertson & Co., 36 Toronto Street, Toronto, Ontario, Canada.
Carr, Frank G. G., Esq., National Maritime Museum, London, S.E. 10.
Carter, Captain T. G., O.B.E., R.N., c/o Glyn, Mills & Co., Kirkland House, Whitehall, London, S.W. 1.
Catlow, A. J., Esq., Sunnydene, Bounds Cross, Biddenden, Ashford, Kent.
Caufield, W., Esq., B.Sc., M.R.C.V.S., 26 Regent Place, Rugby.
Chandler, Commander R. B., R.N., Recruiting Office, Royal Navy & Royal Marines, 7 St. John's Lane, Liverpool, 1.
Charig, Captain (E.) Peter, R.N., Orchard House, Claverton, Bath, Somerset.
Chatfield, Admiral of the Fleet the Rt. Hon. Lord, G.C.B., O.M., K.C.M.G., C.V.O., D.C.L., The Small House, Farnham Common, Bucks.

Chichester, Commander M. G., R.N., 83 Barkston Gardens, London, S.W. 5.
Child, Commander D. W., O.B.E., R.N.V.R., 2 Carlton Court, Knole Road, Bexhill-on-Sea, Sussex.
Clarke, Mrs. K. B., Lower Hitch, Whitchurch Hill, Pangbourne, Berks.
Cleveland-Stevens, W., Esq., Q.C., Winchet Hall, Goudhurst, Kent.
Cleyndert, J. B. De J., Esq., 4 Strand on the Green, London, W. 4.
Cole, Commander (S.) J. H. Melvin, R.N., c/o Westminster Bank Ltd., 26 Haymarket, London, S.W. 1.
Cole, Commander P. F., R.N., H.A.F. Med., F.M.O., Malta.
Congleton, The Rt. Hon. Lord, Minstead Lodge, Lyndhurst, Hants.
Costeker, Miss E. P., 15 Marlborough Road, Bournemouth West.
Coulehan, N., Esq., Burke Road North, Ivanhoe, Melbourne, Australia.
Creswell, Captain John, R.N., Ellerslie, Gattistock, Dorchester.
Crick, Commander T. G. P., O.B.E., D.S.C., R.N., c/o Barclays Bank Ltd., Peterborough.
Critchley, Lieutenant (S.) W. L., R.N., 94 Brookmead, London Road, Tonbridge, Kent.
Cunliffe, Captain R. L. B., C.B.E., R.N., Pakenham Lodge, Bury St. Edmunds, Suffolk.
Cunningham-Graham, Vice-Admiral Sir A. E. M. B., K.B.E., C.B., Ardoch, Cardross, Dunbartonshire.

Daly, Associate Professor R. W., U.S. Naval Academy, Annapolis, Md., U.S.A.
Davidson, The Rt. Hon. The Viscount, G.C.V.O., C.H., C.B., Norcott Court, Berkhampstead, Herts.
Davis, B. J., Esq., F.C.A., 10 Ridgway, Wimbledon, London, S.W. 19.
Daw, Instructor Commander L. J., R.N., Fair View, 514 Crownhill Road, Higher St. Budeaux, Plymouth.
Dawson, Instructor Commander E. R., M.A., R.N., 9 Guest Road, Cambridge.
de Beer, Esmond S., Esq., F.R.Hist.S., 11 Sussex Place, London, N.W. 1.
de Cosson, Lieutenant-Commander C. Anthony, R.N.V.R., 3062 Mathers Avenue, West Vancouver, B.C.
de Pass, Lieutenant-Commander Robert E. F., New Grove, Petworth, Sussex.
Dewar, Captain A. C., C.B., O.B.E., B.Litt., F.R.Hist.S., R.N., Junior Army and Navy Club, Horse Guards Avenue, London, S.W. 1.
Digby, D. A., Esq., Flat 1, 17 Cathcart Hill, London, N. 19.
Dorling, Captain H. Taprell, D.S.O., R.N., F.R.Hist.S., 97 Rivermead Court, Hurlingham, London, S.W. 6.
Douglas, Alan, M.D., F.R.C.P.(C), 289 Dufferin Avenue, London, Ontario, Canada.
Dowell, Squadron-Leader W., Restenet, Lenzie, Glasgow.
Drake, K. M., Esq., 17 King's Drive, Birstall, Leeds.
Draper, A. S., Esq., "Lindum", Green Lane, Spennymoor, Co. Durham.
Drent, Sub-Lieutenant J., R.C.N., Wardroom, H.M.C.S. *Stadacona*, Halifax, N. Scotia.
Driscoll, The Reverend W. J., R.N., St. Joan of Arc's, Torpoint, Cornwall.
Dye, Commander Ira, U.S.N., Commander Submarine Division Fifty-two, c/o Fleet Post Office, San Francisco, California, U.S.A.

Eames, A., Esq., M.A., Hafryn, Belmont Road, Bangor, Carns., N. Wales.
Eastwick, Miss C. L., Curlew Bank, Brittas Bay, Co. Wicklow, Eire.
Eccleshall, Leslie C., Esq., 148 Priory Road, Hardway, Gosport, Hants.
Eckford, Lieutenant (S.) P. J., R.N., c/o Lloyds Bank Ltd., Sparkhill, Birmingham.
Edwards, Messrs. Francis, Ltd., 83 High Street, Marylebone, London, W. 1.
Egerton, Rear-Admiral Brian, The Manor House, Ringwood, Hants.
Ehrman, John, Esq., M.A., F.R.S., Sloane House, 149 Old Church Street, London, S.W. 3.
Eldridge, R. G., Esq., 18 Forest Street, Yarmouth, Nova Scotia, Canada.

Elphinstone, Kenneth V., Esq., Artillery Mansions, Westminster, London, S.W. 1.
Ensor, Lieutenant Moreton J., U.S.N.R., 30 Charles Street, Lexington 73, Mass., U.S.A.
Erskine, The Hon. David, 50 Argyll Road, Kensington, London, W. 8.
Evans, Commander (S.) L. C., V.R.D., LL.B., F.C.A., R.N.V.R., 1 Windsor Place, Liskeard, Cornwall.
Evershed, The Right Hon. Lord, Royal Courts of Justice, Strand, London, W.C. 2.

Fardell, Commander K. M., R.N., Hartfield, Littleham Cross, Exmouth, Devon.
Farrington, Instructor Lieutenant-Commander L., H.M.C.S. *Venture*, H.M.C. Dockyard, Esquimalt, British Columbia, Canada.
Fenwick, K., Esq., 22 Grosvenor Road, Scarborough.
Ferrigno, Anthony V., 29 Caldy Road, Aintree, Liverpool, 9, Lancs.
Feteris, Vice-Admiral P. J., C.B.E., Royal Netherlands Navy, Van Boetzelaerlaan, 57B, The Hague.
Fisher, Lieutenant-Commander R. C., R.N., c/o Westminster Bank Ltd., Clarendon Road, Southsea, Hants.
Foxley, G. H., Esq., 10 Westcraig Avenue, Moston, Manchester, 10.

Gascoigne, Instructor Commander J. C., O.B.E., R.N., H.M.S. *Dryad*, Smethwick House, nr. Fareham, Hants.
Gaunt, R. H., Esq., Dane Court School, Pyrford, nr. Woking, Surrey.
Gibbs, Professor N. H., All Souls College, Oxford.
Gilbert, Commander (S.) A. D., R.N., St. John's Cottage, She Field, nr. Southampton.
Gilchrist, Lieutenant W. L. R. E., R.N., H.M.S. *Crofton*, c/o G.P.O., London.
Gill, Lieutenant-Commander G. Herman, R.A.N.V.R., Inveresk, 258 Beaconsfield Parade, Middle Park, Melbourne, S.C. 6.
Gillespie, Commander (S.) T. P., M.B.E., R.N., c/o The Manager, Lloyds Bank Ltd., Commercial Road, Portsmouth.
Glossop, Lieutenant Commander J. J., R.N., H.M.S. *Dryad*, Southwick, nr. Fareham, Hants.
Godfrey, Admiral J. H., C.B., White Stacks, Wilmington, nr. Polegate, Sussex.
Goulding, Lieutenant-Commander B. H., R.N., The Tannery, Kintbury, Newbury, Berks.
Graham, Professor Gerald S., M.A., Ph.D., University of London, King's College, Strand, London, W.C. 2.
Graham, N. W., Esq., Suilven, Kings Road, Longniddry, East Lothian.
Grant, Alistair Ian, Esq., c/o Grant & Cia Ltd., Rua XV de Novembre 194, P.O. Box 707, Santos, Brazil.
Graves, Miss F. M., Cocknowle, Wareham, Dorset.
Grice, Lieutenant H. R. C., R.N., H.M.S. *Ariel*, Worthy Down, nr. Winchester, Hants.
Gwilliam, R., Esq., 9 Eccleston Avenue, Handbridge, Chester.

Hale, Colonel F. W. H., Box 913, G.P.O., Melbourne, Victoria.
Hall, Instructor Rear-Admiral Sir Arthur E., K.B.E., C.B., 10 Liskeard Gardens, Blackheath, London, S.E. 3.
Hanson, Lieutenant-Commander R. J., D.S.O., D.S.C., R.N., Cliff House, Leckhampton Hill, Cheltenham, Glos.
Harding, Gilbert, Esq., 9 Mulgrave Road, London, N.W. 10.
Hazel, Senior Commissioned Gunner E. W., Ward Room Mess, Royal Naval Barracks, Chatham, Kent.
Hegarty, Lieutenant-Commander (E.) R. D. M., R.N., 475 Maidstone Road, Wigmore, Gillingham, Kent.
Herbert, M., Esq., The White House, Perry Street, Chislehurst, Kent.
Hill, Surgeon Lieutenant-Commander R. C. J., R.N.V.R. (Retd.), 606 Essenwood Road, Durban, Natal, South Africa.

Hill, Mrs. S. F., 181 Rayleigh Road, Hutton, Essex.
Holder, Lieutenant D. K., R.N., 24 Crooks Lane, Alcester, Warwickshire.
Hood, The Viscount, c/o The Foreign Office, Whitehall, London, S.W. 1.
Hope, Admiral Sir George, K.C.B., K.C.M.G., Common House, Plaistow, Billinghurst, Sussex.
Hordern, Lieutenant-Commander M. C., R.A.N.R., B.A., c/o Comm. Banking Co. of Sydney Ltd., Old Jewry, London, E.C. 2.
Hornsby, F. L., Esq., Bletchley, Moulyining, Western Australia.
Horsburgh, George D. L., Esq., c/o Messrs. Swift Levick & Sons Ltd., Clarence Steel Works, Sheffield, 4.
Horton, Captain C. Ivan, R.N., Fenwick Cottage, Emsworth, Hants.
Howatt, Sub-Lieutenant C. G., R.N., 6½ St. Peter's Grove, York.
Howieson, Lieutenant L. S., R.N., 98 Shandon Road, Broadwater, Worthing, Sussex.
Hughes, Arthur J., Esq., Pages, Chigwell Row, Essex.
Hughes, Professor Edward, The Manor House, Shincliffe, Durham.
Hume, J. M., Esq., c/o The Royal Northumberland Yacht Club, Blyth.
Humphreys, Commander L. A., R.N., Elm Lodge, Biddestone, Chippenham, Wilts.
Hussey, John, Esq., Farleigh, East Albany Road, Seaford, Sussex.

Ingram, Captain Sir Bruce S., O.B.E., M.C., Ingram House, 195/198 Strand, London, W.C. 2.
Irrmann, Professor Robert, Ph.D., Department of History, Beloit College, Beloit, Wisconsin, U.S.A.
Iveagh, The Rt. Hon. The Earl of, C.B., C.M.G., Pyrford Court, Woking, Surrey.
Ivliev, N. V., Esq., 89 Addison Road, London, W. 14.

Jackson, Instructor Captain T. E., R.N. (Retd.), 131 Gudge Heath Lane, Fareham, Hants.
Jackson, Rear-Admiral W. L., D.S.O., Soberton Mill, Swanmore, Hants.
Jacob, Commander J. C., R.N., The Red House, Woodbridge, Suffolk.
James, Admiral Sir William M., G.C.B., The Road Farm, Churt, Surrey.
Jennings, Lieutenant-Commander E. D., R.N., Camperdown, Melvil Road, Lee-on-Solent, Hants.
Jenson, Commander L. B., C.D., R.C.N., 26 Renfrew Avenue, Ottawa, Ontario, Canada.
Jewell, J., Esq., c/o Lloyds Bank Ltd., Devonport, Devon.
Johnson, S. H. F., Esq., University College of Wales, Aberystwyth, Cards.
Jones, Lieutenant-Commander (S.) A. M., R.N., Suffield, Albert Drive, Deganwy, Caernarvonshire.
Jones, Commander C. G. Pitcairn, R.N., The Old Vicarage, Farningham, Kent.
Jones, Commodore Gerald N., C.B.E., D.S.O., R.D., R.N.R., Westwinds, Deganwy, N. Wales.
Jones, Commander Whitson M., U.S.N.R., 2350 Calle Corta, La Jolla, California, U.S.A.

Kelsey, J. A. C., Esq., 46 Ambleside Gardens, South Kenton, Wembley, Middx.
Kemp, Commander P. K., R.N., Malcolm's, 51 Market Hill, Maldon, Essex.
Kennedy, L., Esq., Piers Place, Old Amersham, Bucks.
Kingsford, The Rev. Maurice R., M.A., B.Litt., The Rectory, Nuneham Courtenay, Oxford.
Kinnahan, Admiral Sir H. R. G., K.B.E., C.B., Severn Ridge, Gloucester Road, Almondsbury, Bristol.
Kirk, Admiral Alan Goodrich, U.S.N. (Retd.), The Dakota, 1 West 72nd Street, New York 23, New York, U.S.A.
Knight, R. W., Esq., P.O. Box 56, Port Louis, Mauritius.
Knox, Captain D. W., U.S.N., Navy Historical Foundation, c/o Navy Department, Washington 25, D.C., U.S.A.

Ladner, Thomas E., Esq., 4610 Connaught Drive, Vancouver, B.C., Canada.
Laing, E. A. M., Esq., 73 Barrow Point Avenue, Pinner, Middx.
Lambe, Vice-Admiral Charles, Knockhill House, Newport, Fife.
Lambert, H. V. A., Esq., c/o Barclays Bank Ltd., 54 Lombard Street, London, E.C. 3.
Lampen, Commander D., D.S.O., O.B.E., R.N., White Rocks House, Garway Hill, Hereford.
Lang, Sir John G., K.C.B., The Admiralty, London, S.W. 1.
Larsson, Hans, Esq., c/o Svenska Dagbladet, Stockholm, Sweden.
Lavett, Lieutenant J. L., R.A.N., c/o Department of External Affairs, Canberra, A.C.T., Australia.
Law, H. G., Esq., Spring Grove, Ranelagh Drive, Bracknell, Berks.
Lawder, Commander (S.) M. C., R.N., Brook House, Wrington, nr. Bristol, Somerset.
Leach, Lieutenant J. B., R.N., c/o Barclays Bank Ltd., Tredegar, Mon.
Leck, John E., Esq., M.R.S.T., 3 Stanley Avenue, Latchford Without, Warrington, Lancs.
Leinster-Mackay, D. P., c/o Midland Bank Ltd., Witney, Oxon.
Lemon, H., Esq., 48 Moutcharles, Belfast.
Lenox, Patrick G., Esq., Suite 401, The Canadian Bank of Commerce Building, 640 West Hastings Street, Vancouver, 2, B.C., Canada.
Lester, Lieutenant Richard M., R.C.N.(R.), 20 Chipping Road, Don Mills, P.O., Ontario, Canada.
Lewis, Captain A. F. P., R.N., Garden Cottage, Hindhead, Surrey.
Lewis, J. Parry, University College, Cathays Park, Cardiff.
Lewis, Professor Michael A., C.B.E., M.A., F.S.A., F.R.Hist.S., 36 Dartmouth Row, Greenwich, London, S.E. 10.
Lister, R., Esq., Grey Friars, Kent Road, Harrogate.
Little, Admiral Sir Charles J. C., G.C.B., G.B.E., The Old Mill, Ashurst, nr. Steyning, Sussex.
Lloyd, Professor C. C., M.A., F.R.Hist.S., Royal Naval College, Greenwich, London, S.E. 10.
Lloyd, Mrs. K. B., Pilgrims House, Knockholt, Kent.
Lloyd, Commander L. G. B., R.N.V.R., Battledown View, Oakley Road, Cheltenham.
Lloyd, Lieutenant-Colonel W. A. S., M.B.E., Mucklowe House, 53 Strand-on-the-Green, London, W. 4.
Loram, R. G., Esq., Land House, Blind Lane, Mersham, Ashford, Kent.
Lorimer, Surgeon Commander J., M.B., Ch.B., R.N.V.R., Hazlewood Creetown, Kirkcudbrightshire, Scotland.
Love, Major Stuart, D.S.O., M.C., 31 Irving Road, Toorak, Melbourne, S.E. 2.
Lowe, Brian S., Esq., 1877 Haro Street, Vancouver, B.C., Canada.
Lowther, Lieutenant L. W. H., R.N.V.(S.)R., The Old Vicarage, Wix, nr. Manningtree, Essex.
Lucas, J. C., Holly Lodge, Croxfield Green, Petersfield, Hants.

McCormick-Goodhart, Commander L., O.B.E., V.R.D., R.N.V.R., 610 East Boulevard Drive, Alexandria, Virginia, U.S.A.
McDougall, Commander A. R., R.N.V.R., Stone House, Highmoor Cross, nr. Henley-on-Thames, Oxon.
Macdougall, Miss K. Lindsay-, 25 Hans Place, London, S.W. 1.
Mackay, R. F., Esq., 7 Mt. Boone, Dartmouth, Devon.
Mackenzie, Instructor Lieutenant-Commander D. D., c/o Royal Bank of Canada, Douglas Street, Victoria, B.C., Canada.
McKee, Lieutenant Fraser M., R.C.N. (R.), 33 Hansen Avenue, Beaconsfield, Quebec, Canada.
McKeown, Commander (E.) R. J., R.C.N., c/o Principal, R.C.N. Technical Representative, Harland & Wolfe, Belfast, N. Ireland.

Martin, Captain C. J. P., 41 Lish Avenue, Whitley Bay, Northumberland.

Mason, Colonel F. van Wych, Enfield, Ely's Harbor, Somerset, Bermuda.

Mathew, The Most Rev. Archbishop, M.A., Litt.D., F.S.A., Athenæum, Pall Mall, London, S.W. 1.

Mathieson, Writer A. H., 12 Eglington Street, Saltcoats, Ayrshire.

Mendenhall, Professor T. C., 128 High Street, New Haven, Connecticut, U.S.A.

Merriman, Commander R. D., D.S.C., R.I.N., Somerdown, 26 Somers Road, Reigate, Surrey.

Millar, Commandant E. Hoyer, O.B.E., W.R.N.S., Queen Anne's Mansions, London, S.W. 1.

Minchin, Sub-Lieutenant P. D., R.N., Waterbrook, Sevington, Ashford, Kent.

Moe, Colonel Albert F., U.S.M.C. (Retd.), 4729 N. Washington Boulevard, Arlington 5, Virginia, U.S.A.

Moir, Lieutenant-Colonel A. C. D., Woodham, Manor Road, Chigwell, Essex.

Monsarrat, Nicholas, Apt. 807, Sandringham Appts., Ottawa, Canada.

Montgomery, Commander J. R. C., R.N., Kinnabus, The Oa, Port Ellen, Isle of Islay, Scotland.

Moore, Sir Alan, Bart., Hancox, Whatlington, Battle, Sussex.

Moore, Admiral Sir Henry R., G.C.B., C.V.O., D.S.O., Junior United Service Club, London, S.W. 1.

Morgan, John M., 2118 Robinwood Avenue, Toledo, 2, Ohio, U.S.A.

Morse, Rear-Admiral Sir John A. V., K.C.B., C.B., D.S.O., Union Club, Carlton House Terrace, London, S.W. 1.

Mote, Captain Paul, U.S.N.R. (Retd.), Box 1275, Fairhope, Alabama, U.S.A.

Mountbatten of Burma, Admiral of the Fleet The Earl, K.G., P.C., G.C.S.I., G.C.I.E., G.C.V.O., G.C.B., D.S.O., First Sea Lord, Admiralty, London, S.W. 1.

Moxly, Commander S. H. S., The Stone Frigate, Belmore Lane, Lymington, Hants.

Muderlugu, Deniz Muzesi, Dolmabrahce, Istanbul, Turkey.

Naish, Lieutenant-Commander George P. B., R.N.V.R., National Maritime Museum, London, S.E. 10.

Nijhoff, Mr. Martinus, Lang Voorhout 9, The Hague, Holland.

Nugent, Vice-Admiral R. A., C.M.G., The Field House, Lee-on-Solent, Hants.

Ogelsby, Captain J. C. M., U.S.M.C.R., 317 Lakeside South, Seattle 44, Washington, U.S.A.

Overton, E. M., Esq., 54 Somerset Road, Edgbaston, Birmingham, 15.

Owen, Commander J. H., F.R.Hist.S., R.N., 41A Roland Gardens, London, S.W. 7.

Packer, Vice-Admiral Sir H. A., K.C.B., C.B.E., Fourth Sea Lord, Admiralty, London, S.W. 1.

Palmer, Lieutenant-Commander J. A., R.N., Langham Hill Cottage, Ivybridge, S. Devon.

Parker, Lieutenant V. A., R.A.N., 14 East Crescent Street, MacMahons Point, nr. Sydney, Australia.

Parker, Lieutenant-Commander E. V., V.R.D., R.N.V.R., 61 Marlborough Crescent, Sevenoaks, Kent.

Parkinson, C. Northcote, Esq., Ph.D., D.R.Hist.S., Department of History, University of Malay, Cluny Road, Singapore.

Pearsall, A. W. H., Esq., 6 Pemberton Drive, Morecambe, Lancs.

Pelling, John L., Esq., Messrs. T. Bickerstaff & Son, A9 & 10 Queen Insurance Buildings, 10 Dale Street, Liverpool, 2.

Penn, C. D., Esq., F.R.Hist.S., 4 Grantley House, 30A Florence Road, Boscombe, Bournemouth.

Penney, Major-General W. R. C., C.B., C.B.E., D.S.O., M.C., Brooks House, Stanford Dingley, Berks.
Perren, G. E., Esq., 64 High Street, Burnham-on-Crouch, Essex.
Petree, J. Foster, Esq., 36 Mayfield Road, Sutton, Surrey.
Petrie-Hay, Lieutenant-Commander (S.) A. J., R.N., H.M.S. *Harrier*, Kete, nr. Haverfordwest, Pembrokeshire.
Pett, Lieutenant W. C. G., R.N. (Retd.), 4 Ralph Devlin Drive, Halifax, Nova Scotia.
Peyton-Burbery, Rev. Canon R. J. P., S.G.M., R.N., St. Mary's Rectory, March, Cambridgeshire.
Phillips, Bertram, Esq., 7A Crown Circus, Downahill, Glasgow, W. 2.
Phillips, Lieutenant J. M., R.N., Maresfield Lodge, Maresfield, nr. Uckfield, Sussex.
Phillips, Lieutenant-Commander M. H., V.R.D., R.N.V.R., The Bombay Co. Ltd., P.O. Box 201, Bombay.
Plunkett-Ernle-Erle-Drax, Admiral The Hon. Sir Reginald A. R., K.C.B., D.S.O., Charborough Park, Wareham, Dorset.
Pool, Bernard F., Esq., C.B., C.B.E., 81 Bromley Road, Shortlands, Bromley, Kent.
Pope, Dudley, Flat 774, 67 Chancery Lane, London, W.C. 2.
Potter, John A., 14 Sandringham Gardens, N. Finchley, London, N. 12.
Powell, The Rev. J. R., 85 Carlisle Mansions, London, S.W. 1.
Price, Lieutenant G. D. A., R.N.V.R., Barlow Fold, Heybridge Lane, Prestbury, Cheshire.
Prime, Alfred C., R.D.I., North Valley Road, Malvern, Penn., U.S.A.
Pring, Commander (S.) L. W., R.N., Stoneways, 60 Aldenham Avenue, Radlett, Herts.
Pullen, Rear-Admiral H. F., O.B.E., R.C.N., 15 Lorne Terrace, Halifax, Nova Scotia.

Raikes, Commander Iwan G., D.S.C., R.N., Mantley, Newent, Glos.
Ranft, B. McL., Esq., Royal Naval College, Greenwich, London, S.E. 10.
Rayner, Commander D. A., R.N.V.R., Earlstone Manor, Burghclere, nr. Newbury, Berks.
Regnart, Lieutenant H. J., R.N., H.M.S. *Fulmar*, Lossiemouth, Moray.
Reid, Captain W. R. G., R.N., Bordein, West End, Woking, Surrey.
Rivers, P. J., Esq., c/o The Chartered Bank, Singapore.
Robinson, T. I., Esq., Braishfield Manor, Romsey, Hants.
Robson, Brian, Esq., 31 Hangleton Way, Hove, Sussex.
Rodger, A. B., Esq., Balliol College, Oxford.
Roper, Captain E. G., D.S.O., D.S.C., R.N., Polmayne, St. Minver, Cornwall.
Roskill, Captain Stephen W., C.B.E., R.N., Blounce, South Warnborough, Basingstoke, Hants.
Ross, Commander R. D., R.N., c/o Westminster Bank Ltd., 26 Haymarket, London, S.W. 1.
Rowbotham, Commander, W. B., R.N., 22 Ashley Gardens, London, S.W. 1.
Rutherford, Miss G., 2 Phillimore Place, London, W. 8.
Ryan Anthony N., Esq., 8 Prince Alfred Road, Liverpool, 5.

Sanders, Commander C. B., V.D., R.N.V.R., 59 Winchester Court, London, W. 8.
Sandwich, The Rt. Hon. The Earl of, Hinchinbroke, Huntingdon.
Sarell, Captain R. I. A., D.S.O., R.N., Braeside, Ashurst Road, East Grinstead, Sussex.
Saunders, Lieutenant-Commander Raphael, D.S.O., R.N.V.R., 6 Douglas Mansions, Quex Road, London, N.W. 6.
Saxby, R. C., Esq., 3 Helena Road, Ealing, London, W. 5.
Scarr, D. A., Esq., 49 Bartlemy Road, Newbury, Berks.
Schurman, D. M., Esq., 402 Mcewen Drive, La Salle Park, Reddendale, Ontario, Canada.
Scott, Surgeon Lieutenant-Commander W. I. D., M.D., Ch.B., R.N.V.R., 30 Curzon Park, Chester.

Scrivenor, Lieutenant-Commander R. J., R.A.N., c/o Navy Office, Melbourne, Australia.
Selkirk, Rt. Hon. The Earl of, O.B.E., A.F.C., Rose Lawn Coppice, Wimborne, Dorset.
Sergeant, Captain T. A., R.D., R.N.R., No. 1 The Brow, Friston, nr. Eastbourne.
Sheen, Commander C. E., D.S.C., R.N., H.M.S. *Dodman Point*, H.M. Dockyard, Devonport, Devon.
Shelley, Rear-Admiral R., C.B., C.B.E., The Pickeridge, Stoke Poges, Bucks.
Shelmerdine, Malcolm G., 36 Moncktons Avenue, Maidstone, Kent.
Sheridan, R. N., 148/45 89th Avenue, F.I., Jamaica 32, N.Y., U.S.A.
Short, S. J., 12 Elms Road, Stoneygate, Leicester.
Shute, Lieutenant-Commander R. H. N., R.N., c/o Commercial Bank of Scotland, Campbeltoun Branch, Campbeltoun, Scotland.
Somerville, Lieutenant-Commander J. A. F., R.N., Hoefield House, The Leigh, Coombe Hill, Gloucester.
Somerville, Commander I. F., R.N., c/o National Provincial Bank Ltd., Portsea.
Southcott, Lieutenant-Commander T. Ian G., c/o Mrs. E. Spencer-Niarn, Burham, Cupar, Fife.
Spaull, L. C., Esq., 21 St. Martins Avenue, Epsom, Surrey.
Spicer, Captain S. D., R.N., Salt Mill House, Fishbourne, Chichester.
Stanford, Peter, Esq., Essex, Connecticut, U.S.A.
Stanhope, The Rt. Hon. Earl, K.G., D.S.O., M.C., D.L., Chevening, Sevenoaks, Kent.
Stephens, Lieutenant-Commander Richard Alan, R.N., The Old Vicarage, Easebourne, Midhurst, Sussex.
Stevens, B. D. N., Esq., 79 Somerset Road, Mead Vale, Redhill, Surrey.
Stubbs, Lieutenant R. D. S., R.N., Chelmsford Hall, Eastbourne, Sussex.
Sturdee, Commander A. R. B., D.S.C., R.N., R.N.A.S. Culrose, Helston, Cornwall.
Style, Lieutenant-Commander G. W., D.S.C., R.N., Gilhams Birch, Jarvis Brook, nr. Crowborough, Sussex.
Swinley, Lieutenant J. G. B., R.N., Lypiatt Hill House, nr. Stroud, Glos.
Symes, Commander E. D., R.N., Dymoke House, Easton, Winchester, Hants.

Talbot, Vice-Admiral Sir Cecil P., K.C.B., K.B.E., D.S.O., Chynance, St. Buryan, nr. Penzance, Cornwall.
Tanner, Captain (E.) G. W., R.N., Royal Naval Air Station, Yeovilton, Somerset.
Taylor, Rear-Admiral A. Hugh, C.B., O.B.E., The Manor House, Diss, Norfolk.
Taylor, T. G. T., B.A., Cobbler's Last, Holy Cross Green, Clent, nr. Stourbridge, Worcs.
Tennyson, The Lord, White's Club, St. James's Street, London, S.W. 1.
Thistleton-Smith, Vice-Admiral G., G.M., R.N., H.M.S. *Vanguard*, c/o G.P.O., London.
Thorndycraft, John, 87 Chester Drive, North Harrow, Middx.
Thursfield, Rear-Admiral H. G., F.S.A., Creake Abbey, Fakenham, Norfolk.
Timings, E. K., Esq., M.A., Public Records Office, Chancery Lane, London, W.C. 2.
Tizard, Sir Henry, G.C.B., F.R.S., Keston, Hill Head, Fareham, Hants.
Tolley, Lieutenant-Commander R. P., R.N., 37 Edenfield Gardens, Worcester Park, Surrey.
Toy, Ernest W., Esq., Jr., 5456 Wayman Avenue, Riverside, California, U.S.A.
Trentham, Captain David, R.N., Red House, Yateley, Hants.
Trevelyan, Professor G. M., O.M., C.B.E., F.B.A., Litt.D., LL.D., F.R.Hist.S., 23 West Road, Cambridge.
Trier, Commander P. A., R.N., 77 Bambra Road, Caulfield, Melbourne, Victoria, Australia.
Trotter, W. P., Esq., 78 Kenilworth Court, Putney, London, S.W. 15.
Troubridge, Lieutenant-Commander Peter, R.N., Middle Oakshott, Hawkley, Liss.

Villiers, Commander Alan, D.S.C., "Windrush", Davenant Road, Oxford.

Walker, Commander (Sp.) G. E., O.B.E., R.I.N.V.R., 26 Rutland Street, London, S.W. 7.
Walling, Captain R. V., R.A., Sunnyholme, Bigbury-on-Sea, Kingsbridge, S. Devon.
Wallis, Frederick A. E., Esq., 22 Queen's Keep, Clarence Parade, Southsea, Hants.
Warner, F. P., Esq., "Spymay", Langton Matravers, Dorset.
Webber, G. E. G., 325 Waterloo Street, Winnipeg, 9, Canada.
Weir of Eastwood, The Rt. Hon. Viscount, G.C.B., LL.D., D.L., Holm Foundry, Cathcart, Glasgow.
White, E. A., Esq., B.A., 1 Park Avenue, Deepdale, Preston, Lancs.
Whiting, Instructor Commander R. O., M.A., R.N., Berwick Lodge, Barnham, Bognor Regis, Sussex.
Wickham, Captain E. T., O.B.E., R.N., Rokeby Lodge, Bathford, Somerset.
Wiggins, Harold P., Esq., Hans Cottage, Henley-on-Thames, Oxon.
Willis, H. C., Esq., Boulders House, Simon's Town, C.P., South Africa.
Wilson, W. R., Esq., 1659 46th Avenue, Oakland, 1, California, U.S.A.
Woodrooffe, Commander T., 11 Allen House, Allen Street, London, W. 8.
Woodward, Chief Officer S. M., 43 Shaftesbury Road, Southsea.
Wreford, J. G., Gloucester House, Cornwall Gardens, London, S.W. 7.
Wright, Rear-Admiral (S.) Noel, C.B., O.B.E., The Thatched House, 27 The Avenue, Alverstoek, Hants.
Wyatt, Lieutenant (E.) A., R.C.N.(Rtd.), 148 Cottonwood Drive, Don Mills, Ontario, Canada.

LIBRARIES, INSTITUTIONS, ETC.

Aberdeen, University Library, Aberdeen, Scotland.
Amsterdam, Nederlandsch Historisch Scheepvaart Museum, De Lairessehoek Corn, Schuytstraat, Amsterdam, Holland.
Antiquaries of London, Society of, Burlington House, Piccadilly, London, W. 1.
Ariel, H.M.S., Wardroom Mess Treasurer, Winchester, Hants.
Athenaeum, The, Pall Mall, London, S.W. 1.
Australia, Commonwealth National Library, c/o Australia House, Strand, London, W.C. 2.
Australia, South, Public Library of, Adelaide, S. Australia.

Baltimore, The Enoch Pratt Free Library, c/o Messrs. Edw. G. Allen & Son, Ltd., 12 & 14 Grape Street, Shaftesbury Avenue, London, W.C. 2.
Baltimore, Johns Hopkins University Library, c/o Hubert Wilson Ltd., 161 Borough High Street, Southward, London, S.E. 1.
Bath, Victoria Art Gallery & Municipal Library, Bath, Somerset.
Bath Club, The, 74 St. James's Street, London, S.W. 1.
Belfast, Linen Hall Library, Donegall Square North, Belfast.
Belfast, Queen's University.
Birmingham, The Library, The University, Edmund Street, Birmingham, 3.
Birmingham Public Libraries (Reference Library), Birmingham, 1.
Burgersdijk & Niermans, Leiden, Holland.
Bolton Central Reference Library, Bolton, Lancs.
Boston Athenaeum, The, c/o Messrs. Edw. G. Allen & Son, Ltd., 12 & 14 Grape Street, Shaftesbury Avenue, London, W.C. 2.
Boston, The Public Library, c/o Messrs. Bernard Quaritch Ltd., 11 Grafton Street, London, W. 1.
Bristol Public Libraries, Central Library, College Green, Bristol.
Bristol, University Library, Bristol, Somerset.
British Columbia, The Serials Division S-3170, The Library, The University of British Columbia, Vancouver, 8, Canada.
Brown University Library (Rhode Island), c/o Messrs. Henry Sotheran Ltd., 2, 3, 4 & 5 Sackville Street, Piccadilly, London, W. 1.

California, Serials Department, General Library, University of California, Berkeley 4, California, U.S.A.
California, Acquisitions Department, University of California Library, Riverside, California, U.S.A.
Chatham Public Library, Chatham, Kent.
Cambridge, Christ's College.
Cambridge, St. John's College.
Cambridge, Seeley Historical Library, The Old Schools, Bene't Street, Cambridge.
Cardiff, The Public Libraries.
Chicago, Newberry Library, 60 W. Walton Street, Chicago, 10, Illinois, U.S.A.
Chicago, The University of Chicago Library, Continuation Record, Harper M.21, Chicago, Illinois, U.S.A.
Chichester, West Sussex County Library, County Hall, Chichester.

Cincinnati, Public Library, Cincinnati, Ohio, U.S.A.
Cincinnati, The University of, c/o George Harding's Bookshop, Ltd., 106 Great Russell Street, London, W.C. 1.
Claremont College Library, Harper Hall, Claremont, California, U.S.A.
Columbia University Library, The, c/o Messrs. G. E. Stechert & Co., 2 Star Yard, Carey Street, London, W.C. 2.
Congress, Library of, Washington, D.C., c/o Messrs. Edw. G. Allen & Son Ltd., 12 & 14 Grape Street, Shaftesbury Avenue, London, W.C. 2.
Copenhagen, The Library of the Royal Danish Navy, Overgaden Oven Vandet 60, Copenhagen, Denmark.
Copenhagen, The Royal Library, c/o Messrs. Francis Edwards Ltd., 83 Marylebone High Street, London, W. 1.
Cornell University Library, Ithaca, N.Y., c/o Messrs. Edw. G. Allen & Son Ltd., 12 & 14 Grape Street, Shaftesbury Avenue, London, W.C. 2.
Croydon, The Public Libraries.
Cruising Association, The, Chiltern Court, Baker Street, London, N.W. 1.

Dartmouth College Library (Hanover U.S.A.), c/o Messrs. Edw. G. Allen & Son Ltd., 12 & 14 Grape Street, Shaftesbury Avenue, London, W.C. 2.
Dolphin, H.M.S., Ward Room Mess, Gosport, Hants.

East Sussex Record Office, County Archivist, Pelham House, Lewes, Sussex.
Edinburgh Public Libraries, George Fourth Bridge, Edinburgh.
Edinburgh University.
Emory University Library, Georgia, U.S.A.
Esquimalt, H.M.C.S. *Naden*, Esquimalt, B.C., Canada.
Exeter City Library, Castle Street, Exeter.

Folger Shakespeare Library (Washington D.C., U.S.A.), c/o George Harding's Bookshop Ltd., 106 Russell Street, London, W.C. 1.

Glasgow, Institute of Chartered Accountants of Scotland, Glasgow Local Committee, 142 St. Vincent Street, Glasgow, C. 2.
Glasgow, The Mitchell Library, Glasgow Corporation Public Libraries, Glasgow, C. 3.
Glasgow University.
Guildhall Library, London, E.C. 2.

Hague, The, Holland, The Royal Library.
Halifax, H.M.C.S. *Stadacona*, Command Reference Library, Halifax, Nova Scotia, Canada.
Halifax Memorial Library, Halifax, Nova Scotia, Canada.
Harrier, H.M.S., Wardroom Mess, Kete, nr. Haverfordwest.
Harvard College Library, Cambridge, Mass., U.S.A., c/o Messrs. Edw. G. Allen & Son Ltd., 12 & 14 Grape Street, Shaftesbury Avenue, London, W.C. 2.
Hull Public Libraries, Hull, Yorkshire.
Huntington, Henry E., Esq., Library and Art Gallery, San Merino 15, California, U.S.A.

Illinois University Library, Urbana, Illinois, U.S.A.
Indiana University Library, The, c/o Messrs. G. E. Stechert & Co., 2 Star Yard, Carey Street, London, W.C. 2.
Iowa, The State University of (Library Annexe), c/o Iowa City, Iowa, U.S.A.
Ireland, National Library of, Dublin.

Johannesburg Public Library, Market Square, Johannesburg, Transvaal, S.A.

Karlskrona, Kungl., Orlogsmanna Sällskapet Bibliotek, Karlskrona, Sweden.

Leeds University Library.
Leicester, University of, University Road, Leicester.
Liverpool Public Libraries, William Brown Street, Liverpool, 3.
Liverpool University Library.
London Library, St. James's Square, London, S.W. 1.
London University, Institute of Historical Research, Senate House, Bloomsbury, London, W.C. 1.
London University Library, Senate House, Bloomsbury, London, W.C. 1.
Lund, K. Universitets-Biblioteket, Lund, Sweden.

Maine University Library, Orono, Maine, U.S.A.
Malta, The Commissioner of Police, Valetta.
Malta, Royal Malta Library, Valetta.
Manchester, The John Rylands Library, Deansgate, Manchester.
Manchester Public Libraries, St. Peter's Square, Manchester.
Manchester, The Victoria University of Manchester.
Manitoba, The University of Manitoba Library, Winnipeg, Canada.
Mariners' Museum Library, The, Newport Mews, Virginia, U.S.A.
Massachusetts Historical Society, The, 1154 Boylston Street, Boston, Mass., U.S.A.
Melbourne, Public Library of Victoria, c/o Messrs. Truslove & Hanson, 153 Oxford Street, London, W. 1.
Melbourne University, c/o Messrs. David Nutt, 156 High Holborn, London, W.C. 1.
Michigan, The General Library, University of Michigan, c/o Messrs. Henry Southeran Ltd., 2, 3, 4 & 5 Sackville Street, Piccadilly, London, W. 1.
Minnesota, University Library, c/o Messrs. G. E. Stechert & Co., 2 Star Yard, Carey Street, W.C. 2.
Missouri, University Library, Columbia, c/o Messrs. G. E. Stechert & Co., 2 Star Yard, Carey Street, W.C. 2.
Montreal, Redpath Library, McGill University, 3459 McTavish Street, Montreal, P.Q., Canada.
Marine Nationale Bibliotheque Principale, Du Port De Lorient, Morbihan.

Nebraska, University General Library, c/o Messrs. Henry Southeran Ltd., 2/5 Sackville Street, Piccadilly, London, W. 1.
Newcastle-upon-Tyne Public Library, New Bridge Street.
Newcastle University College Library, N.S.W. University of Technology, Tykes Hill, 2N, N.S.W.
New South Wales Public Library, c/o Messrs. Truslove & Hanson, 153 Oxford Street, London, W. 1.
New York Public Library, c/o Stevens & Brown, 77/79 Duke Street, Grosvenor Square, London, W. 1.
New York State Library, The, c/o Messrs. G. E. Stechert & Co., 2 Star Yard, Carey Street, London, W.C. 2.
New York University, General University Library, 100 Washington Square East, New York, 3, N.Y., U.S.A.
New York Yacht Club Library, 37–41 West 44th Street, New York City, New York, U.S.A.
New Zealand, Alexander Turnbull Library, Bowen Street, Wellington, C.I., New Zealand.
New Zealand General Assembly Library, Wellington, c/o The High Commissioner, New Zealand Government Offices, 415 Strand, London, W.C. 2.
Nottingham Central Public Library, Sherwood Street, Nottingham.

Ohio State University Library, Columbus 10, Ohio, U.S.A,
Ontario, National Defence Library, Royal Military College of Canada, Kingston, Ontario, Canada.

Otago University Library, Dunedin, N.I., New Zealand.
Ottawa, Departmental Library, (Naval Section) "C" Building, Department of National Defence, Ottawa, Ontario, Canada.
Ottawa, National Library of Canada, Public Archives Building, Ottawa 2, Canada.
Oxford, All Souls College Library.
Oxford, Exeter College Library.
Oxford, Rhodes House Library.
Oxford, Trinity College Library.

Paddington, Maida Vale Library, Sutherland Avenue, Paddington, London, W. 9.
Paris, Bureau Des Acquisitions, La Bibliotheque Nationale, 58 R. de Richelieu, Paris, 5.
Paris, Service Historique De La Marine, 3 Avenue Octave Greard, Paris, 7eme, Seine, France.
Pennsylvania Historical Society, 1300 Locust Street, Philadelphia, Pennsylvania, U.S.A.
Pennsylvania University Library, c/o Messrs. George Harding's Bookshop Ltd., 106 Great Russell Street, London, W.C. 1.
Perth, The State Library of Western Australia, James Street, Perth, Western Australia.
Pittsburgh, University Library, Room 517, Cathedral of Learning, University Library, Pittsburgh, Penn., U.S.A.
Plymouth Central Library, Tavistock Road, Plymouth.
Portsmouth Central Public Library.
Portsmouth, H.M. Navigation School (H.M.S. *Dryad*), Portsmouth, Hants.
Princeton University Library, Princeton, New Jersey.
Public Record Office Library, Chancery Lane, London, W.C. 2.

Queensland University Library.
Quebec, College Militaire Royal de St. Jean Library, Saint-Jean, Quebec, Canada.

Reading University Library, Reading, Berks.
Reading Central Library, Blagrave Street, Reading.
Rice Institute Library, c/o Messrs. G. E. Stechert & Co., 2 Star Yard, Carey Street, London, W.C. 2.
Rochester University Library, Rivea Campus Station, Rochester 20, N.Y., U.S.A.
Royal Cruising Club, 1 New Square, Lincoln's Inn, London, W.C. 2.
Royal Empire Society Library, Northumberland Avenue, London, W.C. 2.
Royal Historical Society Library, 96 Cheyne Walk, Chelsea, London, S.W. 10.
Royal Marine Barracks Officers' Library, Eastney, Portsmouth, Hants.
Royal Naval Club, Portsmouth.
Royal Roads, H.M.C.S., The Librarian, Victoria, B.C., Canada.
Royal United Service Institution, Whitehall, London, S.W. 1.

San Francisco, The Public Library, c/o Messrs. G. E. Stechert & Co., 2 Star Yard, Carey Street, London, W.C. 2.
Schenectady, Union College Library, Schenectady 8, New York, U.S.A.
Sheffield University Library, Western Bank, Sheffield, 10.
St. Andrew's University Library, Scotland.
Stanford University Libraries, Stanford, California, U.S.A.
Swets & Zeitlinger, Messrs., Amsterdam C, Keizersgracht 471, Holland.

Tasmania, Agent General for, 457 Strand, London, W.C. 2.
Tecumseh, H.M.C.S., Wardroom Mess, Calgary, Alberta, Canada.
Toronto Legislative Library, Department of Education, Parliament Buildings, Toronto 2, Ontario, Canada.
Toronto, Reference Division (General), The Public Library of Toronto, College and St. George Streets, Toronto 2B, Ontario, Canada.

Toronto, Royal Canadian Military Institution, 426 University Avenue, Toronto 2B.
Travellers Club, 106 Pall Mall, London, S.W. 1.
Trinity House, Tower Hill, London, E.C. 3.

United Service Club Library, 116 Pall Mall, London, S.W. 1.
Universitetsbiblioteket, Uppsala, Sweden.
University College Library, The, Gower Street, London, W.C. 1.
U.S. Naval Academy Library, Annapolis, U.S.A.

Venture, H.M.C.S., Recreation Fund, H.M.C. Dockyard, Esquimalt, British Columbia, Canada.
Vernon, H.M.S., Ward Room Mess, Portsmouth.
Victoria Provincial Library, Parliament Buildings, Victoria, B.C.

Wales, University College of, Aberystwyth, Wales.
Washington University Library, Acquisitions Division, Seattle 5, Washington.
Westminster Public Library, St. Martin's Street, London, W.C. 2.
Winchester, Moberly Library, c/o H. E. Walker, Esq., Winchester College, Winchester, Hants.
Wisconsin University, General Library, c/o Messrs. Henry Southeran Ltd., 2/5 Sackville Street, Piccadilly, London, W. 1.
Witwatersrand University Library, Milner Park, Johannesburg, S. Africa.

Yale University Library, New Haven, U.S.A., c/o Messrs. Edw. G. Allen & Son Ltd., 12 & 14 Grape Street, Shaftesbury Avenue, London, W.C. 2.

Printed by Spottiswoode, Ballantyne & Co. Ltd., London and Colchester